THE NAZI ELITE

The Nazi Elite

Edited by

Ronald Smelser

and

Rainer Zitelmann

Translated by Mary Fischer

NEW YORK UNIVERSITY PRESS
Washington Square, New York

© Wissenschaftliche Buchgesellschaft, Darmstadt. 1989
English translation © The Macmillan Press Ltd 1993

First published as *Die Braune Elite: 22 Biographische Skizzen,* 1989

First published in the U.S.A. in 1993 by
NEW YORK UNIVERSITY PRESS
Washington Square,
New York, N.Y. 10003

Library of Congress Cataloging-in-Publication Data
Braune Elite.   English
The Nazi elite / edited by Ronald Smelser and Rainer Zitelmann.
p.   cm.
Includes index.
ISBN 0–8147–7950–6
1. National socialists—Biography.   2. Germany—Politics and
government—1933–1945.   I. Smelser, Ronald M., 1942–   .
II. Zitelmann, Rainer.   III. Title.
DD244.B7313   1993
943.086'092'2—dc20
[B]   92–37036
                                         CIP

Printed in Hong Kong

Contents

Notes on the Contributors

Josef Ackermann studied at the Universities of Munich and Göttingen. He received his doctorate in 1969 with a work on Heinrich Himmler and has been working since 1983 as Head of the Department of Social Sciences at a grammar school in Göttingen. His publications include *Heinrich Himmler als Ideologe* and *Kemal Atatürk. Wegbereiter des Fortschritts* (in preparation).

Peter W. Becker studied history at Stanford University and completed his doctorate in 1971 with a work on the German war economy in the Second World War, *The Basis of the German War Economy under Albert Speer, 1942–1944*. Since 1966 he has taught German history at the University of South Carolina. He has published numerous articles on the Third Reich and the German war economy in the Second World War and is joint editor of the *Historical Dictionary of Napoleonic France 1799–1815*.

Peter Black studied history at the University of Wisconsin and at Columbia University. In 1981 he received his doctorate with a work on Kaltenbrunner. He works as a historian with the American Justice Ministry in Washington DC. He is the author of *Ernst Kaltenbrunner: Ideological Soldier of the Third Reich*.

Reinhard Bollmus studied history, German, and political science at the universities of Tübingen, Bangor and Heidelberg. He received his doctorate in 1968 with a work on the Rosenberg Bureau. He is currently at the University of Trier. His books include, *Das Amt Rosenberg und seine Gegner, Studien zum Machtkampf im Nationalsozialistischen Herrschaftssystem*; *Handelshochschule und Nationalsozialismus, Das Ende der Handelshochschule Mannheim und die Errichtung einer Staats- und Wirtschaftswissenschaftlichen Fakultät an der Universität Heidelberg*.

Gustavo Corni studied history and political science at the University of Bologna. He received his doctorate in 1974 with a work on agriculture and politics in Germany from Absolutism to Dictatorship. Since 1989 he has been Professor of Modern History at the University of Chieti. His publications include *Stato assoluto e società agraria in Prussia nell'età di Federico II* and *Cultura politica e società borghese in Germania fra Otto e Novecento* (co-editor).

Günther Deschner studied at the University of Erlangen-Nuremberg, and received his doctorate in 1967 with a work on Gobineau. He works as a journalist, author and executive in a publishing firm. His most important publications are *Menschen im Ghetto; Reinhard Heydrich. Statthalter der totalen Macht; Saladins Söhne. Die Kurden – das betrogene Volk.*

Jost Dülffer studied history, Latin, and political science at the universities of Hamburg and Freiburg. He received his doctorate in 1972 with a work on politics and the building of the navy, and completed a post-doctoral degree in 1979 with a work on the Hague Peace Conferences. Since 1982 he has been Professor of Modern History at the University of Cologne. His books include *Weimar, Hitler und die Marine. Reichspolitik und Flottenbau 1920–1939, Hitlers Städte. Baupolitik im Dritten Reich. Eine Dokumentation* (with J. Thies and J. Henke); *Regeln gegen den Krieg? Die Haager Friedenskonferenzen von 1899 und 1907 in der internationalen Politik; Nationalsozialismus und traditionelle Machteliten; Bereit zum Krieg. Kriegsmentalität im wilhelminischen Deutschland 1890–1914* (co-edited with K. Holl).

Conan Fischer studied modern history, sociology and German at the University of East Anglia and history at the University of Sussex. He received his doctorate in 1980 with a work on the SA. He is presently Senior Lecturer in History at the University of Strathclyde, Glasgow. His publications include *Stormtroopers: A Social, Economic and Ideological Analysis, 1929–35* and *The German Communists and the Rise of Nazism in the Weimar Republic.*

Elke Fröhlich studied history and political science, and completed a doctorate. Since 1973 she has worked at the Institut für Zeitgeschichte, Munich. She is joint editor and co-author of the series *Bayern in der NS-Zeit*, 6 vols, and editor of the *Tagebücher von Joseph Goebbels, Teil I*, 4 vols.

Udo Kissenkoetter studied at the universities of Bonn, Cologne and Düsseldorf. He gained his Doctor of Philosophy in 1975. He is the author of *Gregor Strasser und die NSDAP.*

Christoph Klessmann studied history, classical philology and political science at the universities of Göttingen, Tübingen and Munich. He received his doctorate in 1969 with a work on Nazi cultural policy and the Polish resistance. Since 1976 he has been Professor of Contemporary History at the University of Bielefeld. Amongst his many publications are *Die Selbstbehauptung einer Nation. NS – Kulturpolitik und polnische Widerstandsbewegung im Generalgouvernement 1939–1945; Streiks und Hungermärsche im Ruhrgebiet 1946–48* (with P. Friedemann); *Polnische Bergarbeiter im Ruhrgebiet. Soziale Integration und nationale Subkultur einer Minderheit in der deutschen Industriegesellschaft; Gegner des Natio-*

nalsozialismus (co-edited with F. Pingel); *Die doppelte Staatsgründung. Deutsche Geschichte 1945–1955*; *Zwei Staaten, eine Nation. Deutsche Geschichte 1955–1970*.

Alfred Kube studied history, art history and German at the universities of Trier, Heidelberg and Berlin. He received his doctorate in 1983 with a work on Hermann Goering. Since 1987 he has worked as a historian and director of exhibitions in the 'Haus der Geschichte Baden-Württembergs' in Stuttgart. His publications include *Pour le mérite und Hakenkreuz. Hermann Goering im Dritten Reich*; *Die Veräusserung der Nationalgüter im Rhein-Mosel-Departement 1803–1813* (with Wolfgang Schieder); *Südwestdeutschland und die Entstehung des Grundgesetzes* (with Thomas Schnabel).

Jochen von Lang has written numerous books and television documentaries on the Third Reich. He received the DAG Television Prize for his programme *'Das Verhör des Adolf Eichmann'*. He was awarded the Federal Merit Cross First Class for his researches in the field of National Socialist history and his contribution to German-Jewish reconciliation. His most important publications include *Der Sekretär. Martin Bormann: Der Mann, der Hitler beherrschte*; *Das Eichmann-Protokoll* (editor); *Der Adjutant. Karl Wolff, der Mann zwischen Hitler und Himmler*; *Der Krieg der Bomber. Dokumentation einer deutschen Katastrophe*; *Der Hitlerjunge, Baldur von Schirach: Der Mann, der Deutschlands Jugend erzog*; *Die Partei. Mit Hitler an die Macht und in den Untergang*; *'und willst Du nicht ein Deutscher sein . . .' Terror in der Weimarer Republik*.

Wolfgang Michalka studied history, German and education at the universities of Heidelberg and Mannheim. He received his doctorate in 1976 with a work on Ribbentrop. Since 1988 he has worked as an editor at the *'Militärgeschichtliches Forschungsamt'* in Freiburg. His books include *Nationalsozialistische Aussenpolitik* (editor); *Ribbentrop und die deutsche Weltpolitik 1933–1940*; *Gustav Stresemann* (co-editor with M. Lee); *Nationalsozialistische Machtergreifung* (editor); *German Foreign Policy 1917–1933: Continuity or Break?* (with M. Lee).

Patrick Moreau studied history, philosophy and political science at the Universities of Paris I and IV, the Sorbonne and at the Institut d'Etudes Politiques de Paris. He received his doctorate in 1978 with a work on the Otto Strasser Group. In 1984 he received a post-doctoral degree with a work on the NPD. Since 1987 he has been a civil servant in the French Foreign Office and has worked for the CNRS since 1983. He is a member of the *Mission Historique Française* in Germany. His publications include *Nationalsozialismus von links. Die 'Kampfgemeinschaft Revolutionärer Nationalsozialisten' und die 'Schwarze Front' Otto Strassers 1930–1935*.

Dietrich Orlow studied history at Ohio University and at the University of Michigan. He received his doctorate in 1962 with a work on National Socialist policies on the Balkans. Since 1971 he has been Professor of European History at the University of Boston. He is the author of *The History of the Nazi-Party 1919–45*, 2 vols; *Weimar Prussia 1918–25. The Unlikely Rock of Democracy*; *A History of Modern Germany, 1871 to the present.*

Franz W. Seidler studied history, German and English at the universities of Munich, Cambridge and Paris. He received his doctorate in 1955 with a work on the concept of revolution. Since 1973 he has been Professor of Contemporary History, especially social and military history, at the University of the *Bundeswehr* in Munich. His publications include *Die Abrüstung*; *Frauen zu den Waffen?*; *Wehrdienst-Zivildienst*; *Das Militär in der Karikatur*; *Fritz Todt. Baumeister des Dritten Reiches*; *Die Organisation Todt. Bauen für Staat und Wehrmacht 1938–1945*; *Deutscher Volkssturm 1944/45.*

Ronald Smelser studied history at the University of Wisconsin. He received his doctorate in 1970 with a work on Nazi foreign policy and the Sudeten problem. Since 1983 he has been Professor of History at the University of Utah. He is past President of the German Studies Association. His books include *Das Sudetenproblem und das Dritte Reich 1933–1938. Von der Volkstumspolitik zur Nationalsozialistischen Aussenpolitik*; *Robert Ley: Hitler's Labor Front Leader.*

Hanno Sowade studied at the universities of Göttingen and Munich. Since 1984 he has worked at the *Institut für Zeitgeschichte*, and he is currently writing a doctoral thesis. He is joint editor of *Die Eingliederung der Bundesrepublik in die westliche Welt.*

Albrecht Tyrell studied political science, history and Latin at the universities of Bonn and Munich. He received his doctorate in 1972 with a work on Hitler. He has worked since 1986 as a director of the 'Schaufenster Schlesien' (museum, library, archive) in the *Haus Schlesien*, Königswinter. His publications include *Führer befiehl . . . Selbstzeugnisse aus der 'Kampfzeit' der NSDAP* (editor); *Vom 'Trommler' zum 'Führer'. Der Wandel von Hitlers Selbstverständnis zwischen 1919 und 1924 und die Entwicklung der NSDAP*; *Bibliographie zur Politik in Theorie und Praxis*; *Grossbritannien und die Deutschlandplanung der Alliierten 1941–1945.*

Michael Wortmann studied history and German at the University of Cologne. He received his doctorate in 1980 with a work on Baldur von Schirach. He has worked since 1981 as an editor with the *Westdeutsche Rundfunk*. His books include: *Baldur von Schirach: Hitlers Jugendführer.*

Rainer Zitelmann studied history and political science at the Technische Hochschule in Darmstadt. He received his doctorate in 1986 with a work on Hitler's concept of himself as a revolutionary. Since 1987 he has been Research Fellow at the Freie Universität, Berlin, in the *Zentralinstitut für sozialwissenschaftliche Forschung*. His works include *Hitler. Selbstverständnis eines Revolutionärs*; *Adolf Hitler. Eine politische Biographie*.

Translator's Note

The language of the Third Reich is highly specialised and often incomprehensible to the general reader. In translating the contributions to this book I have sought to put the specialised terminology and vocabulary of the period into an accessible form of English, while at the same time trying to retain the original sense of that terminology. German terms have been retained only where no meaningful English equivalent exists, as for example in the case of *Gauleiter*, who were the National Socialists' regional leaders. Where organisations are referred to by their initials (e.g. KPD, KGRNS) I have translated the name of the organisation into English and thereafter referred to it by its German initials, following the practice of most English language books on this period.

Chapters 13 and 16 were submitted in English by their authors.

MARY FISCHER

Glossary of German Terms and Abbreviations

AG	Arbeitsgemeinschaft der nordwestdeutschen Gaue der NSDAP – Study Group North West of the NSDAP
BAK	Bundesarchiv Koblenz – Federal Archive, Koblenz
DAF	Deutsche Arbeitsfront – German Labour Front
DAP	Deutsche Arbeiterpartei – German Workers' Party, forerunner of the NSDAP
DNVP	Deutschnationale Volkspartei – German National People's Party
DVFP	Deutsch-Völkische Freiheitspartei – German Ethnic Freedom Party
Freikorps	Free Corps
Frontbann	Cover organisation for the banned SA, 1924–5
Gauleiter	NSDAP regional leader
GG	Government General (in German-occupied Poland)
IfZ	Institut für Zeitgeschichte – Institute for Contemporary History, Munich
IMT	International Military Tribunal (at Nuremberg)
Kampf Verlag	Strasser publishing house
KDAI	Kampfbund Deutscher Architekten und Ingenieure – Fighting League of German Architects and Engineers
KfdK	Kampfbund für deutsche Kultur – Fighting League for German Culture
KGRNS	Kampfgemeinschaft Revolutionärer Nationaler Sozialisten – Battle Group of Revolutionary National Socialists
KPD	Kommunistische Partei Deutschlands – Communist Party of Germany
NSBDT	Nationalsozialistischer Bund Deutscher Technik – National Socialist League of German Technology
NSBO	Nationalsozialistische Betriebzellen Organisation – National Socialist Factory Cell Organisation
NSDAP	Nationalsozialistische Deutsche Arbeiterpartei – National Socialist German Workers' Party

NSKD	Nationalsozialistische Kampfgemeinschaft Deutschlands – Nationalist and Socialist Fighting Association of Germany
OKW	Oberkommando Wehrmacht – Supreme Command of the Armed Forces
OT	Todt Organisation
PO	Politische Organisation – Political Organisation of the NSDAP
Reichskriegsflagge	'Imperial War Flag' (paramilitary league)
Reichsredner	National speaker (elite of Nazi public speakers)
RFSS	Reichsführer SS – National Director of the SS
RHSA	Reichssicherheitshauptamt – Supreme National Security Office
ROL	Reichsorganisationsleitung – National Administrative Headquarters (of the NSDAP)
SA	Sturmabteilung – Storm Section (of the NSDAP)
SD	Sicherheitsdienst – State Security Service
SPD	Sozialdemokratische Partei Deutschlands – Social Democratic Party of Germany
SS	Schutzstaffel – Guard Squadron (of the NSDAP)
Stahlhelm	Steel Helmet – monarchist paramilitary organisation
Stürmer, Der	Anti-semitic Nazi newspaper
USPD	Unabhängige Sozialdemokratische Partei Deutschlands – Independent Social Democratic Party of Germany
VDI	Verein Deutscher Ingenieure – Association of German Engineers
völkisch	Populist ethnic
Völkischer Beobachter	Official organ of the NSDAP

1 Introduction
Ronald Smelser and Rainer Zitelmann

Who were the leaders of the NSDAP and the Third Reich? What were the experiences which led them to embrace National Socialism? What role did they play in the National Socialist state? How can the success – and the failure – of National Socialism be explained? What were the motives which determined the actions of these men, what do we know of their personalities and the philosophy which guided them?

In this book historians from Germany, France, Italy, Scotland and the USA attempt to give answers to these questions. All the authors have undertaken in-depth studies of the personalities they discuss. Years of archival research, often resulting in extensive monographs, form the basis of the contributions presented here; indeed in many respects they go beyond the longer studies. In every case they take the most recent research into account. However this book is not simply intended for historians, but is aimed in the first instance at teachers, students, school pupils – a broad readership with an interest in history. The authors have tried to write academically reliable studies in language which is accessible to all. They have dispensed with any scholarly apparatus. However at the end of each contribution there are notes for those who would like to find out more about any of the personalities discussed.

The sequence of the contributions is not a comment on the importance of the person concerned. To a certain extent the alphabetical arrangement is a means of side-stepping a source of difficulty but at the same time it is the expression of a historical fact; in the NSDAP and the Third Reich formal responsibilities, rank and position did not necessarily give any clue to real influence, and therefore in many cases they do not give any reliable indication of a Nazi leader's position within the hierarchy of the Nazi elite. Today, historical research talks of a 'polycratic system' or of a 'confusion of powers', in which different personalities within the leadership and institutions struggled for power and influence – with varying degrees of success. Many of the Nazi leaders held quite important positions before the seizure of power but no longer had a role to play in the Third Reich. This is true, for example, of the brothers Otto and Gregor Strasser. Otto Strasser quarrelled with Hitler in 1930 and left the party. His brother, the powerful National Organiser, resigned his post in December 1932 and was shot on 30 June 1934. The mercurial political career of the SA leader, Ernst Röhm, who was murdered by the SS shortly afterwards, ended on the same day. Ideologues who were accorded some influence in the NSDAP before 1933, like Gottfried Feder and Alfred Rosenberg (both of whom had belonged to the party since 1919), did not play the important role they had hoped for in the Third Reich. On the other hand, others, who did not embrace National Socialism until later, like the foreign Minister Joachim von Ribbentrop or Hitler's architect and Armaments Minister Albert Speer (both joined the party in 1931/32), held significant and powerful positions in the Third Reich for a time.

However, as in the case of Hermann Goering, who was regarded for a time as the 'second man' in the Third Reich and in 1934 was named by Hitler as his successor, advancement was often followed by a rapid loss of power, which in many cases was not least the expression of Hitler's loss of faith in them. Many of the acts of the Nazi leaders have to be seen as attempts to enhance their standing with Hitler by means of extra-ordinary deeds. This was possibly one of Joseph Goebbels motives for initiating the so-called *Reichskristallnacht* on 9 November 1938. His standing with Hitler had suffered considerably because of his love affairs. Rudolf Hess, the Deputy Führer, certainly thought he was acting in accordance with Hitler's wishes when he flew to Britain in 1941. He probably hoped that if he succeeded in bringing Hitler his long sought-after alliance with Britain, this would increase his standing with the Führer and therefore also his influence in the Nazi leadership. The cult of the Führer in the Third Reich was probably not a coolly calculated, artificially stage-managed propaganda ploy: all those who propagated the 'Hitler myth' were themselves in its thrall. Nonetheless this did not prevent people from criticising many of Hitler's actions and ideas. But in general Hitler's miscalculations and wrong decisions were regarded by his supporters as resulting from the Führer having been 'influenced' by 'bad company' (by which they meant other party leaders with whom they were in competition) and they hoped to mitigate this tendency through their own influence.

For all the figures we discuss here their relationship with Hitler was the main factor on which their political career depended. Personal access to Hitler was more important than their own – often only ill-defined – terms of office. This indicates the extraordinary importance of the Führer in the National Socialist system. Coversely, this book makes it clear that it would be oversimplistic to equate National Socialism with Hitler. Emphasising the 'Hitler Factor' need not be synonymous with considering Hitler in isolation. Any examination of the Nazi leadership extends beyond the personalities concerned. Areas of policy formulation and the structures of the Nazi system of government are described as explicitly as the by no means coherent ideology which has been termed 'National Socialist philosophy'.

Structural factors, the importance of which is heavily emphasised in current historical research, are however not abstract concepts, totally separate from the people involved. The notion that 'the conscious will of the actors makes history' (Treitschke) is regarded today as the expression of an understanding of history which is too naive, personalised, even anachronistic. Structural factors, or according to the doctrines of Marxist historiography, the laws of economic causality, it is said, are more important than the people involved. An understanding of the significance of these factors undoubtedly marked an advance in attempts to understand the motive forces of history. But we must not 'throw out the baby with the bath water'. A view of history which works solely within a structuralist context and treats the people involved as an insignificant factor is as unconvincing as a psychological view which regards the 'nature' or 'character' of influential personalities as the sole keys to the understanding of history. The unqualified use of *one* methodological approach or theoretical construct leads to a selective understanding of the historical process.

Anyone whose aim is to explain history must accept the necessity of a pluralistic methodological approach. Structural analysis, social and economic history, constitutional history, intellectual history, the history of everyday life and other methods which make history accessible do not necessarily have to be mutually exclusive and each can be justified just as historical biography can. These approaches are only counter-productive when they are no longer regarded as being complementary but are set against one another. Thus it is unhelpful to set 'history from below' *against* 'history from above', as many historians of everyday life do, or to construct illusory alternatives between the biographical method and the structural approach, as is sometimes attempted by representatives of the so-called 'history of society'.

Alongside these general observations the importance of the biographical method is underlined by two distinct arguments. The first is a didactic one. Historical research is not the only task for historians; they also have to make their results accessible and comprehensible to a wider public. However this wider public often tries to gain access to history by trying to understand the people participating in it. An interest in the individuals who have had an effect on history can often be the incentive to develop a deeper interest in factors above or beyond personalities, to press forward from the particular to the general and from the individual person to structural factors. This is however more than a didactic concept, it corresponds to the way in which knowledge unfolds. For, and this is a second reason which underlines the justification of the biographical method, it is possible to proceed from the particular to the general, but there is no path from general theory which 'leads to the contemplation of the particular' (Ranke). The substantive history of National Socialism in the years 1919–45 cannot be derived from the often very abstract 'theories of facism'. But as the contributors to this book demonstrate, an understanding of key National Socialist personalities can lead to more general insights, even if the outcome does tend to suggest the need to take more care with generalisations and blanket pronouncements.

Taken as a whole, the contributions compel the reader to take leave of many current stereotypes. For example it is no longer possible to maintain the theory that Nazi ideology is anti-modernist in character. There were of course Nazi leaders in whose thinking anti-modern, agrarian utopias played a role – often those who are not commonly associated with such goals by many historians – like for example Otto Strasser. Men like Fritz Todt, Robert Ley, Albert Speer and Joseph Goebbels were, like Hitler himself, by no means supporters of an anti-modernist ideology, but to some extent pursued wholly modern ideas.

The 'mysticism' represented by Rosenberg and Himmler should not simply be equated with Nazi ideology as such. There were contradictions between the version of National socialist philosophy they propagated and the self-image and world view of Hitler (and other Nazi leaders), which were in many respects more 'rationalistic' in nature and these contradictions can no longer simply be evaluated as the varying emphases within a unified ideology.

Some of the men who held the reins of power in the Third Reich and were responsible for propaganda and the realisation of the National Socialist philosophy did not accept central elements of its racial ideology or saw themselves more as apolitical technocrats of power. The first is true of Joseph Goebbels who repeatedly lashed out at the racial ideologues who held that it was possible to draw conclusions about a person's capabilities from his external appearance. In his critique of this 'racial materialism' Goebbels knew himself to be in agreement with Hitler. The second applies to Richard Heydrich, one of the main initiators of the 'final solution', for whom the ruthless implementation of technocratic efficiency and the greatest possible effectiveness were more important than the beliefs of *völkisch* (populist ethnic) ideology. He was thus the opposite of the 'blood and soil' theorist Walther Darré. It is worth noting that Darré's Secretary of State Herbert Backe and Heydrich laughed together at the philosophical idiosyncrasies of their respective superiors, Darré and Himmler, just as Hitler and Goebbels mocked Rosenberg's and Himmler's 'mysticism'.

Alongside differences such as these there was of course common ground: the fundamental rejection of bourgeois values, anti-semitism, the rejection of Marxism and liberalism and a conviction of the absolute primacy of the needs of the 'ethnic community' before those of the individual, were imprinted to a greater or lesser degree on the minds of most National Socialists. Nonetheless it is necessary to differentiate even with regard to these basic tenets. It would be wrong, for example, to reduce National Socialism primarily to anti-semitism. Anti-semitism played a pre-eminent role for many Nazi leaders, but for many other motives came to the fore. The vision of a synthesis of Nationalism and Socialism, of a 'third way' between communism and capitalism led many people to National Socialism and as a motive was often of greater significance than hatred of the Jews.

The experience of the First World War played a part for many men who later formed the leadership corps of the Nazi party. The 'ethnic community of the trenches', in which there seemed to be no differences in status or rank, was to be carried over into society as well.

That anti-Jewish feelings were not necessarily a determining factor is also indirectly confirmed by the fact that from 1930 at the latest, anti-semitic themes became less dominant in Nazi propaganda. The National Socialists were evidently aware that they would not attract a mass following in Germany with radical anti-semitic slogans.

Even the motive recently suggested by Ernst Nolte of 'anti-communism' or 'fear of bolshevism' was by no means the decisive factor for most of the Nazi leaders discussed here in their decision to join the Hitler movement. Supporters of the so-called Nazi left, like the Strasser brothers or Goeb-bels, even entertained considerable sympathy for Russian bolshevism. It is also worth noting that Hans Frank, later the Governor-General of Poland, was originally an enthusiastic admirer of Kurt Eisner, and that the 'econ-omic theoretician' of the NSDAP, Gottfried Feder, gave his programme for the 'abolition of interest slavery' to Eisner's government in the hope that it would take steps to implement the plan. The recognition that idealistic motives played an important role not only for many supporters of National Socialism but also for many of its leaders does not in any way render National Socialism and its crime 'harmless'. But it makes a more precise understanding of them possible. This is the aim of the authors of the present volume. Of course the contributions also reflect the great variety of differing approaches to historical writing. The question of the role played by moral judgement in the discipline of history is answered in many different ways in the debate among historians. But even in the case of authors who regard an *explicit* moral assessment as important and even inescapable, the emphasis is not on accusation and moral condemnation but on an effort to achieve a more precise understanding of past events and hence to make them more comprehensible. Naturally it goes without saying that all the authors included here have no truck with attempts at apologism or justifying Nazism on moral grounds. However the frequent demonisation of Hitler and other prominent Nazis is also unproductive. Anyone who measures history solely by the standards of morality, even the history of the Third Reich, who categorises the leaders of National Social-ism solely under the heading of 'moral depravity' or even simply as the 'incarnation of evil' is putting barriers in the way of his/her access to an understanding of their career and of historical events as a whole.

This book represents only the first part of a larger project. Further volumes are in preparation which, like this one, contain contributions on the dominant personalities of the NSDAP and the Third Reich. The selection made for this volume does not therefore claim to be comprehen-sive in any sense of the word. One might well ask why Nazi leaders like, for example, Max Amann, Philipp Bouhler, Wilhelm Kube, Hans Heinrich Lammers, Viktor Lutze, Julius Streicher and Otto Wagener or alternatively leading members of the armed forces, like for example Werner von Blomberg, Alfred Jodl and Wilhelm Keitel are not discussed here. The selection in this volume is not representative nor is it intended to convey anything about the relative importance of the persons discussed, or not discussed, here. Along with the limits set by a compact volume, the following consideration was felt by the editors to be crucial: where there was any doubt, a person was not included if there was no really competent author available. For, in contrast to many reference works on the Nazi elite, it remains a fundamental aim of this project that contributions should only be accepted if their authors can be regarded as experts on the Nazi leader under discussion. Unfortunately no biographical studies exist as yet for countless leading figures in the NSDAP and the Third Reich. This project should be seen as an initiative to fill this gap.

The editors would like to take this opportunity to thank both the authors, who to a great degree have done justice to the aims of this book, and the History Editor at the Wissenschaftliche Buchgesellschaft, Hermann Cürten, without whose untiring efforts this study would not have been possible. Among the many colleagues who gave their help in the realisation of this project, the editors wish to thank in particular Dr Gerhard Schreiber, Freiburg, and Dr Hans-Heinrich Wilhelm, Berlin.

2 Martin Bormann: Hitler's Secretary
Jochen von Lang

At the end of October 1945, as they lay rotting and starving in the rubble of their cities, with no hope for the future, the Germans heard that twenty-four of the most important men in the Third Reich were being prosecuted as criminals. The names were all familiar to them, except one: Martin Bormann. Now for the first time they learned of his many functions: National Director of the NSDAP, General of the SS, Chief of the Party Chancellery, Secretary to the Führer, and still more besides. In the indictment of the International Military Tribunal at Nuremberg he was accused of having contributed to the 'Nazi conspirators' seizure of power' before 1933 and thereafter of having taken part in a conspiracy against peace, the Geneva Convention and humanity.

This indictment was as vague as the whereabouts of the man himself; he was the only accused for whom the victors were still looking. They did not find him, in spite of 200 000 copies of a 'wanted' circular, newspaper appeals and radio announcements. He had always worked in the background and now he had melted away into it. The Allies had no idea of what they were losing in the process: as perfect a National Socialist as Hitler himself could have asked for. Because of this he had become Hitler's shadow over the years; in many respects he even became a man who directed the dictator, by deciding what his Führer was allowed to know. Hitler, who barely trusted anyone, trusted him almost unreservedly, and with good reason. From Hitler's point of view Bormann was his most loyal follower – to the very end.

To all external appearances Hitler's pre-eminent functionary was totally unremarkable, the average German in every respect: 170 cm tall, dark eyes and prematurely greying dark hair, a round head, bull necked, he had become overweight from attending banquets and drinking. He was as good at taking as at giving orders and he carried them out without scruples. If he gave an order there was no mistaking it; anyone slow on the uptake might be helped on his way with a kick. He understood quickly and immediately grasped essentials. Both at work and at home he ruled absolutely. If a woman took his fancy he made no attempt to restrain himself and had taught his wife that she had to accept his affairs with a good grace. In a party which reserved all the important decisions for men this behaviour caused no offence.

His origins and Wilhelmine ideals predestined Bormann to be the ideal official. Although the son of a National Socialist petty bourgeois family, he boasted of coming from a Prussian military dynasty. In fact, his father was a post office clerk and had only been a trumpeter for a time in a Hussar regiment. His year of birth in 1900 should have singled out Martin Bormann as one of those heroic youths who overran enemy positions in the last year of the war. In fact, until his demobilisation he was batman to an officer in the Naumberg garrison. The profession he then studied was farming. He worked first as a trainee on a big estate in Mecklenburg and then as a farm manager; he was however never a real farmer, who according to Nazi dogma would be the life source of the nation. He was director of two large concerns in the Third Reich, but the only work he did there was with his index finger.

Even as a young man he said he wanted to sooth the sufferings of his vanquished people. In fact, he was convicted of having misdirected rationed foodstuffs. He made a more ominous contribution to German revival when he joined a North German *völkisch* (populist ethnic) league, became a member of an 'Association against the Arrogance of the Jews',[1] and from his farm manager's desk he administered hordes of shadowy figures whom the estates had given lodging. They were demobilised soldiers who had been unable or unwilling to gain a foothold in civilian life, who as Volunteer Units defended the exposed eastern border against Polish irregulars, and who were tolerated or even secretly supported by the governments of the Reich as a counterweight against communist revolutionary schemes. Years later Martin Bormann wrote in an NSDAP questionnaire that he had been 'sectional leader of the Rossbach Organisation in Mecklenburg'. This was a mark of honour in the NSDAP, for in its early days it was a rallying point for this kind of super-patriot. Bormann even said he went to prison with some Rossbach members for 'love of the Fatherland.' In fact, the rabble on the estate accused a comrade of conspiring simultaneously with the Bolshevists and the French occupying power in the Ruhr. That was in spring 1923. They tried the supposed traitor according to their principles: he fell victim to the Vehme. They filled him with gin, took him into the woods, where they smashed in his skull, cut his throat, and, just to finish the job, put two bullets in his brain.[2] The State Court in Leipzig reduced the charge of 'patriotic' murder to one of grievous bodily harm resulting in death. Bormann's part in the deed remained unclear; he got away with one year in prison. A few years later he described his martyrdom in the dungeons of the Republic in the *Völkischer Beobachter*. The thanks of the Fatherland caught up with him ten years later in the shape of a gleaming silver medal: the Blood Order of the NSDAP.

According to Hitler's wishes, this decoration, to be worn on a red ribbon, was originally to be given only to those who had taken part in the attempted putsch of 8 and 9 November 1923. However after the invasion of

Austria anyone was allowed to adorn themselves with it if they had been deprived of their freedom for at least one year in the service of the swastika. When Bormann's Party Office devised this condition in 1938 he too availed himself of this honour. He never wore other decorations, although, like all of Hitler's constant companions, protocol allowed him to wear all sorts of exotic insignia during state visits.

When he was released from prison in February 1925 a reward like this was still a long way off. Neither the aristocratically inclined *völkisch* leagues in the north nor the more plebeian National Socialists in the south were more than insignificant political sects. So, to begin with, all the anti-republicans gathered in paramilitary leagues. Bormann went to Weimar, because his mother was well placed there, and since Captain Ernst Röhm's *Frontbann* was particularly active there, he joined it. By July of the following year, 1926,[3] at the National Convention of the newly-established NSDAP in Weimar, he could already be seen standing in his brown shirt uniform alongside Hitler's big Mercedes, in which, as was to become the custom, the Führer saluted his followers' march past.

Six months later the Party became Bormann's employer – and remained so until the end. In Weimar he became the general factotum for the Party District Executive: in exchange for pocket money he helped keep alive a struggling weekly newsheet by being its advertiser, representative, accountant, cashier and driver, because he had succeeded in buying himself a small car. He also drove speakers out to the villages. His first and last attempt to win supporters in a busy pub ended in stuttering and ultimately silence after ten minutes which he had laboriously managed to fill with the party's propaganda slogans. From then on he knew that he would get to the top in this party of fire-eaters, orators, saviours of the world and fighting cocks only if he developed his own strengths: assiduousness, the ability to settle complex matters quickly, to organise, to be a bureaucrat. Fanatical brutality towards opponents, ruthlessness with friends and devoted obedience towards those in command soon marked him out as suited for greater tasks.

When the director of a Nazi relief fund in the SA High Command in Munich did not give the contributions to wounded fellow activists but put them in his own pocket instead, Bormann was given his job. In an amazingly short time he became an expert on insurance schemes. He dispensed with the secondary cover provided by investment companies, collected the contributions of all party members in one special fund and paid out for loss or injury at his own discretion and without allowing recourse to law. When the Party could yet again not balance its accounts for propaganda material, a loan from Bormann's reserves made them solvent once more.

He also made sure of his career in other ways. He married Gerda Buch, the daughter of a former major and Party member from the earliest days of the NSDAP whom Hitler had nominated as Chief Justice of the Party. At the wedding[4] nearly all the men wore brown shirts, including the Party boss, who came to the celebration to act as witness and put his car, the big Mercedes, at their disposal. Rudolf Hess, at that time (1929) the Führer's secretary, had also come to the celebration, and because Bormann did not meet with the approval of the rowdies of the SA High Command – the true blue fighters of the *Freicorps* and the former officers – in future the guardian of the relief fund addressed his criticisms of the SA coterie to Hess. In this way he showed himself to be a loyal citizen, intent on political morality, a German Everyman.

This reputation stood him in good stead when, with the seizure of power in 1933, the Party mushroomed in size. This, and the earlier fall from grace of the former National Organiser Gregor Strasser prompted Hitler to restructure the Party hierarchy.[5] Rudolf Hess, a political fool and therefore no rival, was now allowed to serve the Party as Hitler's deputy, but it was probably thought advisable to allocate him a Chief of Staff with a practical understanding of human nature, with burning ambition and unshakeable loyalty to the Führer: Bormann. As one who prided himself on his modesty, Hess had no need to fear that his new colleague could steal even a fraction of the glory of his new duties; Bormann stayed in the background. For this too he was rewarded; when Hess became even more demonstratively modest by dispensing with any mark of rank on his brown shirt – this was moreover just what the Führer had done – Bormann received the title of National Director of the Party and naturally along with it the tab with the golden eagle on a red ground on his brown jacket.

In 1933 there were sixteen such dignitaries in the Party. Later their number increased to nineteen. To all appearances they were equal in rank, so they were constantly fighting amongst themselves about their powers and annoying the Führer with their insistence on arbitration. They did not suspect that in the not too distant future their new colleague would spare them all this unpleasantness by announcing – in Hitler's name, naturally – that the affairs of the Party could only be brought before their very busy Führer if they had first been brought to the attention of his deputy (or of *his* deputy, Bormann). Hess the dreamer naturally did not want to be concerned with trivia; he liked to float above the clouds – and not just as an aircraft pilot. Hitler therefore preferred to collaborate with Hess's Chief of Staff. Bormann presented him with short documents which lent themselves to swift decisions, had been evaluated for their implications for Party policy and were legally watertight – thanks to the steadily growing band of assistants in his steadily growing department.

Hitler had given assurances to people in Munich that the Party National Directorate would stay in Munich. Hess therefore felt obliged to stay there. Bormann however gradually moved to Berlin where he was allowed to set up a small office in the Reich Chancellery. Later a larger office was added close by, so that he had all the documentation at hand when the Führer needed something. Bormann soon had a regular place at Hitler's lunch table.[6] There his devotion occasionally compelled him to take a meal from Hitler's vegetarian menu, in spite of his own preference for juicy steaks, and then he could not refrain from assuring those at the table how much he was enjoying it.

He admired the Boss, – as Hitler was called in the small circle of those constantly with him – honestly and unreservedly, far more than most national or Party comrades. Overpowered by his charisma and confirmed in this feeling by the successes of the first years of government, he and countless other Germans transferred to their Führer one of the tenets of religious faith: whatever he does is good, even if we fail to recognise it at first. However Bormann had yet another reason for toasting himself in the glow of Hitler's favour; his unexpected rise in the Party and the nature of his duties constantly increased the number of his enemies and those jealous of him, and any who realised that Bormann himself was not to blame were offended by his brutal manner and the inconsiderateness of his methods. These too met with the Führer's approval. When he once happened to hear Bormann shouting at a colleague over the phone a grin spread across Hitler's face and he exclaimed 'That's letting him have it!' Many months later however he fended off complaints about Bormann, explaining that he needed this ruthless follower to win the war.

This comment reveals that even this constantly loyal follower, who was always ready for duty, was never more than a tool for Hitler, to be used as long as he needed it, and which he would have regarded as so much scrap when he no longer had any use for it. If Bormann had ever hoped that in time the Führer would treat him with more than goodwill embellished with a sprinkling of carefully calculated marks of distinction, for all his efforts he never gained anything more than a benevolent patron. Armaments Minister Albert Speer had sadly proclaimed the truth: 'Hitler did not have any friends'.[7] The feminine intuition of the then twenty-three year old Eva Braun led her to suspect this as early as March 1935. 'He needs me only for specific purposes . . .' she wrote in her diary.[8]

Because of Bormann's blind devotion Hitler regarded him as suited to organising private matters as well. The Führer concealed these almost more carefully than his state secrets; evidently he feared that he would lose the aura of being superhuman if he showed all-too-human traits. He left the administration of his fortune to the financial administrator who had proven his worth with the Relief Fund; given his artistic temperament he never bothered about financial matters. In this case his lack of respect for Mammon paid dividends: because the financial director collected whenever there was anything to be had. He also administered the millions from an 'Adolf Hitler Fund' from big business – honestly, but not entirely selflessly, since it increased his influence if he could give a hand to the leading lights of the Party after the expense of attaining new offices had led them into difficulties.

For Hitler the private citizen he obtained land at Obersalzberg above Berchtesgaden; the Führer had bought a holiday house there and was now having it converted into a holiday Residence. With a good deal of money and where necessary by wielding the power of the state, Bormann acquired all the landholdings in the village, had them entered in his name in the land register and turned the mountain environment into a long-term building site. In accordance with plans drawn up by Hitler, the frustrated architect, his small house was extended upwards, downwards and outwards and fitted out with an enormous window which could be lowered to give a majestic view from the conference room over the expanse of the Unterberg. The Bormann family, with a final tally of nine children, a large number of domestic servants and frequent visitors moved into a former children's home up there – after suitable alterations. Goering too obtained a building site and Albert Speer was given a studio. The upper valley soon filled up with buildings: a guest house, SS barracks, a Party department, accommodation for employees, a farmhouse with outbuildings for cattle and horses, a plant for producing fruit juice, an apiary. Bormann himself managed the farming. It provided Hitler as first priority with hot house vegetables, milk products and honey, but also fed his retinue. However it ran at a great deficit; it would have been cheaper to buy the products at a shop. Amused, the lord of the manor one day presented his major domus with a bill.

The most expensive object at Obersalzberg was the Kehlstein House, a private guest house on the summit of a rock outcrop, reached by a mountain road, built solely for this purpose, and by a gleaming brass lift. The cost: in today's money a few hundred million marks. Since the Führer was held up to the people as a shining example of the modest life style, any mention of this building required special permission. A rumour was spread by word of mouth that Bormann had given it to the Führer for his birthday. In fact Hitler only paid a couple of visits to this 'Eagle's Nest', as it was known by the American occupying forces. The roads and footpaths which Bormann had built across the formerly peaceful pasture land were of more practical use. With kilometres of high wire fencing gates and guards he prevented the hoi polloi from disturbing the Führer's peace.

Bormann displayed particular vigilance towards those who were in his opinion the most dangerous enemies of the Germans: Jews and priests. Party policy committed him to the persecution of the Jews in any case; a convinced National Socialist could do nothing wrong in that respect. The battle against the authority of the church and its servants was however more difficult; they sheltered behind the 'positive Christianity' which the Party had promised to protect. So Bormann had to confine himself to trimming back the traditional rights of the churches,[9] such as religious education in the schools. He had protestant clerics, who had once supposed National Socialism to be an enemy of atheism, driven out of the Party. He promoted groups who depicted Jesus as a Jew and overthrew his teaching. He banned everything Christian from his own family. His wife Gerda was instructed to protect the children from church influences at school or from playmates. Among the *Gauleiter* were some who disapproved of such a rigorous attitude. Most of them had gathered together their supporters themselves in the early days and only felt obliged to obey Hitler. With the agreement of the latter, Bormann intended to teach them to be more biddable. To this end each had a District Chief of Staff introduced into his office, a new functionary responsible to Bormann. They were no longer allowed to meet as a group without Bormann's permission. Their prerogative of free access to the Commander-in-Chief was restricted; they were now only allowed to invite themselves to lunch but they were not allowed to bring up matters pertaining to their duties there. Anyone who made himself unpopular went in fear for his office and prerogatives. Thus Julius Streicher, the 'Chief of Franconia' and editor of *Der Stürmer*, who was acting particularly high-handedly, was driven out of his Nuremberg *Gauleiter*'s office back to his farm. In Bormann's office lists were compiled of functionaries held in reserve to replace disobedient *Gauleiters*. Anyone who wanted to gain promotion in Party or state needed the approval of Bormann's chancery.

No-one was better informed about Hitler's plans than he was. He was in Prague when the remnants of Czechoslovakia were made into a Protectorate. He was Hitler's shadow at the launch of a new battleship, a tour of inspection of the West Wall and at SS battle manoeuvres. He helped prepare for war. At the end of July 1939 Bormann was honoured when, in his family home in Pullach, Hitler informed a few selected members of the Party that within a few days he would change from being a rabid anti-Bolshevik into Stalin's accomplice. When the SS Personnel Office enquired of Bormann whether he already had a position, should war break out, he answered 'Not necessary, since if mobilisation occurs I will be at Hitler's side'.

On the evening of 3 September 1939, therefore, he boarded Hitler's special train, the first Headquarters. He had dressed up in field grey in an SS General's uniform, and in it he played at soldiers until the closing minutes of his life. However he never shot at the enemy, fighting instead on the 'home front' against defeatists, parasites, hangers-on, Christians and Jews. The Führer's military entourage were miserly in their respect of his Party office, but since he clung doggedly at Hitler's heels and could only be excluded from military briefings, he scarcely missed a single tip-off. He took care of important matters immediately, other paperwork ended up in a card index which he could refer to some future date. If Hitler happened to be busy at Headquarters as Commander-in-Chief, then for all practical purposes Bormann was the first and last authority in civilian matters. If the Boss retired to the Berghof, even generals had to stay down below on the plains. Party leaders were categorically only allowed to come when Bormann invited them, and he was a witness to nearly every conversation. Even Goering, Goebbels and Himmler had to accommodate themselves to his omnipresence. At Hitler's nightly monologues he was usually the only Party grandee among the listeners. It was typical that Hitler's initial, spontaneous reaction was to call Bormann when he was told that Hess had flown to Britain.

Two days later, on 12 May 1941,[10] Hess's deputy to all intents and purposes moved into his former patron's place. As the director of the Party Chancellery he followed his Supreme Commander into the 'Wolfsschanze', set deep in the forest, where Hitler reduced his team of advisers to a 'Committee of Three': Keitel, Lammers and Bormann, whose influence soon far exceeded that of his two colleagues. In April 1943 he fell heir to yet another title which Hess had held from the early days of the NSDAP: Secretary to the Führer; it allowed him to take part in every decision. Bormann intervened in the matter of exploiting the occupied lands to the east, in the decision to allow Polish children no more than a rudimentary schooling, and when the fate of shot-down enemy pilots was being discussed. When Goebbels proclaimed 'total war' to be the means of rescue from defeat after the catastrophe of Stalingrad, Bormann flung himself energetically into the plan and succeeded in playing a leading role in the 'levée en masse'.

After the attempt on Hitler's life on 20 July 1944 the Führer trusted almost him alone. The Army had committed high treason. The Air Force and its Commander-in-Chief had lied to him and failed. Ministers were unwilling to break laws as ruthlessly as their Führer demanded of them. The Waffen SS was no longer providing the expected victories, the Gestapo was not capturing the enemies of the state in time and even the leader of the SS, who always carried the oath of loyalty about with him on his belt buckle, was no longer free of suspicion of cultivating links with enemies within and without. Since the massacre of June 1934 the SA had sunk to the level of a rifle club. And Germany's Allies? They had appeared after victories; now after defeats they were disappearing, one after the other. Even the Duce of Italy, once an admired model, was now a dictator without land or people. Enemy forces were advancing towards the German borders from the east, west and south and their aeroplanes were destroying the Reich almost unopposed. That might have made many a follower waver, but Bormann remained reliable and willing.

When reason had long since declared the war lost[11] Bormann still, in spite of his understanding of the true situation, believed in Hitler's luck, in his supposed genius and even in miracle weapons. An imagined providence could not, in his belief, permit six years of privation, distress, fear, sacrifices of health and life to remain unrewarded. Bormann and his wife often encouraged each other to this effect in their letters. They sought prophetic consolation in historical novels and, like their Führer, after military defeats they kept up their spirits by remembering events from the reign of King Frederick II of Prussia.

On 5 February 1945 he wrote to Gerda from the destroyed Reich Chancellery: 'You would have to be quite an optimist to say we still had a chance. But we are. We trust our destiny. It is quite simply inconceivable that fate would lead our people and its leader along this wonderful path, for us finally to stumble and disappear'. For this staunch Party member there could be no defeat which would precipitate the nation into a super-Versailles and which would confront him himself with the many crimes he had committed or simply condoned.

Finally he only had heroic rhetoric left with which to strengthen his resolve. On 2 April he wrote to his wife 'We will do our sworn duty to the end; and if we perish, as the old Nibelungs once did in Attila's Hall, let us go proudly and unbowed!' He knew of course that nothing else could be gained by bowing. All he too had left was hope in the miracle on which Hitler the gambler was still speculating.

The more the Reich dwindled during the last few weeks of the war into the Reichs Chancellery and the bunker underneath it, the closer Hitler and Bormann must have felt to each other. He was allowed to write down the latter's will and send it by courier to the Obersalzberg. He could assign a few troops to each of his fanatical Party officials and send these small forces to strengthen morale in areas near the front – as executioners for defeatists. He instructed members of the Hitler Youth (boys and girls)[12] to allow the enemy to sweep past them and then to commit acts of sabotage as Werewolves. His activism did not slacken as long as he still had the tools of his trade at his disposal: batteries of teleprinters, through which he sent commands, proclamations, entreaties and abuse almost without pause into the world above. Just as his Führer could only call upon shattered divisions for his 'blow for freedom', so Bormann's messages were at the end transmitted into a void. The ministers, *Gauleiter*, National Party Leaders, even Albert Speer, Heinrich Himmler and Hermann Goering were now only concerned with saving their own skins – from the enemy and from him too.

The faithful Bormann stayed in his Führer's underworld until the latter's body was half consumed in the flames. It is open to doubt whether he was sustained at this time by his ardent heroism alone. Tradition has it that, along with two generals he was friendly with, he drew courage from the cognac which was available in abundance – top quality French produce, of course. At the same time, in the last days of his life he had the satisfaction of being, along with Hitler, who had lost interest, the unrestricted ruler of the Reich. Of course it now measured only a few square kilometres.

In the night of 1 to 2 May 1945[13] the inhabitants of the bunker attempted to break through the encircling Red Army. During this time Bormann disappeared. He wanted to take Hitler's political testament to Flensburg to Admiral Karl Dönitz and take up his office there at the same time. Hitler had nominated Dönitz as his successor and named Bormann as Party Minister. He never arrived in Flensburg. The Nuremberg judges would have been able to find Bormann's body if the Americans had believed the statements of the National Youth Leader, Artur Axmann. At the hearings he had stated that he had seen the Führer's Secretary dead at the first light of dawn, after the night he fled, in the vicinity of the Lehrter Station in Berlin. As it later transpired, Bormann had made use of the Nazi suicide pill, the capsule filled with prussic acid, which Hitler too had used. The corpse was buried as a nameless soldier not far from where it was found; after breaking out of the Führer's bunker Bormann had removed all marks of rank and all clues to his identity. Perhaps he would have had a chance of surviving unrecognised in prison. He had always remained a typical petty-bourgeois in every respect and was scarcely distinguishable from the millions who had trustingly followed Hitler.

Bormann was condemned to death in his absence on 1 October 1946 in Nuremberg, one of twelve accused. His skeleton lay undiscovered under the earth of the Exhibition Grounds in the Invalidenstrasse Berlin until 7 December 1972.

NOTES

1. Bormann's own entries on the Party questionnaire (Berlin Document Center).
2. From the verdict of the State Court, Leipzig (Berlin Document Center).
3. Information given to the author by Hans Severus Ziegler, former deputy *Gauleiter* of Thuringia.
4. Information given to the author by Albert Bormann, Martin Bormann's brother; wedding photographs.
5. Letters from Bormann to Rudolf Hess dated 5.10.1932 and 27.3.1933 (Bundes-archiv Koblenz and the personal file on Martin Bormann in the BDC).
6. Information given to the author by Baldur von Schirach and Albert Speer.
7. Information given to the author by Albert Speer.
8. Eva Braun's diary, entry dated 11.3.1935, in: W. Maser, *Adolf Hitler. Legende-Mythos-Wirklichkeit* (Munich and Esslingen, 1971) p. 317.
9. Letter from Bormann to Bernhard Rust dated 20.5.1939 (Berlin Document Center).
10. Circular from Bormann to the National Directors *et al.* dated 15.5.1941 (Berlin Document Center).
11. Correspondence between Bormann and his wife Gerda.
12. Statement made to the author by Artur Axmann.
13. Statement by Artur Axmann, IMT files, Ermittlungen der Staatsanwaltschaft Frankfurt am Main.

BIBLIOGRAPHY

Primary Sources

For his publication on Bormann the author had available to him documents from the following agencies: the final report of the Frankfurt State Prosecutor filed under Js 11/61 (GStA Frankfurt am Main) in the 'prosecution for murder of Martin Bormann' dated 4 April 1973. These findings were written by the Senior State Prosecutor, Joachim Richter, who had been conducting the search for Martin Bormann for over a decade on behalf of the Frankfurt State Prosecutor's Office. Because of his involvement in the clearing up of the Bormann case, the Hesse Justice Minister, Karl Hemfler granted that the author could be the first to publish this final report. Apart from archival research, the author's biography of Bormann (see below) and this present contribution are based primarily on interviews with contemporaries. Among others, the author questioned Artur Axmann, Friedrich Bergold, Adolf Martin Bormann, Albert Bormann, Sepp Dietrich, Karl Dönitz, Alfred E. Frauenfeld, Hans Fritsche, Heinrich Heim, Ilse Hess, Heinrich Hoffmann Jr., Karl Kaufmann, Robert M.W. Kempner, Otto Kranzbühler, Wilhelm Mohnke, Hanni Morell, Werner Naumann, Henry Picker, Karl Jesko von Puttkamer, Hanna Reitsch, Hans-Ulrich Rudel, Gustav Adolf Scheel, Baldur von Schirach, Henriette von Schirach, Richard Schulze-Kossens, Lutz Graf Schwerin von Krosigk, Lord Shawcross, Otto Skorzeny, Albert Speer, Felix Steiner, Otto Strasser, Ehrengard von Treuenfels, Karl Wahl, Walther Wenck, Karl Wolff, Wilhelm Zander, Hans Severus Ziegler. The Bormann-Sammlung (27 volumes) is in the author's private archive. The British historian H.R. Trevor Roper has edited a book containing Bormann's letters: *The Bormann Letters. The private correspondence between Martin Bormann and his wife* [Gerda Bormann] *from January 1943 to April 1945* (London, 1945).

Secondary Literature

In 1987 the third, completely revised new edition of the Bormann biography written by the present author appeared: J.v. Lang, *Der Sekretär. Martin Bormann: Der Mann, der Hitler beherrschte* (with the collaboration of Claus Sibyll) (Munich/Berlin). For Bormann see also the two volumes edited by L. Besymenski: *Auf den Spuren von Martin Bormann* (Berlin, 1965); *Die letzen Notizen von Martin Bormann. Ein Dokument und sein Verfasser* (Stuttgart, 1974). See also the study by J. Wulf, *Martin Bormann-Hitlers Schatten* (Gütersloh, 1962).

3 Richard Walther Darré: The Blood and Soil Ideologue

Gustavo Corni

Richard Walther Darré stands out in a number of ways from the other National Socialist leaders. Firstly he joined Hitler's Party very late, more precisely in summer 1930, almost at the same time as he was admitted to the inner circle of the National Socialist elite. He did not therefore have to work his way up the Party during the 'heroic phase' when it led a marginal existence, but went straight to the top. Secondly Darré never belonged to the Führer's immediate circle, the entourage which, particularly from the late thirties onwards, took on the role of a second government and was able to influence Hitler's decisions. Darré's distance from the intrigues of the 'court circle' around Hitler can be explained by his honesty, an under-developed inclination to flattery and his firm ideological convictions.

Moreover, it is interesting that Darré had a degree of political power only during the limited period between 1930 and 1936. This period en-compassed the series of electoral successes, during which Darré was able to fulfil a decidedly important function, and the consolidation of power, when he had control of agricultural policy. When the Four Year Plan was initiated, involving the full militarisation of the Third Reich, Darré's political career went into a marked decline. After the outbreak of war he disappeared for good from the German political scene.

Do these factors justify the thesis that Darré should be classed as a fellow-traveller, a conservative politician who, as was argued recently, cannot be regarded as a National Socialist? Or does the eccentric figure of Darré not simply confirm the complexity and variety of a regime which history has for too long presented as being all too unified and homogeneous? In what follows we will attempt to provide a partial answer to these alternative possibilities.

Born in July 1895 in Belgrano (Argentina), the son of prosperous parents who had temporarily moved abroad shortly before, Darré studied until the outbreak of the First World War with the aim of specialis-ing in colonial agriculture. Like other National Socialist leaders, he served with distinction in the war. And like them he had considerable difficulty in the post-war period in taking up his profession, difficulties which were in stark contrast to his solid middle class background. Nonetheless he suc-ceeded in completing his studies in agriculture and animal husbandry at the university of Halle, even if he was not able to realise his academic and scientific ambitions. In the late twenties, when he was engaged in official government fixed-term contracts in the field of animal breeding, Darré won distinction with some publications on selective breeding, which became the basis of his subsequent racist anthropological theoretisation. In complete accord with the agrarian and irrational tendencies of the *völkisch* (populist ethnic) movement, including H.F.K. Günther's theories on the Nordic race at the end of the decade, Darré produced a coherent theoretical construct glorifying the peasantry, who were regarded as the racial focus of the German people. The reorganisation of agriculture, not so much from the point of view of economics, but more from spiritual and racial considerations, was for him the decisive precondition for giving back to the German people its outstanding racial qualities, which had gone into marked decline as a result of the increasing pace of industrialisation. In this context Darré coined the expression 'Blood and Soil', by which he intended to demonstrate the reciprocal relationship between the quality of the race and the peasant life.

The two volumes *Peasantry as the Life Source of the Nordic Race* (1929) and *The New Aristocracy of Blood and Soil* (1930), in which he presented his theoretical considerations in a supposedly scientific and unassailable manner, produced a wide, and for the most part, positive response, which points to the fact that they slotted entirely and unreservedly into a specific cultural climate. In the first work Darré intended to show that the fundamental difference between the German and the Slav races lay in the steadfastness and peasant-like nature of the former. In the second book he deploys an extensive battery of anthropological and philosophical tools in order to prove that the internal structure of ancient German society in the mythical era did have class divisions but that they were purely functional. They did not imply that the peasant was inferior to the aristocrat. Darré drew practical conclusions from his theorising: the renewal of peasant society in Germany, by means of reversing the hitherto dominant trend of industrialisation and, moreover, in the long term, measures for the creation and selection of a new aristocracy with the best racial qualities, which would raise the German Reich again to the status of a great power in the heart of Europe.

The question of racial renewal brought Darré into close contact with Himmler and the SS. Thus for many years he was the Director of the Headquarters for Race and Resettlement, which was charged with defining the selection mechanism which was to make the SS the 'new aristocracy' of the Germanic race. The long term perspective which this implied however remained vague in Party propaganda, which from 1930 under Darré's direction paid particular attention to the rural electorate. It concentrated on the general glorification of the peasantry and promised to save it by reversing existing trends. The themes of race and aristocracy on the other hand were left out, because they might have prompted unfavourable reactions from the intended audience.

In spite of these prudent tactics it is not possible to disregard the racial and ideological elements in Darré's thinking. It would be equally mistaken to forget that the anti-urban and pro-rural intellectual currents corresponded unreservedly with National Socialist thinking. After an active period in various groups on the extreme right, among which were the *Artamen* and the *Stahlhelm*, Darré's political career brought him into contact with Hitler's movement. Thanks to the good offices of the architect Paul Schultze-Naumburg and the degree of renown he had acquired through his writing, Darré came into contact with Hitler himself in spring 1930. And the Führer spontaneously asked him to take over the directorship of a new section of the Party's political executive devoted to peasant affairs. It was only after this, in July of the same year, that Darré became a card-carrying member of the NSDAP.

From Headquarters in Munich Darré began to build up a network of specialist advisers who operated across all the states in the Reich and whose job was to pick ideas from the grass roots and pass them on to Headquarters. From these a political and ideological programme was to be worked out which was aimed specifically at the rural population, in whom the NSDAP had hitherto shown scarcely any interest. The overwhelming success Hitler's Party achieved in the following elections in September, an electoral success which was evident to a marked degree in the countryside in particular, cannot however be ascribed to Darré's organisational abilities, because at this time he was involved in efforts to build up his agricultural policy network. The massive success seems to be linked more to the deep crisis, not exclusively economic, in which rural society found itself. It must be regarded as a protest vote.

In the following years, up to the seizure of power, Darré's strategy evolved along two converging lines. On one hand he launched massive propaganda campaigns in the countryside, to disseminate soothing messages of deliverance, and on the other hand he infiltrated the traditional interest groups from below. In this way he intended to produce a mass consensus which would serve as a means of pressurising the old ruling elites. But at the same time he was aware of the significance that these interest groups had with regard to national agricultural policy. In the case of the former Darré created an effective and well-integrated propaganda machine which had the advantage of being spread over almost the entire country and could therefore address social groups which had hitherto remained largely excluded from the far-reaching processes by which society was being mobilised. Darré's organisation made use of a network of publications of varying standards. Over and above this, speakers, suitably trained by Darré, journeyed tirelessly through the countryside propagating slogans about the guaranteed deliverance of the peasantry in the coming

'Third Reich'. It is not easy to tell how far the activities of Darré's organisation won votes and support for the National Socialists. It is not enough to rely on facts such as the steady increase in votes for the NSDAP at regional and national elections, the growth in Party membership in the countryside or the constant successes enjoyed by the National Socialist list in elections for the executives of various interest groups. For these uncontestable facts do not allow us to tell how far National Socialist propaganda was effective, as against general factors such as the severe economic crisis and the decline in the preeminence of the rural elites.

In any event the rural population's contribution to Hitler's election successes is undeniable and this was bound to have a direct effect on Darré's political role when the new regime was set up. Moreover it is worth noting that he succeeded in a few years in building up a propaganda machine which he personally supervised, and in working out a relatively consistent ideology, in which he was unique among the top members of the National Socialist elite. Darré's disappointment must therefore have been all the greater when Hitler agreed for tactical reasons that in his coalition government the agriculture ministry Darré prized so greatly should be entrusted to the leader of the DNVP, Alfred Hugenberg. His disappointment notwithstanding, Darré completed the process of coordination and integration begun in the previous years, through which he quickly took over full control of all the representative bodies in the realm of agriculture.

In this way he laid a secure basis for further progress, at the end of which he was Minister and undisputed leader of a sphere which included nearly one third of the total population. Hugenberg's downfall at the end of June 1933 was in the first instance the consequence of his foreign policy adventurism. But the absolute hegemony which Darré had long since achieved in the agricultural sector may well also have contributed to it. Appointed Minister at last, Darré got down to implementing his ideology of 'blood and soil' and making it one of the pillars of the Third Reich. The fundamental features of this first phase of government, during which Darré may be considered master of the situation – unharmed even by serious conflicts – were: the creation of a corporate body encompassing all producers and even those associated with agricultural production, then the drafting of new laws for the inheritance of land, thirdly the revival of land settlement, above all in the eastern regions and, finally, the regulation of the domestic market in foodstuffs (including imports).

As regards the first point, the idea of uniting all peasants in a single group equipped with greater bargaining power was not really new but had been in the air for some time as a leitmotiv in German rural society. However Darré undertook to implement it quickly and decisively. From July until September 1933 he enacted a series of outline measures on which he based the National Food Corporation. Of course this new organisation was far removed from the ideals of corporate self-administration, it adhered to the Führer principle and was strictly subordinate to the Party. The basic idea was not unambitious. For instead of limiting himself to organising agricultural producers Darré intended to gather together within the National Food Corporation all those who had something to do with the provision of foodstuffs: from production via processing to the point of sale. The principles of self-administration were corrupted in the process of actual implementation in favour of Darré's and National Socialism's predominant political aims. Within the context of his programme Darré of necessity came into collision with the interests of other areas, each of which had its own political representative in the leadership of the Third Reich. Particularly violent were his disputes with the *Gauleiter*, who would not contemplate accepting the existence of organisations at regional level which were free of their supervision, with Robert Ley's German Labour Front, which was attempting to gain control of all German 'workers' and with associations concerned with the interests of youth, women, the retail trade and so on. In all these disputes Darré succeeded up to a point in defending the primacy of his own organisation and his personal power base. However he often engineered a pronouncement in his favour from Hitler, who quite simply had to have regard for an organisation which provided and marshalled such an important section of his support. Speaking against an interpretation which explains these confrontations as the defence of corporate autonomy and therefore sees Darré as the supporter of self-administration for the peasants is the fact that the National Food Corporation was hierarchically structured, and that its chief purpose was to secure the support of the rural population for the regime. The conflicts mentioned become more comprehensible with reference to the polymorph and polycratic nature of the Third Reich.

The second pillar of Darré's policies as Minister and leader of the peasantry concerned the reform of the laws of inheritance, which were implemented in the National Entailed Farms Act, enacted on 29 September 1933. The purpose of the law was to put an end to the fragmentation of land ownership inevitable in a system where land was divided equally between the various sons of the land owners. By creating a new system of inheriting farms, whereby they could not be split up and could only be passed on to one heir – the most deserving one – National Socialism did not just intend to change forms of inheritance but also to anticipate the concept of an ideal form of land ownership. The farms were to be self-sufficient economic units, independent of the vagaries of the market and solely intended to bring into being again a peasantry which in due course would be refined by the principles of natural selection and be able to shoulder the grandiose tasks which Darré intended for it. In fact in his eyes the hereditary farm represented the core of the 'aristocracy' theoretically conceived of years before, which was to form the new leadership group not just in the agricultural sector but in the Third Reich as a whole. Such principles were so radically ideological that they were not acceptable to the majority of peasants, in spite of the advantages that the status of hereditary farmer afforded them.

The implementation of the law therefore came up against significant obstructions, beginning with the number of properties which, as against the overall tally, could be categorised as entailed farms. It was therefore unavoidable that the special courts which Darré had established to resolve any possible disputes about the entailed farms relaxed the most stringent stipulations. They allowed more leeway for regional practices and the rights of those who were not entitled to inherit (primarily women). Even those responsible for the National Food Corporation were forced to admit, in answers to a questionnaire Darré distributed towards the end of 1938, that the law was failing to achieve its objectives, particularly with regard to Darré's ideological plan. In fact it promoted inactivity and opportunism on the part of the producers instead of emphasising their good points and it had unfavourable consequences in that it reduced the birth rate.[1]

One of the most important weaknesses of the law on farm inheritance concerned the possibilities offered to those sons who did not inherit to become farmers in their own right, which could have strengthened the peasantry both qualitatively and quantitatively. These prospects were contained in the third pillar of Darré's political plan: colonisation, or land resettlement. Here too, as in the two other areas discussed, the National Socialists were establishing links with a tradition with deep roots in German society: the strengthening of agriculture, above all in the eastern territories, in order to set up a barrier against the advance of the Slav nations. There was a further element over and above this in Darré's plans, particularly in his idea of a new aristocracy, of enmity towards the class of estate owners who for centuries had dominated the eastern provinces of Prussia. Finally it should be remembered how hard the agricultural crisis of the late twenties had hit precisely those estates in the east which had made their living from the extensive cultivation of grain. All in all conditions were well suited to dealing a final blow to the moribund aristocracy and setting up a large number of small farms in the eastern territories. The resettlement programme launched by Darré was given a new name intended to emphasise the new racial content: the concept of restructuring the German peasantry was introduced in place of the idea of resettlement. The policies of this restructuring promised completely to reform the peasantry by the redistribution of land holdings. In spite of the Minister's high-flown declarations – one which especially springs to mind is the extremely hard-hitting speech delivered on 11 May 1934 in Storkow against the aristocracy, which in the past had destroyed the peasant's means of existence[2] – in practical terms the implementation of colonisation was completely unsatisfactory. On average the number and size of the new settlements did not surpass the results recorded during the years of the despised Republic. Moreover, considerations of quality prevented the implementation of the principle according to which two thirds of the new farmers were to come from the eastern provinces. Finally, colonisation as implemented by Darré failed totally to achieve its aim of offering new opportunities for social advancement to men who did not own land, that is day labourers and those who did not inherit.

What were the reasons for this failure (especially with regard to planning)? One of the individuals responsible for this planning[3] wrote that the 'general political considerations' which can be regarded as causes of its failure consisted essentially of three elements: 1) Hitler's deep-rooted conviction that the problems of domestic food shortages and overpopulation could only be solved by an expansion of living space. This idea was then put into practice during the war by the SS in the occupied eastern provinces. 2) The fact that it was politically inopportune to damage the interests of the Prussian aristocracy, which still had strong links with the officer corps and the bureaucracy. 3) Finally many economic experts, especially those involved in the Four Year Plan, were concerned that large estates would be more efficient from the point of view of production and the creation of strategic reserves than small peasant properties.

In short, all of the points in Darré's programme for a new agricultural policy which derived directly from his ideology were implemented only sketchily and in a manner which must undoubtedly have disappointed him. The fourth point of the programme, concerning the regulation of the internal market was less closely linked to his ideological preconceptions, although Gustav Ruhland, an economist and proponent of the cartelisation of the agricultural markets active around the turn of the century, was one of Darré's treasured 'spiritual fathers'. In fact, during those years, in the face of the economic crisis almost all the industrialised states applied forms of more or less strict economic planning and control in the agricultural sector. In Germany's case, thanks to trade barriers against imports, the type of market order Darré aspired to was able to keep supplies of goods and prices under control. But even in this context it must be emphasised that although on the one hand regulation of the market made it possible for agricultural producers to enjoy relatively stable returns, as years passed it was increasingly adapted to suit the interests of consumers, whose needs had to take precedence for the regime in the period of the build-up to war.

Moreover the returns assured to the peasantry paled into insignificance compared to the considerably more marked improvements in other groups' incomes. This situation quite soon produced widespread unrest in the countryside, and Darré was forced to direct despairing appeals to Hitler to intervene decisively in the looming 'general agricultural crisis'.[4] And so the cornerstones of the peasants' renaissance Darré had wished to see collapsed one after the other. Moreover since the creation of the administrative machinery for the Four Year Plan, the Minister had seen Herbert

Backe's star rise in threatening fashion. Backe had formerly been his chief deputy and, deriving strength from the support of Goering and Himmler, Backe put himself forward as a technocrat in open opposition to the 'ideologue' Darré. He quickly succeeded in snatching away a part of the absolute power Darré had possessed until then. However the change in the balance of power between the two, which contributed to the hardening of Darré's reservations about the ruling elite, should not be regarded as a radical turning point. The policies which were translated into action thereafter were as much the Minister's doing as the work of his dangerous rival. One only has to remember that the fundamental measures taken to intensify the dirigiste supervision of agricultural activities actually originated during the time when Darré controlled the regime's agricultural policy: the law of 26 June 1936 on apportionment, which enabled the state to consolidate landholdings which belonged to various owners in order to rationalise production; or the law of 23 March 1937 (but already formulated in the previous year), which subordinated the economic interests of individual landowners to the higher aims of the state. In addition one could cite the satisfaction with which Darré greeted the appointment of Goering as Commissioner for the Four Year Plan.[5]

Darré's progressive loss of power in the years after 1936 is not echoed by, for example, a drastic transition from a land policy favourable to the peasantry to one which 'militarised' them, which the decrees quoted above might lead one to suppose. In fact agricultural policy continued on a wavering and uncertain course between dirigiste pressures on the one hand and the maintenance of privileges conceded to the peasants in previous years on the other. The reasons for this indecision lay in part in Hitler's desire not completely to squander the support of a considerable part of the German population, especially not in the face of the coming war. On the other hand, thanks to the close trading links with the Balkan countries which produced agricultural surpluses, it was possible to keep the agricultural economy as it were 'on hold' in comparison to the basic course of economic policy in the Third Reich without fundamentally altering its precarious balance. Indeed it was possible to import foodstuffs and raw materials from the Balkan countries and the Danube basin at very favourable prices. This allowed the transference abroad of internal contradictions in the realm of agriculture. And it should be remembered that Darré took an active part in this policy.

Nevertheless, grounds for dissatisfaction were accumulating in the countryside and Darré was increasingly powerless in the face of them. The labour shortage, triggered by the higher wages offered by industry, began to have worrying consequences: there was a threat that not only would productivity be reduced but also that the racial characteristics of the peasantry, so highly valued by the Minister, would be adversely affected, not least because of the increased workload on women. In view of the deep crisis in the agricultural economy the concession allowed between 1937 and 1938 of some price increases, in parallel with a decrease in the cost of fertilisers and machinery, was nothing other than an inadequate sop.

The outbreak of war brought a fundamental change in the situation, for now the Third Reich could exploit the resources available in the occupied territories without limit. However Darré's executive powers had long since disappeared. In March 1942 the office of Minister was also taken from him. At this time he began to develop a picture of himself as a 'victim' of National Socialist 'warmongers', which he then presented at the trials brought by the American military administration against a number of 'minor' ministers – a picture which in no way represents the problematic role Darré played for at least three to four years, when he was supervising agricultural matters and subordinating them to the interests of the regime. Sentenced to seven years imprisonment for crimes relating to the unleashing of the war, he was released early on health grounds. Darré died on 5 September 1953 in embittered isolation, totally engrossed in plans for 'organic' agriculture. This gave his defenders both then and now the opportunity to portray him as a forerunner of the ecological movement, who during the course of his meteoric political career was solely concerned for the well-being of the peasantry. But in the light of evidence given here, however compressed, this hagiographic description has no basis in historical fact.

NOTES

1. See the extensive correspondence in the Bundesarchiv Koblenz (BAK), R16, vol. 1272.
2. See press reports, including the *Kölner Zeitung* of 12 May 1934.
3. See the letters from Kurt Kummer in BAK, Nachlass Darré, vol. 56.
4. See, among other things, Backe's reports of 24.2.1938 (BAK, R2, vol. 18732) and Darré's dated 27.8.1938 (BAK, R43II, vol. 200) and 20.2.1939 (Deutsches Zentralarchiv Potsdam, 99 US 7, vol. 393).
5. Darré's letter to Hitler dated 5.8. and to Goering dated 1.11. in: BAK, NS 10, vol. 103, and Stadtarchiv Goslar, Nachlass Darré, vol. 146, respectively.

BIBLIOGRAPHY

Primary Sources

Sources for a biography of Darré, which has yet to be written, are relatively extensive. A considerable archive of papers is available, divided into a section dealing with the period before 1933, which is held in the Stadtarchiv Goslar, and a more comprehensive and significant section dealing with his activities in the government, which is in the Bundesarchiv Koblenz. Backe's papers are also held in Koblenz, and although incomplete, they are nonetheless useful for clarifying the difficult relations which existed between the two men. The papers on the National Food Corporation and the Ministry for Food and Agriculture, on the other hand, of which only fragments survive in Koblenz and in the Zentralarchiv, Potsdam, are totally inadequate. However it is possible to find sources on Darré's activities as the leader of the peasantry in the Third Reich in the collections of other archives: these include the files of the National Ministry of Finance and the Chancellery in Koblenz, the Press archive of the National Agricultural League, the Prussian Ministry of Agriculture in the Zentralarchiv in Merseburg, the files of the Foreign Office, which are dispersed in Berlin and Potsdam, and those on the membership files in the Berlin Document Center.

Secondary Literature

There is no complete biography of Darré, although there are two voluminous studies which deal with him: Horst Gies, *R. Walther Darré und die nationalsozialistische Bauernpolitik 1930 bis 1933* (Frankfurt am Main, 1966) and A. Bramwell, *Blood and Soil. Walther Darré and Hitler's Green Party* (Abbotsbrook, 1985) (both are theses). Gies later published a series of very comprehensive essays, among which are: 'Der Reichsnährstand: Organ berufsständischer Selbstverwaltung oder Instrument staatlicher Wirstschaftslenkung?', in *ZAGAS* 21 (1973) 216–33; 'Aufgaben und Probleme der nationalsozialistischen Ernährungswirtschaft', in *VSWG*, 22 (1979) 466–99 and 'Die Rolle des Reichsnährstandes im Nationalsozialistischen Herrschaftssystem', in G. Hirschfeld, L. Kettenacker (eds), *Der Führerstaat. Mythos und Realität* (Stuttgart, 1981) 270–303. Bramwell's book, which puts forward the thesis that Darré was an outsider in the regime, and fundamentally its victim, was convincingly attacked by critics.

With regard to the regime's general agricultural policy there is very little literature. I can only point to J.E. Farquharson's study, *The Plough and the Swastika: The NSDAP and Agriculture in Germany* (London, 1976), that of F. Grundmann, *Agrarpolitik im Dritten Reich* (Hamburg, 1979) and my own book which is currently at press: G. Corni, *Hitler e i contadini. La politica agraria del Terzo Reich* (Milan, 1989).

4 Gottfried Feder: The Failed Policy-Maker

Albrecht Tyrell

In historical writing about National Socialism the figure of Gottfried Feder occupies a singularly ill-defined position. General descriptions usually make do with the observation that the propagandist who coined the slogan 'the eradication of interest slavery' and was co-author of the 1920 Party Programme had been Hitler's economic and financial adviser, but that his influence had declined from the end of the twenties onwards when Hitler turned towards big business. Feder was employed for a time in inconsequential posts in the National Executive of the NSDAP and in 1933/34 within the government, before he disappeared into anonymity. It is striking that even in more specialised treatises on the internal development of the Party, or Hitler's links with groups within economic life, the authors never really succeed in achieving a clear understanding of Feder's relationship with Hitler and his part in the Party's rise to power. It therefore seems advisable to describe Feder's attitude to the NSDAP from its beginnings and to show the circumstances which shaped his political activism. A discussion of Feder's aims and his attempts to have his specific programme adopted in the NSDAP will ultimately give a clearer picture of the preconditions under which ideologues or 'policy-makers' were active in the Party.

There is scarcely anything in the first thirty years of Gottfried Feder's life which gives any indication of the political idealist who stepped into the public domain in 1918/19 in Munich. Feder came from Franconia. His grandfather and his father, privy counsellor and senior government official respectively, had achieved positions of respect as senior civil servants in the Kingdom of Bavaria. Feder was born on 27 February 1883 in Wurzburg and completed his Higher School Leaving Certificate in Ansbach. Up until 1905 he studied building science at the technical institutes in Munich, Charlottenburg and Zurich, specialising in the promising subject of building in reinforced concrete. After completing his diploma he spent the time until 1908 gaining practical experience with a building firm.

In 1901 Feder had joined the renowned 'Isaria Corps', an eighty-year old students' association of the type which practised duelling. His reputation as the then 'best-known swordsman of the Munich student body'[1] leads one to suspect, as was later confirmed on many occasions, that he had an excitable temperament and sensitivity, combined with vanity, which led him as a student into many affairs of honour and later involved him in endlessly recurring rows with Party members in the NSDAP. In one duel he suffered a head injury which made him ineligible for military service.

In 1908 Feder joined the civil engineering firm of Ackermann and Co. as a partner and director of their Munich branch. In the following years he built warehouses, bridges and other large buildings in Germany, Italy and Bulgaria; after the beginning of the war he added munitions stores and aircraft hangars. Since Feder and his firm only had limited capital of their own at their disposal, considerable loans were needed to complete each of their projects. We know from Feder's later descriptions of the 'demoralising' experiences the young entrepreneur with his ambitious plans had with foreign money-lenders. That they themselves were partly to blame because of their own naivety and arrogance can be left to conjecture. Nevertheless it was some time before he derived universally valid insights from his experiences with big banks and his observations abroad about the 'pitiless iron grip of the impersonal power of money, which first of all offers and gives the desired credit, but then in each economic crisis acts only in the self-seeking interests of capital'.[2]

In the first years of the war there were extensive state contracts to be fulfilled. Moreover the lack of shipping tonnage and steel turned Feder's enterprising spirit towards a project of building a reinforced concrete ship, and he devoted himself energetically to achieving this project at the risk of his personal fortune. Since he was not called up for military service, the project left him enough time to think about the social situation in Germany after the war. In an essay written in 1917, 'Compensation for German Soldiers at the Front', which, significantly, he distributed at once among the highest authorities, he took up the idea of reducing social tensions with an enhanced rural setttlement programme and the encouragement of small-holdings. Feder who was self-taught in these matters began to concern himself with questions of financial theory. The resentment he already felt was increased by concern about the increasing indebtedness of the German Reich as a consequence of war loans. But for a long time he evidently shared with many of his fellow-countrymen the hope for a victorious peace, which would allow the debts to be passed on to the losers. Only when this self-deception was no longer possible after the unambiguous defeat in 1918 does the way to salvation seem to have occurred to Feder in a flash of 'intuition'. He 'suddenly clearly recognised' the perniciousness of interest payments as the root of all the evil which had befallen Germany.[3]

> The principle of charging interest on loans is the devilish invention of the big credit institutions, it alone makes it possible for a minority of powerful financiers to live as indolent drones at the expense of the productive nations and their workforce, it has led to deep, unbridgable conflicts, to class hatred, from which civil wars and wars between brothers are born.

So said the introduction to the 'Manifesto for the Eradication of Financial Interest Slavery', which Feder committed to paper in the days after the capitulation in November 1918 and published as a pamphlet in 1919.[4]

An economic theory, at the heart of which is the demand for the 'eradication of interest slavery' by means of the abolition of all interest payments and the nationalisation of banking and the stock exchange, certainly does not fully do justice to the complexity of its subject-matter. But one should not overlook the fact that it possessed a certain attraction in the prevailing revolutionary climate precisely because it offered bearings in a socio-political landscape which had at a stroke become completely confused, and as an apparently ingeniously simple, radical solution Feder was not the only one to be fascinated by it. Members of the middle classes, who had been badly affected by the lack of goods, price increases, unemployment and other consequences of the war, were barred by their national and non-proletarian self-image from seeking salvation in the political and social revolution demanded by the socialist parties. In this context 'eradication of interest slavery' offered itself as the battle cry of a third way between capitalism and Marxism towards 'German socialism'.

Feder did not object to capital and private ownership as such, but wanted to link it to both individual achievement and social obligation and to give the state priority where the well-being of the whole demanded it. With a rather artificial distinction, which had been developed decades before in *völkisch* (populist ethnic), anti-semitic circles, he distinguished 'rapacious' capital from 'creative' capital. By the first he meant commercial and finance capital which 'grew ceaselessly' from returns on interest, which was concentrated in the hands of a few 'power-hungry international plutocrats' – for example the Rothschilds – and subjugated more and more countries by giving loans of all kinds.[5]

By contrast, Feder wanted to made money a tool of the economy again, instead of it being an end in itself. The necessary working funds for national industrial production, the 'creative capital', was in future to be distributed and controlled by the state itself. In order to make Germany independent of the 'financial powers above and beyond the state', Feder demanded a strict renunciation of all loans. Even he could see no possibility of escaping the financial burdens which the victorious powers would inflict on Germany. But when these had been paid, at the latest, Germany would have to release herself from international interest slavery. A new beginning at national level by means of declaring the state bankrupt and nationalising monetary affairs would break the fateful chain and give other countries a model of how to pull the rug from under the feet of the international capitalists.

The beneficial effect of the battle for the 'eradication of interest slavery' would not only manifest itself in increasing independence from the outside world, according to Feder, but also in the removal of the internal divide in the nation. In agreement with many who were looking to defuse the class war by means of 'German socialism', Feder proclaimed: 'Workers and employers belong together'. Their mutual interest in the output of the national economy was greater than the differences between them, which could be solved 'by means of contractual pay scales and the management of companies to their mutual satisfaction'.[6]

Even in his first publication Feder left no doubt that he did not simply see himself as a financial reformer but as the founder of a new political doctrine of salvation with a claim to universal validity. The description of his pamphlet as a 'manifesto', and, even more clearly, the linguistic references to the 'Communist Manifesto' in its closing sentences are characteristic of his claim to be in competition with Marxism.

Feder's dissociation from the marxist version of anti-capitalism was unmistakable. On the other hand anti-semitism played a less distinct role. Feder did not resist the temptation of presenting 'the conscious co-operation of the power-hungry plutocrats of all nations'[7] as a component part of a world-wide Jewish conspiracy, if for no other reason than that it opened up greater prospects of success for his demands. Nonetheless even in the following period, for Feder the economic aspects of his doctrine always ranked above the anti-semitic ones. He was more inclined to regard the Jews as a representative of the evil, but one whose removal would not bring about any fundamental change. Instead, from 1918/1919 onwards he held unerringly to the view that only the 'eradication of interest slavery would strike at the root of the world's ills, and the tap root at that.'[8]

This realisation had the effect of a political awakening for Feder. He took steps to put it into practice without delay. On 20 November 1918 he handed his first draft to the new Bavarian government under the independent socialist Prime Minister Kurt Eisner, because it seemed to him to be of vital importance that the issue of interest was tackled immediately.

The shattering of his delusion that he would find some agreement here, at least in his rejection of high finance, was followed by the discovery that his public activities were more in tune with the political right. For the time being Feder fought on his own for publicity, with total personal commitment. In the course of 1919 he retired from his firm. As the head of a family with three children this was not a step to be taken lightly, in view of the economic uncertainty which surrounded him, even if one can assume that his business prospects were now on the gloomy side, given the decline in foreign and armament contracts. In 1920 he gave up his home in Munich and moved into a small newly-built country house in Murnau on the Staffelsee. As time went on, however, Feder's sense of independence corresponded less and less to his actual material situation. He was increasingly compelled to link his work publicising his idea with the necessity of safeguarding his family's livelihood. The resulting mixture of idealistic pretensions, criticism of the 'bigwig' economy of the republican parties and demands for high fees for the lectures he gave did not always meet with understanding of his hosts and his later colleagues.

Nonetheless from 1919 on his battle-cry met with considerable interest. Feder sought to influence the public mainly in two ways. He became very active as a journalist and made appearances as a speaker when he had the opportunity. He did not disdain even a small audience. In both cases the *völkisch* movement, with its many groupings – in Munich alone there were more than two dozen of them in 1919/20 – offered a fruitful arena for his activities. Even before he had published his 'Manifesto' and 'State Bankruptcy – the Way Out' as separate pamphlets, radical right wing Munich papers had put their pages at his disposal. He quickly came into contact with the 'Thule Society' and the anti-semitic author Dietrich Eckart, who both played their parts in the early history of the NSDAP. The news, press and propaganda division of the Regional Army Command 4 – for the time being the highest military authority in Bavaria – employed Feder as an adviser and director of training for the education of personnel who were to use propaganda to combat socialist tendencies in the provisional army.

The corporal Adolf Hitler, who was among those taking the course in June, was deeply impressed by Feder's expositions. Feder's central idea is reproduced in the first piece of writing which survives from his early days in politics, although transposed into the direct incitement to anti-semitism characteristic of Hitler. In a statement on the Jewish question written on 16 September 1919, Hitler makes an unmistakable link between credit capital and Jewry, a link Feder had tended to hint at discreetly. 'His [the Jew's] power is the power of money, which effortlessly and endlessly grows in his hands and forces nations to take on that most dangerous of yokes, because of its initial golden sheen; a yoke they come to realise is so heavy in its later sad consequences.'[9]

Four days earlier Feder's and Hitler's paths had crossed once again at a meeting of the German Workers' Party (DAP), at which Feder was talking about his ideas. Both subsequently became members. But there the similarities ended. For while Hitler made his political base in the DAP, which was soon renamed the NSDAP, and quickly became its driving force and the public face of its propaganda, Feder remained an outsider. In the following period the Party interested him only in as far as it could be exploited as a platform for the dissemination of his idea. In 1920/21 his contact with the Party was limited to occasional speeches at Munich Party meetings.

Nonetheless the Party's Twenty-Five Point Programme of 24 February 1920 contained, in points ten and eleven, the demand:

10   The first duty of every state citizen must be to be physically or intellectually productive. The activity of individuals should not conflict with the interests of the generality, but must take place within the

framework of the whole, and for the benefit of all. Therefore we demand: 11   the abolition of income not generated by effort or labour. Eradication of interest slavery.

Primarily on the basis of these demands and the correspondence of some further economic points in the programme with the ideas disseminated by Feder, it has been suspected that he was the author, or at least the co-author of the programme along with Hitler and the Party founder Drexler. Indications that this was the case are however thin on the ground and do not tip the balance in the face of evidence which argues against his direct participation.

During the following years Feder went his own way. By 1920 he had already founded the 'German Fighting League for the Eradication of Interest Slavery', but it had very little influence. In 1920 his speakers took part in a total of thirty meetings. Feder only had moderate success, too, in influencing like-minded organisations in Germany and Austria. He came into direct competition with the NSDAP at the end of 1920 when he wanted to take over the dead-end newspaper, the *Völkischer Beobachter*, which was up for sale, and use it for his own ends. However Hitler and Drexler beat him to it. When Drexler subsequently wrote to Feder that he hoped 'that your ideas become ours and our ideas become yours'[10] this clearly reflects the distance between Feder and the NSDAP.

Feder's attempts to win a wider audience for his ideas by going it alone, as it were, were without success. However it was inconceivable for him to give up the fight. So he had no other option than to reactivate his loose, but never entirely severed links with the NSDAP in the course of 1922 and to seek support there.

He was always very welcome there as a means of bridging over the weak spots in the policies of the purely demagogic party. The NSDAP was enjoying success in this guise in Munich. At the Party Convention in January 1923, before the guests invited from outside the Party made their speeches, and immediately after Hitler who elaborated the three fundamental philosophies of the future Germany – socialism, nationalism and anti-semitism – he spoke about National Socialism's fiscal programme and set out the 'nature and goals of the fight for the eradication of interest slavery'.

In his new role as the economic and fiscal policy spokesman of the NSDAP Feder continued to play his old role with unbroken self-confidence. He saw himself as a forerunner of the Nazi movement because he had entered the public arena earlier than Drexler and Hitler – indeed he had even up to a point provided the latter with his first basic political insights, as he subsequently never tired of emphasising. At the same time he could claim that by his writing he had given substance to the vague policy profile of the NSDAP on its path towards 'national revolution'. That was not really the case until he was able to inform Hitler that he had 'finished the new book, after months of toil . . . a book which undertakes to describe the entire structure of the coming National Socialist state.' For Feder it was a matter of course from the outset that his book *The German State on a National and Socialist Foundation* (with the significant sub-title *New Directions in State, Finance and Economy*) would be regarded as the 'authoritative publication for the Party as a whole.'[11]

Feder realised of course that the NSDAP's success up until then was primarily the result of Hitler's actions, but he believed that the policy-makers were bound to get their chance, at the latest when the NSDAP seized political power. Therefore he expressly demanded of Hitler that he should form an 'intellectual general staff' from the most important of his colleagues and that he should listen to their advice, for, 'although we are willing to grant that you are supreme, you are only supreme among those who are otherwise your equals and independent, in the best old Germanic tradition'.[12]

In a short introduction, which Feder almost had to force out of him, Hitler did describe the book as the 'catechism' of the Nazi movement,[13] but this was as little a clear acknowledgement of Feder's pretensions as was his nomination as Minister of Finance on 8 November 1923, or the words which Hitler found for him in *Mein Kampf* in 1925, which seem positive only at first sight. Later, when Feder repeatedly referred to *Mein Kampf*, he prudently overlooked the unambiguous reservations which Hitler wrote into it on him and all theoreticians with narrow pretensions to exclusivity in the NSDAP:

> Every idea, even the best, becomes dangerous when it deludes itself that it is an end in itself, when in reality they are a means to an end – for me however, and for all true National Socialists, there is only one doctrine: Folk and Fatherland. . . . Everything must be measured against this standard and used or rejected according to its practicality.[14]

From Hitler's point of view the revival of Germany could not be brought about by devising and proclaiming concrete programmes; instead its basic precondition was a successful counter-revolutionary campaign against domestic political enemies, because only that would make concrete changes possible. He allowed policy-makers like Feder, Rosenberg, Arthur Dinter and Otto Strasser, to name but a few, to be active in the NSDAP because they secured supporters and fulfilled other useful functions, mainly in propaganda. For at least as long as they did not prejudice the Party's propagandistic impact to an intolerable extent with disputes over dogma, or publicly put his own position as leader in question, to a large degree they had a free hand. However without Hitler's express support their demands were not officially binding.

The distance between Feder and Hitler, rooted in their differing points of view, and also in mutual personal reservations, determined their relationship in the following period. Under these circumstances, if Feder wanted long-term success in the Party, it was vitally important for him to achieve a position in it which would force Hitler to make his ideas his own, or at least to give him a free hand. If he did not achieve this by influencing Hitler directly, then another way remained open for Feder; that of propagating his doctrine so successfully within the NSDAP and among its sympathisers that the desire to put it into practice became strong enough to win Hitler over. This second possibility, however, pre-supposed that Feder was not only an active and successful propagandist, but also required that he made himself indispensable by means of relatively stable support in the Party and that he attained a certain amount of independence. The outcome was already obvious; in spite of all his efforts Feder failed on both counts.

Feder did not receive an official Party post with clearly defined duties and powers after the re-establishment of the NSDAP in February 1925. From 1924 (until 1936) however, he was a member of the *Reichstag* representing the *völkisch* fraction of the National Socialists and from that time on he used it as a platform for making speeches and petitions in order to press forward towards his goal of 'eradicating interest slavery' and to implement measures related to it. Moreover the *Reichstag*'s Deputies' allowances and the free travel pass made his propaganda work much easier. In 1926 alone he spoke at 107 public Party meetings.

At the turn of the year 1925/6 he was also able to demonstrate his value as an ideological watchdog to Hitler. Feder saw great danger for the 'internal stability of the movement'[15] in the efforts of Gregor Strasser and the 'Study Group of the NSDAP North West' to define more precisely National Socialist goals which were only inadequately expressed in the old Twenty-Five Point Programme. Strasser had his reasons for not involving Feder in the deliberations. This made the latter all the more determined to set Hitler against them. Therefore the famous Bamberg Leader's Conference of the NSDAP on 14 February 1926, at which Hitler put an end to the first and only attempt to set up a formal forum within the Party for political discussion, was entirely due to Feder. To a certain extent it was as a reward for his watchfulness that Hitler entrusted him in Bamberg with the 'upholding of the programmatic fundamentals' of the NSDAP,[16] without however defining more precisely the extent of this commission, based as it was on the exigencies of the moment.

In any case Feder described himself from then on as the author of the movement's programme and had himself named as such in the Party press and on posters for meetings.[17] At this stage, in order to achieve a firm foothold within the leadership of the Party, in the months after Bamberg he especially advocated the 'urgent necessity of limiting the authority of individual Party offices' of the National Executive.[18] However his renewed call for the 'formation of a so-called intellectual general staff' and for regular Leader's conferences à la Bamberg, which he proposed with the support of most of the leading Party functionaries at the 1926 Party Conference,[19] was ignored by Hitler. On the other hand he came into his own with a call for the establishment of an official Party publication series, the 'National Socialist Library', of which he became editor in 1927.

Taken as a whole, the years from 1926 to 1928 may have been the most satisfactory in Feder's Party career. The gradual consolidation of the NSDAP gave him for the first time the prospect of putting his ideas into practice. He was fully occupied as a speaker; his commentary on the Party programme, which was published as volume one of the NS Library at the Party conference at Nuremberg in 1927, went onto its fifth edition in February 1929. The *German State* secured an edition of 20 000 copies at the end of 1928. The demands it made in the field of economic policy met with a positive response in the Party. Unpleasantness, which resulted partly from Feder's inclination on his journeys to intervene in the affairs of other Party members which had little or nothing to do with him, was kept within bounds. Disputes with Rosenberg, Otto Strasser and Dietrich Klagges about the concept of National Socialism and the content of individual points of policy were conducted relatively matter-of-factly.

As Feder knew, his position was by no means secure in the long term. He still had not found a place in the framework of the Party organisation around which his close friends could gather and establish themselves. And there were certainly no executive powers which corresponded to his role as watchdog. For this reason he seized his chance when the opportunity arose at the end of 1928 for him to take over the publishing house of four south German Nazi district newspapers. This turned out to be a complete fiasco, in which Feder even lost in three years what remained of his personal fortune. Hopes for the post of *Gauleiter* in Hessen-Darmstadt were dashed in 1931/32 as were those for a ministerial post in the Free State of Hessen.

Finally Feder received a few posts within the Party leadership during the organisational expansion of the NSDAP's National Executive from 1930 onwards; most importantly he became the director of the National Economic Council in November 1937. This title sounds much more important than the powers associated with it actually warranted, and once more Feder proved he was not a man who could protect and extend them on his own initiative. In addition, in Otto Wagener, the director of the Economic Policy Section established at the end of 1930, he faced a competitor who at least for the time being maintained stronger links with Hitler. Moreover Feder's ideas were always completely disregarded in Hitler's efforts to gain support from representatives of big business, one of the influential groups who were to clear the way for him to take over power.

Feder played a lamentable role in the Strasser crisis in December 1932. First of all he protested in an agitated letter to Hitler against his own sphere of duties also being cut back during the restructuring of Strasser's National Organisational Executive, and requested 'several weeks leave' – the following day he took everything back in a devoted declaration of loyalty to Hitler.

All the rest was simply a postscript. From July 1933 until the take-over of the National Economics Ministry by Hjalmar Schacht in August 1934, Feder fulfilled duties there as Secretary of State and along with this held office for a while as the State Commissioner for the Rural Resettlement Programme and as the President of the National Socialist League of German Technology. Then from November 1934 until his death in 1941, far removed from politics, he was simply Professor of Rural Settlement and Town Planning in Berlin.

NOTES

1. A.R. Herrmann, *Gottfried Feder. Der Mann und sein Werk* (Leipzig, 1933) p. 12.
2. G. Feder, 'Innere Geschichte der Brechung der Zinsknechtsschaft', in *Völkischer Beobachter* no. 72 dated 12.8.1920.
3. Ibid.
4. Diessen by Munich, 1919, p. 5 (reprinted in a shortened form in G. Feder, *Kampf gegen die Hochfinanz* (Munich, 1933) p. 51ff.)
5. Feder, Manifest p. 11.
6. Ibid., p. 55f.
7. Ibid., p. 12.
8. Ibid., p. 61.
9. Hitler to A. Gemlich, 16.9.1919 (published in E. Jäckel/A. Kuhn (eds), *Hitler. Sämtliche Aufzeichnungen 1905–1924* (Stuttgart, 1980) p. 89).
10. Draft of a letter from Drexler to Feder, 13.2.1921, sent 9.3.1921 (BA, NS26/76).
11. O.J. Hale, 'Gottfried Feder calls Hitler to order: an unpublished letter on Nazi Party affairs', in *Journal of Modern History*, **30** (1958) p. 362.
12. Ibid.
13. This preface is missing in the first and second editions, since Hitler kept Feder waiting for it for a long time.
14. A. Hitler, *Mein Kampf*, 504th–508th edition (Munich, 1940) p. 234.
15. Feder to Hitler 2/3.5.1926 (published in A. Tyrell (ed.), *Führer befiehl* . . . (Dusseldorf, 1969) p. 125).
16. Feder to Goebbels, 26.2.1926 (BA, NS 1–338); see also G. Feder, *Das Programm der NSDAP und seine Weltanschaulichen Grundlagen*, 184th/185th edition (Munich, undated, originally 1927) p. 19.
17. See for example *Illustrierter Beobachter* series 3, no. 2, dated 28.1.1928, p. 28.
18. Feder to Hitler, 2/3.5.1926 (p. 127).
19. BA, NS 26–389.

BIBLIOGRAPHY

Primary Sources

The best survey of Feder's ideas on economic and financial policy are to be found in
his collection of essays: *Kampf gegen die Hochfinanz* (Munich, 1933). The sixty-
four page pamphlet: *Das Programm der NSDAP und seine weltanschaulichen
Grundgedanken* (Munich, 1927) had already been printed by the Party publishers
Eher Nachf. before 1933 in an edition of several hundred thousand copies. Feder's
town-planning activities, which aimed to '. . . establish new country and small
towns as a new form for social existence . . . and to secure the economic base for
their existence' were given written expression in: *Die neue Stadt. Versuch der
Begründung einer neuen Stadtplanungskunst aus der sozialen Struktur der Bevölker-
ung* (Berlin, 1939).

Secondary Literature

Feder's person, policies and career have only twice been the subject of thorough
academic investigation: A. Tyrell, 'Gottfried Feder and the NSDAP', in P.D.
Stachura (ed.), *The Shaping of the Nazi State* (London, New York, 1978) p. 48–87,
and M. Riebe, *Gottfried Feder, Wirtschaftsprogrammatiker Hitlers. Ein biographis-
cher Beitrag zur Vor und Frühgeschichte des Nationalsozialismus*, unpublished
thesis from the University of Erlangen-Nuremberg, 1971. A. Barkai, *Das Wirt-
schaftssystem des Nationalsozialismus, Der historische und ideologische Hinter-
grund 1933–1936* (Cologne, 1977), is of the opinion that Feder's basic ideas 'were
more valid from the point of view of modern economic thinking' than contemporary criticism of them. For Feder's role in engineering and construction after 1933
see K.H. Ludwig, *Technik und Ingenieure im Dritten Reich* (Dusseldorf, 1974), and
E. Forndran, *Die Stadt- und Industriegründungen Wolfsburg un Salzgitter* (Frankfurt am Main–New York, 1984).

5 Hans Frank: Party Jurist and Governor-General in Poland

Christoph Klessmann

Hans Frank, the star jurist of the NSDAP and Governor-General of occupied Poland during the Second World War, is not one of the truly powerful men in the hierarchy of the Third Reich. Nevertheless he was one of those chiefly responsible for the bloody German reign of terror in Poland. This was where Frank played his 'historic role', for which he was condemned to death at the Nuremberg trials in 1946 and hanged. By comparison his role as jurist in the NSDAP before and after 1933 can be regarded as peripheral. Yet this first phase of his political biography, too, shows certain traits and links characteristics of a middle class intellectual who joined the National Socialists after some prevarication, and made his career in their Party.

Hans Frank was born on 23 May 1900 in Karlsruhe, the son of a lawyer. He attended the Grammar School in Munich and from 1916–17 he was for a while a pupil at a grammar school in Prague. Details about his political activities after completing his Higher School Leaving Certificate in Munich in 1918 are confused, but to a certain extent they reflect his problems in orienting himself politically. In 1918 Frank joined the '*König*' infantry regiment but was too late to be sent to the front. In 1919 and 1920 he was a member of the *völkisch* (populist ethnic) secret association, the 'Thule Society' and took part in the suppression of the Munich Soviet as a volunteer in the *Freikorps Epp*. According to the statements of a fellow pupil Frank was also elected to the Soldiers' Council in November 1918. Enthusiastic admiration for Kurt Eisner, at least, emerges from his early personal diaries. However this enthusiasm was directed entirely to the person and his admiration was based on a remarkable misunderstanding of the actual content of Eisner's socialist programme.

'Eisner was a hero,' Frank wrote, after the murder of the revolutionary leader, '. . . he died in the battle for his ideals. Yet what he died for has not died with him: the flame he fanned and nourished burns on: Socialism!' In the eyes of the middle class Hans Frank the goal of this socialism was not to be class war but the reconciliation of the classes, and it was to be realised not by the collective action of the masses but by a leader: 'the man who will finally remove the curse of classes from humanity. . . People are small and weak, one man is all!'[1]

The way from thoughts like this about a national socialism which would reconcile the classes, to joining the NSDAP seems to have been mapped out early in Frank's life. In September 1923 the student of economics and jurisprudence joined the SA; one month later he became a member of the NSDAP. He was an active member during the Hitler Putsch of 9 November 1923, fled afterwards for a short time to Austria, but returned to Munich in 1924 and in the same year received his doctorate in jurisprudence in Kiel.

After leaving the NSDAP for a short time in 1926 because of Hitler's attitude to the South Tirol question, Frank's career as a lawyer in the Party and within the state system began when he rejoined in 1927 (or 1928). He defended destitute Party members in countless court proceedings. The establishment of the National Socialist League of Jurists, the purpose of which was to coordinate the defence in political trials developed from his initiative. It later turned into the 'National Socialist League for Upholding the Law'. As a result of defending cases for Hitler himself, in particular, Frank was able to assure himself of a position in the Party. The Leipzig trial in September 1930 against army officers from Ulm accused of high treason became particularly famous. Hitler consistently pursued his strategy of strict observance of legality as means of achieving power and Frank offered him an effective public forum to reinforce this policy under oath.

A degree of trust between Hitler and Frank seems to date from this time. Of course the latter apparently never realised how much his Führer simply used the law as part of his political calculations but otherwise despised jurists and never took Frank's ideas of 'a renewal of German justice according to the ideas of National Socialist philosophy' very seriously. However Frank played a relatively substantial role not only in the context of the legality policy during the seizure of power, but also in the phase of the consolidation of power after 1933, although his various functions and offices carried little weight in political terms.

For a short time he was Bavarian Justice Minister and then in 1934 he brought about the liquidation of the regional state justice systems as 'State Commissioner for the Uniformisation of Justice in the *Länder* and the Renewal of Law and Order.' He was a member of the national government as Minister without Portfolio until the end of the Third Reich. According to his own statements he attempted to resist the encroachments of the political police in the early thirties, opposed the establishment of the Dachau concentration camp and protested against the execution without trial of SA leaders in connection with the so-called 'Röhm Putsch' in 1934.[2] How far such intervention went and how serious it was can not be determined. In any event it remained completely unsuccessful and was probably like the later conflicts of Governor General Frank with the SS, which were less concerned with justice and morality than with authority and asserting his own position. In the thirties, after he had played the role of legal accomplice for the seizure of power, Frank let himself be pushed aside into the politically relatively insignificant field of ideological judicature.

In October 1933 he founded the 'Academy for German Law', the task of which was to be the creation of a 'German Community Law' to replace Roman law, as was demanded in the Party manifesto. In addition the Academy was to instigate and prepare the drawing up of draft laws to promote and standardise the training of lawyers. In 1937 the Academy had approximately 300 members and forty-five committees. That Frank himself, as President, together with the Director of the Weimar Nietzsche Archive, directed the jurisprudence committee is a characteristic detail which reflects Frank's soaring ambition and actual ineffectiveness. Apart from a few of the Academy's activities, which are primarily of interest to a more specialised history of the discipline of jurisprudence (for example the *National Socialist Handbook for Law and Legislation*, 1935; the *Year Book of the Academy for German Law*, Iff, 1933ff), this institution is of particular interest with regard to Frank's later activities in two respects. Part of the staff of the Academy was transferred to the occupation administration in Poland (for example the Chief of Staff of the Government General (GG), Secretary of State Josef Bühler, district governors Karl Lasch (Radom), and Ludwig Fischer (Warsaw), Wilhelm Coblitz as the director of the 'Institute for German Activities in the East' among others). Furthermore, within the framework of his Academy, Frank developed contacts with Poland in the form of a Working Party for Polish-German Legal Links (1937). The background to this was apparently attempts to form a 'new Polish policy' along the lines of an anti-Bolshevik alliance of the German state, with Poland as the junior partner, which he unreservedly supported.

However these contacts did not have any demonstrable inherent link with Frank's nomination as the leader of the GG in 1939. This has to be seen more as Hitler's 'reward' for a Party veteran whose loyalty seemed assured. In any case neither his previous links with Poland nor the idea of a 'revival of Germanic law' had any visible influence on Frank's activity in his new role as Governor General. Instead, like some of the *Gauleiter* and District Chief Executives for the areas of Western Poland annexed into the German state, he unleashed a reign of terror which put all other forms of territorial annexation by the National Socialists into the shade and gave tangible proof of the new character of the 'ideological war of extermination' (Ernst Nolte). 'Frank is behaving like a megalomaniac pasha', Ulrich von Hassell, former ambassador in Rome, noted in his diary on 25 December 1939.[3] This remained an apt description of Frank during his whole period of office in Poland.

Only a few details about Frank's short period as Leader of the Administration during the martial rule of General von Rundstedt in September/October 1939 are available. According to a note added later to the front of his office diary, on 15 September he received an oral command from Hitler 'to take over the entire civil administration in the former Polish territories as Supreme Head of the administration'.[4] By decree of the Führer on 12 October he was made Governor General for those parts of Poland not absorbed into the German state, with effect from 26 October. Two weeks after the termination of the military administration and the official establishment of the GG he moved to Cracow, where the Wawel, the old Polish royal castle, was to be his imposing seat of government. Frank was directly responsible to Hitler and so formally held a strong position. Later, in various disputes, he repeatedly referred to the wording of the decree, without however being able to secure his political position, which in reality was weak. For the central departments of the German state in Berlin possessed far-reaching powers, in particular Goering as the President of the Ministerial Council for the Defence of the Nation and Commissioner for the Four Year Plan. One of the more serious, lasting disputes came about as a result of the quasi-independent status of the Supreme SS and Police Chief in the GG, who was nominated by Himmler in his role as 'State Commissar for the Consolidation of the German Race' as his commissioner in this territory. This put a huge question mark over the 'unity of government' which was Frank's aim. Through the commissioner, Himmler gave orders direct to the district SS and police chiefs, without the headquarters of the civil government in the GG having been advised in advance. 'The inherent tendency towards a distinctive territorial regime run by the SS and Police grievously threatened Frank's position'.[5]

One characteristic of the internal structure of the GG, and to a lesser extent of the Third Reich, was therefore already built into its configuration when it was established; the 'departmental polyocracy' (Martin Broszat), accurately described by Frank as an 'anarchy of plenipotentiaries', which made the effective exercise of rule impossible. Whether this system formed a central plank of a strategy of 'divide et impera', or was the expression of a sort of naturally occurring administrative chaos, following from the parasitical dismemberment of traditional administrative structures, is debatable. In any event Hitler never made any definitive decision on the future status of the GG or on the personal power structure and so left the field clear for rivalry and disputes about authority.

Frank's activities as Governor-General were therefore primarily shaped by the attempt to assert his function as based on the Führer's decree of 12 October and to gain compensation for his diminishing authority. His office diary, kept from 1939–45, is unique of its kind as a source and has been preserved in its entire thirty-eight volumes. It gives ample evidence of both of these factors. Conceived of as a document to the vanity of an unstable power broker who wanted to leave a testimony to his 'construction work' for posterity, instead it documents the increasingly 'marked marginalisation of and lack of scope'[6] for the GG. In detail which verges on the ridiculous, it describes how Frank attempted to model himself into a replica of the Führer he idolised and to conceal the fact that his position was in reality increasingly being undermined by the SS, the economy and the army, by making long rhetorical speeches and uninhibited public appearances. To this extent the diary also reflects the pathology of the person of the Governor General as well as the structurally determined chaos of his domain.

Until summer 1940 the status of the GG was still undecided, in as far as plans to create a 'residual Polish state' as a factor for bargaining with the Western powers had not yet been completely shelved. It was only after this that the administration was consolidated and Poland was economically and politically more tightly integrated into the Greater German Reich, but without the GG being tied in to the structure of the German state in the same way as other occupied territories in Poland or Czechoslovakia. In this first phase Frank attempted, with some success, to fend off the demands of the German state authorities and to ensure the autonomy of his administration. At the same time these first months were distinguished by a policy of unrestrained plundering and exploitation, and a share of this could only be obtained on the precondition that the GG functioned not as an integrated part of the German state but as a reservation and resettlement zone for expellees. Not only were large sections of the Polish population resettled here from the 'annexed territories', but initially vague plans to create a 'Jewish reservation' in the east also formed part of this nexus of ideas.

At first this development was welcomed and supported by Hans Frank, the fanatical National Socialist, in spite of the fact that it went against his ambitions to build up a unified German administration. In the phase of German *Blitzkrieg* victories, above all, he had allowed his uninhibited imagination free rein. The image of the 'Butcher of the Poles' was therefore taking shape at an early stage. An interview with the *Völkischer Beobachter* dated 6 February 1940, in which he discusses the basis of Polish policy, is among his most infamous statements. In one passage – not published by the *Völkischer Beobachter* – to a question on the differences between the Government General and the Protectorate of Bohemia and Moravia, Frank declared:

> I can tell you one concrete difference. For example, in Prague big red posters were put up, on which you could read that seven Czechs had been shot that day. I said to myself, if I were to put up a poster for every seven Poles that had been shot, the forests of Poland would not be big enough to produce the paper for these posters. Yes indeed, we had to take severe measures.[7]

Such statements and others like it are not only an indication of the policy of terror which Frank made possible or helped to initiate, but of his personality, which Joachim Fest has aptly described as a 'carbon copy of a terrorist'. Frank's attitude to violence always contained unreal, theatrical, contrived elements, and his ordinary rhetorical invective, too, was obviously intended to conceal his psychological instability. However he was never the pugnacious hero he pretended to be. The desired ideal was always far in advance of the reality.

The second phase of the development of the Government General was determined by a change of function during the course of the preparation and implementation of 'Operation Barbarossa' and the restructuring of the German economy from the *Blitzkrieg* strategy to a total war economy with armament in depth. The direct seizure of the resources of the GG by the various special commissioners of the German state increased. Frank attempted to do justice to the increased demands of the war economy by intensifying his methods of exploitation. The resistance of the Polish population, which initially had been restricted largely to the intellectuals, inevitably became more widespread because of this, and increasingly encompassed the peasantry, who until then had been relatively passive, politically. The severe demands of the delivery quotas could now only be enforced by terror, but the terror produced resistance and counterviolence, which increasingly put into question the ordered administration to which Frank aspired. In his political goals he was scarcely distinguishable from his rivals in the SS and the Party Chancellery. On the other hand he was evidently not blind to the visible consequences of a policy which was rigorously enforced according to the maxim that the Poles were to be treated as a slave nation. Therefore for the purpose of realising the interests of the German state's war economy he tried to implement a course which was to some extent more flexible and ultimately more effective. Because of this he came into even greater conflict with Himmler's SS. Various cases of corruption, in which Frank was implicated, gave Himmler and Bormann welcome excuses to push him into a corner and to strengthen the position of the Supreme SS and Police Chief in the GG, Friedrich-Wilhelm Krüger.

In summer 1942 in four lectures at the universities of Berlin, Vienna, Munich and Heidelberg, Frank took the risk of making a remarkably open attack against the arbitrary rule of the police state and pleaded for the 'observance of justice'. Even although, after his previous behaviour in Poland, Frank was anything but a credible champion of norms of justice – however these were understood, against the background of his bitter conflicts with the SS these speeches were provocative. He was therefore banned from speaking in the German state and lost all his offices in the state with the exception of his role as Minister without Portfolio. At this point his political demise seemed to be inevitable, and in the SS they were already casting about for a successor. In this situation Frank offered Hitler his resignation in November 1942, but it was refused.

In spite of the consistent weakening of his personal position in the

National Socialist power structure, by remaining at his post Frank had gained a starting point for a renewed confrontation with Himmler's Racial Policy, which reached a new high-point in autumn 1942 and spring 1943 in the Zamość campaign. A ring of German settlements was to be created in the Zamość district in the upper reaches of the Bug in anticipation of the later Germanisation of the GG. To this end Polish peasants had been arrested in their thousands from November 1942 onwards, forcibly evacuated and replaced by ethnic German settlers. In the eastern GG the security position worsened acutely, the Polish resistance movement gained a spontaneous rush of support and the delivery of quotas declined. In this situation Frank finally managed to have his way and as far as possible put a stop to the campaign as well as achieving the removal of his main competitor, the Supreme SS and Police Chief Krüger and the chief of the SS and Police in Lublin district, Odilo Globocnik.

When, after the German defeat at Stalingrad, Propaganda Minister Goebbels announced his decree 'regarding the treatment of European nations, including the eastern nations', Frank believed he could see an opportunity for far-reaching policy changes in Poland too. Considerably overestimating the possibilities of being able to deviate from the previous political line of total suppression of the Poles, he pleaded in countless memos to Hitler, some of which were extensive, for better treatment for the Polish forced labourers because their catastrophic living conditions and discriminatory work situation in the German state was providing constant new fodder for the resistance movement in Poland. Over and above this he recommended an improvement in food rations and a reduction in the delivery quotas, the reopening of Polish secondary schools and the participation of Poles in administration at district level. However open and courageous some of these petitions look against the background of Polish policy as it was officially practised, in the final analysis they all have to be seen as tactically motivated and coming too late; attempts to extricate himself from a military situation which was becoming increasingly precarious. In Berlin Frank could achieve practically nothing.

Of course the verbal radicalism of the statements in his diary only reflects one side of Frank's activities and personality. But he was, and remained, representative and executor of an occupation policy in Poland which was fundamentally criminal and politically lacking in foresight. It was this which left its mark on the image of Hans Frank the National Socialist. This image can be more clearly defined, although not relativised, by drawing attention to the 'other' Frank, who was not the same as the criminal and to whom contemporaries who were close to him have also drawn attention. The Italian author, Curzio Malaparte, who got to know Frank during his stay in the GG in 1942 and presented his impressions of this time in his novel *Bust*, encapsulated this ambivalence in these sentences: 'Not a man who could be dismissed with a hasty judgement. The unease I always felt in his company originated precisely from the many layers apparent in his nature, from the unique mixture of cruel intelligence, a refined and a vulgar character, of brutal cynicism and exquisite sensibility.'[8]

The juxtaposition of cynicism, cold brutality and 'correctness' on the one hand and sentimentality and the middle class intellectual's avidity for culture on the other is a well-known pattern for many senior Nazi functionaries, and is particularly alarming in its ability to combine these attributes without visible contradiction. The expense of running German culture, which Frank brought to the GG, with his own state theatre and symphony orchestra, the 'Institute for German Activities in the East' and his newspapers, the extensive correspondence he conducted with musicians and intellectuals in the German state and his extravagant need for grand public appearances therefore in the final analysis complement his image as the Butcher of the Poles and lend it particularly macabre features.

In this respect Frank remained true to himself until his end on the gallows in Nuremberg. At the Nuremberg Tribunal he was one of the few major war criminals who confessed their guilt. When he heard that masses of Germans were being driven out of the eastern territories and the Sudetenland, however, he revised his statement of Germany's 'thousand years of guilt'.[9] The autobiographical reflections he wrote in prison in Nuremberg, in spite of all attempts at self-criticism, document helpless excuses for his own role and an attempt to regard Hitler and Himmler as the only truly guilty ones. Even in his attempts to distance himself from his Führer he remained enslaved to him.

NOTES

1. Personal diary, entries for 11.12.1918 and 12.4.1919, Bundesarchiv Koblenz, Nachlass Frank.
2. H. Frank, *Im Angesicht des Galgens* (Munich, 1953) p. 146f, 150ff.
3. U. von Hassell, *Vom anderen Deutschland* (Zurich, 1946) p. 112.
4. W. Präg, W. Jacobmeyer (eds), *Das Diensttagebuch des deutschen General-gouverneurs in Polen 1939–1945* (Stuttgart, 1975) p. 45.
5. Ibid., p. 26 (Introduction).
6. Ibid., p. 29 (Introduction).
7. Ibid., p. 104.
8. C. Malaparte, *Kaputt* (Karlsruhe, 1961) p. 143f.
9. International Military Tribunal, Nuremberg, *Der Prozess gegen die Haupt-skriegsverbrecher*, vol. XXII, p. 438.

BIBLIOGRAPHY

Primary Sources

The most important source for Hans Frank's role as Governor-General is: W. Präg W. Jacobmeyer (eds), *Das Diensttagebuch des deutschen Generalgouverneurs in Polen 1939–1945* (Stuttgart, 1945). A short sample from the diary, which is basically identical to the document produced by the Polish representative for the prosecution at the trial in Nuremberg, USSR–223, is given in S. Piotrowski: *Hans Franks Tagebuch* (Warsaw, 1963). Also useful are the transcripts of the proceedings of the Nuremberg trials: *Internationaler Militärgerichtshof Nürnberg, Der Prozess gegen die Hauptkriegsverbrecher*, 42 volumes (Nuremberg, 1947–1950), here: Volume XII, XXII (Verhandlungen gegen Frank). There are revealing passages about his personality in the document he wrote in prison: *Im Angesicht des Galgens. Deutung Hitlers und seiner Zeit aufgrund eigener Erlebnisse und Erkenntnisse*, edited by O. Schloffer (Munich, 1953). The memoirs of Division Leader (Innere Verwaltung) in the Government General, F.W. Siebert, were written as the result of direct observation of Frank: 'Versuch einer Darstellung der Persönlichkeit Franks', Bundesarchiv Koblenz, Ost-Dok. 13 GG 1a/13.

Secondary Literature

The study by M. Broszat, *Nationalsozialistische Polenpolitik 1939–1945* (Frankfurt am Main, 1965) is still the main source, although its section on the GG is very short. It is complemented by: G. Eisenblätter, *Grundlinien der Politik des Reiches gegenüber dem Generalgouvernement 1939–1945*, thesis (Frankfurt am Main, 1969), which contains a great deal of material. The literature on the Polish side is so vast as to be almost unmanageable. The most important works are: C. Madajczyk, *Die Okkupationspolitik Nazideutschlands in Polen 1939–1945* (Cologne, 1988) (a more complete Polish version, 1970). The cultural policy context is discussed by C. Klessmann: *Die Selbstbehauptung einer Nation. NS-Kulturpolitik und polnische Widerstandsbewegung* (Dusseldorf, 1971). The conversations of the Nuremberg prison psychologist G.M. Gilbert give important insights into Frank's personality: *Nürnberger Tagebuch* (Frankfurt am Main, 1962). Portraits which attempt to give a personal and political description of the lawyer and Governor General are to be found in J. Fest: *Das Gesicht des Dritten Reiches. Profile einer totalitären Herrschaft* (Munich, 1963) and C. Klessmann: 'Der Generalgouverneur Hans Frank', in *VfZ* 19 (1971) p. 245–60.

6 Joseph Goebbels: The Propagandist
Elke Fröhlich

'Why does fate deny me what it grants to others? How my heart aches. God, God, why have you abandoned me?'[1] – thus went the despairing, plaintive lamentations of the twenty-eight year old Joseph Goebbels in his diary at the beginning of his meteoric career. At the end of it, twenty years later almost exactly to the day, in March 1945, when he would have had every reason for despair, given the millions of dead and incalculable devastation, he maintained a posture of fanatical battle-readiness until the very end. From 1944 he had been promoted to the post of State Plenipotentiary for the Prosecution of Total War, and during this time he wrote in his diary: 'In Berlin, at least, the defence continues to be organised, and it is my firm resolve that, if it comes to it, I will give the enemy such a fight here that it will be unique in the history of war.'[2] Like these quotes, all his diaries bear testimony to the contradictory tensions united in their author: an inferiority complex along with evangelical self-confidence, a longing for salvation with a desire for total annihilation, maudlin sentimentality with calculating cynicism, whingeing self-pity combined with brutal cruelty to others. Goebbels had a singular effect on his contemporaries and even on historians; at once repulsive and fascinating. For a long time he was regarded as – with the exception of Hitler – the most interesting personality among the prominent National Socialists. The reasons for this were very varied: because of the aura of the many love affairs which hung about him; because of the unique position he held for two decades as Hitler's intimate and the most effective promoter of the Führer myth; because of the spectacular end to this loyalty in the form of a family suicide in the Führer's bunker at the Reich Chancellery, in which he and his wife Magda, who was as devoted to Hitler as he was, also involved six thriving children. Among the leadership of the National Socialists, most of whom were only moderately gifted, the State Propaganda Minister, seriously disabled by a club foot, stood out primarily because of his sarcastic intellect and his polished rhetoric. But his rather 'latin' style of intelligence, and the physical disability, so inappropriate to the Nazi ideal of the Germanic man, made Goebbels an outsider throughout his life.

Joseph Goebbels was born on 29 October 1897 in Rheydt, a small industrial town on the Lower Rhine. His father had succeeded by dint of hard work and patience in rising from being a commercial clerk to the chief clerk in a firm which made wicks. Even though every penny had to count twice in the Goebbels household, there was sufficient to buy a small terraced house and to educate the children well. The young Goebbels did not experience social misery, and he could be as certain of the love of his good Catholic parents as his four siblings. His weak stature and the stigma of his serious disability even confirmed him as the favourite at home. As the most gifted of his siblings Joseph not only received piano lessons – a positive luxury in 'white collar' circles – but was also allowed to attend grammar school. He, for his part, as his diary shows, always had fond memories of his parental home and still tried to be a 'good' son to his mother, even when he had long since risen to be the famous and notorious State Propaganda Minister. If his childhood and youth were often joyless, as he wrote on 1923 in his *Reminiscences*, [3] this was primarily because of his club foot, which gave rise to much spiteful teasing at school and on the street. Isolated as he was by this, he for his part developed qualities, especially a tendency to intrigue and to pushiness, which made him unpopular with the teachers too, although he was a good pupil.

In 1917 he completed his Higher Leaving Certificate. Afterwards, free of war service because of his disability, he studied German at five universities. He could not really afford these frequent changes in his place of study, given his meagre allowance from the parental home and a small loan from the catholic Albertus Magnus Society. The chief reason for them was his great and ultimately unhappy love for Anka Stahlherm, whom he had followed unswervingly from place to place. She was the first of a long series of women at the fringes of his life. Women were attracted to him even when he was still unknown and before he had any roles in films to distribute. Conversely he had male friends only during the short time while he was a student and up to the beginning of his political career, and then no more at all. One exception was Richard Flisges, who died young, and for whom the diary novel Goebbels wrote in 1920 was a memorial. He sacrificed his few other friendships to his paramount ambition, which was above all else to make himself important and have a successful career.

Having attained the degree of PhD in 1921, with a literary dissertation on the Romantic Wilhelm von Schutz at Heidelberg under the Jewish Germanist Max von Waldberg, in the future Goebbels set great store by always adorning his name with the title 'Doctor'. For the present, however, the newly-fledged 'Doctor' was still financially dependent on his father; the young man considered himself too good for any uninteresting means of simply earning a living, having from an early stage believed himself to have a vocation for a special mission. He only persevered in a job, obtained by his then girl-friend, in the Dresdner Bank in Cologne, for a few months in 1923. However he was very quickly drawn back again into his attic room in his parents' house, devoted to literary endeavours and the constant meditation in his diary. Nonetheless he suffered from his unresolved situation. The self-confident certainty that he was called to higher things alternated with outbreaks of the deepest self-doubt, which intensified to the point where he considered suicide. For the rest, he occupied himself as the man of letters he considered himself to be. Even as a student he had written several plays and novels. Stylistically bombastic and banal in content, none of them was convincing.

Goebbels was late in beginning to take an interest in politics. The First World War period, the Revolution and the period after the war scarcely left a trace in his diary. His personal associations with the year 1918, so catastrophic for the Germans, were of 'blissful memories' of his great love for Anka. The fact that the lame man intended to join up in the last year of the war was probably mainly an act of pathetic self-stylisation and hardly intended seriously. In as far as Goebbels took notice of politics at all in this period, it was in the manner of the resentful philistine of his day: 'Politics is sad. In London the rich bankers dispose of Germany's workforce for the next forty years. Gently, gentlemen!'[4] At that time he could also write: 'Today I have no interest in anything. Just leave me in peace.'[5]

That changed abruptly with his debut on the political stage. Having been introduced into various *völkisch* (populist ethnic) circles by a prosperous friend, Fritz Prang, who had also joined the NSDAP as far back as 1922, Goebbels experienced his political awakening in summer 1924 on the occasion of a joint party conference of the *Völkische* and the banned NSDAP in Weimar. Immediately after his return he became extremely active politically. The very next day he formed a local branch of the National Socialists in Mönchengladbach (21.8.1924). At the same time he discovered his gift for public speaking. Thoughts just flew into his head while he was speaking, the spark which he was able to fan in his listeners jumped over to him and gave wings to his rhetorical achievements. He was, he wrote at that time, proud, but also shocked that he had become a 'demagogue of the worst sort'.[6] However as his success quickly became established, this self-criticism deserted him, never to return. In August 1924 Goebbels was engaged as the editor of the Saturday newspaper *Völkische Freiheit*, for which he wrote nearly all the articles himself. His renown as a political columnist and speaker for the Party grew, and seven months later, when the NSDAP District Rhineland North was founded in Eberfeld in March 1925, he was already one of the prominent regional Party members. Compared with other leading National Socialists, Goebbels had found his way into the Party relatively late and after quite a long period of political gestation – still without having got to know Hitler.

Not only did he make a favourable impression in the 'Movement', but he was soon known as shrewd, arrogant and scheming. In conservative-*völkisch* circles he was soon denounced as a National Socialist Robespierre. Together with his friend Karl Kaufmann he intrigued successfully against the other leader of the District, Axel Ripke, with the result that Kaufmann became *Gauleiter* and Goebbels his business manager. He commented bitterly: 'I do the work and he is the "leader"'.[7] The only close friendship Goebbels ever had among Party leaders suffered a rift which developed into deadly enmity. Soon Goebbels was working against Kaufmann, too, – successfully – and driven by ambition, let the friendship be ruined. It was much the same with his politically admittedly much more significant relationship with Gregor Strasser, the powerful leader of the North German NSDAP. For this 'magnificent chap' with his 'wonderful sense of humour',[8] Goebbels soon became the main mouthpiece of the socialist left of the Party – its most radical and articulate 'comrade in arms'. They were primarily united in their negative judgement of the Munich headquarters as a 'stinking, rotten system'.[9] Goebbels became the most important contributor to the *Nationalsozialistische Briefe*, edited by Strasser, probably the most intellectually demanding Nazi newspaper, for which he wrote some of his most brilliant articles.

For a year and a half Goebbels played a leading role as demagogue and radical spokesman of the left wing of the NSDAP, which in contrast to the rival German *Völkisch* Freedom Party, primarily emphasised the socialist element in the NSDAP's programme. Then, however, came his conversion on the road to Damascus, at the Leader's Conference at Bamberg in February 1926, where he met Hitler for the first time and fell under the sway of his rhetorical powers of suggestion, even though at this conference Hitler sharply condemned the socialist drift of the Party. From then on for the Strasser wing of the Party he was the much despised deserter to Hitler. Goebbels did not by any means give up his radical anti-bourgeois convictions, but he instinctively sensed Hitler's political superiority to Gregor Strasser and, to the surprise of his political friends, without much ado he went over to Hitler's side. The latter knew how to impress the 'little doctor' with the splendour of the Munich Party and win him for himself. Soon Goebbels was completely under Hitler's spell. He wrote in his diary at that time: 'I bow to the greater man, the political genius',[10] 'Adolf Hitler, I love you because you are both great and simple.'[11] Hitler rewarded Goebbels' devotion by assigning him to Berlin, where he was to take over the vacant post of *Gauleiter* and the particularly difficult duty of reorganising the Party in the national capital.

In the cosmopolitan metropolis of Berlin there was initially almost no hope of gaining even a degree of public recognition for the small and feuding branch of the NSDAP. It took the demagogical inventiveness and pugnacious temperament of a Joseph Goebbels to gain even a spark of attention from a city used to sensation. The ambitious young man first of all purged the squabbling Party rabble with special authority from Hitler, accepting a further loss of membership in the process, and built up a small but loyally devoted staff of co-workers. After a few weeks Goebbels was able to hold his first public meeting. His campaign methods were distinguished by boldness, aggression and – extreme effectiveness. Right from the beginning Goebbels made a point of provocatively challenging the socialist parties which were particularly strong in Berlin (SPD, KPD) by imitating their own methods.

When he had been in Berlin for just three months, after a short preliminary skirmish he took the risk of making the attack on his main opponents, the communists, which has gone down in National Socialist annals as the 'Battle of the Pharus Rooms'. The new *Gauleiter* of the NSDAP had arranged a meeting to attract workers in, of all places, the communists' traditional public house in the red district of Wedding, which must have thoroughly enraged them. The 'Sowing with Blood', as he later titled one of his literary products, had begun. The evening ended in a wild meeting-hall brawl. Goebbels and the NSDAP became the talk of the town. Using the belligerence of the SA, the 'backbone of the movement' as he called it, Goebbels staked his tactics on terrorism in meeting rooms and on the street. His SA men fought with Red Front activists and physically molested Jewish passers-by in the middle of Berlin. Brown terror began to spread. The energetic leadership of the Prussian Police Headquarters did not of course let this continue for long. A ban on the NSDAP, long since demanded by the democratic Berlin press, was enacted in May 1927. It lasted nearly a year, until March 1928, and drastically reduced the *Gauleiter*'s newly tested opportunities for agitation. As a consequence Goebbels moved the battle from the streets to the press. The man who had formerly been rejected by various newspapers founded his own District newspaper with the significant title *Der Angriff* (The Attack). However, by so doing he was breaking into the Strasser brothers' territory, and that of Otto Strasser in particular, whose Kampf Publishers produced a series of regional Nazi news-sheets for north and central Germany.

The style and content of *Der Angriff* were copied from marxist newspapers: its motto was 'no information, just agitation'. If the subject was the Jews *Der Angriff* was scarcely distinguishable from the notorious *Stürmer*. When verbal agitation became vulnerable to legal redress through the Law for the Protection of the Republic, Mjoelnir (Hans Schweitzer) continued the infamous attacks in caricatures.

Goebbels did not just try to counter the political lull with prepared speeches, but also by means of calculated insults and defamation. He was often convicted and fined, but what did that matter against the gain in public attention which the criminal proceedings and courts afforded him? Goebbels did not disport himself on these occasions as the petty accused, but with the demeanour of the plaintiff, and this assured him of almost regular headlines in the newspapers. He was often only saved from prison by the immunity he had acquired in May 1928 by virtue of his seat in parliament, immunity he mocked quite openly in public secure in the knowledge that he would receive cheap applause from the many who despised democracy.

He could also count on applause for his infamous campaign against influential Jews. His battle against the Jewish Vice President of the Berlin police, Dr Bernhard Weiss, became a satirical stereotype. He picked out this man as the representative of the hated 'system', branded him 'Isidor' and constantly and cleverly tried to make his activities appear ridiculous. Weiss did win most of the court cases he brought against Goebbels, but these also kept the nickname 'Isidor' in circulation and provided Goebbels with a long-running source of effective demagogy, which Berlin laughed about for months.

In September 1928 Goebbels held a successful mass rally in Berlin's Palace of Sport, which held over 15 000 people: a 'historic hour'; from then on this venue was the preferred location for large-scale National Socialist events in the national capital until the end of the Third Reich. The series of Party conventions, political rallies and speeches, each following hard on the heels of the last, began in the summer of 1929. The NSDAP, for the first time since the Hitler Putsch of 1923, had the opportunity of participating in an issue of national importance within the context of emerging radical right-wing opposition to the Republic, in the campaign for a national referendum on the American Young Plan for restructuring German reparation payments. Further opportunities to exploit the unease over the incipient agricultural and economic crisis were afforded by the regional elections in Thuringia (December 1929) and Saxony (June 1930), communal elections in November 1929 and above all the elections to the *Reichstag* in September 1930, which brought the decisive breakthrough for the National Socialists – even in Berlin. If Goebbels could be content with the Berlin communal elections, for he had raised the vote for the NSDAP from something over one hundred to far in excess of 100 000 in three years – for one year of which he was almost excluded from the struggle because of the ban, the result of the *Reichstag* elections was a political sensation. One of the smallest splinter parties (1928: 2.6 per cent) had become the second strongest party in the *Reichstag*. Without doubt Goebbels, who was nominated National Propaganda Director of the NSDAP in spring 1930 had, by means of his electoral strategy and his tireless application, played a considerable part in the success.

1930 became a milestone for Goebbels in another respect. Fortified by his success in 'red Berlin', a special NSDAP initiative to 'conquer the factories' was set in train under Goebbels' supervision and it became the model for a later nation-wide Party trade union organisation. Goebbels made the young SA leader Horst Wessel, who had been shot by a communist, the symbol of heroic sacrificial death in the fight against the communist movement. Although the murder had had personal motives and Wessel's disreputable life style was well known, Goebbels was able to stylise him as a national hero and the chief martyr of the 'movement'. The Horst Wessel song '*Die Fahne hoch*' ('Fly the banner high'), originally an SA marching song, became the National Socialist national anthem after 1933, alongside the official anthem.

During this phase of the struggle for power Goebbels was a stronger advocate of the revolutionary road to power than Hitler, who often hesitated and relied on a tactic of formal legality. For all his admiration of Hitler he nonetheless expressed some forthright criticism and concern in his diary. He described Hitler as a magician and idler who, instead of working, sat in coffee houses with his philistine Munich entourage and asked anxiously what would happen 'if he had to play the dictator in Germany?'[12] However much Hitler disappointed him, Goebbels, who had proved his capacity for disloyalty to others, remained unconditionally true to Hitler.

Goebbels ended the successful year of 1930 with an unseemly political racket on the occasion of the Berlin premiere of Ernst Maria Remarque's pacifist film 'All Quiet on the Western Front'. With disguised SA men and Party officials he organised a so-called spontaneous eruption of popular anger, which prevented any further showing of the film. The spectacle not only enhanced the popularity of the 'Chief Bandit of Berlin', as he liked to call himself, seizing on one of his opponents' insults, but also provided proof that his methods enabled him to have his way against the Berlin police. He wrote jubilantly in his diary: 'National Socialism on the streets dictates the government's actions'.[13]

If it had not been for quarrels with the SA, the *Gauleiter* could have been content. However his style of fighting meant that the main burden of the struggle fell on the strong-arm troops of the SA. They were the revolutionary potential of the movement and therefore Goebbels was on their side. But Hitler, who was primarily courting the bourgeois members of society and who did not want to be pushed again into a coup d'état as he was in Munich in 1923, was not willing to meet the demands of the SA for greater concessions. In order to give these demands more weight the SA twice stormed the District office of the Berlin NSDAP – in August 1930 and April 1931 – significantly on both occasions during the absence of the *Gauleiter*. Hitler saved the politically and psychologically wounded Goebbels, thereby making him even more dependent.

Goebbels' marriage at the end of 1931 to Magda, a beautiful and rich woman of the world, also led to a strengthening of his relationship with Hitler. The years of material and social starvation were now finally at an end for Goebbels. He moved into his wife's apartment and she, adored by Hitler, became a guarantee of greater closeness between the two men. The Goebbels' well-kept home and their charming children attracted Hitler again and again, and offered a substitute for the family he himself did not have.

Even the many crises in the Party could not shake Goebbels' conviction that the National Socialists under Hitler's leadership would soon gain power. In early 1932 Hitler and Goebbels discussed the distribution of government posts, as if they already held power. After the July elections in 1932, when the NSDAP had become the strongest Party in the country, Hitler demanded, among other things, seven ministerial posts and the Chancellorship for himself, in his negotiations with General von Schleicher, the influential adviser of President von Hindenburg. Goebbels, who was marked down for the posts of Prussian Minister for Cultural Affairs and National Minister for Education, wrote in his diary: 'What it means is – total power or nothing! That's as it should be. Just don't let's think small. . . .'[14] We will never give up power again, they'll have to carry out our corpses'.[15] He was to be right, he had only got the timing wrong. Hindenburg still did not want to concede the 'Bohemian corporal' anything more than the Vice-Chancellorship. When Hitler was then finally nominated as Chancellor on 30 January there was at first no post in the government for Goebbels. His bitter disappointment about this is expressed bluntly in his diary: 'Magda is very unhappy. Because I'm not making any headway. I'm being frozen out. Now Rust is getting the Culture job. I'm whistling in the dark.'[16] And three days later: 'Hitler is scarcely helping me. I have lost heart. The reactionaries lay down the law – the Third Reich!'[17] Always slightly irritable and quickly thrown off balance, Goebbels was nonetheless wrong. Hitler continued to be dependent on his most talented propagandist. After Goebbels had delivered yet another masterly example of his demagogic skills during the preparations for the national elections on 5 March 1933 he did not remain unrewarded. Two days after the election Hitler informed his astonished ministerial colleagues that there was to be a Ministry for Public Enlightenment and Propaganda. On 13 March the President signed the decree appointing Goebbels. In the autumn of 1924 the then hounded pauper had confided to his diary: 'I will continue on an upwards path. I hereby make that solemn, sacred vow. Upwards! To the stars!'[18] In less than a decade he had achieved his goal. From now until the destruction of the Third Reich he remained, after Hitler and Goering, one of the great stars in the brown firmament.

He established the new Ministry, as befitted its status, in the Leopold Palace, built by Schinkel on the Wilhelmsplatz, and set to work with total 'joy and devotion'.[19] With great inventiveness he attempted to retain at least a few aspects of cultural and intellectual brilliance for the system of compulsion and anti-intellectualism, but in his refined way he contributed all the more to the repression of intellectual freedom. With the establishment of the National Chamber of Culture in the autumn of 1933, he prepared the decisive blow against any free artistic or journalistic activity. The National Chamber for Culture, with its sub-departments for creative art, music, theatre, film, radio, writing and the press decided who was in the future to be permitted to practise their profession in the field of culture. The doors of the Chamber of Culture remained forever shut to non-

Arians, incorrigible anti-fascists and many other non-conformists. If anyone did not conform politically they were thrown out and lost the right to
continue practising their profession. Book-burnings and blacklists contributed to the denuding of the National Socialist cultural landscape.
Although Goebbels had retained a certain feeling for modern trends, for
example for expressionist art, and knew too, what a damaging effect the
negative selection process was having on cultural life, he pressed on with
the outlawing of modern art, partly in order to continue to endear himself
to Hitler. His was the plan for the 'Exhibition to Discredit Corrupt Art',
and he refused to be prevented from opening the exhibition of cultural
'degeneracy' in summer 1937, even though Hitler reserved for himself the
actual programmatic speech, in which he proclaimed a 'merciless purge' of
modernism.

His name is associated above all with the nature of National Socialist
propaganda. As early as August 1932 he wrote pithily in his diary; 'The
national education of the German people is being put in my hands. I will
master it.'[20] Two days after his appointment as Minister he announced in
public that as he understood it this meant the total standardisation of
thought and feeling in the population. He explained to the press that
people must be 'worked on' until they 'fell under the sway' of National
Socialism. His particular form of Nazi propaganda consisted less of philosophical indoctrination than in the use of suggestion to mobilise euphoric
or aggressive emotions, and in this he was a master. There were soon
(1937) 1000 civil servants and clerks devoted to the manipulation of the
German population in the fast expanding Ministry. In the field of propaganda Goebbels had unlimited supremacy over other leaders of the Nazi
regime. He remained second only to Hitler in this sphere, – albeit an
uncommonly talented and inventive second. Hitler established the basic
features of propaganda, large-scale plans and events were always discussed
jointly, but their execution was in Goebbels' hands. His ingeniousness in
the concoction of propaganda slogans and events seemed unlimited and
scarcely any other leading National Socialist caught the mood of the people
as well as he did. Among the most successful vehicles for propaganda were
the national holidays he organised. The holiday calendar of the National
Socialist year, modelled on the stations of the Catholic Church, scarcely
gave Germans a chance to come to their senses. The Day of the Seizure of
Power, the Führer's Birthday, National Labour Day, the Bückeburg
Peasants' convention, the Nuremberg National Party Rally, the Day of
Remembrance for the March to the Feldherrnhalle and others provided a
round of suggestive and imposing images of society as a national community (one people, one state, one leader), which were conveyed by radio,
the press and the weekly cinema news into every District in the country and
were far more effective than ideological evening classes. Events staged on
the grand scale, like the Olympic Games in 1936 or the state visit of

Mussolini in 1937 even sparked off enthusiasm abroad. In the realm of music, theatre and above all film, Goebbels succeeded to an amazing degree in overcoming the cultural haemorrhaging which had arisen through the demonisation of modernism and the emigration of many very talented Jewish authors and artists, with a superficially glittering facade. But even in the defamation and denunciation of opponents and so-called enemies of the people he showed a diabolic virtuosity which had been well-tested during the 'Era of Struggle'. One of his first 'official acts' as Propaganda Minister was the call for a boycott of Jewish businesses on 1 April 1933. In a shameless distortion of cause and effect the boycott was presented as a 'response' to the so-called' Jewish demands for a boycott [of Germany]', that is to the criticism which flared up all over the world of the new regime's anti-semitic measures after the seizure of power. The campaign proved a mistake; the majority of the population rejected it and distanced themselves from it. Further campaigns which had already been announced were therefore called off.

Goebbels was behind the repulsive Priests' Trials too. The Nazi leadership staged these as a reaction to pronouncements critical of the regime, primarily from the Catholic Church, in the years 1937 and 1938, in order to stigmatise Catholic priests and monks with political crimes (for example against the foreign exchange laws) and above all with offences against morality. But here too Goebbels utterly failed to achieve his propagandistic aim. Precisely because of the repulsive methods designed to reveal these short-comings the smear campaign of the Priests' Trials led to great anger among Catholic church-goers and actually had the effect of intensifying the criticism of the regime. For this reason Hitler had the campaign stopped in 1938.

In the same year however Goebbels tried again with another spectacular campaign. The occasion for it was the assassination attempt by a young Jew on a diplomat in the German Embassy in Paris at the beginning of November 1938. When it became known, on the evening of 9 November, on the occasion of the traditional celebration by veterans of the Hitler Putsch in Munich's old town hall, that the German Secretary to the Legation had died of his wounds, Goebbels took the floor in front of the assembled party leaders to make an ingenious, inflammatory speech, which made clear in barely disguised terms that the SA and the Party were to initiate a nationwide pogrom against the Jews that very night. The result was the devastating events of the so-called *Reichskristallnacht*, in the course of which countless synagogues were set on fire, thousands of Jewish businesses and apartments demolished and looted, Jewish cemeteries desecrated and Jewish citizens murdered.

Goebbels probably intended to win Hitler's personal approbation with this action, for at this time his relationship with Hitler was not at its best. Goebbels had fallen seriously in love with a Czech film actress. His wife, who had generously overlooked many of her husband's other affairs, now wanted a divorce. But Hitler, who could not afford any new scandal within the leadership of the regime, after the embarrassing marriage of the Minister for the Army, General Field Marshall von Blomberg to a lady of the night at the beginning of the same year, forced Goebbels to drop his mistress and continue to live with Magda. In the inner circle of the Nazi leadership Goebbels' rating at this stage was at zero. Rosenberg, cordial enemy of the Propaganda Minister, discussed the affair with various people and recorded the following observation in his diary about Hitler's attitude: 'He (Hitler) has kept on Dr Goebbels for reasons of state, but personally he has had enough of him. He knows that he supports him at the expense of his own standing.' And Rosenberg commented: 'We see every day that our revolution has a running sore which is infecting the healthy blood. Dr G. has no friends, no comrades, and as for his lackeys, they too, are abusing him.'[21]

In autumn 1938, in order to win back Hitler's favour, Goebbels began to write a hagiographical study of Adolf Hitler. After a few months, thanks to his propagandistic virtuosity, he finally succeeded in regaining Hitler's respect. The grandiose stage-management of Hitler's fiftieth birthday on 20 April 1939 evidently contributed effectively to this. In fact none of the leading figures of the Third Reich was able to spread and enhance the Hitler myth with such pseudo-religious intensity as Joseph Goebbels. He was probably only able to do this so effectively and credibly because Hitler had for a long time been a kind of political god for Goebbels himself, on whom 'the little doctor' had become totally dependent, even in his personal life and in his capacity for judgement. In view of the considerable intellectual ability Goebbels possessed, this growing enslavement to Hitler is an astonishing phenomenon, of which there is much evidence in the Goebbels diaries.

Without Hitler's favour, which he always regained, Goebbels could only with great difficulty have remained so unchallenged within the inner circle of power until the end of the regime. However he was in a permanent state of conflict, not only with Rosenberg but with nearly all his ministerial colleagues. This could partly be adduced by the fact that the Propaganda Ministry, as a completely new establishment, was almost bound to come into conflict with other ministries and Nazi authorities already in existence, who were in their own way attempting to disseminate propaganda for themselves and the Nazi regime. Particular friction arose with the Minister for Science, Education and Popular Training, Rust, and also with the Foreign Office, where propaganda for foreign consumption remained a bone of contention until the end of the regime. In Rosenberg, Goebbels saw a rival in the field of culture, in particular writing, in Goering a competitor in the sphere of art, Dr Dietrich in press matters. In addition, Goebbels was not highly regarded by his ministerial colleagues and comrades in the Party leadership because of his scheming personality, even if his achievements in propaganda had to be acknowledged. He found real support in the leading Nazi clique from Hitler alone.

When the war began, however, Goebbels did noticeably seem to lose influence. He was not a party to the decisive consultations and decisions on foreign and military policy. Goebbels the civilian, who was only allowed to fight out his *Blitzkrieg* in the press, seemed to have been banished to the second rank of the leadership élite. But when the first military defeats began, after the great initial successes, the second great 'Era of Struggle' began for Goebbels. If his combative powers had visibly atrophied during the period of the consolidation of power, now he won back the ground he had lost. Now too, he won back to a great degree the trust of those who had been badly disappointed by the generals. The war, which became more difficult from 1941 onwards, demanded a new form and a new tone of propaganda, which Goebbels was able to make all the more intense since Hitler now only seldom spoke to 'his people'. Goebbels initiated a large-scale offensive against the population's illusions that the war would end quickly, as well as against the decline in the political will for the war. One of his 'new ideas' was a call for the collection of items of winter clothing to equip the soldiers at the front in 1941. He reached the apogee of his new manipulation of hearts and minds in the speech he gave after the capitulation of Stalingrad at the Palace of Sport on 18 February 1943, in which he wrung emphatic approval for total war from the German people and its Nazi representatives, a master-stroke, as he himself called it.

Goebbels gave this speech knowing that political leadership was lacking, perhaps knowing there was a leadership crisis. He was convinced that the total mobilisation of all available resources had not by any means been fully realised and that therefore the war might be lost. The Palace of Sport speech was intended to be a turning point. In order to take the defence of the nation away from the court camarilla around Hitler and secure it in his own hands, he came to an understanding with Speer, Funk, Ley and Goering, but ultimately without success. His attempt to seize the office of Foreign Minister, too, was unsuccessful.

His popularity, on the other hand, was increasing. If Hitler, and, as yet, Goering, had been highest in the esteem of the German population until the catastrophe of Stalingrad, Goebbels gained respect as the war became more difficult and imposed greater and greater sacrifices and burdens, by virtue of the solemnity and frankness of the tone with which he appealed to the willingness of the people to make sacrifices, and with which he offered comfort. He was also one of those at the top of the Party who did not hide away after defeats, but were always there when the first relief measures had to be set in train in a town afflicted by large-scale bombing raids, and comfort given to the relatives of the victims. After the attempt on Hitler's life on 20 July 1944 Goebbels was appointed State Commissar for the

Implementation of Total War. The more Hitler's star went into decline, the more Goebbels tried to maintain the collapsing regime by his powers of suggestion and persuasion.

At times of conflict and crisis Goebbels and Hitler were magnetically attracted to each other. So it was not without an inner logic that, when the Red Army closed in on Berlin and the war began to draw to a close, Goebbels and his family joined Hitler in the Bunker. He was the only one there who followed Hitler's example and, after having been Hitler's successor as Chancellor for one day, took his own life.

NOTES

1. Goebbels Diaries, entry dated 27.3.1925.
2. Ibid., entry dated 28.3.1945.
3. Ibid., Erinnerungsblätter, p. 2.
4. Ibid., entry dated 21.7.1924.
5. Ibid., entry dated 29.8.1924.
6. Ibid., entry dated 4.9.1924.
7. Ibid., entry dated 28.9.1925.
8. Ibid., entry dated 21.8.1925.
9. Ibid., entry dated 21.8.1925.
10. Ibid., entry dated 13.4.1926.
11. Ibid., entry dated 19.4.1926.
12. Ibid., entry dated 28.3.1930.
13. Ibid., entry dated 10.12.1930.
14. Ibid., entry dated 5.8.1932.
15. Ibid., entry dated 7.8.1932.
16. Ibid., entry dated 3.2.1933.
17. Ibid., entry dated 6.2.1933.
18. Ibid., entry dated 3.10.1924.
19. Ibid., entry dated 12.3.1932.
20. Ibid., entry dated 9.8.1932.
21. *Das politische Tagebuch Alfred Rosenbergs*, edited by H.G. Seraphim (Munich, 1964) p. 80, entry dated 6.2.1939.

BIBLIOGRAPHY

Primary Sources

The basic source for research on Goebbels is his extensive diaries: *Die Tagebücher von Joseph Goebbels. Sämtliche Fragmente*, edited by E. Fröhlich, Part I 1924–41 (Munich, 1987). Part Two is in preparation. Fragments of the entries in the diaries from the years 1942–5 have been published in: *Goebbels Tagebücher aus den Jahren 1942–43. Mit anderen Dokumenten*, edited by L.P. Lochner (Zurich, 1948);

Joseph Goebbels, Tagebücher 1945. With an introduction by R. Hochhuth (Bergisch Gladbach, 1980). A comprehensive bibliography of Goebbels' essays and books can be found in Bärsch (see below). The articles published in *Angriff* and in *Reich* are of particular interest. The propaganda minister's speeches have been collected in: *Goebbels-Reden 1932–1939*, vol. I, edited by H. Heiber (Dusseldorf, 1971); *Goebbels-Reden 1939–1945*, vol. II, edited by H. Heiber (Dusseldorf, 1972).

Secondary Literature

There are numerous biographical studies of Goebbels. The one which is still the best was reprinted in 1988: H. Heiber, *Joseph Goebbels* (Berlin, 1962). The following should also be mentioned: C. Riess, *Joseph Goebbels* (Baden-Baden, 1950); H. Fraenkel/R. Manvell, *Goebbels* (Cologne, 1960); C.-E. Bärsch, *Erlösung und Vernichtung* (Munich, 1987). In the realm of propaganda the reader is referred to the work by E.K. Bramsted: *Goebbels und die nationalsozialistische Propaganda 1925–1945* (Frankfurt am Main, 1971).

7 Hermann Goering: Second Man in the Third Reich

Alfred Kube

Given the increasingly sophisticated formulation of historical issues and the use of structuralist approaches to research as a basis for examining the long term causes which made the Third Reich and its system of rule possible, an analysis of the role of Hermann Goering acquires particular importance. Between 1933 and 1939 Goering was the 'number two' in the Third Reich. During this period he played an extremely active political role, because after 1933 Hitler did not allow any other politician as much free play. At the same time Goering's position within the National Socialist leadership was not uncontroversial. Party comrades were often irritated, not only by his political views, which were often idiosyncratic, but also by his glittering life style and self-satisfied demeanour. His contradictory nature provoked contradictory assessments of him. Many contemporaries described him as the 'iron man', others saw him as a 'paper tiger'. However Goering was undoubtedly popular with the population, and even Hitler accepted Goering's extravagances, unwillingly, but without fuss. He appointed Goering as his deputy and successor at an early stage, underlining Goering's political importance in the Third Reich.

In the following study, section one will sketch the social and ideological preconditions for Goering's advancement. Section two offers a chronological outline of five stages of Goering's career, since Goering's position in the Nazi state changed with the realignment of the internal balance of power during the course of the Third Reich. The third section describes Goering's relationship with Hitler and with the NSDAP and analyses Goering's function in the Nazi system of government.

I

Hermann Wilhelm Goering was born on 12 January 1893 at the Marienbad Clinic in Rosenheim, and given a Protestant baptism. Even in his youth he developed a domineering, egocentric character, which led his mother to remark: 'Hermann will either be a great man or a great criminal'.[1] His father, Dr Heinrich Ernst Goering, who came from Westphalia, was a senior official in the Wilhelmine colonial service. He was the first to make his mark on his son's basic philosophy, passing on to him his nationalistic, economic imperialist ideology, along with unconditional loyalty to the Greater German Fatherland.

The military colleges in Karlsruhe and Grosslichterfelde in Berlin, which Goering attended with enthusiasm and distinction from 1905 to 1911, underpinned his Prussian identity with the consciousness of being a soldier. Although he was born in Upper Bavaria Goering always considered himself to be a Prussian, and first and foremost a Prussian soldier.

The First World War laid the basis of Goering's fame as a notable fighter pilot. With the rank of First Lieutenant, he was decorated on 2 June 1918 with one of the highest orders, the 'Pour le Mérite', for outstanding bravery. Goering's place in the ranks of the best known World War One fighter pilots was secured not only by this rare distinction, but by his promotion, which followed shortly afterwards, to Commander of the famous 'Manfred Baron von Richthofen' fighter squadron.

The Wilhelmine influences of his parental home, his education as a Prussian officer and the comradeship among flyers in the First World War fundamentally shaped Goering's early outlook on life. During this time basic political concepts were emerging which constantly recurred during his later speeches: 'loyalty', 'comradeship', 'Prussian virtues', 'love of the Fatherland' and 'the strong state' were concepts which derived from the political repertoire of a status-conscious Prussian officer of the younger generation.[2]

The end of World War One and discharge from the army precipitated Goering into a personal and professional crisis. After fleeting contacts with paramilitary leagues and the *Freikorps*, Goering earned his keep in Denmark and Sweden by means of a series of jobs in the air travel business. On 3 February 1922 he married a Swede, Carin von Kantzow, with whom he moved to Munich. Here, at the end of 1922, a certain Adolf Hitler conferred a new task on him, one which appealed to his qualities as an officer.

II

Goering's political career is characterised by distinct periods. Five stages can be discerned, each of which has very differing characteristics and are closely linked with the changing power relationships within the Nazi State. The *first stage* encompasses the years 1922 to 1924 and represents Goering's first attempt to win a new sphere of action for himself as a professional politician.

At the end of 1922 Goering came into contact with Adolf Hitler at a political rally in Munich, and decided shortly afterwards to work in Hitler's party. His order 'Pour le Mérite' was demonstrably the decisive factor in leading Hitler to assign to Goering the organisation and leadership of the party's Storm Troopers. Goering's enthusiasm for the philosophical goals of Hitler's NSDAP was not unlimited. It seems rather that it was more by chance that the unemployed officer sought a new area of employment specifically in Hitler's party.

As a self-confident representative of the Prussian officer school, Goering soon came into conflict with the Bavarian core of the NSDAP, whom he despised as a 'crowd of rucksack-wearing beer drinkers with narrow minds and provincial horizons'.[3] In view of his many disputes with Party agencies it is not surprising that Goering became isolated after the NSDAP's failed Munich putsch attempt in November 1923.

During the 'March on the Feldherrnhalle' Goering had suffered a potentially fatal gunshot wound to his hip. He escaped political pursuit by fleeing via Austria to Italy, where he tried to make contact with the Italian fascists. In the spring of 1925 he returned with his wife to Sweden. Here he was compelled to make several visits to a clinic for nervous disorders to be cured of the addiction to medical morphine he had acquired during his flight.

From his exile in Stockholm, Goering complained bitterly about the Party members who had in the meantime actually had his name deleted from the membership list and were refusing to allow him to be granted support. In Goering's opinion 'loyalty' and 'comradeship' were just 'hollow words'[4] in Party circles. Goering's first attempt to make a career as a professional politician had failed at the first hurdle. He had aroused Hitler's interest but had not succeeded in establishing himself in the NSDAP.

The *second stage* in Goering's political development encompasses the period from the end of 1927 until 1934 and is marked by Goering's battle for power and his successful rise to power with Hitler. After his return to Germany in 1927, Goering established himself in Berlin as the representative of a supply company to the up-and-coming air transport industry in Berlin. Only when he had achieved this economically secure position did he make contact with Hitler again. Goering became an NSDAP candidate for the *Reichstag* and had been elected by May 1928.

The distinctive feature of Goering's renewed political activity was that he only felt himself under obligation to Hitler personally, but not to the Party. The greater the likelihood of Hitler entering into talks on coalition with other parties via influential mediators, the more valuable Goering's extensive social contacts became to him. The former war hero contributed decisively to National Socialism's growing acceptability in 'polite society' and to its entrée into the higher reaches of political society.

Goering suffered a personal set-back with the death in Stockholm on 17 October 1931 of his wife Carin, who had been ill for some time. Goering seemed to want to compensate for the loss of the wife he had so cherished by increased political involvement. A visit to Mussolini, innumerable political negotiations with the German Nationalists and leaders of the *Stahl-*

helm in the winter of 1931/2 and finally his election as President of the *Reichstag* after the elections of 31 July 1932 all added to his political contribution to the rise of the NSDAP.

On 30 January 1933 Goering reaped the reward of his efforts. Alongside Hitler and Frick he was the third National Socialist in the coalition government. He was however simply Minister without Portfolio, National Commissioner for Air Traffic and National Commissar for the Prussian Ministry of the Interior. His ministerial position in the Cabinet was therefore of dubious value.

As a result of his own efforts Goering was named Minister For Air Transport on 5 May 1933 and promoted to Infantry General on 30 August 1933. At the same time he campaigned ruthlessly for a break-through by the NSDAP in domestic politics. His infamous firearms decree of 17 February 1933 ordered the Prussian military police to proceed against political opponents with all available force, without regard to the consequences of the use of firearms. In the same way he used the *Reichstag* fire on 27 February 1933 to get rid of his political opponents. However Goering had nothing to do with starting the fire, directly or indirectly.

After some skilful manoeuvring, Goering was named by Hitler, after some hesitation, as Prussian Prime Minister and Prussian Minister of the Interior. The Prussian State Government now became Goering's private organisational headquarters. Here he could call on his own circle of colleagues, who were brought together not through membership of the National Socialist Party, but by their personal oath of allegiance to Goering.

His participation in the elimination of the old SA leadership marked a key episode in Goering's consolidation of political power within the National Socialist system of government. Goering's police force, which was outside the Party and built around the State Secret Police, (the Gestapo), which he had created, played a central part in the murders and arrests in July 1934. After the purge of the SA leadership, Hitler and Goering presented themselves to the public as comrades bound by oath. Hitler rewarded his 'most loyal Palladin'[5] by making Goering 'his deputy in all aspects of national government', in the event of his being prevented from carrying out his duties.[6] This was accomplished in a decree dated 7 December 1934 which has barely been considered by researchers. The 'law concerning the successor to the Führer and Chancellor' of 13 December 1934 is almost equally unknown. In this, Hitler nominated Goering as his successor with the words: 'Immediately after my death he is to take an oath of personal allegiance from the members of the national government, the army and SA and SS units.'[7] With this act Goering was already secretly installed as the designated successor to Hitler by the end of 1934.

Thus a new departure in his political career began for Goering in 1935. In this *third stage*, which extends to the end of 1938, in terms of his power

Goering can easily be described as 'the state within the state'. He now gave up his role as Hitler's Minister for Police and on 20 November 1934 he officially handed over the leadership of the Gestapo to Heinrich Himmler. Before this, by way of compensation, Goering had received the office of National Director of Hunting and Forestry, which ranked as one of the senior state agencies. Goering now sought to achieve a role as Hitler's diplomat and as political representative of the nation. His marriage to actress Emmy Sonnemann on 11 April 1935 contributed materially to the image he was making for himself. The 'wedding of the year' attracted international interest and secured the role of the nation's 'First Lady' for Goering's wife. On 2 June 1938, Goering's only child, his daughter Edda, was born.

In 1935 Goering also succeeded in making a breakthrough in military politics. As a result of lobbying he was appointed Commander-in-Chief of the newly formed Air Force on 1 March, in addition to being Minister for Air Transport. In this way Goering became a prime force in military politics and, following the Italian example, he presented the Air Force for the first time as an independent third arm of national defence alongside the Army and the Navy.

From the time of Goering's involvement in armament issues concerning the Air Force, economic goals were also given greater consideration in his politics. Accordingly he insinuated himself into the realm of economic policy decision-making. One important staging post in this was his nomination as Commissioner for Currency and Raw Materials on 4 April 1936. The concept which Hitler and Goering devised together of a 'Four Year Plan' to secure the economic dimension of rearmament, was the lever Goering wanted to make himself the German 'economic dictator'. This was followed on 18 October 1936 by his nomination as Commissioner for the Implementation of the Four Year Plan.

With this Goering had succeeded in taking control of economic policy-making in the Third Reich. Forcing the face of rearmament and a privileged status for the Air Force were his most important aims in this sphere. Goering's temporary take-over of the Economics Ministry (from November 1937 until February 1938) essentially allowed the Ministry to be transformed into an executive agency of the Four Year Plan. The growth of the 'Hermann Goering Works' from July 1937 into the biggest steel enterprise in Europe demonstrated Goering's personal economic power.

In the mid-thirties Hitler often praised Goering as his 'best man'. Foreign opinion agreed, regarding him as the most powerful man after Hitler. His important position made it easier for Goering to gain entry to the sphere of foreign affairs. He was Hitler's foreign affairs 'Special Plenipotentiary' for Italy and tried to implement imperialist economic expansionary policies in south east Europe in the manner of Stresemann's central European policies. Goering's plans for south east Europe were rounded off to the north east by an active policy towards Poland, which he was trying to win for an anti-bolshevik alliance.

Until the Second World War, Goering regarded east and south east European policies as his very own foreign policy domain. His ideas about the scope and possibilities of economic penetration of neighbouring countries were as vague and flexible as his overall vision of foreign policy. However his concept of a large economic block was clearly different in its essentials from Hitler's idea of 'living space'.

At the beginning of March 1938 Goering's first big foreign policy project became reality: the annexation of Austria into the German state. Goering had made a considerable contribution to this and later described himself with a degree of justification as the 'organiser of the annexation'.[8] With the realisation of the Munich Agreement in September of the same year, Goering had proved his success on the diplomatic stage. He played a fundamental role in the preparatory talks for the agreement.

With the signing of the Munich Agreement, however, it became apparent that Goering's foreign policy agenda no longer coincided to the same extent as before with Hitler's policy of rapid expansion. The Sudeten crisis was the first time Goering urged a solution which did not satisfy Hitler. The 'cowardly generals' and Goering, too, were later heaped with invective by Hitler.

While Goering believed until the summer of 1939 that Hitler would return to a non-military policy of blackmail, the latter paid no more attention to Goering's moderate political line from the beginning of 1939. During the occupation of Prague in March 1939 Goering was no longer taking any part in policy-making. His place was now taken by Ribbentrop, who was less hesitant that Goering and considered the risks of a localised war to be calculable. In this he was in agreement with Hitler's political judgement.

At the beginning of 1939, therefore, Goering entered the *fourth stage* of his varying position of influence in the Third Reich. His political retreat and his gradual displacement from the centre of political decision-making were complete by the end of 1941. Goering reacted to the beginning of war in the same way as the majority of the conservative elite in leading positions in Germany: their loyalty to Hitler and the mechanisms of the Nazi leadership structure outweighed their own political traditions and fundamental political beliefs. It was in keeping with Goering's political philosophy that he should blindly follow 'his leader' at this time of conflict, with a soldier's allegiance to 'the very end'.[9]

However from the beginning of the war it became impossible to overlook the fact that Goering's attitude was basically pessimistic. He was fully informed about the armaments situation and thought it was inadequate for a long war. The trauma of losing the First World War was still clear in his mind. But Goering did not dare to present these worries bluntly to Hitler and instead tried to avoid everything which would discredit him with the

Führer. Goering only experienced one temporary, uncritical bout of euphoric belief in victory, thanks to the successful campaign in France. In his opinion all that was needed now were a few targetted air attacks on the British Isles, in order to force the British government to come to the negotiating table. However, after the failure of the Battle of Britain, Hitler's doubts about Goering's capabilities as Chief of the Air Force increased. This not only led to an even greater loss of prestige with Hitler, but from now on Goering was increasingly pushed into a minor role in shaping military policy.

Goering followed the attack on the Soviet Union in June 1941 with little interest. Even before the Soviet counter-attack in December 1941 Hitler indulged in several outbursts of anger against Goering on account of the ostensible failure of the Air Force. When Hitler took over the Supreme Command of the army on 19 December 1941 the Air Force was downgraded to an auxiliary arm of the Army.

In 1942 the *fifth* and *last stage* in Goering's political career began. From 1942 the circle around Goering noticed that the *Reich* Marshall was increasingly lethargic and took little pleasure in his work. From the turn of the year 1942/3, Goering was evidently convinced that the war could no longer be won. In the period that followed he flew as often as possible to his hunting lodge 'Karinhall' or relived the romanticism of his youth at Burg Veldenstein. His chief concern now was collecting art treasures from all over Europe.

At the beginning of 1943 there was an open breach between Hitler and Goering. The British air offensive on the Ruhr in March turned Hitler's full fury on Goering. However although Hitler did not balk at sacking a whole series of other officers for supposed incompetence, he still retained Goering. Hitler rejected demands to replace Goering with a more capable air force chief with the words: 'I cannot do that for reasons of state'.[10] But it was primarily Goering's continued intense popularity with the population and Hitler's fear of the negative consequences for the prestige of his leadership cadre in world opinion which prevented Goering's dismissal. It was not until the hopeless situation of the last few days of the war that Hitler expelled Goering from the NSDAP and relieved him of all duties, in his so-called 'Political Testament' of 29 April 1945.[11]

From March 1946 onwards Goering had to answer to the Allied Military Tribunal at Nuremberg. Cured of a drug addiction, Goering had regained some of his original vitality and quick-wittedness. He did not present himself as the humble loser, but worked on his own memorial in grandiloquent manner. On 1 October 1946 the court found Goering guilty on all four counts on which he was accused and sentenced him to death by hanging. On 15 October 1946, during the night before the planned execution of the sentence, Goering escaped the judge's writ by committing suicide in his cell, by means of a poison pill.

III

Goering's political rise and fall reflects the changing political situation in the Third Reich and thus also reflects the progressive radicalisation of National Socialist politics. In this context Goering's supposed political affinities with National Socialism are representative of large sections of the pan-German, economic imperialist inclined elite, whose political identity gradually dissolved in the face of the increasing consolidation of Hitler's power.

Until the end of 1938, in the realm of politics a series of short-term revisionist nationalistic goals provided sufficient basis for an expedient, opportunistic alliance between the late imperialist Goering and the racist political proponent of 'living space', Hitler. Goering did know Hitler's book, *Mein Kampf*, but thought that Hitler's programmatic exposition, explaining his policies, was irrelevant.[12]

Although Goering did little to try to prevent the increasing brutality of the anti-Jewish measures, he was not the motive force behind them. He was basically only interested in the economic aspect of the 'Jewish question'. The central opponent in Goering's philosophy was not Jewry, but communism. In his foreign policy deliberations and negotiations during the thirties, the formation of a Central European Bloc as a buffer against the Soviet Union, which was to extend from Poland to the Balkans, is mentioned again and again. In the longer term, he saw Europe threatened by the 'bolshevik menace' and considered that a war against Russia during the forties was inevitable.[13]

It may have suited Goering that Hitler's programme, freshened up from time to time in confidential monologues, was much more radical. In the context of this alliance between National Socialists and national conservatives Goering was a capable intermediary, and Hitler's radicalism was ideally suited for demonstrating the resoluteness which would help Germany to attain a new significance in the world.

In his perception of the relationship between the NSDAP and the state, too, Goering was fundamentally at odds with Hitler and the other Party leaders, among whom the view prevailed that the state was to be gradually demolished. In Goering's political ideology, on the other hand, the state clearly played the leading role vis à vis the Party. Goering supported the idea of the 'state as a militant entity'[14] and made use of state powers and organisations to build up his power base.

Because it was rooted like this in rather conservative, authoritarian philosophical categories, Goering's political ideology was based on different fundamentals from those of the Party theoreticians. His confrontations with Goebbels, Hess, Himmler and Rosenberg on questions of power politics and ideology even caused comment abroad. Goering made no secret of the fact that he had no time for politics based on racist social Darwinism.

Goering's role in the Nazi leadership structure has one fundamental distinguishing feature, which differentiates him from other national conservative politicians who entered into an alliance with Hitler. Goering was so useful to Hitler because his position in power politics straddled the four pillars of the state: the Party, armed forces, the economy and the bureaucracy. Goering's exceptional status in the Third Reich rested on the fact that in terms of power politics he belonged to both the military and the Party, the economic leadership as well as the bureaucracy. However it is characteristic that in spite of this he was not the representative of these individual pillars of power, but united something of all of them. The antagonism of these power blocs characterised Goering's specific position in the Nazi state. Goering moved between four poles like a magnetic needle.

In the initial phase of their collaboration Goering was a useful tool for Hitler on his road to power, because of his contacts and skilled conduct of negotiations. Later, because of his independent position, between the power blocs, Goering became an important instrument for the exercise of dominion and the integration of all the separate elements which made up the Third Reich. In many areas he could be appointed as Hitler's 'right hand man' and implement decisions which Hitler himself tried to avoid in his policy of 'divide et impera'.

Goering, for his part, profited from his exceptional position between the extremes of power politics. He could intervene in several areas of national politics and often quote quite ominous directives from Hitler in his support. This not only secured for Goering his own sphere of dominion but also created for him considerable room for political manoeuvre.

One important precondition for Goering's relatively independent power base was that he did not need to fall back on NSDAP leadership cadres for the recruitment of personnel. His conduct of his staff office, his own press and intelligence agency, the internal administration of Prussia, the directorship of the air force and the Four Year Plan were not as a rule in the hands of Party functionaries. The leaders in Goering's entourage consisted of former war-time colleagues, personal friends from the time before the seizure of power or specialists not linked with the Party from the administration, the economy and industry.

However Hitler always took care that none of Goering's power bases became so big that they could present a potential threat. When Goering was hoping to take over Blomberg's office as Minister of War in 1938, Hitler resisted his request. The firmness with which he turned Goering down in this matter proves that Hitler was aware of the potential danger posed by his designated successor's great powers.

However Goering's political role in the Third Reich and his dominant position in individual areas within the Nazi leadership structure demonstrate that up to 1938 it was perfectly possible to combine old-style imperialistic, or at least revisionist, politics and radical expansionary politics based on social Darwinism. The implementation of Hitler's reckless racial-biological 'concept' went hand in hand with the gradual process of removing power from the national conservative elites, which led from Papen by way of Hugenberg, Schmitt, Schacht, Neurath, Blomberg and Fritsch to Goering and even Ribbentrop.

As the last significant representative of the late imperialist revisionist politicians, Goering was excluded from the centres of decision-making at the beginning of 1939. From then on his political significance in the state was reduced to a role as figure head and rallying point in the realm of propaganda. The 'Führer State' had now also become reality in the heart of government.

NOTES

1. Comment by Franziska Goering in: G.M. Gilbert, 'Hermann Goering. Amiable Psychopath', *Journal of Abnormal and Social Psychology*, 43 (1948) 211–29, 213.
2. For Goering's idea of the state see his speech dated 26 October 1935 in: *H. Goering, Reden und Aufsätze*, edited by E. Gritzbach (Munich, 1938) p. 208, and especially Goering's speech in Potsdam of 10 March 1934 in Nacht-Ausgabe des deutschen Nachrichtenbüros, no. 518, Politisches Archiv des Auswärtigen Amtes, Bonn, Büro RM/18–1, vol. 20, sheet 414.
3. Goering's remark in E. Hanfstaengl, *Hitler. The Missing Years* (London, 1957) p. 72.
4. Goering's note to Lahr dated 26 June 1925, Geheimes Preussisches Staatsarchiv/Stiftung Preussischer Kulturbesitz, Berlin-Dahlem, Rep. 90 B/No. 286.
5. Goering's 'paladin' comment in a speech dated 18 May 1933 in: *Ursachen und Folgen. Vom deutschen Zusammenbruch 1918 und 1945 bis zur staatlichen Neuordnung Deutschlands in der Gegenwart. Eine Urkunden- und Dokumentensammlung zur Zeitgeschichte*, edited by H. Michaelis, E. Schraepfler and G. Scheel, vol. IX (Berlin, 1968) p. 114.
6. Hitler Decree of 7 December 1934, Bundesarchiv Koblenz, R43II/1660, B1.26.
7. Nuremberg document NG-1206(2), Archiv des Instituts für Zeitgeschichte, Munich, MA-5(2).
8. Goering's remark of 14 March 1946 in: *Der Prozess gegen die Hauptkriegsverbrecher vor dem Internationalen Militärgerichtshof Nürnberg, 14 November 1945 bis 1 Oktober 1946* (Nuremberg, 1947) vol. 9, p. 333f.
9. Goering's closing remarks at the sitting of the Reichstag on 30 January 1939, in: M. Domarus, *Hitler. Reden und Proklamationen 1932–45. Kommentiert von einem deutschen Zeitgenossen* (Munich, 1965) vol. 2, p. 1067.
10. Hitler's comment in: H. Guderian, *Erinnerungen eines Soldaten* (Heidelberg, 1951) p. 405.
11. Hitler's Political Testament dated 29 April 1945, Bundesarchiv Koblenz, NS20/129, 7f.

12. Goering's statement in: *Der Prozess gegen die Hauptkriegsverbrecher*, vol. 9, p. 297f, and in E. Bross, *Gespräche mit Hermann Goering während des Nürnberger Prozesses* (Flensburg, 1950) p. 110.
13. Goering's speech of 28 October 1933 in *H. Goering, Reden und Aufsätze*, 96; memo on file about a meeting of the senior air force officers with Goering on 2 December 1936 in *Ursachen und Folgen*, vol. XI, p. 453f.
14. Statement by SS General Karl Friedrich Otto Wolff dated 7/8 September 1952, Archiv des Instituts für Zeitgeschichte, Munich, ZS317, B1.1.

BIBLIOGRAPHY

Primary Sources

Because of difficulties with sources, scholarly research on Goering did not start until about ten years ago. There is no file of documents which gives a detailed account of Goering's activities. Instead the many written testimonies to his policies have been dispersed among nearly all the German historical archives. Part of Goering's missing political archive was found by me in the National Archives in Washington. Personal notebooks found at the same time contain hardly any political comment.

Published sources are in short supply. The work edited by Th. R. Emessen, *Aus Goering's Schreibtisch. Ein Dokumentenfund* (Berlin, 1947) is barely worth mentioning. There are some published speeches and essays which can be consulted on his political ideology: *Aufbau einer Nation*, 2nd edition (Berlin, 1934); 'Der Kampf gegen Marxismus und Separatismus' in W. Kube (ed.), *Almanach der nationalsozialistischen Revolution* (Berlin, 1934) 155–60; *Reden und Aufsätze*, edited by E. Gritzbach (Munich, 1938).

Contemporary propaganda biographies give an indication of how Goering saw himself: J. Matthias, 'Der Flieger Hermann Goering', in *Unter Flatternden Fahnen*, vol. 4 (Berlin, 1935) 55–90; M.H. Sommerfeldt, *Goering, was fällt Ihnen ein! Lebensskizze* (Berlin, 1932); E. Gritzbach, *Hermann Goering. Werk und Mensch* (Munich, 1937).

Goering's comments at the time of the Nuremberg trials are comparatively well documented: *Der Prozess gegen die Hauptkriegsverbrecher vor dem Internationalen Militärsgerichtshof Nürnberg*, 14 November 1945 bis 1. Oktober 1946 (Nuremberg, 1947) vol. 9; P.M. Bleibtreu, *Hermann Goering: Ich werde nichts verschweigen . . .* (Vienna, 1950); W. Bross, *Gespräche mit Hermann Goering während des Nürnberger Prozesses* (Flensburg, 1950); G.M. Gilbert, 'Hermann Goering. Amiable Psychopath', in *Journal of Abnormal and Social Psychology*, **43** (1948) 211–29.

The memoirs of Goering's second wife give scarcely any information on his politics: F. Goering, *An der Seite meines Mannes. Begebenheiten und Bekenntnisse* (Göttingen, 1967).

Secondary Literature

The first studies of Goering to appear after the war came predominantly from the pen of journalists. Without any claim to scholarly exactitude, they largely consisted of rumours and anecdotes about Goering, for example; E. Lange, *Der Reichsmarschall im Kriege. Ein Bericht in Wort und Bild* (Stuttgart, 1950); E. Butler and

G. Young, *Marshal without Glory. The Troubled Life of Hermann Goering* (London, 1951); W. Frischauer, *Goering. Ein Marschallstab zerbrach* (Ulm, 1951); Ch. Bewley, *Hermann Goering* (Göttingen, 1956); L. Mosley, *Goering. Eine Biographie* (Munich, 1975). H. Fraenkel and R. Manvell, *Hermann Goering* (Hannover, 1964) are an exception, since they do base their work on source material, albeit a limited range.

More recent works show that the journalists' rumours about Goering's way of life still have greater attractions than scientific objectivity: G. Böddeker and R. Winter, *Die Kapsel. Das Geheimnis um Goerings Tod* (Munich, 1983); W. Paul, *Wer war Hermann Goering? Biographie* (Esslingen, 1983). This is in many respects also true of the comprehensive work by D. Irving, *Goering* (Munich, 1987) which presents a series of mistakes and doubtful judgements in the form of a historical novel.

Richard Overy was one of the first historians to come to grips with Goering as a whole, but without, however, being able to free himself from many of the clichées in his assessment of Goering, since the study was not adequately based on source material: R. Overy, *Goering, The 'Iron Man'* (London, 1984).

At the same time, but independently of each other, Martens and I published our works on Goering's role in the 'Third Reich': S. Martens, *Hermann Goering. 'Erster Paladin des Führers' und 'Zweiter Mann im Reich'* (Paderborn, 1985); A. Kube, *Pour le merite und Hakenkreuz. Hermann Goering im Dritten Reich*, 2nd. edition (Munich, 1987). Both these works evaluate unpublished material for the first time. The interpretations do not diverge greatly; Martens lays greater emphasis on an examination of Goering's foreign policy, while my work attempts to take account of several of the domestic policy areas Goering was involved in. Both combine biographical and structuralist history.

Single aspects of Goering's politics are dealt with in: H. Boog, *Die deutsche Luftwaffenführung 1935–1945. Führungsprobleme, Spitzengliederung, Generalstabsausbildung* (Stuttgart, 1982) (until now the only reliable study of Goering's work in the Air Force); A. Kube, 'Aussenpolitik und "Grossraum-wirtschaft". Die deutsche Politik zur wirtschaftlichen Integration Südosteuropas 1933 bis 1939' in H. Berding (ed.), *Wirtschaftliche und politische Integration in Europa im 19. und 20. Jahrhundert* (Göttingen, 1984) 185–211 (on Goering's 'large-scale economy' planning); S. Martens, 'Die Rolle Hermann Goerings in der deutschen Aussenpolitik 1937/38', in F. Knipping and K.-J. Müller (eds), *Machtbewusstsein in Deutschland am Vorabend des Zweiten Weltkrieges* (Paderborn, 1984) 74–92 (on Goering's efforts in foreign policy 1937/38).

8 Rudolf Hess: Deputy Führer

Dietrich Orlow

Our picture of Rudolf Hess is still characterised by vagueness and contra-dictoriness. Hitler's private secretary in the 'Era of Struggle', in the Third Reich Hess became Minister of State and the Führer's deputy for Party affairs. At the beginning of the Second World War Hitler put him in second place, after Goering, in the list of his successors. In spite of this prolifera-tion of offices and honours, historians are by and large in agreement that Hess only had slight influence on the political decision-making process before and after 1933. This is particularly true of foreign policy. In spite of this, his name is probably still most firmly linked with the spectacular (although of course senseless) foreign policy mission he undertook in person.

So who was this man? At first sight Hess appears to be a National Socialist of the first order. Like several of the leading 'old warriors' he was born abroad, in his case on 26 April 1894 in Alexandria (Egypt): his father had been living there for several years as the representative of various German firms. On his father's side the family belonged to the upper middle class; his mother came from a more petty-bourgeois milieu. Both parents had their homes in Wurttemberg.

Hess's youth was shaped by a sustained conflict with his father. Although the boy showed an early interest in the natural sciences, his father wanted him to enter a commercial career. Hess did submit to his father's will for a while, but at the beginning of the First World War he broke off his commercial training and volunteered for military service. Like Hitler he was an enthusiastic and bold soldier. At the end of the war he was a lieutenant in the Air Force.

After the defeat, Hess, like thousands of his comrades, found himself without a job or a future. He became a student at Munich University, probably for want of anything better to do. Hess attended lectures by the political geographer Karl Haushofer. His geographical-determinist teachings provided an answer to Hess's search for a theoretical way out of Germany's shame, but Hess was also personally on good terms with his teacher. As a student he also got to know his future wife, Ilse Pröhl. The marriage they contracted in 1927 was a completely happy relationship.

Hess was always thought of as a difficult, inscrutable man. He was one of the few leaders of the Third Reich who did not use his position as a means of enriching himself or fostering adulation. To all outward appearances, and probably in his own estimation, too, he remained a 'simple Party member'. Other important Nazis, like Joseph Goebbels, however, regarded him for precisely this reason as boring and weak.

Hess's moral and aesthetic thinking had its roots in the bourgeoisie of the Wilhelmine era. His views on art and culture, women and his personal taste, too, were those of a typical member of the bourgeois middle classes. Goebbels and Hitler, who after 1933 developed a preference for a grandiose style of furnishing their living quarters, made fun of the Deputy's lack of 'taste for grandeur' in his interior decorations.[1]

Hess was an out-and-out loner. His obsessive concern for his health points to certain deep-seated psychological problems; he was a confirmed hypochondriac. He tried to assuage what were often pschosomatic ailments with a range of alternative cures. Among these were obscure diets. 'The food was quite dreadful,' Goebbels noted in his diary after a visit to the Hess family.[2]

Rudolf Hess became politically active at an early age. Soon after his arrival in Munich he plunged into the turmoil of extreme right wing associations. He joined the Thule Society and the *Freikorps Epp*. According to all available witnesses he was a rabid anti-semite even before he got to know Hitler and accepted unconditionally the theory of an 'International Jewish Conspiracy'.

Nonetheless Hess was not a typical 'old warrior'. His attitude to Nazi doctrine and especially to the 'Teacher' was stamped to greater extent than in the case of other Nazi leaders with quasi-religious feelings. Hess regarded National Socialism as a signpost pointing towards a utopian age and Hitler as an infallible prophet. Again and again, contemporaries remarked that he did not talk in his speeches, he preached. His pathetic proclamation: 'Führer, my leader, my faith, my light', was not play-acting, but expressed the content of the relationship between Hitler and his Deputy.

His first meeting with Hitler took place at an early NSDAP meeting and was a key experience for Hess. He fell into ecstasy and immediately saw in Hitler not just the dictator the extreme right wing had been waiting for with such longing, but also a religious Messiah.

Soon after this first meeting Hess was a member of the group around the future leader. After the failure of the Hitler Putsch, in which Hess had taken an active part, he was sentenced to a short time in jail, which he served at Hitler's side in the fortress of Landsberg. Hess more and more took on the role of Hitler's secretary.

After his release from prison, Hess became one of the Party leader's constant companions. A restless personality, Hitler loved to surround himself with a small group of colleagues, to whom he delivered endless monologues on philosophical and political themes, as he was to do later with his nightly supper guests. Hess and Hitler also had contact in their private lives. In 1927 Hitler was a witness at Hess's marriage to Ilse Pröhl, while Hess took touching care of Hitler when the latter was plunged into a serious nervous crisis after the suicide of his niece, Geli Raubal, in 1931.

As Hitler's private secretary Hess increasingly became the man the junior leaders of the movement had to speak to. He was conscious of his role as Hitler's mouthpiece and spoke of himself as the 'Hagen' of the Party. In an analogy to the later 'If the Führer knew that' syndrome, junior Party leaders blamed Hess for decisions which undoubtedly emanated from Hitler himself. In addition, Hess propagated the Hitler cult within the Party. It was primarily he who elevated the statement that the Führer 'was always right and always would be' to the level of a Party maxim.

The Nazi seizure of power, which for Hess was the fulfilment of his personal faith, predestined by fate and willed by God, brought the Private Secretary power and honours, but also distanced him increasingly from his idol. From 1935 on he had less personal contact with Hitler; sometimes months passed before he was allowed a personal audience with his Führer.

This alienation did not lead to any change in his relations with the dictator. Hess remained a believer. However Hitler's relationship with his Deputy raises considerably more questions. What did Hitler think of the man who had been among his closest colleagues for more than a decade and whom he made his Deputy for Party Affairs? Hitler was only capable of one-sided relationships. A relationship based on mutual equality and inclination was impossible for him. Beyond a doubt he valued Hess's absolute devotion and the stage-management of the Hitler cult. Above and beyond this Hess embodied something akin to the early 'idealism' in the Party, which Hitler remembered sorrowfully, especially in the years of the defeats during the Second World War. Hess almost shed tears when his wife informed him in Spandau that during the war Hitler had put forward the view that he was the only idealist in the Party. But there are other witnesses according to whom Hitler was increasingly disappointed in his Deputy. Goebbels took a certain amount of satisfaction in recording Hitler's criticism of Hess's petty-bourgeois manner and his lack of assertiveness.

In the final analysis, Hess, like all the dictator's colleagues, was only the means to an end. In the 'Era of Struggle' Hess played an important role as Hitler's mouth-piece and tamer of the Party radicals. Later, when Hitler was increasingly preoccupied with plans for his war of aggression, Hess's constant reminders of the 'ideals' of National Socialism became a nuisance and Hess himself became increasingly dispensable. He had done his duty.

For almost a decade Hess was the highest ranking functionary in the NSDAP. He was responsible for matters of Party administration, from the selection of the NSDAP's body of functionaries to their installment in the machinery of state. On paper at least he was something of the order of a General Secretary of the NSDAP. In reality of course nothing in the Third Reich was as it appeared on paper. In practice plenary powers had little meaning.

Of particular interest is in how Hess came to office and what influence he had in the Third Reich. There is no doubt that Hess had an emotional relationship with the Party; he was an enthusiastic and convinced Party comrade. One of his speeches, which even the hypercritical Goebbels described as 'gripping' was a memorial address Hess delivered at the beginning of 1941 on the occasion of the state memorial service for the 'old warrior', Hermann Kriebel. (Like Hess and Hitler, Kriebel had been imprisoned for a while in Landsberg.) Beyond this, Hess, convinced that Hitler thought as he did, regarded the Party as an elite organisation for shaping the coming National Socialist age which was to replace the rotten, mendacious bourgeois world.

However, none of this predestined him for an established career in the Third Reich.[3] Hess had neither a personal nor territorial power base. The beginning of his spectacular rise was without a doubt the Strasser crisis in December 1932.

As always in a crisis, Hitler attacked rather than retreated, and announced that in future he would direct the Party administration himself. This of course was a fiction. The greater part of Strasser's duties were taken over by his deputy, Robert Ley. He now had the title of 'Director of Staff of the Political Organisation of the NSDAP' (PO). However Hitler evidently had reservations about conferring all of Strasser's powers on Ley. For this reason he gave orders for the establishment of a Political Central Commission (PCC) and appointed Hess as its director. The duties of the PCC in the first instance were negative. It was to prevent the PO developing a taste for independence. Hitler regarded Hess, who was entirely devoted to him, as the suitable leader for this purpose.

Supposing that they could now issue orders to state and society, immediately after the seizure of power the Party organs interfered more or less at will in the various spheres from public administration to the economy. In the late spring of 1933 the situation was getting increasingly out of control. To prevent threatened anarchy Hitler conferred on Hess the newly created office of Deputy Führer. To begin with Hess again had negative duties to carry out: he circulated a ruling to all Party authorities that they were not to initiate any intervention in state or society without his prior approval and this was supposed to keep the ambitious Party organs within bounds. But Hess and his colleagues developed far-reaching plans for the future too. They understood the office of Deputy Führer as a kind of general staff for the development of the future Third Reich.

Now there were many such plans and ideas in Hitler's Reich. They all came to grief, not just because of their programmatic inadequacies and the aggressive intentions of the regime, but also because of Hitler's basic administrative principle: 'divide et impera'. Hess fared no differently from his rivals. His title notwithstanding, he was by no means senior to the other Party leaders. In practice he was only one of sixteen national directors, who all, like the *Gauleiter*, had direct access to Hitler. As Hitler had presumably intended, this resulted in constant friction between the office of the Deputy Führer and other Party organs. In his efforts to restrain his rivals among the national directors, mainly Ley and his fast-growing empire, the Deputy gave the *Gauleiter* a great deal of freedom to manoeuvre.

Any discussion of the role Hess played as the senior Party functionary in the Third Reich is made more difficult by the person and function of his most important colleague, Chief of Staff Martin Bormann. In the Bormann-Hess-Hitler triangle Hess progressively lost influence. By 1935 at the latest the Deputy was increasingly pushed into the background. But Bormann's growing shadow also makes it difficult for the historian to differentiate between Hess's institutional role and his personal influence. In the second half of the thirties in particular, when Hess had to stay at home for weeks in far-off Harlaching with stomach pain (probably psychosomatic in origin), Bormann probably took decisions in the name of, but without the knowledge of his superior. However this state of affairs is not true for the early stage of the Nazi regime. In at least one key event Hess's personal help was decisive for Hitler's actions.

The matter in case was the so-called Röhm affair. Here Hess was one of the driving forces who pushed Hitler into taking action against the supposed shortcomings of the SA leader. He had both personal and political reasons for this. In contrast to Hitler, who regarded the personal affairs of his lieutenants primarily from the point of view of their net contribution to his rule, Hess evidently really was morally outraged about the widespread homosexuality among SA leaders. What is more, he was convinced that Röhm's ambitions to secure the role of the SA as the political and military elite of the Third Reich could seriously endanger the position of the political functionaries. In the end Hitler's decision to sentence people to death without reference to the law or the courts accorded with Hess's idea of a dictator behaving responsibly.

According to Hess's understanding of the matter, the office of Deputy Führer formed the intersection between state and Party in the 'dual state' of the Third Reich. Its public duties were secured in law. In December 1933 Hess (along with Röhm) was appointed Minister of State without Portfolio. At the same time Hitler determined that all ministries were to present copies of laws and decrees to the office of the Deputy Führer before they were published or issued. Over and above this Hess's office received consultative rights in all personnel matters affecting the senior civil servants. In practice, however, the department experienced considerable difficulty in asserting its consultative rights in legislation and personnel matters. Both Hess and Bormann were soon forced to acknowledge that political fanaticism and a racially impeccable family tree could not replace expertise and practical ability.

However in the area of legislation on the Jews the department was to a large extent able to realise its ambitions. It played a decisive role in the formulation of the so-called Nuremberg laws of September 1935, which among other things deprived the German Jews of their civic rights. Here, it must be said, Hess's personal influence is more difficult to prove than in the Röhm affair, but it can probably be assumed that as a fanatical anti-semite he fully welcomed the attacks the Party initiated against the German Jews. In the implementation of these laws, too, his department again and again demanded the most severe treatment possible.

If Hess's influence on domestic policy gradually decreased, this is even more true of foreign policy. There is no indication that Hess influenced Hitler's foreign policy decisions. After the outbreak of World War Two Hess was pushed into an even more marginal role. It is doubtful whether he was informed at all about the details of German plans of attack from the invasion of Poland up to the Russian campaign. The Norwegian campaign, for example, came as a complete surprise to him.

Remarkably, after a series of years during which he was often ill and depressed, at the end of 1940, not least as a result of the victorious French campaigns, he seems to have been completely in touch again. Goebbels, who in past years had often complained about Hess's personnel policies and the lack of decisiveness in his department, noted on 16 October after a meeting with the Deputy Führer: 'He is now completely cured. A good dependable man. Hess made the best possible impression on me: he is calm, rational, communicative and very trusting'.[4]

In the early evening of 10 May 1941 Rudolf Hess took off in an ME 262 aircraft which had been specially converted for him personally, on course for Britain. A few hours later, after a flight which is still regarded today as a masterpiece of flying, he landed by parachute in Scotland. The aircraft crashed to the ground. The longest and most insignificant period of his life had begun.

This sensational flight still preoccupies historians and contemporaries today. What is especially disputed is his motivation. Hess's own statements seem too contradictory to be credible. Of particular interest is the question of whether and to what extent Hitler was aware of his deputy's intentions. Hess himself, as well as the official propaganda of the Third Reich, denied that Hitler had any knowledge of his actions. On the other hand, Ernst Bohle, the director of the NSDAP's Foreign Affairs Organisation, and Hess's brother were convinced at least until the official denial, that Hess had flown to Britain with a secret peace proposal from Hitler.

A closer examination of the circumstances appears to exclude Hitler's participation. Hitler's outrage at Hess's initiative was genuine, because at this point he was bound to be afraid that any such action would be interpreted as weakness. The conviction of the leaders of the Soviet Union (which they maintained until his death), that Hess flew to Britain to secure

British participation in Hitler's planned attack on the Soviet Union is equally incorrect. Everything points away from this interpretation. In the first case, it is by no means clear whether Hess had any knowledge of Operation Barbarossa, for in the months before his flight he had very little contact with Hitler and the other leaders of the Third Reich. Moreover there is no indication in the British transcripts of his interrogation that Hess even mentioned the Soviet Union.

The solution to the riddle is found in Hess's relationship with Hitler and the latter's vision of a global balance of power among the 'Germanic' peoples. In short the Deputy Führer flew to Britain in order to make an offer to the 'peace faction' there, an act he was convinced both corresponded with Hitler's intentions and was in Britain's interest. Such a 'peace offer' could not be made through diplomatic contacts, because – according to Hitler's frequently expressed conviction – Winston Churchill and the British 'war faction' would prevent serious discussion of it. Hitler believed that the 'peace faction', which in his estimation included parts of the British aristocracy and possibly even members of the Royal Family among its members, had been deprived of political power by Winston Churchill and his supporters.[5] In reality of course there was no such gulf between the peace and war factions in the British ruling classes, but then Hess never doubted Hitler's brilliant powers of judgement.

With this spectacular course of action Hess hoped to find his way directly to the 'peace faction'. His unsuspecting middle man was Albrecht Haushofer, the son of his old teacher Karl Haushofer. Haushofer worked in the Foreign Office and before the war he had had close links with a number of British aristocrats, including the Duke of Hamilton. Hess flew for Hamilton's estate, hoping to be able to use him to contact the real leader of the supposed 'peace party'.

Hitler's assessment of Britain and its military prospects were a decisive factor in Hess's decision. Goebbels repeatedly noted in his diaries Hitler's conviction that Britain had lost the war, but that he, Hitler, was nonetheless ready to make a fair peace offer to his opponent. The proposals which Hess presented to his British audience were identical to Hitler's ideas. The German dictator only demanded two conditions for a peace agreement between Britain and Germany: Germany demanded undisputed hegemony on the continent and the return of the German colonies. These colonies were however, as a punishment as it were for Versailles, to be 'rounded up' somewhat. Iraq, for example, was 'of course' to pass into German hands.

Understandably the British showed little interest in Hitler's/Hess's generous offer. After they had established into the bargain that Hess could not reveal any military secrets, silence fell after a few days around the prominent prisoner. The British decision to play down the Hess affair coincided with the intentions of the Nazi leadership. For Goebbels, Hess's flight was a propaganda nightmare which he wanted to be rid of as quickly as possible. The Propaganda Minister declared on the spot that Hess was mentally confused, a version of events which moreover Hess himself had suggested in the event of his mission failing, by his letter of farewell to Hitler.[6]

During his imprisonment in Britain Hess's hypochondria increased and he displayed a series of psychopathic symptoms. He suffered from paranoia and claimed his guards were trying to poison him. He also complained of loss of memory. However Hess later wrote that he had only been pretending to suffer from these conditions in order to make the British send him back to Germany as a mental patient. But the British thwarted these plans and did not repatriate him. At the end of the Second World War they transferred the former Deputy Führer to Germany as one of the twenty-two accused in the Nuremberg Trials. The order of seniority in the dock was exactly the same as it had been in the Third Reich: Hess sat beside Hermann Goering. He faced the court on four charges: conspiracy and crimes against peace, war crimes and crimes against humanity.

Hess regarded the entire judicial proceedings as a farce. He did not show a trace of repentance, as for example Speer or Schirach did, but did not attempt either to justify his behaviour. He appears to have had two reasons for his (pretended?) apathy. Firstly, he regarded the trial as victor's justice staged by the Jews, although he was by no means alone in this among the accused. His belief that the Western Allies, too, regarded their participation in the Inter-Allied Military Tribunal at Nuremberg as a public relations exercise, however, was probably his alone. In a macabre continuation of Hitler's delusions in his bunker. Hess, too, was persuaded that the Western Allies would either sentence him to death or entrust him with the political leadership of the three western zones of occupation. The Deputy still regarded himself as Hitler's legitimate successor. In his final speech before the passing of his sentence, he emphasised that he still remained true to his idol, Hitler, in spite of everything. In the course of lengthy and very confused statements he declared: 'I was privileged to work for many years under the greatest son my people has produced in its thousand year history. I have no regrets. If I had to start again I would act as I have done, even if I knew that at the end a funeral pyre would be burning for me'.[7]

The court found Hess guilty on two of the four counts (conspiracy and crimes against peace) and sentenced him to life imprisonment (the Russians appealed for the death sentence). Hess did not react to the judgement; in fact he wrote that it did not affect him at all. True to his belief, that he would soon resume a leading role in politics, he spent the months between being sentenced and being transferred to Spandau incessantly preparing documents for his future role in the three western zones. Hess thought of everything: the preparation of office accommodation in Munich, his speech on the occasion of the first meeting of the *Reichstag*, guards of honour for the graves of the accused executed at Nuremberg and his own title. To begin with Hess intended to do without the title 'Führer'. This was to be reserved for Hitler.

Rudolf Hess spent forty-one years of his life as a prisoner in the Military Prison in Spandau, the last twenty-one of these as the sole occupant of the huge complex.[8] Guarded by a squad selected monthly from each of the four Allied powers, he became the most expensive prisoner in the world. What sort of person was he during this time, which comprised almost half of his life? In fact little about him changed. The letters to his wife and son as well as the memories of the French prison chaplain and the American commander show a well-read, by no means unsympathetic person with wide-ranging interests. But other less positive characteristics are still evident too. Hess was still a hypochondriac and, as far as can be achieved in prison life, a loner. There were weeks when he scarcely said a word to his fellow prisoners. Above all, however, he remained a political fanatic. In contrast to the other prisoners Hess refused for years to agree to visits from his wife and son, because in his opinion this would amount to a recognition of the judgement of the victorious Allies. It was only on Christmas Eve 1969, when he was genuinely seriously ill and had to undergo a stomach operation in the British Military Hospital in Berlin that he agreed to a visit from his family. It was to be the only time he saw them again in his life.

Although the Western Allies were ready to pardon him in the final years of his imprisonment, the Soviets refused to release the old man. At the end, however, Hess succeeded in evading the attention of his guards for a short time. A few weeks after his ninety-third birthday, on 17 August 1987, he strangled himself with the electric cable of a heater which the prison administration had had built into a summerhouse in the garden, to make it more pleasant for the aged prisoner to stay out in the open. The announcement from the Allied powers which had been formulated years earlier, stating that Hess had died of natural causes in Spandau, had to be revised.

Hess's significance in history? He himself was probably convinced right up to the end of his life that he would be a symbol of the renaissance of National Socialism if he left prison alive, a martyr uniting the generations after his death. He would have been deeply disappointed by the reality. A few Neo-Nazis demonstrated in Spandau and in various locations in the Federal Republic after his death had been announced, but the general public in Germany certainly did not mark the death of this last representative of a past era in the manner he may have dreamed of. Hess overestimated his place in history, because he overestimated the long-term influence of his idol Adolf Hitler. As the actual originator of the Führer cult Hess literally saw National Socialism and the person of Adolf Hitler as one and the same thing. Paradoxically by so doing he achieved the opposite of what he had intended. The exclusive identification of the Nazi regime and its ideology with the person of Hitler was decisive in National Socialism's loss of appeal, when it became obvious that Hitler would not only fail to achieve his aims, but was also personally driving Germany into the abyss. And with the downfall of Hitler, Hess had also lost the place he hoped for in history.

NOTES

1. *Die Tagebücher von Joseph Goebbels, Teil I: Aufzeichnungen 1924–1941*, ed. by E. Fröhlich (Munich, 1987) vol. 2, p. 694 (6.10.1936).
2. Ibid., vol. 3, p. 283 (30.9.1937).
3. On Hess's role in the Third Reich see: P. Diehl-Thiele, *Partei und Staat im Dritten Reich* (Munich, 1969); D. Orlow, *The History of the Nazi Party 1933–1945* (Pittsburgh, 1973).
4. *Goebbels-Tagebücher*, as above, vol. 4, p. 366ff. (16.10.1940).
5. Ibid., p. 121 (21.4.1940), p. 126 (25.4.1940), p. 218f. (26.6.1940), p. 236f. (11.7.1940).
6. Ibid., p. 638–49 (10.5.1941–20.5.1941).
7. Hess's 'Final word' is repeatedly quoted in the literature, more or less in its complete form. See: J.C. Fest, 'Rudolf Hess oder die Verlegenheit der Freiheit', in J.C. Fest, *Das Gesicht des Dritten Reiches* (Munich, 1964) p. 269; I. Hess (ed.), *Ein Schicksal in Briefen* (Leoni am Starnberger See, 1971) p. 112; E.K. Bird, *Prisoner No. 7: Rudolf Hess* (New York, 1984) p. 55, contains a selection of Hess's 'decrees' and 'proclamations' in English translation.
8. For the 'Spandau Years' see: Bird, as above, and the memoirs of the French chaplain in Spandau, C. Gabel (Paris, 1987).

BIBLIOGRAPHY

Primary Sources

Unfortunately we only have a few primary sources which enable us to gain an insight into the life and character of Hess. He did not keep a diary, and there are no large files of internal documents from his time as Hitler's private secretary. The correspondence edited by his wife and his son aims unambiguously at apologism: I. Hess (ed.), *Ein Schicksal in Briefen* (Leoni am Starnberger See, 1971); W.R. Hess, *Rudolf Hess, Briefe 1908–1933* (Munich, 1987). The Goebbels Diaries tower above the memoirs and journals of his contemporaries. Goebbels had frequent contact with Hess before and after 1933 and was a very shrewd observer. However it is generally true of his diaries that the reader must be aware of his efforts to give himself prominence. On the subject of Hess as a minister and Deputy Führer the following editions of sources should be consulted: *Akten der Reichskanzlei. Die Regierung Hitler, Teil I, 1933/34*, 2 vols ed. by K.H. Minuth (Boppard am Rhein, 1983); *Akten der Reichskanzlei*, ed. by Institut für Zeitgeschichte, 4 vols (Munich, 1983ff). However when using these sources one must always be aware of the difficulty of distinguishing Hess's views and decisions from those of Bormann and other colleagues.

Secondary Literature

There has, up till now, been no satisfactory academic study of Hess's life. W. Schwarzwäller, *Der Stellvertreter des Führers. Rudolf Hess, der Mann in Spandau* (Vienna, 1974) is somewhat extreme in style. A more balanced analysis, although less comprehensive, is to be found in: J.C. Fest, 'Rudolf Hess oder die Verlegenheit vor der Freiheit, in Fest, *Das Gesicht des Dritten Reiches* (Munich, 1964) p. 257–70. Hess's spectacular flight to Britain has caused many British authors to take an interest in the person of Hess. Of these, J.R. Rees (ed.), *The Case of Rudolf Hess. A Problem in Diagnosis and Forensic Psychiatry* (London, 1947) is something of an exception. It deals with the medical and psychiatric aspects of the Hess case. The author of *Motive for a Mission. The Story behind Rudolf Hess's Secret Flight to Britain* (New York, 1987) is J. Douglas-Hamilton, the son of the man Hess wanted to reach by his flight. The most recent biography comes from the pen of the 'enfant terrible' of modern historians; D. Irving, *Hess. The Missing Years* (London, 1988). Like all the works of this author, this book too contains a wealth of interesting details, but its apologist tendency is problematic. Finally, the contribution of H. Höhne, *Mordsache Röhm* (Reinbek bei Hamburg, 1984) should be mentioned. Höhne's book contains what is probably the best description of Hess's role in the Röhm affair.

9 Reinhard Heydrich: Security Technocrat

Günther Deschner

Reinhard Tristan Eugen Heydrich was a child of music. He was born in Halle on Saale on 7 March 1904. His mother called him Reinhard (good counsellor) after a hero in one of her husband's operas. His father, a composer and director of the Conservatory in Halle, called him Tristan, after the opera by Richard Wagner. And thirdly, and finally, the boy was named Eugen (well born) after his grandfather on his mother's side, who, as the founder of the world-famous Conservatory in Dresden, had achieved the greatest musical renown the Heydrich family had known up till then.

But Heydrich's Fates were to be wrong: his life had nothing to do with music. He did learn to play the violin, so that it brought tears to the eyes of his listeners; as well as grammar school he attended classes at the Conservatory in piano, cello and composition – but after taking his Higher Leaving Certificate the eighteen-year-old school leaver fled his unremittingly musical and eternally pious parental home – his parents had been converted to Catholicism – to enter his first career: he became a sea cadet in the first post-war crew in the navy of the Weimar Republic. For nearly ten years he dreamed of being an admiral. Then the navy, concerned for its reputation, dismissed him on account of trouble with a girl, a trifling matter, even by the standards of honour of those times. In April 1931, at the height of the world economic crisis, Sublieutenant Heydrich was dishonourably discharged. He was unemployed.

His second career went into vertical take-off. It made history. At the age of twenty-seven (1931), he became Chief of the Security Service (SD) of the *Reichsführer – SS*. After the seizure of power, the twenty-nine year old went first to the Bavarian Political Police; at the age of thirty-two he was in charge of the Secret State Police and the entire Criminal Police and at the beginning of the war the National Security Head Office in Berlin, a gigantic security apparatus, was created specially for him. Using the policy of the carrot and the stick, he succeeded in a few months in transforming the rape of the Czechs into a seduction. For this reason the Czech government in exile had him assassinated in May 1942 by two agents flown from London and dropped by parachute. Along with all his other duties Heydrich was also put in charge of the 'final solution of the Jewish question', which he organised from the emigration phase up to the extermination stage in the policy. He became a manifestation of the SS State like no other.

It is hard to assess the sum total of his life. Some saw him as the driving force behind the extermination of the Jews, others spun a yarn that he himself had a Jewish grandmother. For his whole life his voice was that of an adolescent boy, but he sent thousands to concentration camps with a single signature. He was an exceptional and competitive sportsman, decathlete, fencer and bold fighter pilot, who took leave to go to the front and found it a form of recreation.

No wonder that such a figure has long eluded the usual attempts to come to terms with Nazism during the post-war period. After 1945 the vultures picking over the remains of the Third Reich joined forces with those who had served him in prominent positions. They made Heydrich globally responsible for all stages of the Nazi reign of terror, the former by perpetuating Allied war-time propaganda, the latter rushing to find alibis in order to cleanse themselves of blame. Many of the accused and witnesses at the Nuremberg Tribunal had, for example, come to an agreement to 'push as much blame as possible on to Heydrich – after all he's already dead'.[1] Soon every evil the Third Reich had produced seemed to have originated in Heydrich's demonic mind. Quite absurdly, he was made responsible for events he only became aware of after they had happened. In the meantime it has become common knowledge that he was not behind the assassination attempt on Hitler in the Bürgerbräu Keller, nor did he orchestrate the so-called *Kristallnacht* – even though these claims will feature in 'standard' works for a long time to come.

Wiser observers saw, in Heydrich's lifetime as well as in later historical reflections, the inner contradictions which opened up in him, between brutality and sensitivity, between sober power political considerations and romanticism. Both contemporaries and post-war authors built a narrow bridge by which they hoped to cross this gulf. For them, Heydrich's was a totally fractured personality: 'he recognised his secret fears and regarded himself as being constantly plagued by tensions, bitterness and feelings of self-loathing.'[2] However this approach to Heydrich could only work if the strut provided by the legend of the supposed Jewish origins of the divided hero was left in place. But these stories, mainly gossip, have in the meantime been consigned to the realm of fairy-tale. Heydrich, the master of all security in the Third Reich, was by no means 'afflicted with an indelible stain and in a condition of mortal sin'.[3] He had no Jewish ancestors he would have had to hide from his superiors and he was neither melancholic nor capable of being blackmailed on account of such an accusation of a lack of racial purity, as was claimed by Himmler's masseur, Felix Kersten, who was consulted by historians for a long time.

One is compelled to accept the exact opposite as the true sum of his life: instead of being marked out by an indelible flaw, Heydrich was indistinguishable from the portrait National Socialism liked to paint of itself. He possessed the quality of worldly impressiveness which was the primary requirement in the image of National Socialist man. Even in his external appearance: if National Socialism had looked into a mirror, Reinhard Heydrich would have looked back out of it. The historical vision of a racially-defined geographical heartland, which can be regarded as the encapsulation of the National Socialists' view of a future utopia, had at its core the selection of a human type whose external appearance has best been described by the racial theorist of the Third Reich, Hans F.K. Günther, as blond and tall, with a long head and a narrow face, 'a pronounced chin, a narrow nose with a high bridge, soft fair hair, deep-set pale eyes and rosy skin-colouring'.[4] The minimal extent to which leading National Socialists conformed to this ideal led to curious contortions in public relations in the Third Reich. Popular humour quickly and precisely summed up the facts in the lines 'blond like Hitler, tall like Goebbels, slim like Goering and able to hold their drink like Ley.' Countless of the leading representatives of the Third Reich were, as Ernst Nolte put it, 'non-conformist in their conformity'.

Heydrich was one of the exceptions: the SS newspaper *Das Schwarze Korps* (*The Black Corps*) celebrated him in an obituary in June 1942 as 'a man without defects'. 'Even in his external appearance he was the kind of SS man the public expected'.[5] As the ideal prescribed, Heydrich was tall, fair-skinned and blond, an exceptionally successful competitive sportsman, combining high intelligence with that metallic trait in his personality which was taken to be the proof of particular racial endowment. For all their criticism of their boss's disagreeable or repulsive characteristics, his early colleagues were agreed in their judgement of his personal lifestyle. It corresponded without qualification to the checklist of the ideal Nazi. The historian of the SD, Spengler, summed it up: 'All that he demanded of his men in the way of achievements, tenacity and endurance, ceaseless self improvement, cleanliness and simplicity in their personal life, Heydrich had not only demanded of himself, but had achieved in exemplary manner.'[6]

However, the magical coincidence of the general with the particular which Burckhardt spoke of was expressed in Heydrich far more in his deeper characteristics than on the surface. Here we find what Ernst Nolte felt was lacking in most of the fascist movements of the era: all the historical and structural elements of fascism were represented in Naval Sublieutenant Heydrich (retd). Giovanni Zibordi, an incisive critic of Italian fascism had stated as early as 1922 in his study '*Critica socialista del fascismo*', that fascism was primarily the 'violent revolution of declassé soldiers'.[7] His theory was scarcely more true of any of the leading National Socialists than of Heydrich. It was the loss of his officer's uniform alone, which, after his initial rejection of it, made National Socialism and the SS seem a desirable vehicle for the self-fulfilment of a declassé soldier.

The fact that Heydrich's gigantic police organisation, beginning with the

SD and ending with the National Security Headquarters, was so heavily militarised has its origins not least in Heydrich's love of the soldier's life, which had been so ignominiously rewarded and to which he could now finally devote himself again in National Socialism. It is not a coincidence, either, that he did not reach the height of his power in peace time, but in the midst of war. 'War was its real element', as Ernst Schüddekopf wrote, not about Heydrich, but about fascism.[8] The condition of nationhood was conceived of as being one of permanent crisis. This naturally had consequences for domestic policy and policing: the idea of a pre-emptive police force which in due course rendered harmless all conceivable categories of 'undesirable elements', of a criminal as well as political kind, was developed by Heydrich to the height of perfection and translated into fact.

Heydrich had found his way into the Security Service of the National Leader of the SS thanks to the social decomposition of the German bourgeoisie after the defeat in the First World War, and he gathered round him the most intelligent men National Socialism was ever able to employ. They were the rear-guard of a bourgeoisie whose values, minted before the First World War, they were no longer able to share.

They left the values of this declassé bourgeoisie behind them without any great soul-searching. This abandonment of past values was even more marked in Heydrich because of the conventional negative attitude of the average officer to politics, his formal abstinence from them, perfectly compatible with an anti-democratic state of mind; Heydrich fully shared this dominant characteristic of the Seeckt era during the first years of his SS career. With the fragments of ideology he found within the SS, mostly based on a romanticised vision of the past, he combined the principle of effectiveness – in this he resembled to a great extent present-day value-free technocratic managers – and he made this combination into an unmistakable amalgam.

Heydrich utilised the methods of left-wing revolution and the technology of the machine age for the purpose of revolutionary upheaval and the National Socialist state. This is part of the reason for the giddy ascent of Heydrich's star, and with it Himmler's, in the Third Reich. After a difficult initial period, in which he was fobbed off with subordinate posts, the turning point came for Heydrich with his flawless adoption of the modern. In the years during which the Nazi state was being consolidated, which were marked by the events surrounding the Röhm Putsch, Heydrich set his wagon on the right track. Thereafter it arrived at its goal of its own accord, its course being identical to the overall direction of the Third Reich.

Unlike the squarely-built go-getter Ernst Röhm, unlike the SA, which after the seizure of power, as Heydrich mockingly said, faded into 'senseless, directionless, personal illegality',[9] the Heydrich-Himmler team silently occupied the most important key positions within the police and administration. In his consistent pursuit of this technocratic administrative policy, Heydrich, acting quietly in the background, was revolutionary in a far more modern sense than the revolutionary fetishist Ernst Röhm. Heydrich understood that the only thing that mattered in a revolution in highly developed central Europe in the middle of the twentieth century was to occupy the institutional structures. Whoever conquered them held power. The effects of this were felt first by the political opponents of National Socialism, then Röhm and the SA, and finally even other National Socialists themselves, like Frick, the Minister of the Interior, for whom, although he was nominally Heydrich's superior, little more remained than a thin cast-off shell, while the institutional structures had long since been integrated into Heydrich's network of power.

However much one or another element of National Socialist philosophy, within the context of which Heydrich had to implement his policy, may have derived from the nineteenth century, he himself was more rooted in the twentieth century and its technocratic spirit, indeed he represented it. He himself had no roots in the past. In Karl Kraus's 1933 definition of fascism, he embodied 'the contemporaneousness of everything that is and is no more'. It was beyond doubt: of all the leading National Socialists, Heydrich at least 'conformed to the ideal'.

This raises the question of whether Heydrich had any roots, and where they were, if not in the past. He was evidently not at home in any of the philosophies produced by the Judaeo-Christian world. The religions of divine revelation remained inaccessible to him, in spite of, or perhaps because of his bigoted upbringing in an atmosphere of false religiosity, often found in families of converts. For class reasons he felt no affinity with Marxism, a surrogate religion, the repulsive features of which he came across during the Weimar period; after he had had to get to know it after 1933 in the SD he rejected it for intellectual reasons. He openly confessed his contempt for all possible 'Christianities' and strands of belief from Moses and Christ up to Marx, just as Mussolini had done after his electoral defeat in 1919, mocking all the red, white and black charlatans and soon frowning on the brown ones. Encyclicals, he informed the officers of his SD, were now issued by two Vaticans: one in Rome and the other in Moscow. 'We are the heretics in both these religions'.[10] Ultimately he was not only against the church, but against Christianity too.

In him and many other National Socialists, there was a type of person who had not experienced the current primary values which held the West together. They had come to power and, in the search for 'secondary links' consciously dispensed with those which formed the basis of questioning throughout their century: the classical view of mankind, the Judaeo-Christian west and the liberal democracy of previous centuries. He was, however, receptive to ideas about the coming of the biological age, of 'heroic vitality', of which the SS itself was such an eloquent symbol. The individual human being became uninteresting and the object of racial or national calculations which gave a new definition to the principle of *raison d'état*. Heydrich was never 'pious' his whole life long; he never searched for the unknown God who would have set a goal and given direction to his vitality. The main motive forces of life, as D.H. Lawrence saw them, passion and the desire for power, were Heydrich's law. A certain arrogant racism, the symbolism of death and the veneration of war were an inherent part of him.

These characteristics practically destined him for success in the black-shirted SS: in their catechism, too, biological notions of vitality, the hero-worship of war and the hard-headed dogma of *raison d'état* had fused together into 'a dynamic fundamentally without doctrines, a technology of domination', as Höhne attested for the SS.[11] His dynamism, which drove him on, and the restlessness which possessed Heydrich, his urge and ambition to achieve, which would tolerate no rival at fencing, the decathlon, the flights to the front line – things which no-one had demanded of him, in his intelligence-gathering stratagems, all these testify that for Heydrich the decisive factor was not the NSDAP's programme but the vitality and élan of the modern philosophy of life, activism and finally the unscrupulous use of force.

Another of his decisive motivating forces was by no means at odds with this: his existential fear, linked in Heydrich with a specific fear of the future. 'If we don't do it, who will? We must do it'.[12] Those who have studied fascism have come to suspect that these fears are then transmuted into violence and terror against real or only imaginary enemies. The suppressed themselves become the suppressors, the tormented the tormentors. For Heydrich power of itself became a new moral norm, it became the duty of the new elite, who were to make the dream of the new state into a lasting reality.

In Heydrich's eyes this goal had to be commensurate with 'unprecedented' brutality ('unprecedented' was his favourite word). Despite that aspect of his personality which people like to describe as metallic, the brutality he preached was not in fact always forthcoming, since his personality tended towards sensitivity rather than stoicism, as has been attested to by Carl Jacob Burckhardt, after several long conversations with Heydrich. Burckhardt, who in his capacity as League of Nations Commissioner had demanded from Heydrich a visitor's permit for the German concentration camps and had received it after some prevarication, reports that the latter stood in front of him during the conversation about political detainees in the concentration camps and 'looking over my left shoulder he said in a choked voice, "They think we're bloodhounds, abroad, don't they?" and then, "It is almost too hard for one person, but we have to be as hard as granite, otherwise the work of our Führer will be destroyed. In the distant future they will thank us for what we have taken upon ourselves"'.[13]

This obligation to be brutal was a fundamental element of the elite to which Heydrich belonged. In their self-image they were an elite in two senses: elite by birth on the basis of racial selection and elite in functional terms because of their claims to high achievement, ability and discipline. Heydrich himself demanded of the true SS man in his essay *Wandlungen unseres Kampfes* (The Course of our Struggle) that he should be the best in all spheres. The new order of the Third Reich, which Heydrich was prepared to secure, was to reflect the spirit of these elitist principles in its internal structure and in its representatives. This drove Heydrich to be disdainful and sometimes sharply negative in his attitude to the Party, where primitive lust for power and opportunism were gaining ground. The 'peacock type', more than any of the political opponents of the new system became an object of deep antipathy to him.

Heydrich the technocrat got on much better with the technological functionaries, who, in spite of the key positions they might hold in the National Socialist state, only had a superficial veneer of Nazi ideology. That was particularly true of the Secretary of State in the Ministry of Agriculture, Herbert Backe, who injected cold rationality into all the wild fantasies of his boss, Darré, and secured the country's food supply even under the most difficult circumstances by his outstanding achievements in the planning and administration of his department. Heydrich was a friend of his and many times they had occasion to debate on the philosophical fads of their respective superiors, Darré and Himmler.

This also applied to Hitler's Armaments Minister, Albert Speer. Heydrich: 'He is good. He knows what he is doing'.[14] This evaluation was entirely mutual. Speer remembered his first conversation with Heydrich: the chief of the security police and of the SD had been preceeded by his reputation for being 'cruel and unpredictable'. But Speer was pleasantly surprised. He had not been able to detect any of this odiousness during the conversation. Heydrich had been 'very polite, his manner was not arrogant and above all very assured and matter-of-fact'. Speer was most impressed by his matter-of-factness:

> He was not at all like these *Gauleiter* or other potentates, who on other occasions have clung to *idées fixes*, to something which was architecturally or technically impossible, perhaps to a dream from their youth or one of their wife's wild notions and then doggedly insisted on it. . . . By contrast Heydrich was uncomplicated, he had only a few objections to my suggestions, which taken as a whole showed that he was considering the problems intelligently. If his objections were technically unfounded then he could be persuaded of this at once.[15]

Research has indicated that Hitler would soon have had problems with the young SS, which was imbued with the spirit represented by Heydrich.

The gulf which had opened up between the sober, rational, technocratic coldness of Heydrich, his squad of intellectuals at the SD on one hand, and the endlessly swaggering resentful Party bosses on the other, between pure intellect and mere prejudice, was probably only covered up and prevented from becoming a historical fact by the outbreak and course of the war.

All of Heydrich was visible in the way in which, for example, he approached the solution to the 'Czech question' in the autumn of 1941, a problem which had become intractable for everyone else. Xenophobia or hatred of the Slavs was not an issue for him. The words with which he introduced himself as the new State Protector in a secret speech to German officials in Prague probably had many a dyed-in-the-wool Party member doubting the time of day: nothing was of interest to him here except that the area was made peaceful and useful to the German war economy. He would, therefore, cooperate with all Germans who worked towards this aim and he would dispose of all those who put obstacles in its way. And then, 'What is essential is that we proceed with all severity against those things which are not acceptable. For there is no purpose in beating up the Czechs and using a great deal of effort and police pressure to force them to go to work if they are not actually getting what they need.'[16]

The 'elite of central Europe', as Heydrich understood it, a mixture of the engineer with the figure of the soldier, as he was described in Ernst Jünger's '*Stahlgewitter*' (Storm of Steel) – intelligent and cunning, strong and decisive, pitiless towards himself and others, a completely new race – could not of course be reproduced at will in the required numbers. And moreover: not all of his SD intellectuals could stand it for long in the frigid zones into which Heydrich had advanced in the course of his rise to power, mainly because of the radicalisation of war, which became progressively more extensive. The Gestapo lawyer, Dr Werner Best, was forced out of office after difficulties with Heydrich. Although he was a passionate National Socialist and SS leader from the 'Era of Struggle', Dr Best had insisted that the requirements of state security should not completely liquidate the integrity of the law, that there were outer limits which Heydrich's soulless perfectionism and rigorousness had to respect. Scruples like these were alien to Heydrich. He completed the tasks allotted to him by any means which seemed suitable. For him the continued existence of the state justified measures of every kind. The question 'did the movement make him or did he provide the drive for the movement?' is superfluous: Heydrich and National Socialism had looked for and found each other. In spite of his 'conformity to the ideal', which was uncommon in the leadership of the Third Reich, Heydrich was, and remained, a loner. His colleague Best stated simply: 'Heydrich cannot be type-cast'. 'He embodied elemental characteristics which made him seem more like a natural phenomenon than a political and social one.'[17] Heydrich was filled with 'boundless vitality' in Best's judgement, which surged out into his surroundings, constantly looking for new activity and acknowledgement. In this constant surging advance everything he did and achieved was only a means to even more distant goals.

Even his appearance gave an initial indication of his disposition. As his colleagues and subordinates all said, the look in his close-set blue eyes 'was usually cold, enquiring and mistrustful and their flickering restlessness was often irritating.'[18] His appearance and the look in his eye alone unsettled many people, subordinates and superiors alike. Right from the outset, his abrupt, hasty manner of speaking, combined with his domineering, lordly, challenging gestures revealed an attitude which placed an uncommon emphasis on the will. Best had the impression that 'he suggested his ideas and intentions at the outset with a forcefulness which caught one unawares, and by this means he forced the other into a position where he either had to comply or mount a counter-attack'.[19] Thus, Heydrich forced his own rules of engagement on to every partner from the outset and forced him to take up a position as friend or foe.

In the selection of his colleagues his own instinct was more important than the evaluations of past careers which were presented to him. His instinct chose those characteristics he was looking for and valued, that is a soldier's bearing, aggressiveness, intelligence and, to a lesser extent, racial appearance and possibly also sporting inclinations. 'Candidates who impressed with their subjective personality also appealed to Heydrich's subjectivism and were accepted',[20] even, we are told, when their contradictoriness later revealed them to be 'uncomfortable' subordinates. This contrariness was one of the main factors in rationalising Heydrich's entourage during his rapid rise to power. The lawyer Best, who thought along conventional lines, left Heydrich's service; the young, impressionable and 'subjective' Walter Schellenberg, similar to Heydrich in many ways, was discovered.

What this subjectively-defined Heydrich sought was power, more and more power. But he did not seek it like the opportunists of all political systems, in order to achieve material gains and the limelight, but in order to confirm his own identity and the nature of his own personality. This impetuous striving found expression not only in his political and police career; his very body demanded success. This is one of the reasons for his passion for sport; fencing, shooting and the decathlon. He tried to succeed in horse-riding too, but that was bound to fail – no horse reacts to the alternative of friend or foe.

In his intelligence Heydrich had a tool suited to his personality, which paralleled his physical vitality. It was the intelligence of a conqueror and hunter. He made a clear assessment of situations and problems right at the beginning. Where others were still thinking about technical problems, Heydrich 'went into another gear' – that was his own expression for it – at once, that is he examined the significance of the matter for his own purposes. This analysis of utility was linked to such an extent with his quick comprehension of the matter itself that he almost always had a head start on any others from the outset.

In the full enjoyment of his own dynamic powers Heydrich had little need of the companionship of other people. A colleague testified: 'People were either obstacles on his path or means to his ends'.[21] Those who denied him his desired success and full recognition he regarded as obstacles: parts of the Party, the bureaucracy and the army. His means were his superiors and his subordinates. He barely had any personal hatred for the enemies of the state, whom he fought with the tools at hand and largely eliminated as a political factor; instead he hated those who threatened his rise to power. Best believed that even when he took over the commission for the 'final solution to the Jewish question', he scarcely thought of hating the Jews, 'but only considered the extent of the task, which stretched over many countries, and the necessity of proving his energy and skill in fulfilling it.'[22]

He would expend zeal and intelligence on a task like that. It led him first of all to the idea of defining the 'final solution' as emigration, by a systematic harrying of the Jews out of Germany. Then when the war made this impossible, came deportation to destinations which were constantly changing and alongside this, and systematically from 1942, extermination. There is much to indicate that he accomplished this phase of his task with very mixed feelings. He saddled subaltern subordinates like Adolf Eichmann with its planning and implementation. While he took on the detailed work inherent in his intelligence-gathering intrigues with loving care, the 'final solution' was everyone's responsibility. The terminology which was supposed to keep the business of genocide secret came from him.

He was of course ruled by complete indifference to the inviolability of human life – including his own. That was a characteristic of both revolutionaries and technocrats. Death by means of a shot in the back of the neck was for him as normal as death in a bomb explosion and not less abnormal than death by pneumonia or cancer. But cunning suited him more than brutality and an opponent's unsuspecting step into a skilfully-built trap gave him a satisfaction he never experienced from an act of direct brutality.

This even lends credibility to Himmler's remark about Heydrich's scruples about organised genocide, to be found in his memorial speech on the occasion of the state ceremony for the 'God of Death' (Carl Jacob Burckhardt) after he was assassinated. 'From countless conversations with Heydrich,' Himmler said, 'I know how this man, who had to be outwardly so hard and severe, often suffered and wrestled in his heart and what it often cost him, nonetheless, to shape his decisions and actions again and again according to the law of the SS, by which we are duty bound to spare neither our own blood nor the blood of others, when the life of the nation demands it'.[23]

Heydrich had for the first time in history developed for the national leadership, by dint of much hard work, a unified national police force and a comprehensive political intelligence service, which overcame the fragmenting effect of state and territorial traditions. These pursued an entirely new set of goals, and were constantly at the ready – effective, reliable, objective and extensive tools.

But again and again the tasks which were imposed on him, precisely because of his – in Nazi terms – successful police reforms, caused him inner conflicts. His role in the liquidation of Röhm, the only man in the Party to whom he had offered friendship, and the murders committed by his task forces and finally his function as the executor of the 'final solution' all made him aware of the profound incompatibility of means and end. He complained cynically that he was sometimes only the 'chief rubbish collector of the German Reich'. 'It is remarkable,' his widow stated, 'that he was fully aware of his work as executioner and even had a ready justification for it'.[24]

He thought of his work as being like a deed which involved great personal sacrifices and burdens, which he felt he had to accomplish for the sake of the matter in hand, for the future of the Reich. 'I feel that I am free of all guilt,' Heydrich regularly concluded after wrestling with his conscience. 'It is my job to make myself available and it is for others to pursue egotistical goals'.[25] A comparison with Saint-Just, the revolutionary tribune of 1789 is obvious. It is said of him that he held his head high, like a sacred vessel, as he demanded one head after the other. Heydrich's attitude was similar and in his approach he was a revolutionary. The combination of cold rationality with efforts to achieve technical perfection, the longing for a life which was – in the vitalistic sense – heroic and dangerous à la Saint Just, 'between mortal dangers and immortality', and a ridge-walk of the soul which accepted the existence of the deepest abysses: that is what Heydrich was.

NOTES

1. The author's interview with Bruno Streckenbach on 21.5.73 and with Lina Heydrich on 20–23.3.1973.
2. J.C. Fest, *Das Gesicht des Dritten Reiches* (Munich, 1963) p. 142.
3. F. Kersten, *Totenkopf und Treue* (Hamburg, 1952) p. 128.
4. H.F.K. Günther, *Rassenkunde des deutschen Volkes* (Munich, 1922) p. 34.
5. 'Das Schwarze Korps', Berlin, dated 11.6.1942.
6. W. Spengler, 'Reinhard Heydrich – Wesen und Werk' in, *Böhmen und Mähren*, 5/6 (Prague, 1943) p. 23.
7. G. Zibordi, *Critica socialista del fascismo* (Milan, 1922) p. 15.
8. O.-E. Schüddekopf, *Bis alles in Scherben fällt* (Gütersloh, 1973) p. 101.
9. R. Heydrich, *Wandlungen unseres Kampfes* (Berlin, 1936) p. 4.
10. Interview with Streckenbach.

11. H. Höhne, *Der Orden unter dem Totenkopf* (Gütersloh, 1967) p. 196.
12. Interview with Lina Heydrich.
13. C.J. Burckhardt, *Meine Danziger Mission 1937–1939* (Munich, 1960) p. 97.
14. Interview with Lina Heydrich.
15. The author's interview with Albert Speer on 19.1.1972.
16. Secret speech by Heydrich on 2.10.1941, published in *Die Vergangenheit warnt* (Prague, 1960).
17. W. Best, Notes on Reinhard Heydrich dated 1.9.1949, Copenhagen.
18. The author's interview with Walter Wannemacher on 21.3.1972.
19. Best, as above.
20. Ibid.
21. Ibid.
22. Ibid.
23. Heinrich Himmler, Memorial Speech, dated 9.6.1942 in: R. Heydrich, *Ein Leben der Tat* (Prague, 1944) p. 64.
24. Interview with Lina Heydrich.
25. Lina Heydrich, *Leben mit einem Kriegsverbrecher* (Pfaffenhofen, 1976) p. 48.

BIBLIOGRAPHY

Primary Sources

Sources which are central to an investigation of Heydrich are to be found in the files of the Hauptarchiv der NSDAP, Hoover Collection (Stanford) as well as in the files of the Personal Staff of the National Leader of the SS and the Chief of the German Police in the National Archive (Washington). Also of importance are the unpublished sketches of Heydrich by Werner Best (1.9.1949) and Karl von Eberstein (15.10.1965). Of Heydrich's own publications, the following should be mentioned: R. Heydrich, 'Der Anteil der Sicherheitspolizei und des SD an den Ordnungsmassnahmen im mitteleuropäischen Raum', in, *Böhmen und Mähren*, 5/1941 (Prague, 1941); 'Die Bekämpfung der Staatsfeinde' in, *Die deutsche Rechtswissenschaft*, vol. 1, no. 2 (1936) and 'VB' dated 28.4.1936; *Ein Leben der Tat* (Prague, 1944); Gedenkschrift der RHSA (Berlin, no year); speech, 'Die Wenzelstradition' in, Reinhard Heydrich, *Ein Leben der Tat* (Prague, 1944); speeches dated 2.10.1941 and 4.2.1942 in, *Die Vergangenheit warnt* (Prague, 1960); 'Rede zum Tag der deutschen Polizei', published in Reinhard Heydrich, *RHSA*, no year; *Wandlungen unseres Kampfes* (Berlin, 1936). Himmler's memorial speech on Heydrich's death is published in R. Heydrich, *Ein Leben der Tat* (Prague, 1944).

Secondary Literature

For a long time history has only been interested in Heydrich in an eclectic way. The historical person has been fragmented into countless essays, chapters or footnotes, scattered across numerous monographs about the SS and the Gestapo, the German secret service, twentieth century spying, the persecution of the European Jews. In the memoirs of former National Socialists published after the war, by Heydrich's colleagues or other contemporary witnesses, the reports frequently consist simply of office gossip with no value to researchers. Sometimes misleading information about Heydrich's supposed Jewish background is given. That is true for example of: W. Hagen (Höttl), *Die geheime Front* (Linz, 1950); F. Kersten, *Totenkopf und Treue* (Hamburg, 1952); W. Schellenberg, *Memoiren* (Cologne, 1956); O. Strasser, *Hitler und ich* (Constance, 1948).

The first attempt at a biography of Heydrich was published twenty years after his death: C. Wighton, *Heydrich – Hitler's Most Evil Henchman* (London, 1962). Wighton's study is unsatisfactory not just because of the lack of accessible source material at that time, but more especially because the line the author takes still relies entirely on Allied war propaganda. Only when access to original files had become easier was it possible to make a serious study of aspects of Heydrich's biography. Thus U.D. Adam, *Judenpolitik im Dritten Reich* (Dusseldorf, 1972) was the first to give a comprehensive scholarly analysis of the various, competing or chronologically consecutive attempts to devise a 'final solution', and in the process he shed light on Heydrich's role. An Israeli historian has described the first years of Heydrich's SS career (up to 1934) in a convincing juxtaposition of archive material and 'oral history' and his work contains a great deal of material: S. Aronson, *Reinhard Heydrich und die Frühgeschichte von Gestapo und SD* (Stuttgart, 1971). Having temporarily gained access to files held in Czechoslovakia, D. Brandes was able to deal in detail with the background to and course of Heydrich's activities in Prague: D. Brandes, *Die Tschechen unter deutschem Protektorat, Teil I: Besatzungspolitik, Kollaboration und Widerstand im Protektorat Böhmen und Mähren bis Heydrichs Tod. 1939–1942* (Oldenburg, 1969). It was not only the work of 'professional historians' which led during these years to convincing studies, derived not from political and propagandistic premises, but from a precise study of the source material. The work of a journalist, too, has proved valuable right up to the present day. He was the first to correct the idea of the monolithic 'Führer state' and to point out that the Jewish policies of the Third Reich should not be interpreted a posteriori: H. Höhne, *Der Orden unter dem Totenkopf* (Gütersloh, 1967). The present author used this work as a tool for his own biography of Heydrich. He was also the first to evaluate newly accessible files, the entire body of secondary literature and interviewed contemporary witnesses who had been close to Heydrich: G. Deschner, *Reinhard Heydrich – Statthalter der totalen Macht* (Munich, 1978). The memoirs of Heydrich's widow include useful details on the human side of Heydrich's personality, but they are teeming with historical misjudgements, wrong dates and a desire to show him in a more positive light: L. Heydrich, *Leben mit einem Kriegsverbrecher. Mit Kommentaren von W. Maser* (Pfaffenhofen, 1976). That history, which has become considerably more dispassionate and 'unideological' in the last twenty years, also provides a way back to the clichées of the anti-fascist leagues of the former anti-Hitler coalition, is demonstrated by the most recent book on Heydrich: E. Calic, *Reinhard Heydrich – Schlüsselfigur des Dritten Reiches* (Dusseldorf, 1982). Here, as was already the case in the first edition of E. Kogon's *SS-Staat*, Heydrich is given an omnipotence capable of determining the course of history, an interpretation for which there is not the slightest support in the sources. Moreover the political and personal peculiarities of this author are revealed in, K.-H. Janssen, 'Calics Erzählungen', in U. Backes *et al.*, *Reichstagsbrand. Aufklärung einer historischen Legende* (Munich, 1987) p. 216–37 (this also contains a critical reference to Calic's biography of Heydrich.) After this no-one can any longer take Calic seriously as a historian.

10 Heinrich Himmler: Reichsführer – SS

Josef Ackermann

It remained a mystery to many of those who knew Heinrich Himmler how this man, timid and indecisive at heart, could have attained a position of extraordinary power in the Third Reich. 'I had the impression,' reports the chief of the Armaments Ministry, Hans Kehrl, 'that he was a small man, not a personality in the grand, let alone diabolical style. Both his influence and the fear of him, which was probably deliberately encouraged, were a mystery to me'.[1] Albert Speer does not claim either that he had any outstanding abilities or characteristics which predestined him for the role he actually played in the Third Reich. He saw in him 'a completely insignificant person, who in some inexplicable way has risen to a prominent position'.[2]

Himmler's career as the 'Grand Inquisitor' of the Third Reich is also a mystery to his former classmates from his school-days in Munich and Landshut. 'It's impossible. . . . , it's impossible,' shouted the German American historian George W.F. Hallgarten, for example, in the common room of the history department at Munich University in 1948, when he identified Himmler, the 'monstrous servant of a dictator' as his classmate and school friend from the Munich school-days they spent together. He remembered him as the personification of 'the gentlest lamb you could imagine, a boy who would not hurt a fly'.[3]

Did Himmler's character therefore undergo a total transformation for the worse or did people fail to recognise a hidden side to his nature already present in his earliest youth? What role did his parental home play in his spiritual development, in an age in which the structure of society had long since begun to destabilise? These questions can only be answered with difficulty.

Heinrich Himmler was born on 7 October 1900 in Munich. He had two brothers, of whom Gebhard was two years older and Ernst a few years younger. He received his Christian names from his godfather, Prince Heinrich of Bavaria, to whom Heinrich Himmler's father was tutor from 1893 to 1897. In a letter dated 13.10.1900 to his 'dearest Prince Heinrich' his father, Gebhard Himmler, informed the former of the date of Heinrich's baptism and asked the Prince for the 'great honour of offering him a glass of champagne' after the baptism.[4]

The Himmler family's connection with Prince Heinrich was maintained by both sides until the time of the First World War, and when the latter was killed in 1916 at the age of thirty-two, his mother remained in contact with the Himmler family thereafter. On 11 June 1917 a cheque to the amount of 1000 Reich Marks in war bonds was sent by the dowager princess's court administration; in the letter to Gebhard Himmler it said: 'Please accept this sum for your son Heinrich as a present from his late godfather, His Royal Highness, the late Prince Heinrich of Bavaria'.[5]

In contrast to the picture Alfred Andersch paints of Heinrich Himmler's father in his account 'The Father of a Murderer', the latter seems, at least in his earlier years, to have been universally well-liked. Joseph Bernhardt, one of Gebhard Himmler's former pupils from the time before the turn of the century, gives a very positive assessment of his former teacher: 'We felt that the refined aura which emanated from him was benificent. He was supple, of medium build and kept his class's attention without a word of rebuke by the strict, but kind, look in his eyes, behind his gold pince-nez. Stroking his small reddish beard, he was prepared to wait quietly until a pupil had found an answer'.[6]

The father seems to have had a strong influence on the intellectual development of his children. In particular he accompanied them through their school-days with benign understanding and encouraging interest. As he did for his elder son, he also prepared a short sketch for Heinrich of his first four years at school in Munich. In it we read:

> On 4 September 1906 Heinrich was enrolled in the first class of the Cathedral School (Salvatorplatz) (at our request, instead of the Amalienschule). On 6 September lessons began with an entirely new syllabus (Kerchenstein). . . . Heinrich was often ill (glandular fever, measles, pneumonia, mumps) 160 absences, but caught up everything by lessons with Miss Rudelt and passed with grade of II, total marks 25. Holidays in Oberaudorf. . . .[7]

That Heinrich's health was not in a very good state is not only demonstrated in these notes, but also in information available from later years. With discipline Heinrich overcame his weak physical constitution, from which he suffered all his life, and which gave his masseur Felix Kersten astonishing influence on him during the Second World War. This is probably also the source of his keen interest in his own sporting achievements, for which he set himself standards he was barely capable of achieving.

As early as the end of the second year of primary school Heinrich Himmler was constantly changed from school to school, which made learning difficult for him. After only two years at the Cathedral School in Munich he moved in 1908 to the Amalienschule, which he attended until the end of the fourth year and then in 1910 he went to the King William

Grammar School. In 1913 he followed his father, who was transferred to be deputy headmaster of the grammar school there, to Landshut, the regional capital of Lower Bavaria.

Alfred Andersch considers it worthy of reflection that Heinrich Himmler 'did not grow up, like the man to whose hypnotism he succumbed, in the lower working class, but in a family from the old bourgeoisie educated in the humanities.' This leads him to ask sadly: 'Do the humanities then not protect us from anything? This question is capable of throwing one into despair'.[8]

What is certain is that the upbringing and education which Himmler enjoyed to such a great extent in the grammar schools in Munich and Landshut, more than almost any other leader in the National Socialist regime, are not an unconditional guarantee of a secure system of humane values, do not necessarily provide a bulwark against political manipulation and being led ideologically astray. This then poses the question as to which intellectual and ideological influences Heinrich Himmler, a model pupil in every respect, was exposed to at grammar school, and, since his father himself represented part of this institution, in his parental home as well.

The type of grammar school which Himmler attended in both Munich and Landshut, was the normal and most common form of secondary school at the time in Bavaria. It emphasised the study of the language and literature of classical antiquity, religious and moral education and the 'cultivation of the German mother tongue'. A single uniform educational goal had been formulated for 'secondary schools' in general – that is 'to raise children to be morally upstanding on the basis of religion, ... to provide a higher general education imbued with a patriotic spirit, ... and to enable them to think independently'.[9]

Harry Graf Kessler has accurately pin-pointed the 'basic failing' of the grammar schools at the end of the nineteenth century and the beginning of the twentieth: 'From the ideal of the humanistic being, carrying the whole of humanity and its culture in his head and heart . . . there remained only the enormous hard work necessary to take in the vast amount of material'.[10]

In the intellectual currents, tensions and battles of the age, the school was also the ideological stage for the interpretation of German history and for the 'rightful claim' to German greatness and economic prosperity. The combative nature of the movement for German unity and the desire to be a world power, were, as was taught in history and German lessons, the basis for, and characteristic of, the enormous vitality of the German Nation. Where was there any room here for political humanity? Prominence was not accorded to what European peoples had in common, but what divided them; they did not teach the senselessness of war, but war as an indispensable element of progress and national self-affirmation.

Heinrich Himmler's father did not see war, any more than his son

Heinrich did, as contradictory to the refining and spiritualisation of cultured life and of Christian humanity. The father called on all his contacts in his vigorous support of his son Heinrich's desire for a career as an officer, for which he was, in fact, still too young. Gebhard Himmler was even ready to set aside his son's schooling to this end. In a questionnaire on his son's application for entry into the officer corps the father made the following remark on June 1917: 'The father of the applicant would *prefer* that his son completed his education at grammar school before entering the army, *with a place reserved in the regiment.* But if it should not be possible to continue his studies after reaching the age of seventeen (because of the continuance of the war or auxiliary service), then he would rather his son entered the army *at once.*' He adds as an explanation for the request for admission: 'My son Heinrich has a strong desire to make a life-long career as an infantry officer'.[11] In some respects, his agreeing to his son pursuing a military career is also a logical consequence of his activities up till then at the school at which he was headmaster and which his son attended. As can be seen from the chronicle of the grammar school in Landshut, in the school year 1914/15 alone he gave eight lectures, the purpose of which was to make the hearts and minds of the pupils more aware of 'the great events of the age'. Even in 1929 he was talking of the First World War as a 'Holy War'.[12]

There is scarcely any doubt that Heinrich Himmler absorbed this false pathos about the nature and necessity of war, which was nonetheless perfectly normal at the beginning of World War One, from both the school and his father, and adopted the glorifying attitude to war which is so hard for us to understand today. From the age of fourteen until the end of his life Himmler tried to endow conflict and war with a higher meaning and to see the plan of God's providence in them.

This can be proved beyond any doubt from the diaries he kept sporadically and from his notes on the books he read: war as the 'greatest time of maturation' and battle as a 'general principle of life' become for Himmler fixed points in his philosophy of life, interwoven into his Social Darwinist ideology. At an SS initiation ceremony in 1936 he reflected on the meaning of battle for his SS: 'Many regard us SS men . . . as a hard-hearted company', said Himmler, referring to the reputation his SS had as a terrorist organisation. 'That is right. We are a hard-hearted community; for we emerged from battle and we exist solely for battle, not just today, but as is our belief and will, for centuries and perhaps for millenia'.[13]

Sadly Himmler mourns the fact that, although he did complete the cadet training course in 1918, he did not take any active part in the events of the war and therefore could not now gather any experience at the front. Instead he offered his services to various paramilitary leagues which were fighting against a 'Marxist dictatorship', democracy and the 'disgraceful Treaty of Versailles'. He finally ended up in the *Reichskriegsflagge* league and became its standard bearer. His later appointment by Hitler as the commander in chief of the replacement army, and of the Upper Rhine army groups in particular, in autumn 1944, fulfilled Himmler's dream of a lifetime. It came as no surprise to long-serving officers in Hitler's army that he was a total failure in this office, because they had cast doubt, probably correctly, on Himmler's military competence from the outset.

We should return, however, to Himmler's youth, during which the foundations of his ideology were presumably laid down. What were the positive norms of behaviour which Gebhard Himmler wanted to inculcate into his son, which characteristics did he intend to develop in him? An answer to this question can only be gained indirectly from pronouncements made by Gerhard Himmler about people he was close to. In an obituary he wrote for a league comrade he singled out his outstanding intellect and his principled, distinguished, pleasant nature, his sensitive soul, his wide reading, philanthropy and helpfulness. 'But above all else he loved his German Fatherland,' Gebhard Himmler wrote:

The youth often spoke enthusiastically with us, his friends, about its greatness, might and magnificence; the man was often fearful for its growth, blossoming and prosperity; for this Fatherland alone he hurled himself again and again into the battle against petty-bourgeois dullness and philistinism, in order to awaken in German youth a sense of understanding of their political duties and tasks, and then, when his Fatherland was under threat, he went forth into the Holy Fight, he wept for his Fatherland's misfortune, but he died on a bed of suffering with an unshakable belief in a revival of Germany's might – a true, a whole German man; a model for us all but especially for our youth![14]

This bombastic patriotism may be scarcely surprising from the mouth of a former tutor to a prince. But it is worth establishing that there were no anti-semitic undertones among Himmler's system of ideas, feelings, character traits and values – even as late as the year 1929. His son Heinrich's anti-semitic attitude certainly did not grow from the intellectual soil of his parents' house, but was inflamed later among like-minded German-*völkisch* (populist ethnic) comrades. It is possible to follow the path along which he developed into an anti-semite in Heinrich Himmler's reading list, which he kept from 1919 until 1934 and embellished with copious commentaries; initially he was very moderate, later however he became more and more radical.[15]

A desire to regard Heinrich Himmler as a stupid, stolid person fits the clichéd view of him which is often invoked but is nonetheless incorrect. 'In spite of his somewhat tangled impenetrability, Himmler had a powerful intellect', as Hallgarten says of his school friend.[16] Himmler the school-boy was always among the best in the class. A grade of 'very good' was often found in his reports. He was particularly interested in history, but he also brought home very good grades in German and the classical languages, Greek and Latin. In the school year 1913–14 his class teacher at the grammar school in Landshut, Professor Hillgärtner, entered the following comment about him in the 'confidential school report': 'Apparently a very gifted pupil, who by dint of tireless hard work, burning ambition and lively participation in lessons, achieved the best results in the class'.[17] His Leaving Certificate, which was awarded on 15 July 1919, from the grammar school in Landshut, is adorned by the comment: 'During his time in this institution he has always displayed good manners and showed conscientiousness and diligence'. He was assessed with a grade of 'very good' in religious education, German, Latin, Greek and history and 'good' in mathematics and physics.[18] He passed the final diploma exams in agriculture, too, which he sat at the end of the summer term 1922 at the Technical High School in Munich, where he had been studying agriculture since 18 October 1919, with an overall mark of 1.7 – 'very good'. The reports on his practical classes in the various branches of agriculture stress his enthusiasm, diligence, conscientiousness, enterprise and pleasant personality.[19]

His attempts to enter active politics at the beginning of the twenties, too, show him to be a zealous enthusiast, who could not get over the fact that the political order under which he had grown up had finally come to an end. We know from his brother Gebhard that the 'stab in the back legend', according to which the victorious German army was betrayed by the Marxists, had a place in his world of ideas.[20] In the various paramilitary leagues he gradually assumed a more and more radical position. He took part in the 1923 Hitler Putsch as the standard bearer of the *Reichskriegsflagge* league, which had the task of occupying the entrance to the Bavarian War Ministry.

A short time later, on 25 January 1924, he wrote to a friend, 'The future is of course one great big question mark, but I am optimistic that we will fight through and reach a quiet place, somewhere a man can build the foundations of his life, even though we will all as a rule be fighters, then as now'.[21] Himmler's professional situation was anything but rosy in those years. He could not find a suitable permanent job and was consequently thinking of accepting a job abroad.

On 23 November 1921 he noted in his diary: 'Today I cut an article about emigration to Peru out of the paper. Where will I be driven to go – Spain, Turkey, the Baltic, Russia, Peru? I often think about it. In two years I will no longer be in Germany, if God wills it, unless there is conflict and war again and I am a soldier.'[22]

How greatly circumstances had brought about a change in Himmler's ideas from his earlier attitudes is demonstrated in a passage from the letter of 25.1.1924 already quoted, in which he conjured up the images of the enemy against whom he and people who thought like him wanted to fight 'as soldiers and confident supporters of the *völkisch* cause', that is 'against the hydra of the black and red International, of Jews and Ultramontanism, of freemasons and Jesuits, of the spirit of commerce and cowardly bougosie [*sic*]'.[23]

Even before Himmler got to know Hitler personally he was already in contact with Ernst Röhm. A meeting with him in January 1922 is noted in Himmler's diary. Himmler gave his first speech for the Party on 24 February 1924 for the 'National Socialist Freedom Movement' in a village in Lower Bavaria near Kelheim. He was discovered as a 'Party speaker' by Heinrich Gärtner, leader of the Party branch at Schleissheim. Himmler was one of the first to buy Hitler's *Mein Kampf*. After reading the first volume he ascertained 'there's an incredible amount of truth in it'. But that he was at this point still very critical of Hitler is shown in a further comment: 'The first chapters on his own youth contain many weak points'.[24]

He was active in the National Socialist Party from 1925. He became Gregor Strasser's secretary, deputy *Gauleiter* of Lower Bavaria and Oberpfalz and in 1926 deputy *Gauleiter* of Upper Bavaria and Swabia and deputy National Director for Propaganda. In 1927 Hitler nominated him Deputy Leader of the SS and in 1929 *Reichsführer – SS*. In this function he was subordinate to the Chief of Staff of the SA, Ernst Röhm, until the latter was brutally eliminated; a process in which Himmler was massively involved. On the basis of its service in the suppression of the 'Röhm Putsch' the SS was elevated on 20 July 1934 to the status of an independent organisation within the NSDAP, which meant an extraordinary upgrading of Himmler's position.

The real history of the SS began when it was taken over by Heinrich Himmler in January 1929. Himmler wanted to build up an organisation which would fuse together into a single political and philosophical entity an Order based on race, a new 'aristocracy of blood and soil'. The aim was to create a 'new type of human being by means of education and selection', who would be capable of 'mastering all the great tasks of the future'.[25] That meant the ruthless, brutal extermination of the Jews, torturing and killing in the concentration camps and death camps, the brutal persecution of dissidents and those who to his mind did not resist the superior enemy forces strongly enough. 'Everything that opens its mouth', Himmler wrote in 1944, 'must be shot without compunction'.[26] Himmler implanted new norms of behaviour into the young SS men, which robbed them of their moral powers of judgement and replaced them with coldheartedness, cruelty, impatience and an excessive, narrow group egoism. 'I know,' he said in a speech in 1935, referring to the fear of the SS, 'that there are many people in Germany who feel unwell at the sight of this black tunic; we understand this and do not expect to be loved by all that many'.[27] Pride instead of shame at the unpopularity of his troops is evident from Himmler's speech. He practically announces it publicly: 'We are brave enough to be unpopular, we are brave enough to be hard-hearted and unfeeling!'

'Who,' writes Nietzsche, 'will ever achieve anything, if he does not feel within himself the power and the will to inflict great pain? To be able to suffer is the least of it: weak women and slaves often achieve mastery in this. But not to be defeated by inner distress and uncertainty if you inflict great suffering and hear the cry of this suffering – that is great, that is part of greatness.' This questionable aphorism could also have been in Himmler's speech, for this was precisely the mental attitude he wanted to inculcate in his SS.[28] How could his SS members have committed mass murders of such unimaginable dimensions without this consciousness of being an elite, indeed without feeling that they were acting 'on the orders of providence'.

This mentality is also revealed in Himmler's speech at Posen in October 1943: 'The extermination of the Jewish people', he explained to his SS generals:

is one of those things which is easily said . . . . 'the Jewish people is being exterminated', some Party member says. . . . Of all those who speak like that, none has watched, none has seen it through. Most of you will know what it is like to see a hundred corpses lying together, or 500 or 1000. To have seen this through, and, if we disregard exceptional cases of human weakness, to have remained decent, that has made us hard. This is a glorious page of our history which never has been and never will be written. . . .[29]

This document is monstrous not only because of the statements it contains, but also in the way it strips the mask from the mental attitude of those who gave the orders in the Third Reich and also of those who obeyed them. None of those present saw any need to object to Himmler's speech or found the courage to do so. And these were SS generals who could have risked saying something. However one should not underestimate the degree of degradation and perversion of thought which had already been achieved in the SS by means of constantly hammering home doctrines with pseudo-priestly authority. The SS Order's total claim on its members left no room for individual philosophies. 'The guideline for us in our struggle is neither the Old or the New Testament in the Bible, but the political testament of Adolf Hitler.'[30]

Himmler consciously chose the religiously loaded term 'Order' for his community, at the centre of which was Hitler, the new 'saviour'. From his initial reservations about Hitler, Himmler built up an image of him during the course of the years, which bore all the marks of a mystical elevation. The altars of the SS were copied from those of the catholic church in their external form only. At their centre however was not Christ, but Hitler, not the cross but the swastika. The christian cross of exaggerated proportions which had hung in Himmler's parents' apartment, and under which Himmler had grown up, was now declared an enemy symbol. 'We must finish with Christianity', Himmler proclaimed, copying his 'god', Hitler. 'This great plague which might attack us at some stage in our history.'[31]

The new faith under the sign of the swastika showed all the signs of being on the opposite pole from Christianity. 'Whoever has the swastika burning in his heart hates all other crosses,' wrote S. Sebecker.[32]

Himmler wanted to replace Christianity with a 'proper religion and morality' which was to be derived from the 'Germanic inheritance'. Ancestor worship, belief in immortality, the 'blood and soil' myth and the belief in an omnipotent god were elements of the new belief. Ritualised holidays, like that on the thousandth anniversary of the death of King Henry I, held in Quedlinburg Cathedral in 1936, show the importance attached to historical personalities and history in general, in Himmler's new paganism. Himmler himself probably felt that he was a reincarnation of Henry I.[33]

Many of Hitler's comments demonstrate that he did not share Himmler's mystical urges. He disowned efforts to 'imitate a religion, in this idiotic, ritualised way' and pointed out that National Socialism was a 'scientific doctrine'.[34] He poured scorn on Himmler's mystical 'fantasies': 'What nonsense! We have finally arrived in an era which has dispensed with all mysticism, and now he's starting at the beginning again. We might as well have stayed with the church. To think I might one day be made an SS saint. Just imagine it! I would turn in my grave.'[35]

Rainer Zitelmann was right to conclude in his latest study on Hitler that the latter's philosophy can not, as is claimed in the literature, be seen as 'antimodernism'. This is not only true of his conception of history, his opinion of religion and its replacement by a neo-pagan cult, but also of his ideology on 'living space' and race. For him, 'living space' was an economic requirement; in his concept of race he believed that he 'was on the firm ground of assured ideological cognition'. In this sense Hitler must be regarded – by his own lights – as being 'entirely modern'.[36]

This cannot be said at all of Himmler, whose ideology was to a large extent shaped by irrationality. The 'eternal marching orders' he gave his SS are an impressive example of this:

We have set off and are marching according to irrevocable laws along that road into a distant future, as a National Socialist, soldierly order of men selected for their Nordic antecedents, and as a sworn brotherhood of that tribe, and we wish and believe that we will not merely be the grandchildren who fought better, but, over and above that, the antecedents of the final dynasty necessary for the eternal life of the German, Teutonic people.[37]

Himmler reduced what SS members had to absorb down to a few points. The most important of them was without doubt the National Socialist racial doctrine. Nonetheless Himmler's dictatorial onslaught on racial doctrine met with universal derision. Even in the twenties he had followed the publications of pseudo-scientific racial researchers with increasing interest, like for example those of H.F.K. Günther, which according to Himmler strick up the 'hymn of praise to glorious Nordic blood'.[38] The noblest thing in the world for them was the Nordic race, for it alone was capable of producing culture. Mixing of races and the drying-up of Nordic blood led inevitably to the death of a people. Apparently this danger was increasingly threatening the German people. This threat could only be avoided by improving the Nordic substance of the race by means of a planned 'breeding programme'. Himmler: I hope we haven't come too late!'[39]

He went about improving the stock and taking in hand human 'breeding' with missionary zeal. He had been intensively concerned with breeding and heredity as a student of agriculture, and so he firmly believed that the methods which ensured success in plant and animal breeding would be applicable to breeding humans. The SS supplied Himmler with his 'human material'. In a much-quoted speech from 1935 he describes the first, exploratory steps in this unlikely terrain. 'First of all, we, like a seedsman who wants to develop a pure strain of a good old type which has been hybridised and weakened, must first go over the field to select his stock, as it is called; we began to sift out the humans who, according to their external characteristics, were not considered to be of use in building up the SS.'[40] He assigned the 'selection process' to a racial commission of the Race and Settlement Headquarters (SS). Represented on the commission were SS officers, experts on race and doctors. According to a catalogue of criteria, the SS applicants were divided into five categories, which extended from the 'pure Nordic' group down to the group which was of 'mixed race of non-European origin'. Only applicants in the first three categories could be accepted. Alongside eye and hair colouring, a particular role in the selection of candidates for the SS was played by height and the phenotypical measure of the degree of Nordic blood. Only those who were at least 1.70m could guarantee to Himmler that they possessed Nordic blood. The commission also gave marks for symmetry of build. In addition, a proof of ancestry had to be provided: for an SS man as far back as at least the year 1800, for an SS officer back to 1750.

By Himmler's lights it would have been nonsensical to collect the 'good blood' of men in his SS without making it bear fruit for future generations in a breeding programme. To this end he issued an 'Engagement and Marriage order' on 31 December 1931, according to which an SS man was only allowed to marry if the *Reichsführer – SS* gave his consent. The allocation of marriage permits was however dependent on an evaluation of the racial and hereditary health characteristics of the marriage partner, which was decided in the Race and Settlement Headquarters (SS). Himmler knew, naturally, that he was exposing himself to ridicule with this order. Nonetheless, imbued with the idea of having to save the Germanic world from degeneration and destruction, he added prophetically: 'The SS is aware that it has taken a step of great significance with this decree. Mockery, scorn and misunderstanding cannot touch us; the future belongs to us.'[41]

On 1.11.1935 he gave Hitler his precise ideas on the future form of the SS. The document is interesting not just for its fanatical content but also for the servility he showed towards Hitler:

> I conveyed to the Führer. . . my ideas that the SS should one day become the German Samurai, by means of the planned procedure for accepting new admissions: that at any time half or two thirds of those newly admitted could be sons of SS families, in order to achieve a filtering process, and at least one third must be from non SS families, so that no good blood, destined for leadership, ever existed among this people and was not utilised. The Führer expressed his total agreement and approval for the ideas sketched here. I also put the question from the 100 Tenets to the Führer: What is the SS? – The SS is a National Socialist Order of men selected for their Nordic characteristics and a sworn blood brotherhood. The Führer was also satisfied with this formulation.[42]

The social revolution of the qualified agriculturalist and former district leader of the Artam League, Heinrich Himmler, therefore began when he became *Reichsführer – SS* with a bundle of abstruse ideas derived from a romanticised vision of history and a false interpretation of biology, opposed to democracy, liberalism and religion, glorifying the Führer principle and a mercenary mentality, with a brutal hatred of the Jews and finally with a dream of Arian Germanic world domination under the leadership of a new caste of aristocrats. The aim of the Artam league was to lead people out of the towns back onto the land, since the 'racial hygienists' believed they detected a biological degeneration in city dwellers. 'Finding roots for people in the soil again' was seen as a means of restoring the nation to health and therefore the peasant' lifestyle was put forward as a prerequisite for the renewal and preservation of the nation.

These ideas, which Himmler adopted in full, led him to a 'people without space' ideology. From this were derived the demands for 'seizure of land' and colonial settlements in the East, which had as their consequence the expulsion, enslavement and extermination of the resident population. The sole justification for this, for Himmler as for Hitler, lay in the principle that 'might is right'. Himmler saw a basic law of nature in the 'battle for existence', and this also found its way into the philosophy of his order. The meaning of such a battle was the destruction of everything weak and inferior. Human beings were also subjected to this law of nature. Within the meshes of the biological system man was to see himself again as a beast of prey, who firmly rejected the tinsel of refined civilisation and the intellect in order not to fall prey to degeneration. Sympathy cannot be expected in a world like this, the threshold of inhibition about killing has become lower. This is particularly clear in an observation Himmler made on a trip to Kiev in 1942: 'The *Reichsführer – SS* said that the social question can only be solved by killing the other man, so that you get his fields.'[43]

By means of so-called racial sifting, Himmler wanted to select from the subjected eastern lands those people who demonstrated the supposed 'good blood', that is to say 'Germanic racial components', in their heredity; the other sections of the population were graded as inferior, even classified as sub-human. The rules and regulations for the treatment of alien nations in the East which he gave to his SS generals on the occasion of an SS generals' conference in Posen on 4 October 1943 show Himmler as a coldly determined, evil, fanatical ideologue:

. . . Take care,' he said to his SS generals, 'that these sub-humans always respect you, always have to look their superiors in the eye. It is the same with animals. As long as it is looking its tamer in the eye, it does nothing. With this approach we will always be dominant over the Slavs, with this approach will be able to exploit the Russians. But not by any other method.[44]

In agreement with Hitler he decreed that the people in the occupied eastern territories had to be suppressed to the lowest level of culture. The liberally educated Himmler, who had read Goethe and Schiller in his spare time in the Twenties and had learnt Klopstock's Odes by heart, had an illustrated brochure produced in an edition of about four million copies titled *Der Untermensch* (The Sub-Human). In it human thoughts and feelings were brutally violated, by radically denying a large group of people their humanity, their membership of the human race. 'The sub-human,' it stated:

that creation of nature which is apparently identical biologically, with hands, feet and a kind of brain, with eyes and a mouth, is in fact a quite different, frightful creature, is only a stone's throw away from humanity, with human-looking features, but mentally, spiritually it is lower than any animal; sub-human, nothing else! For not everything with a human face is the same – woe to whoever forgets it![45]

This pamphlet, which could be bought at every newsstand and was translated into fourteen languages was corrected at least six times by Himmler in his own hand. One may therefore conclude that the content by and large corresponded to his own views and intentions.

The East was to be 'cleared' in order to create a colonial territory of enormous size for the Germanic race. The outlines of this 'teutonic, pan-German Reich' were described by Himmler thus: 'After the Greater German Reich comes the Germanic Reich, then the Germano-Gothic Reich as far as the Urals and perhaps then even the Franco-Gothic Carolingian Reich.'[46]

There was repeated speculation about Hitler's successor, after Hermann Goering had largely lost his standing. Towards the end of the war this debate reached an acute stage. Himmler seemed to be the potential successor with the best prospects, since, as was widely assumed, he stood highest in his Führer's favour. Added to this was the fact that in comparison to other competitors he had the largest power base at his disposal. At this time he was, among other things, Chief of the SS and the Police, Minister of the Interior and Commander of the Reserve Army. During a briefing at the headquarters of the Military High Command on 27 April 1945 Himmler took Hitler's place as a matter of course.

However Hitler construed his unauthorised offer of negotiations for a cease-fire with the Western Allies as treason, expelled him from the Party and relieved him of all his offices of state. His astonishing career had taken Himmler to within a hairsbreadth of the highest office of state. His downfall was abrupt and, for him, a total surprise. 'A traitor shall never succeed me as Führer', Hitler determined shortly before his death.[47]

Hitler's most ardent follower, who wore the motto 'my honour is loyalty' on his belt buckle, survived Hitler and his 'betrayal' of him by only about three weeks. In a British prison he, like his Führer, Adolf Hitler, committed suicide.

NOTES

1. H. Kehrl, *Krisenmanager im Dritten Reich*, (Dusseldorf, 1973) p. 361.
2. A. Speer, *Der Sklavenstaat. Meine Auseinandersetzung mit der SS* (Stuttgart, 1981) p.47.
3. G.W.F. Hallgarten, 'Mein Mitschüler Heinrich Himmler', *Germania Judaica*, 1 (1960/61) part 2, p. 4.
4. Letter from G. Himmler dated 13.10.1900, BA, Nachlass Himmler.
5. Letter from the court administration Arnulf von Bayern dated 11.6.1917, BA, Nachlass Himmler.
6. J. Bernhardt, 'Aus meiner Jugend', *Hochland*, 53/6 (1961) p. 550f.
7. Personal, undated note by G. Himmler, BA, Nachlass Himmler.

8. A. Andersch, *Der Vater eines Mörders. Eine Schulgeschichte* (Zurich, 1980) p. 136.
9. M. Spindler, *Bayerische Geschichte im 19. und 20. Jahrhundert* (Munich, 1974/75) p. 972 and 977f.
10. Quoted in P.E. Schramm, *Neun Generationen*, vol. II (Göttingen, 1964) p. 448.
11. Questionnaire dated 26.6.1917, BA, Nachlass Himmler.
12. Philisterzeitung der Studentenbindung Apollo, München, 53/2 (1929).
13. Himmler's speech at the marriage of SS Major Deutsch, 2 April 1936, BA, NS 19/1092.
14. Philisterzeitung, as above.
15. J. Ackermann, *Heinrich Himmler als Ideologe* (Göttingen, 1970) p. 25ff.
16. G.W.F. Hallgarten, as above, p. 6.
17. A. Beckembauer, 'Musterschüler und Massenmörder' *Verhandlungen des Historischen Vereins für Niederbayern*, 95 (1969) p. 102.
18. Himmler's Higher School Leaving Certificate is published in: ibid., p. 97.
19. Copies of certificates in BA, Nachlass Himmler.
20. G. Himmler, Skizzen und Materialen zu einem Lebensbild Heinrich Himmlers, typescript, 14.3.1954 (Privately owned).
21. Copy of a letter from Himmler dated 25.1.1924, BA, NS26/1222.
22. Himmler's diary, BA.
23. Ibid.
24. Himmler's reading list, 1919 to 1934, BA, Nachlass Himmler.
25. J. Ackermann, as above, p. 104.
26. H. Heiber, *Reichsführer! Briefe an und von Himmler* (Stuttgart, 1968) p. 274.
27. H. Himmler, *Die Schutzstaffel als antibolschewistische Kampforganisation* (Munich, 1936) p. 29.
28. J. Ackermann, as above, p. 123ff.
29. Himmler's speech at the SS generals' conference in Posen, 4.10.1943, IMT, vol. XXIX, p. 148.
30. J. Ackermann, Himmler, as above, p. 40ff.
31. Himmler's speech at the Haus der Flieger, Berlin, in: B.F. Smith, A.F. Peterson, *Heinrich Himmler. Geheimreden 1933 bis 1945* (Frankfurt a. M., 1974) p. 159.
32. Quoted in J. Neuhäusel, *Kreuz und Hakenkreuz* (Munich, 1946) p. 10.
33. J. Ackermann, *Himmler*, as above, 60ff.
34. R. Zitelmann, *Hitler. Selbstverständnis eines Revolutionärs* (Stuttgart, 1987) p.339.
35. Speer, *Erinnerungen* (Berlin, 1969) p. 108.
36. R. Zitelmann, *Hitler*, as above, p. 342.
37. H. Himmler, *Die Schutzstaffel*, as above, p. 531.
38. See especially the commentary in Himmler's reading list, as above.
39. Ibid.
40. H. Himmler, *Die Schutzstaffel*, as above, p. 31.
41. J. Ackermann, *Himmler*, as above, p. 262f.
42. Himmler's note, 1.11.1935, in the author's private archive.
43. J. Ackermann, *Himmler*, as above, p. 273.
44. Himmler's speech in Posen, as above, p. 124.
45. Der Reichsführer SS, SS Headquarters, *Der Untermensch* (Berlin, 1942).
46. Filed comment of R. Brandt on Himmler's conversation at the lunch table, 13.9.1943, BA, NS19/441.
47. J. von Lang, *Der Sekretär. Mārtin Bormann: Der Mann, der Hitler beherrschte* (Stuttgart, 1977) p. 334.

BIBLIOGRAPHY

Primary Sources

Of all the abundant source material about Heinrich Himmler, the most important holdings are in the Bundesarchiv Koblenz. The 'Nachlass Himmler' and the file on the 'Persönlicher Stab Reichsführer-SS' are particularly useful. Alongside the sources scattered in countless court-files (especially in the Nuremberg Trials, some of which have been published) and other publications, there are only a few books of published documents specialising in Himmler. Among these are H. Heiber (ed.), *Briefwechsel. Briefe an und von Himmler* (Stuttgart, 1968), which has a well-chosen sample of letters which Himmler wrote or received. B.F. Smith and A.F. Peterson (eds), *Heinrich Himmler. Geheimreden 1933 bis 1945 und andere Ansprachen* (Frankfurt a.M., 1974) is a worthwhile publication containing Himmler's important speeches. J.C. Fest wrote the very informative foreword. Of the books which appeared before 1945, the following are especially illuminating: H. Himmler, *Die Schutzstaffel als antibolschewistische Kampforganisation* (Munich, 1936); by the same author, *Rede des Reichsführers im Dom zu Quedlinburg am 2. Juli 1936* (Berlin, 1936). The pamphlet published by the SS Headquarters of the Reichsführer-SS, *Der Untermensch* (Berlin, 1942) is a basic source for research on Himmler.

Secondary Literature

Although Himmler was a central figure in the Third Reich, there is still no comprehensive biography of him which meets academic standards. The account by H. Fraenkel and R. Manvell, *Himmler. Kleinbürger und Massenmörder* (Frankfurt a.M., 1965) is easy to read, reliable and intended for a wide audience. It is based on studies of primary sources and interviews with contemporary witnesses and comes to a balanced conclusion about Himmler and his policies. J. Ackermann, *Himmler als Ideologe* (Göttingen, 1970) discusses Himmler's ideology and how it translated into policy. In the process it touches on strands from intellectual history which give access to Himmler's philosophy. A documentary appendix contains a series of basic sources for Himmler's ideology. Himmler's childhood and youth are the subject of B.F. Smith's book: *Heinrich Himmler 1900–1926. Sein Weg in den deutschen Faschismus* (Munich, 1979). Among other things he assesses Himmler's diaries. The following are indispensable for any work on Himmler; the detailed studies by H. Höhne, *Der Orden unter dem Totenkopf. Die Geschichte der SS* (Gutersloh, 1967); E. Kogon, *Der SS-Staat. Das System der deutschen Konzentrationslager* (Frankfurt a.M., 1946) and B. Wegener, *Hitlers Politische Soldaten: Die Waffen-SS 1933–1945* (Paderborn, 1988), which also deals intensively with Himmler.

F. Kersten, *Totenkopf und Treue. Heinrich Himmler ohne Uniform* (Hamburg, no date) and A. Besgen, *Der stille Befehl. Medizinalrat Kersten, Himmler und das Dritte Reich* (Munich, 1960) give an interesting insight into Himmler's everyday life and into his thinking during the time of the Second World War. The book by A. Wykes, *Reichsführer SS Himmler* (Munich, 1981), in the 'Moewig Dokumentation' series, is of no academic value because of the dubious and/ or false claims it makes.

11 Adolf Hitler: The Führer
Rainer Zitelmann

Is 'National Socialism without Hitler' possible, or could Hitler have been replaced by any other great man? Would the World War and The 'Final Solution' have happened, we might ask, if Hitler had been assassinated in 1938 and Goering had succeeded him? Or is it completely impossible to conceive of the 'polycratic' system of the Third Reich without the unifying figure of Hitler at its centre? These and other similar questions have often been asked, but the answers remain speculative, regardless of whether they judge Hitler's role in the Third Reich to be prominent or more limited. Of course, no-one knows what course history would have taken without Hitler. A historian cannot make reliable statements about how (different) it *might* have been; he can only attempt to reconstruct the actual events.

If we confine ourselves to this, it is impossible to avoid the conclusion that Hitler had a position of overwhelming power in the Third Reich and the Nazi movement. Although after the liquidation of the SA leadership and the leaders of the conservative opposition on 30 June 1934, Hitler united more powers in his own hands than almost any other state leader in modern times, and although in formal terms, after the unification of the offices of President and Chancellor, there was literally no longer any office which Hitler was legally obliged to answer to, nonetheless he did not really rule alone, any more than any other dictator.

His rule was based on the suppression of political opposition by terrorism and on the support of an overwhelming majority of Germans. Over and above this, it was also built on the rivalries between the leaders of the Third Reich and the institutions they represented. The 'polycratic' structure of the Third Reich on one hand, and the 'monocratic' character of Hitler's rule on the other, were two sides of the same coin: the permanent conflict between the leaders of the Nazi system made it possible for the Führer to play his role as a universally accepted unifying figure and final authority. Of course his power was also limited by this 'institutional anarchy', but even more by the circumstance that he had to depend to a large extent for his support on the old elites, which he had set out to abolish. Added to this was Hitler's own specific conception of the role of leader, and his highly contradictory personality, which often made him avoid decisions. This has even led some historians to describe Hitler as 'in many respects a weak dictator' (Hans Mommsen). However he remained indisputably the final arbiter. And above all else: power and influence in the Führer's state were derived not least from access to Hitler, and whether one was able to get a hearing from him and win his favour. Simply having access to Hitler was often of greater importance than formal positions of power, which were often in any case imprecisely defined or overlapped with the powers of others. Conversely: if one ever incurred Hitler's displeasure this resulted in a rapid loss of power and influence. The careers of prominent Nazis described in this book give emphatic proof of this.

As these introductory remarks demonstrate, it is not possible to give a single meaningful response to the question of Hitler's importance to National Socialism. Theoretical constructs and generalised pronouncements will not take us any further forward; this is better achieved through the observation of concrete instances of decision-making. Over and above this it is always necessary to keep the importance of Hitler's philosophical ideas in view, the content and premises of which were seen not just by him, but also by many National Socialists, as binding rules for their actions.

So who was this man, whose name is, for posterity as it was for his contemporaries, a synonym for National Socialism?

Adolf Hitler was born on 20 April 1889 in the small Austrian town of Braunau am Inn. If we accept his own reminiscences in *Mein Kampf* and later in *Table Talk*, his childhood and youth were shaped by violent conflicts with authority figures. He fought with his father, because he – a customs official – wanted his son to become a civil servant too. Adolf, however, dreamed of the carefree life of an artist. He found the idea of not being able to be in control of his own time and of 'ever having to sit in an office like a serf'[1] unbearable. The conflict with his father continued at school. Hitler told later of heated confrontations with his teachers, whom he embroiled in arguments during lessons.

After the death of his father (in 1903 at the age of sixty-five) Hitler applied twice for admission to the Academy of Arts in Vienna, but was turned down. Hitler lived in Vienna from 1908 until 1913. He reports that it was here that the basis of his later philosophy evolved, a philosophy characterised by a hatred of Marxists, Jews and the bourgeoisie. In May 1913 Hitler left Vienna and moved in Munich. He was there when the First World War broke out. Although he had avoided military service in the Austrian Army, he now came forward as a volunteer. Like so many of his contemporaries, he too was shaped by the experience of the 'popular community in the trenches', where there were apparently no longer any distinctions of class, and the personal bravery of individuals was all that mattered.

After being blinded by poison gas he was taken to a military field hospital in Pasewalk. It was there that he heard of the revolution and the proclamation of the republic. Hitler looked for those responsible for the defeat. The anti-semitism and anti-marxism he had already developed in Vienna made him receptive to the accusations of guilt widespread in Germany at that time: the Jews and the 'November criminals', so it was said, were responsible for the defeat.

Characteristic of Hitler were, first of all, the radicalism and exclusivity with which he put forward all his opinions, and then, secondly, the way he attempted to find a 'rational' basis for his views and shape them into a self-contained, coherent view of life, offering solutions to all its problems. Feelings which only caused unease in other people drove him to despair. Hitler took a more radical view than many of his contemporaries of real or imagined grievances. And even his prejudices, which to us appear to be highly irrational, were concrete truths for him, or at the very least they appeared to be reliable insights and incontrovertible truths. In Hitler's earliest surviving political document these characteristics are clear. In a letter written on 16 September 1919 he stressed that anti-semitism as a political movement should not be driven by 'moments of emotion, but by the recognition of facts'. Anti-semitism based on emotions would lead in the end to pogroms, while 'rational anti-semitism' must lead to a planned and legal battle against the 'privileges of the Jews' and their abolition. 'But its final aim,' Hitler wrote, 'must steadfastly remain the complete removal of the Jews'.[2]

When Hitler wrote these lines he was still an intelligence agent in an 'educational section' in the German army. In this capacity he was entrusted on 12 September with the task of visiting the convention of a group calling itself the German Workers' Party (DAP) and later the National Socialist German Workers' Party. The DAP was a small insignificant splinter group. As delegates demanded the secession of Bavaria from the German state, Hitler took the floor and violently attacked the previous speaker. The party chairman, Drexler, was enthusiastic about Hitler's rhetorical abilities. A few weeks later Hitler joined the party and was soon its most important propaganda spokesman.

The polemics in Hitler's speeches were directed against the Treaty of Versailles, which muzzled Germany in foreign affairs, and he also castigated the 'November criminals' who had thrown Germany into a state of misery. The views Hitler expressed to his small, but constantly growing audience, were not unusual for that time. He was putting into words what many people thought and felt.

But much of what he said also sounded new and many contemporaries were unsure of what to make of this man and his National Socialist Party. Many did not take him at all seriously. Others thought he was a capitalist lackey, a reactionary or a monarchist. However they were wrong. Hitler was always violently opposed to the right-wing reactionaries, whose main slogan was the restoration of the monarchy; 'One should not imagine that Nationalism is given expression by demanding or wishing that the old flags should fly again, that the old authoritarian state should be resurrected, that the monarchy should be reinstated or that the old circumstances should return in any way.'[3]

Hitler's antipathy to the November revolution had absolutely nothing to do with the fact that it had sealed the fate of the monarchy in Germany. From his later remarks as 'Führer' we know that in many respects he actually regarded the 'men of November', whom he had abused, in a positive light.

Even in his early speeches it is noticeable that his violent, hard-line position is not simply directed against Jews and Communists, but above all against bourgeois forces. Hitler accused the bourgeoisie of antisocial attitudes, greed for profit and dull materialism. By opposing the justified demands of the workers, he said, the bourgeoisie had driven the working class into the arms of the marxist parties. Proletarian class consciousness was simply an understandable reaction to bourgeois class arrogance. The bourgeoisie had falsified and discredited the idea of the nation by falsely identifying its own egoistical class interests with national interests.

Hitler did not see himself as either a right or left wing politician. In an account of a speech delivered in October 1920 it is stated:

Now Hitler turned on the right and the left. The Nationalists on the right lacked social awareness, the socialists on the left lacked national awareness. He appealed to right wing parties – If you want to be national parties, then come down to the level of the people and away with all your class arrogance! To the left he called – You, who are true revolutionaries, come over to us and fight with us for all of our people![4]

Hitler proclaimed his ambition of abolishing the extremes of bourgeois nationalism and proletarian socialism in a new movement, which 'in opposing the two extremes was itself the most extreme'.[5] In September 1922 he said, 'The disinherited of the left and right must come together in the ranks of us National Socialists.'[6] In his speeches Hitler turned violently against the bourgeois parties and their slogan of 'law and order'. 'Our party must be revolutionary in character, for the condition of law and order only means that we continue to preserve the existing pig-sty.'[7]

Hitler refused to participate in elections, since he feared that the party might lose its character as a revolutionary movement by doing so. When in the summer of 1921 some of the leaders were conducting talks about alliances with like-minded groups, Hitler pointedly left the party and issued an ultimatum, making his return dependent on its acceptance. In his letter of resignation he stated: 'I hereby give an explanation of the reason which made me take this step. The National Socialist Workers' Party, as far as I understand it, was originally formed as a revolutionary national movement. Accordingly it is based on extreme *völkisch* [populist ethnic] principles and rejects all parliamentary tactics . . .'.[8] These and other principles had been violated – for example the unalterability of its policies. Hitler demanded the position of senior chairman 'with dictatorial powers' for himself. His conditions were accepted at an extraordinary meeting of members of the NSDAP on 29 July.

Hitler's biographers have interpreted this action as an expression of his unquenchable thirst for power. Against this interpretation is the fact that Hitler had already been offered the chairmanship of the party on a number of occasions, but he had turned it down. But nonetheless there is already a mode of behaviour evident here which determined Hitler's actions in many later crises within the Party and in domestic politics. Confronted by a situation which he felt to be dangerous or complex, again and again the expansion of his own power base seemed to him to provide the only escape. The fact that he succeeded in overcoming difficult problems in this way increased his confidence in this specific means of crisis management. In most cases these crises were not started by Hitler, far less were they part of a long-term plan, even if the end result, which was always the expansion of his personal power, might suggest this.

The tactic of violent revolution, which Hitler had fought for so vehemently in the crisis of July 1921, was in ruins two years later. When tension between Bavaria and the German state intensified in autumn 1923, Hitler attempted to exploit the situation and to win power by means of a coup. On 8 November he proclaimed 'the national revolution' in the Munich Burgerbräukeller and declared the government to be deposed. But his putsch quickly collapsed. Hitler had to face charges of high treason and was sentenced to five years imprisonment. In prison he wrote the first volume of his political manifesto, *Mein Kampf*, in which he systemised his philosophy and set down its goal with astonishing openness.

Hitler's ideas were shaped by the concept of the 'eternal struggle', which was based on Social Darwinism. According to this, nature, but also society and relationships between peoples, was dominated by a constant conflict between the strong and the weak, in which the bold and courageous had to win and the cowardly and weak were defeated. Starting from this Social Darwinist philosophy, Hitler developed his view of history, which was based on the following considerations: the course of history was determined by the eternal opposition between (limited) living space (*Lebensraum*) and the (increasing) numbers of people. At a certain stage of development an imbalance between these factors would come about. Both emigration and birth control, and an economic policy based on exports, which aimed to import food and raw materials of which there were shortages in exchange for manufactured goods, were attempts to resolve this contradiction which in the long term were condemned to failure.

Above all, Hitler took issue with the strategy of the 'peaceful economic conquest of the world'. He considered this possibility to be illusionary, because competition with other countries caused by increases in exports would finally lead to war, as the First World War had demonstrated. In common with many of his contemporaries he regarded Anglo-German trade rivalry, triggered by German economic expansion, as the real cause of the war. 'It was worse than senseless to be provoked by it – but it was entirely in keeping with our own harmlessness – that Britain one day took the liberty of countering our peaceful activities with the brutality of a violent egoist', Hitler wrote in *Mein Kampf.*[9]

In addition there was a narrowly delimited policy of economic expansion, since the industrialisation of hitherto underdeveloped countries would lead to a decline in Germany's export markets. In a speech delivered on 6 August 1927, in which Hitler developed his theory of the contradiction between the number of people and the base for feeding them, he discussed the various possibilities for bringing the two factors back into balance.

> For there is still one possibility, and that is the export of goods. However this possibility is deceptive, for this industrialisation is not just happening in Germany. Germany is not alone in being forced to industrialise – it is just the same in Britain, France and Italy. And recently America has joined the ranks of these competitors, and the most difficult part is not the so-called increases in production, as people are always saying here, the most difficult part is increasing sales. That is the problem in the world today, with everyone industrialising and competing for markets.

Germany's economic difficulties were bound to keep getting worse:

> firstly because world competition increases from year to year and secondly because the remaining states to whom we previously exported goods are themselves industrialising and because the shortage of raw materials puts us in a less and less favourable position at the outset, as against other states and peoples on this earth.[10]

This argument is of fundamental importance for understanding Hitler's philosophy. For it was from the impossibility of solving the contradiction between 'living space' and population by means of an economic policy directed towards exports that Hitler derived the demand that the German people must fight to conquer new 'living space'. The reasons for his demand, as set out above, remained the same in later years and are found unchanged in his talks to leading members of the armed forces in the thirties as well as in the speeches and essays of the 'Era of Struggle'.

Hitler wrote in *Mein Kampf* that it was not simply a question of getting rid of the Treaty of Versailles and restoring the 1914 borders, since that would not solve the problem of 'living space'. He also rejected the continuation of colonial policy. Germany must wage war against Russia to conquer new 'living space'. Hitler did not accept any moral reservations about such a policy: state boundaries were in any case only the expression of current relative strength in the struggle between nations. He regarded wars as being fundamentally justified if they were necessary to remove an imbalance between 'living space' and population. In his *Second Book*, published in 1928, Hitler writes:

> People on impossible pieces of land, as long as they have sound leadership, will basically always feel the need to expand their area of land, and hence their 'living space'. Later, unmotivated wars of conquest developed out of this attempt to match 'living space' with the population increase – the response to this is pacifism. The latter will disappear again once war has stopped being an instrument of individuals or peoples greedy for power or plunder, and once it has again become the weapon of last resort with which a nation fights for its daily bread.[11]

In *Mein Kampf* and the *Second Book* Hitler developed a concept of alliances which were to create the foreign policy constellation which made a war for the conquest of 'living space' in Russia possible. After the experiences of World War One he wanted to avoid a repetition of war on two fronts at all costs. Therefore he demanded that Germany should ally itself with Britain and Italy and forget old differences and difficulties with these countries. Hitler was especially keen for an alliance with Britain. From the end of 1922 or the beginning of 1923 the idea of Anglo-German cooperation was central to the alliance plans of his foreign policy.

However while Hitler was developing these ideas about the future direction of German foreign policy scarcely anyone was taking him seriously any more. His political career seemed to have come to an end with the debacle of 8 and 9 November. When he was released early from prison on probation on 20 December 1924, the Weimar Republic had entered the phase which today we call the 'golden years' and had taken the ground from under the propaganda of the Communists and National Socialists. The NSDAP, which had been banned after the Putsch, was legalised again at the beginning of 1925 and re-established by Hitler, but the internal state of the Party was in chaos. Hitler's first success was in purging the chaotic situation within the Party and enforcing his claim to leadership, even if it was not to remain undisputed in the years to come.

Hitler had learned a lesson from his failed Putsch: he was now in favour of participation in elections, which he had so violently rejected before. He considered that a violent revolution had no prospect of success, especially in view of the evident stability of the political system. Hitler now declared that democracy would have to be defeated by its own weapons.

The first Reichstag elections in which the NSDAP took part (on 20 May 1928) brought it 2.6 per cent of the vote and twelve seats in the Reichstag, a result which Hitler judged a success but which nonetheless underlined the

NSDAP's character as an insignificant splinter party. The breakthrough came with the Reichstag elections two years later, under the shadow of the steadily deepening economic crisis. The NSDAP became the second biggest faction, winning 107 seats in the Reichstag.

By the time of this electoral success, at the latest, Hitler's propaganda had changed. If his early speeches and writings had been characterised by violent anti-semitic slogans and aggressive demands for new 'living space', these themes now retreated completely into the background. This was not because Hitler had deviated from these goals, but resulted from his realisation that he would only win minority support with such radical policies. Hitler wanted majority support. However although the NSDAP managed to win over 13.7 million voters at the Reichstag elections of 31 July 1932, more than any other party before in the Weimar Republic, Hitler was forced to admit that he alone could not take power. However he rejected a coalition in which he was the inferior party. After Hindenburg had refused to make him Chancellor and Papen only offered him the office of Vice Chancellor, Hitler may well have thought of giving up the so-called legality tactic and taking the path of violent revolution. At the very least Hindenburg was to be forced, by the blatant deployment of the SA (Storm Section), and rumours of a coup, to hand over the powers of government to him. However, after the experiences of 1923, and taking the army into consideration, Hitler held firm to the legality tactic.

Hitler finally came to power in January 1933, in coalition with the conservative elements around Papen and Hugenberg. However this alliance was by no means based on mutual affection. The conservative forces, who lacked Hitler's influence on the masses, wanted to harness him for their own purposes, while Hitler had precisely the opposite intention. He had judged the intentions and hidden motives of his coalition partners quite correctly. In the autumn of 1932 he described their ideas as follows:

'The power is there', they are saying. 'How would it be if we harnessed ourselves behind it.' They are gradually realising that we National Socialists are a movement to be reckoned with, that I am a born tub-thumper, whom they can make good use of. Why should this brilliant movement, they think, with its drummer-boy, not also have brilliant field-marshalls. This drummer-boy is the only one who can drum up support; they themselves are the only ones who are capable of government. They all have 'von' in front of their names, the best proof of their capabilities.[12]

But Hitler no longer intended to be satisfied with the role of 'drummer-boy'. Again and again in his speeches he had declared that he wanted power in its entirety, undivided. And once in possession of power he would not give it up again. For many observers at home and abroad it seemed at first as if there had simply been a change of government, the more so since only three National Socialists were presented in the cabinet formed on 30 January. But appearances were deceptive, since Hitler was quickly able to minimise the influence of his conservative coalition partners. Soon the talk was not of a 'national uprising' but, characteristically, of the 'National Socialist revolution'. For Hitler the seizure of power on 30 January only marked the beginning of a long-drawn-out revolutionary transformation, which was by no means to be confined to the political sphere, but over and above this was to encompass the spheres of the economy, law, culture and intellectual life.

First of all, however, Hitler took action against the communists, whom he feared more than any other political party. This fear was the obverse side of his admiration. For in contrast to bourgeois elements, whom he perceived as cowardly, weak and opportunistic, he regarded the communists as worthy opponents. Even in the 'Era of Struggle' he had copied many of their battle tactics and propaganda methods, which he considered to be extraordinarily effective. Again and again he had stressed approvingly that the communists possessed a philosophy for which they were ready to fight 'fanatically'. So it is altogether possible that Hitler himself believed on the evening of 27 February 1933 that the communists had set fire to the Reichstag, thereby lighting a torch for the uprising. In fact it was the deed of an individual, the Dutch anarchist van der Lubbe. The Reichstag fire decrees enacted as a result of this repealed important basic rights, made possible arbitrary police 'preventive custody' without supervision by the judiciary and laid the basis for a permanent state of emergency. This was the first and decisive step on the path to dictatorship.

Nonetheless, SA terrorism, the 'voluntary dissolution' or the destruction of parties and trades unions, the establishment of concentration camps and the 'integration' (*Gleichschaltung*) of political and social institutions was only *one* of the bases of Hitler's power. Hitler emphasised on various occasions that coercion and violence were insufficient as a basis for rule. 'It is like this: in the long term it is impossible to maintain a regime merely by using the police, machine guns and rubber truncheons. You need something else as well. Some sort of pious idea about the philosophical necessity of maintaining the regime.'[13]

It was characteristic of Hitler's dual strategy that he firstly declared the first of May 1933 to be a legal holiday, something the working class movement had fought long and hard for without success, and then on the following day ordered that trade union offices should be occupied. The unions, which Hitler regarded as agents of Marxism, were replaced by the German Workers' Front (DAF). It was not, of course, a trade union in the traditional sense, but nonetheless safeguarded many of the unions' traditional roles, and in the Third Reich it successfully represented working class interests. It was not just the removal of unemployment which won

Hitler approval in wide circles of the working class. At least as important as this was the fact that he gave the working class the feeling that they were a recognised social group whose approval he sought. The ideological re-valuation of 'manual labour' was combined with a social policy which in many areas achieved clear improvements over the Weimar period.

Hitler was a supporter of the idea of elites, but when he talked about 'elites' he did not mean the traditional social groups who dominated society. Instead he was concerned to bring into being a new 'historical minority', which was to be recruited precisely from the working class. Hitler advocated improving possibilities of advancement for members of socially disadvantaged groups, above all workers. For while he despised the bourgeoisie as 'cowardly' 'weak' and 'apathetic', he saw the working class as the embodiment of 'fighting spirit', 'courage' and 'energy'.

Otto Dietrich, Hitler's National Press Officer from 1933–45, writes in his memoirs:

> Hitler wanted this 'classless state of People and Leader', produced by the revolution, to be secured for all time by means of a functional system of selecting the permanent leadership. To this end all barriers of birth and ownership were to be eliminated for the broad masses of people aspiring to leadership. In this state only one monopoly was to rule: achievement! Unceasingly and unconstrained, the best and eternally young elements were to emerge from the people and take their place in the leadership and the vibrant life of the nation – in order to safeguard not only the stability of the state, but also to guarantee its constant advance and the greatest possible degree of development.[14]

However this was only for the members of the 'German national com-munity' as Hitler understood it. Those who did not belong to this 'national community' experienced a quite different version of reality in the Third Reich: not more equality and opportunity but exclusion, persecution, humiliation and oppression. Those affected were political opponents and racial inferiors such as gipsies, those with a hereditary illness, asocial elements and other groups, but most of all the Jews.

Soon after the seizure of power came the first 'measures': the 'boycott of Jews' on 1 April 1933, the so-called 'Professional Civil Service Law' and then later the Nuremberg decrees (1935), 'Arianisation' and finally on 9 November 1938 the so-called *Reichskristallnacht*. There is disagreement about Hitler's part in the individual steps, about the question of whether he instigated them or tried to limit their impact, about whether the National Jewish policies are to be regarded primarily as the realisation of his philosophy or whether they were the expression of a process of radicalisa-tion which created its own momentum.

Hitler's role in the historical origins of the holocaust has not yet been explained. Until well into the Seventies it was regarded, at least in serious research, as an uncontroversial fact that Hitler was the initiator of the 'final solution' and that the mass murder of the Jews can be traced back to his orders. But since no written orders of Hitler's exist for the mass murder of the Jews (comparable for example with the so-called Euthanasia Decree dated 1 September 1939, which provided the basis for the murder of 60–100 000 mentally ill and disabled people) and there is no secure proof that he issued a corresponding oral order for the murders, some historians developed a theory that the holocaust probably did not have its basis in an order of Hitler's, but should instead be interpreted as the outcome of a cumulative process of radicalisation which created its own momentum. Critics of this 'functionalist' thesis point to the decisive importance of Hitler's philosophy, in which the demand for the 'removal of the Jews' played a central role. The events were inconceivable without a clear order from the dictator. A balanced discussion of this controversial explanatory model is not possible here, nonetheless it should be pointed out that the proponents of both theories can both present a large body of circumstantial evidence to support their explanation. However neither one nor other of the theories can be proved. In the author's opinion the so-called 'functionalist' interpretation has a higher degree of plausibility in this area than it deserves as an explanation of National Socialist foreign policy.

An interpretation which explains the radicalisation of National Socialist foreign policy as the consequence of a dynamic resulting from the rivalry between competing holders of power fails to appreciate Hitler's decisive role and that of the foreign policy manifesto he formulated in the twenties, to which he still felt bound even after the seizure of power. At the same time, the impression that in matters of foreign policy 'Hitler was an improviser, experimenter, given to flashes of inspiration' (Hans Mommsen), is not entirely incorrect. Nonetheless this description can only really be applied to the specific way in which Hitler attempted to realise his goals, not to the goals themselves, which for him had been 'immoveable' since the twenties.

In a speech to commanders of potential front-line troops in Berlin on 10 February 1939, Hitler described his foreign policy in these terms:

> . . .none of the individual decisions which have been put into effect since 1933 are the result of momentary deliberations, but represent the implementation of an existing plan, although perhaps not according to the anticipated timetable, that is to say, in 1933, for example, it was naturally not quite clear when we would leave the League of Nations. What was clear was that leaving must be the first step to German renewal. And it was also clear that the first suitable moment for this step had to be taken. It was planned from the beginning that the next step would then have to be internal rearmament, only it was naturally not possible to predict the

timescale precisely from the first moment, or, shall we say, to keep track of the precise extent of rearmament. It was further obvious that after a certain period, after a specific point in time in this rearmament process Germany would take the great risk of proclaiming its right to rearm to the world.

The actual timing of this step could naturally not be foreseen at the beginning. And finally it was also obvious that each further step forward must bring about the remilitarisation of the Rhineland. Here too, the timetable was set for a year later; I had in mind not to implement this until 1937. Circumstances at the time seemed to indicate that this step should be taken in 1936. In the same way it was quite clear that in order further to secure Germany's political future, and particularly its military-political position, the Austrian and Czechoslovakian problems would have to be solved. . . . And therefore these decisions have not been ideas put into effect the moment they were thought up, but they were long-standing plans, which I was resolved in advance to implement at the precise moment at which I thought that the general circumstances would be favourable.[15]

Although Hitler overstates the planned nature of his activity, this description is basically apt. It would be an exaggeration to say that Hitler had a previously worked out foreign policy 'plan', especially as he had initially not developed any firm ideas about how, and in what manner, he could realise his goals. But the example of his attitude to Britain demonstrates the great extent to which he considered himself bound by the foreign policy scheme he developed in the early twenties.

Countless of Hitler's comments show that the idea of an Anglo-German alliance underpinning the conquest of 'living space' he sought in the East remained the central pillar of his foreign policy. Two months after the conclusion of the Anglo-German Naval Agreement, which Hitler regarded as a step in this direction, Goebbels made a note of the outcome of a conversation with Hitler, in which the latter gave a sketch of his future foreign policy goals: with Britain he aimed for a 'permanent alliance', as against 'expansion in the East'.[16] However Hitler increasingly had to recognise that Britain was not ready for an agreement on the basis he laid down. 'The Führer is complaining bitterly about Britain', Goebbels wrote in his diary on 13 November 1936. 'First they will and then they won't. Their leadership has no flair.'[17] The difficulties in the way of the alliance with Britain led Hitler to consider alternative ideas of how he could put his manifesto into effect, if necessary without Britain. For a time he came under the influence of Ribbentrop, who had developed an anti-British alternative to Hitler's policy. However he still clung to the hope that the British would finally see the light and agree to his idea of a division of the world. This is also demonstrated by the proposals he submitted to Britain in the final days before the attack on Poland, in which he declared himself prepared to guarantee British overseas possessions if the British gave him a free hand in the East in exchange.

When Britain and France declared war on Germany on 3 September 1939, two days after Hitler's attack on Poland, the failure of Hitler's foreign policy became obvious. He had been deceived in his hope that he would succeed in isolating Poland and keeping the Western powers out of the conflict. Hitler found himself at war with his desired ally, Britain, and had had to ally himself with Russia, which he really aimed to conquer. But Hitler did not give up hope for the emergence of an Anglo-German alliance even after the outbreak of war. The offers of peace directed to Britain after the end of the Polish campaign and once again after the victory over France were intended quite seriously. On 1 November 1939 Rosenberg noted the results of a talk with Hitler:

> The Führer remarked on several occasions that he still thought an Anglo-German agreement was the correct solution, particularly in the long term, . . . that we had done everything possible but that they were in the grip of an insane minority led by Jews. Chamberlain was a weak old man and it looked as if they would not see sense before they had had a fearful beating. He said he did not understand what they actually wanted. Even if the British did actually win, the real victors would be the United States, Japan and Russia. Britain would be in tatters at the end of a war, to say nothing of what it would be like if it was militarily *defeated*.[18]

Goebbels, too, reports in his diary that Hitler declared after the victory over France that he believed the British Empire must be preserved, if at all possible. The Führer still had a 'very positive attitude' to Britain, 'in spite of everything', and wanted to give it 'one last chance'.[19]

After Britain had indicated that it was not willing to enter into an alliance, a plan to attack the Soviet Union began to take shape in Hitler's mind. He justified this by saying he must anticipate Stalin's plans for expansion and at the same time knock the 'continental dagger' out of Britain's hand. It may be that Hitler had convinced himself and others that war against Russia was inevitable for these reasons. But the attack on Russia was primarily the expression of his long-established 'living space' plans, which he now believed he could tackle, even though the political alliances which were its preconditions were not in place.

Operation Barbarossa differed from the outset from the war against the western powers. Hitler's infamous 'commission order', in which he gave orders that the Red Army was all, without exception, to be shot, if taken in battle or when resisting, proves, as do the murderous activities of the 'task forces', to whom about one million Jews fell victim, that Hitler planned and directed the war against Russia from the outset as an ideological campaign of annihilation.

At the high point of his power, when he could hope to win the war against Russia, he revealed his future plans to his close advisers. He was indifferent to the fate of the people in the 'living space' he conquered.

> There is only one task: to set about the Germanisation of the land by bringing in Germans and to regard the original inhabitants as Red Indians. . . . I am approaching this matter with ice-cold resolve. I feel that I am the executor of the will of history. What people think of me for the moment is completely immaterial to me.[20] . . . According to the eternal law of nature, rights to land belong to whoever conquers it, because their old borders do not offer enough space for population growth.[21]

Hitler's interest in Russian territory was primarily in exploiting it economically. The newly-won territory was to be used to settle farmers, and over and above this Russia's immeasurable supplies of raw materials and energy were to form the basis of a self-supporting supranational economy and make possible a huge expansion in German industry.

The view that Hitler linked the conquest of Russia to renewed agrarianism in German society is not correct. He admired the technical and industrial achievements of the United States and wanted to make Germany into a modern, highly industrialised state. However the model of the private, capitalist economy of the USA did not seem to him to be worth copying. He did value the principle of economic competition, which he interpreted as a manifestation of the Social Darwinist process of selection, but he was increasingly sceptical about the system of the 'free market economy'. Conflicts with industry about the so-called 'Four Year Plan' (1936) and the successful use of the tool of state intervention in the economy made him more and more of a convinced critic of the private enterprise economic system. He even admired the planned economy of the Soviet Union and was convinced of its superiority to a capitalist economic system. In a discussion on 27.7.1942 he declared that Stalin's economic planning was so comprehensive 'that it is probably only bettered by our Four Year Plans.' For him it was beyond any doubt that there had been no unemployment in the USSR, in contrast to capitalist states, like for example the USA.[22]

His attitude to Stalin and the Soviet Union changed fundamentally during the Russian campaign. Where he had spoken earlier of 'Jewish Bolshevism' and of Stalin as the representative of international Jewry, now he had arrived at the view that Stalin was conducting a Russian nationalist policy in the manner of Peter the Great and had freed Russia from Jewish influence. Wilhelm Scheidt reports:

Hitler began to have a secret admiration for Stalin. From then on his hatred was shaped by envy. . . . He clung to the hope that he could defeat Bolshevism with its own methods if he copied it in Germany and the occupied territories. More and more frequently he pointed to the Russian method as a model for his colleagues. 'We cannot conduct this battle for our existence without their toughness and ruthlessness.' He rejected all objections as bourgeois.[23]

After the failed coup attempt of 20 July 1944, in which military leaders from the aristocracy in particular took a leading role, Hitler even regretted that he had not liquidated the old elites, as Stalin had done. In addition it was now becoming clear that Hitler's evaluation of the traditional bourgeois and aristocratic elites had been wrong, when he had thought that they were weak, cowardly and incapable of real resistence. At a convention of National and District leaders on 24 February 1945 he said, 'We have liquidated the left wing class warriors, but unfortunately in so doing we forgot to strike out to the right as well. That is our greatest sin of omission.'[24] In the face of defeat Hitler looked for reasons and for those responsible for his failure.

> In the absence of an elite as we envisaged it we had to make do with the human material to hand. And this is the result! Because the intellectual concept could not be wedded to a practical and practicable implementation of the idea, the war policy of a revolutionary state like the Third Reich necessarily became the policy of reactionary petty bourgeois.[25]

In terms of foreign policy he saw the reasons for his failure in the policy of the British, who had not taken up his offer of alliances, a policy which for him was incomprehensible. He accused Churchill of having conducted the traditional British 'balance of power' policy, in spite of the fact that in its old form it no longer conformed to the requirements of the time.

> It is not possible simply to copy the successful theories of times gone by. Today's reality, which has changed the face of the world, is the existence of two colossi, the United States of America and the Soviet Union. The Britain of the great Pitt was able to hold the world in balance by preventing the emergence of a hegemonial state in Europe. Present day reality ought to have forced Churchill to agree to the unification of Europe in order to secure the political balance of the world of the twentieth century.[26]

At the end of his life Hitler was forced to concede the failure of his entire plan for internal and foreign alliances. It has been said that a decisive factor in Hitler's domestic and foreign policy *successes* was that his enemies in Germany and abroad underestimated him. Papen's idea of 'taming' him, and the British policy of appeasement are given as examples of this misjudgement. It is equally justifiable to say that Hitler's *failure* was a consequence of *his* misjudgement of those who underestimated him. He did succeed in his domestic policy in restraining the influence of the conservatives who wanted to 'box him in' and 'tame' him. But nonetheless he was still forced to rely to a great extent on the old elites in the bureaucracy, the economy and the military. These were only National Socialist to a slight degree. In some spheres and stages of his policies they joined in because they agreed with Hitler. In other spheres however they had an inhibiting influence on the implementation of National Socialist ideology. And leading men in the German resistance were recruited from the ranks of the conservative elites, and from 1938 onwards they made very serious preparations for an assassination and coup. In the face of defeat Hitler's judgement was that:

> our generals and our diplomats are with few exceptions yesterday's men who are conducting the policies and a war of times gone by. This is as true of the sincere ones as it is for the others. Some fail because of lack of ability or enthusiasm, the others fully intend to sabotage us.[27]

In terms of foreign policy Hitler had succeeded with his policy of 'accomplished facts' in scoring a series of triumphant successes and in forcing the Western powers into making decisive concessions. But Britain was never prepared to play the part Hitler intended for it. This caused his entire policy of alliances to collapse.

Would the course of history have been different without these mutual misjudgements? Would another 'Führer' have followed similar policies and would he have been underestimated in the same way? Doubt is admissable, there is no definite answer.

NOTES

1. Hitler, *Mein Kampf*, p. 6.
2. Hitler's letter to Adolf Gemlich dated 16.9.1919, *Sämtliche Aufzeichnungen*, p. 88ff.
3. Ibid., p. 1014, speech dated 16.9.1923.
4. Ibid., p. 250, speech dated 26.10.1920.
5. Ibid., p. 912, speech dated 24.4.1923.

6. Ibid., p. 698, speech dated 28.9.1922.
7. Ibid., p. 247, speech dated 18.10.1920.
8. Ibid., p. 436, Hitler to the committee of the NSDAP, 14.7.1921.
9. Hitler, *Mein Kampf*, p. 157.
10. BA/NS26/52, Bl. 14ff, speech dated 6.8.1927.
11. Hitler, *Zweites Buch*, p. 80.
12. Preiss, p. 189, speech dated 4.9.1932.
13. Hitler's essay, published in *Illustrierter Beobachter*, edition 5, no. 6, dated 8.2.1930, p. 85.
14. Otto Dietrich, *Zwölf Jahre mit Hitler* (Cologne 1955) p. 126.
15. Hitler's speech dated 10.2.1939 to commanders of active service units in Berlin, BA/NS 11/28, now also published in: K.-J. Müller, *Armee und Drittes Reich 1933–1939* (Paderborn, 1987) here p. 365f.
16. *Goebbels – Tagebücher, Sämtliche Fragmente*, vol. II, entry dated 19.8.1935, p. 504.
17. Ibid., p. 724, entry dated 13.11.1936.
18. *Das politische Tagebuch Alfred Rosenbergs 1934/35 und 1939/40*, edited by H.-G. Seraphim (Göttingen, 1956) p. 85, entry dated 1.11.1939.
19. *Goebbels-Tagebücher, Sämtliche Fragmente*, vol. IV, p. 218 (25.6.1940), p. 234 (9.7.1940), p. 225 (3.7.1940).
20. *Monologe*, p. 91, entry: 17.10.1941.
21. Ibid., p. 242, entry: 28/29.1.1942.
22. Picker, p. 452, entry: 22.7.1942.
23. Captain (retd) Dr W. Scheidt, Nachkriegsaufzeichnungen, vol. IV. IfZ Munich, Sammlung Irving.
24. As it appears in N. von Below, *Als Hitlers Adjutant 1937–45* (Mainz, 1980) p. 403.
25. Bormann-Diktate, p. 73, entry dated 14.2.1945.
26. Ibid., p. 42f. entry dated 4.2.1945.
27. Ibid., p. 73, entry dated 14.2.1945.

BIBLIOGRAPHY

Primary Sources

Hitler's early speeches and essays have been most fully documented in E. Jäckel/A. Kuhn (eds), *Hitler. Sämtliche Aufzeichnungen 1905–1924* (Stuttgart, 1980) referred to as: *Sämtliche Aufzeichnungen*). There is no comparable collection for the later years. Neither is there, unfortunately, any critical edition of the book Hitler wrote in 1925/27, *Mein Kampf* (quoted here in the 419th-423rd edition (Munich, 1939)). The essays he wrote for the *Illustrierter Beobachter* have seldom been published, nor have the many speeches dating from the years 1925–32. Some speeches from this period are published in H. Preiss (ed.), *Adolf Hitler in Franken, Reden aus der Kampfzeit* (Nuremberg, 1939). The book Hitler wrote in 1928, *Zweites Buch*, was never published in his lifetime: *Hitlers Zweites Buch. Ein Dokument aus dem Jahre 1928*, edited and with a commentary by G.L. Weinberg (Stuttgart, 1961). For the years 1933–45 scholars often resort to the collection edited by Domarus. Some of the speeches by Hitler collected there have been arbitrarily edited; the editor's commentary is more annoying than helpful: M. Domarus, *Hitler, Reden und Proklamationen 1932–1945. Kommentiert von einem deutschen Zeitgenossen* (Wiesbaden, 1973). Many of the speeches which are only represented by excerpts in Domarus were published as pamphlets by Eher-Verlag (Munich). P. Bouhler compiled an indispensable collection of speeches from the years 1939–42: *Der grossdeutsche Freiheitskampf. Reden Adolf Hitlers, vol. I/II: 1.9.39–16.3.1941, vol. III: 16.3.1941–15.3.1942* (Munich, 1940–3). Some of Hitler's so-called 'secret speeches' can be found in H. Kotze/H. Krausnick (eds), *'Es spricht der Führer'. 7 exemplarische Hitler-Reden* (Gütersloh, 1966). One of the most important sources for the study of Hitler is the Goebbels diaries (see the chapter on Goebbels in this book). Also useful, although with some reservations, are Wagener's memoirs. He held numerous conversations with Hitler in the period 1929–32: O. Wagener, *Hitler aus nächster Nähe. Aufzeichnungen eines Vertrauten 1929–1932*. Edited by H.A. Turner (Frankfurt am Main-Berlin-Vienna, 1978). The memoirs of the former president of the Danzig Senate are controversial: H. Rauschning, *Gespräche mit Hitler* (Zurich, 1940). In contrast to Th. Schieder, *Hermann Rauschnings 'Gespräche mit Hitler' als Geschichtsquelle* (Opladen, 1972), F. Tobias and W. Hänel are sceptical of its usefulness as a source: F. Tobias, 'Auch Fälschungen haben lange Beine. Des Senatspräsidenten Rauschnings "Gespräche mit Hitler"', in K. Corino (ed.), *Gefälscht. Betrug in Literatur, Kunst, Musik, Wissenschaft und Politik* (Nördlingen, 1988) pp. 91–105; W. Hänel, *Hermann Rauschnings 'Gespräche mit Hitler' – eine Geschichtsfälschung* (Ingolstadt, 1984). The Hitler-Breiting conversations, which were originally regarded by many historians as an important source, have in the meantime proved to be forgeries: E. Calic (ed.), *Ohne Maske. Hitler-Breiting-Geheimgesprähe 1931* (Frankfurt am Main, 1968). See also K.-H. Janssen, 'Calics Erzählungen', in U. Backes *et al.*, *Reichstagsbrand. Aufklärung einer historischen Legende* (Munich, 1987) pp. 216–38. The much-quoted, presumed record of conversations between Hitler and Otto Strasser on 21/22 May 1930 (in O. Strasser, *Mein Kampf* (Frankfurt am Main, 1969) pp. 50–68) can only be used with great reservations. On the other hand the record of Hitler's conversations with statesmen and diplomats in the war years is an important, indispensable source: A. Hillgruber (ed.), *Staatsmänner und Diplomaten bei Hitler. Vertrauliche Aufzeichnungen über Unterredungen mit Vertretern des Auslandes 1939–1944*, 2 vols (Frankfurt am Main, 1967 and 1970). Hitler's 'Tischgespräche' give a valuable insight into Hitler's thinking. While the so-called 'Koeppen-Vermerke' are accessible in the Bundesarchiv Koblenz (R/6/34a, Fol. 1–82), the records of Heim and Picker have been published: *Monologe im Führer-hauptquartier 1941–1944. Die Aufzeichnungen Heinrich Heims*, edited by W. Jochmann (Hamburg, 1980) (referred to as *Monologe*); *Hitlers Tischgespräche im Führerhauptquartier 1941–42* (Wiesbaden, 1973) (referred to as Picker). Finally, the so-called Bormann-Diktate should be mentioned: *Hitlers Politisches Testament. Die Bormann-Diktate vom Februar und April 1945* (Hamburg, 1981).

Secondary Literature

The best survey of research on Hitler is by G. Schreiber, *Hitler. Interpretationen 1923–83*, 2nd., revised edition, with an annotated bibliography for the years 1984–7 (Darmstadt, 1988). There is also an excellent survey of the controversies of Hitler research in K. Hildebrand, *Das Dritte Reich* (Munich, 1987). However the reader of W. Wippermann (ed.), *Kontroversen um Hitler* (Frankfurt am Main, 1986) learns less about Hitler than about theories on fascism and totalitarianism. I. Kershaw's book *Der NS-Staat. Geschichtsinterpretationen und Kontroversen im*

Überblick (Reinbek bei Hamburg, 1988) is useful for the chapters dealing with the controversies about Hitler's role in Nazi policy on Jews and foreign policy, but other parts of the book are problematical.

Biographies of Hitler are now so numerous as to be almost unmanageable. We can name only K. Heiden, *Adolf Hitler. Eine Biographie. Vol. I: Das Zeitalter der Verantwortungslosigkeit, vol. II: Ein Mann gegen Europa* (Zurich, 1936/37); W. Görlitz/H.A. Quint, *Adolf Hitler. Eine Biographie* (Stuttgart, 1952); A. Bullock, *Hitler. A Study in Tyranny* (London, 1951), new German edition 1967; E. Deuerlein, *Hitler. Eine politische Biographie* (Munich, 1969); J.C. Fest, *Hitler. Eine Biographie* (Berlin, Frankfurt am Main, 1973). Although Fest's study is less firmly rooted in original source studies, it is a milestone in National Socialist historiography, because it marks out a convincing interpretative framework and at the same time integrates its results with those of contemporary research. David Irving, in his biographical study, *Hitler's War* (London, Sydney, 1977), examined countless new sources, but the book has to be viewed with some scepticism, especially those sections dealing with Hitler's role in the 'final solution'. Irving deals with the years 1933–9 in *Hitlers Weg zum Krieg* (Munich-Berlin, 1979). Anyone with an interest in the personal details of Hitler's life should look at the biographies by Maser and Toland, although these contribute little, if anything to our understanding of Hitler the politician: W. Maser, *Adolf Hitler. Legende, Mythos, Wirklichkeit* (Munich, 1974); J. Toland, *Adolf Hitler* (Bergisch Gladbach, 1981). A. Tyrell, *Vom 'Trommler' zum 'Führer'. Der Wandel von Hitlers Selbstverständnis zwischen 1919 und 1924 und die Entwicklung der NSDAP* (Munich, 1975) is essential for an understanding of Hitler's early years in politics. R. Zitelmann, *Adolf Hitler. Eine politische Biographie* (Göttingen-Zurich, 1989) is based on the author's more comprehensive work (see below). In this biography the Goebbels diaries are for the first time extensively consulted, as befits their importance. More concerned with the 'image' than the person is I. Kershaw, *Der Hitler-Mythos. Volksmeinung und Propaganda im Dritten Reich* (Stuttgart, 1980).

On the subject of Hitler's philosophy, we should mention E. Jäckel, *Hitlers Weltanschauung* (Stuttgart, 1969, new, revised and expanded edition, Stuttgart, 1981). However it is important not to read this work uncritically, since Jäckel gives a very one-sided view of the dictator's philosophy, reduced to its racial and foreign policy components. Before Jäckel, E. Nolte had pointed to the consistent nature of Hitler's ideology: *Der Faschismus in seiner Epoche. Action Française, Italienischer Faschismus, Nationalsozialismus* (Munich, 1963). At the forefront of the author's work on Hitler are Hitler's social, economic and domestic goals: R. Zitelmann, *Hitler. Selbstverständnis eines Revolutionärs*, 2nd revised and expanded edition (Stuttgart, 1989). An important aspect of Hitler's philosophy is dealt with in V. Tallgren, *Hitler und die Helden. Heroismus und Weltanschauung* (Helsinki, 1981).

Hitler's long-term foreign policy goals are the subject of countless studies; A. Hillgruber, *Hitlers Strategie. Politik und Kriegführung 1940–1941* (Frankfurt am Main, 1965); K. Hildebrand, *Deutsche Aussenpolitik 1939–1945. Kalkül oder Dogma?* (Stuttgart-Berlin, 1980); J. Thies, *Architekt der Weltherrschaft. Die 'Endziele' Hitlers* (Dusseldorf, 1977). In contrast to these works, which come to an understanding of Hitler's 'final goal' as world domination, G. Stoakes, like E. Jäckel (see above), regards Hitler's goals as being 'limited' to the conquest of a continental empire with the annexation of 'living space' in the East: G. Stoakes, *Hitler and the Quest for World Dominion. Nazi Ideology and Foreign Policy in the 1920s* (Leamington Spa, Hamburg, New York, 1986). A.J.P. Taylor reaches a conclusion on Hitler's foreign policy which differs from all the authors mentioned in his 'revisionist' study: *Die Ursprünge des Zweiten Weltkrieges* (Gütersloh, 1962). The following collections of articles contain countless essential contributions about Hitler's foreign policy: W. Michalka (ed.), *Nationalsozialistische Aussenpolitik* (Darmstadt, 1978); G. Niedhart (ed.), *Kriegsbeginn 1939. Entfesselung oder Ausbruch des Zweiten Weltkrieges?* (Darmstadt, 1976); M. Funke (ed.), *Hitler, Deutschland und die Mächte. Materialien zur Aussenpolitik des Dritten Reiches* (Kronberg i. Ts., 1978); K. Malettke (ed.), *Der Nationalsozialismus an der Macht* (Göttingen, 1984).

On the subject of the early history of the holocaust, only sketched in the present contribution: E. Jäckel/J. Rohwer (eds), *Der Mord an den Juden im Zweiten Weltkrieg. Entschlussbildung und Verwirklichung* (Stuttgart, 1985). The 'intentionalist' explanatory model is very vigorously represented by E. Jäckel, *Hitlers Herrschaft. Vollzug einer Weltanschauung* (Stuttgart, 1986). For the 'functionalist' explanatory model see M. Broszat, 'Hitler und die Genesis der "Endlösung". Aus Anlass der Thesen von David Irving', now in H. Graml/K.D. Henke (eds), *Nach Hitler. Der Schwierige Umgang mit unserer Geschichte* (Munich, 1986) pp. 187–229; H. Mommsen, 'Die Realisierung des Utopischen: Die "Endlösung der Judenfrage" im "Dritten Reich"' in W. Wippermann (see above) pp. 248–98.

On Hitler's economic theories, which have only recently become the subject of intensive research, see: H.A. Turner, 'Hitler's Einstellung zu Wirtschaft und Gesellschaft vor 1933', in *Geschichte und Gesellschaft (GuG)*, 1976, pp. 87–117. For a criticism of this which the present author finds convincing: A. Barkai, 'Sozialdarwinismus und Antiliberalismus in Hitlers Wirtschaftskonzept', in *GuG*, 1977, pp. 406–17. The fundamentally important article by P. Krüger, 'Zu Hitlers "nationalsozialistischen Wirtschaftserkenntnissen"', in *GuG*, 1980, pp. 263–82, should also be mentioned. See also L. Herbst, *Der totale Krieg und die Ordnung der Wirtschaft. Die Kriegswirtschaft im Spannungsfeld von Politik, Ideologie und Propaganda 1939–1945* (Stuttgart, 1982) which is also concerned on pp. 84–92 with Hitler's economic policies. A chapter about Hitler and foreign trade 'Hitler und Aussenhandel' (pp. 206–17) is contained in E. Teichert, *Autarkie und Grossraumwirtschaft in Deutschland 1930–1939. Aussenwirtschaftspolitische Konzeptionen zwischen Wirtschaftskrise und Zweitem Weltkrieg* (Munich, 1984). The view of Hitler's 'Nationalökonomie' which H.A. Turner had already developed in other places is now contained in one chapter of his work: *Die Grossaufnehmer und der Aufstieg Hitlers* (Berlin, 1985). However Turner overestimates the agrarian component in Hitler's economic theories.

12 Ernst Kaltenbrunner: Chief of Reich Security Main Office

Peter Black

It is well known that Hitler valued ambitious colleagues whose private and public interests were identical. One such individual was Ernst Kaltenbrunner, the last chief of the Reich Security Main Office (RSHA). This fanatical supporter of Nazi ideology, a single-minded pragmatist within the organisational chaos of the Third Reich, advanced within a few years to one of the most important key positions.

The reasons for Kaltenbrunner clinging so rigidly to Nazi principles such as 'racial purity', the need 'to conquer living space' and the 'Führer state' can probably be traced back to the state of near pathological fear in which many members of the middle classes in German Austria had lived through the final decades of the Habsburg monarchy. A good many German Austrians responded to the constant demands of other nationalities for equal rights in politics, the language issue and the prolonged battles for reasonable proportionality, both in the civil service and in education, with an even more pronounced longing for dependency on the German Reich, even to the extent of having visions of a future 'Greater German Reich', encompassing all people of German race. Based on social Darwinist theories of inequality or of the eternal struggle between 'races', the 'German-minded' extremists of the Habsburg monarchy even then wanted to do away with what they called their 'Cohen-nationals' (by which they meant Jews, nearly all of whom were fully assimilated) and if possible all other non-German fellow citizens, on the grounds that they were biologically and culturally inferior. Anyone who opposed their endeavours – from Catholic priests and liberals, whom they regarded as being far too tolerant, to orthodox Marxists, from Hungarian separatists to those who were pro-Slav or pan-Slavist, up to and including the Zionists, whose movement was then in its early stages – was declared their mortal enemy.

Nowhere in Austria did this 'greater German' chauvinism have such zealous supporters as among the members of the German nationalist student fraternities at the universities. In these duelling societies any 'compromises' were regarded as a betrayal of the 'idea'. The strict rules and the rituals practised in the fraternities (such as duelling and the questioning of honor that permitted one to challenge or accept a challenge to a duel) encouraged a specific mental disposition in their members: severity towards oneself and an arrogant and contemptuous attitude to 'unworthy' people were regarded as virtues. From 1893 to 1898, Kaltenbrunner's father was one of the active members of the German nationalist students' fraternity called 'Arminia' at Graz University. This association had long since barred Jews from membership, took part in anti-Slav demonstrations and supported the policies of Georg von Schönerer, the well-known forerunner of Hitler.

Ernst Kaltenbrunner was born on 4 October 1903, the son of a senior lawyer in Ried in the Inn district. He spent his childhood and youth in Raab (Upper Austria) and Linz and received the stamp of his German nationalism primarily from his parental home. His father, who played a full part in society and who was comfortably off by the standards of the day, was also a passionate supporter of union with Germany. Both in Raab and in Linz he confined his contacts with local Jews to what was professionally unavoidable. As a convinced anti-cleric he was annoyed when his son took part in religious services at school as an altar boy. But the father's concern that his son might come under too great clerical influence was to prove unfounded. Even during his high school days in Linz (1913–21), Ernst was a member of the pronouncedly anti-clerical schoolboys' association called 'Hohenstaufen', and not just as a mere fellow traveller.[1]

From 1921 to 1926, Kaltenbrunner junior studied law in Graz, where he joined the same students' fraternity as his father. Taking a leading role at local and regional level as a representative of the association, along with others he organised not only demonstrations and boycotts directed against Jewish students and professors, but also events directed against the Catholic-monarchist association 'Carolina' and various foreign students' associations. The populist ethnic (*völkisch*) philosophy of the pre-war era and the enemies associated with it had scarcely changed, but the circumstances under which Kaltenbrunner's 'Arminia' believed they had to fight for them probably had. The lost war and the revolution seemed to many of them to be the realisation of the nightmare which had haunted them for half a century: a coalition of churchmen and Marxists seemed to rule over the mutilated remains of Austria, the union of which with Germany had been expressly forbidden by the victorious powers.

Kaltenbrunner and his friends suspected that the real puppet-masters behind the successor states to the Austrian Empire, which feared for their very existence, and behind the governments in Rome, Paris, London, Moscow and Washington were the Jews. They suspected the Jews not only of having incited the Western powers to prevent the German states from joining together by means of the peace treaties, and of holding back the losers economically by means of the unrealistic reparations payments, but also of nurturing in domestic politics the centrifugal forces of social collapse in order further to weaken Austria and render a revival of German Austria impossible. In view of these circumstances, particular mistrust was aroused by all the measures taken by the government in Vienna in favour of the Jews of rump Austria. These measures were not interpreted by dyed-in-the-wool anti-semites alone as an indication of the continued favour given to a minority who, it was said, had made no particular contribution to the common good; in anti-semitic circles, however, they were also represented as direct incitement to 'cultural subjugation' and the 'sexual enslavement of the host people' – as it was called in their inflammatory jargon. Kaltenbrunner himself, for example, decades later took no little pride in the fact that, even as a young member of a students' association, he had traced 'alien influences, detrimental to morality and culture' back to their 'originators' and 'in his readiness to fight the Jews' had not only denounced them but doggedly 'fought against them'.[2]

So, sure as fate, Kaltenbrunner ended up in 1930 in the NSDAP and in 1933 in the SS. In his case economic factors only played a limited role. In 1929, the probationary lawyer from Linz-Urfahr had joined Prince Starhemberg's '*Heimatschutz*' (Home Guard). After Starhemberg's unsuccessful negotiations with the National Socialists, Mussolini and the Christian Social Party, Kaltenbrunner, disappointed with Starhemberg's indecision and the drift of the *Heimatschutz* into clerical issues, made a clear decision to join the NSDAP.[3] His joining the elitist SS can probably largely be explained by the 'anti-proletarian' tradition of the students' fraternities.

Neither the Party's wavering course during the time when it was proscribed, nor his being left out in the cold as Secretary of State for Security or as senior Police and SS Chief in Vienna (1938–43) made him doubt his political convictions. He achieved his desired goal on 30 January 1943, when Himmler appointed him as successor to Heydrich as chief of the Reich Security Main Office, which had been created in 1939 and encompassed the Gestapo, the criminal police and the SD.

His prime aim was, as ever, a united, 'racially pure' Reich. Jews, Slavs, communists, Social Democrats, trade unionists, Catholic clerics, Centre Party supporters, Freemasons, 'serious students of the Bible' and others who would not submit to Nazi ideology were still persecuted as 'enemies of the state'. Things were more complicated in the occupied territories; the course of the war compelled more and more 'deviations' from the former hard line. But even in 1943–4, for as long as the balance of power seemed to permit it, the RSHA was careful not to enter into any agreements with 'sub-humans' simply for the sake of tactical advantage.

The RSHA was least open to making concessions, under Kaltenbrunner's aegis as before, in the 'Jewish question', the solution to which Kaltenbrunner sometimes saw as an even greater priority than did his immediate superior, Heinrich Himmler. When Kaltenbrunner suggested 'reducing the overcrowding' in the 'old people's ghetto', Theresienstadt, by transporting 5000 elderly, infirm Jews to Auschwitz, he was rebuffed by the *Reichsführer* – *SS*.[4] As a lawyer, Kaltenbrunner was always interested in formal legal regulations, even for Jews who were to be deported or had already been deported. Although the Justice Ministry and the Ministry of the Interior already regarded such regulations as partially obsolete in 1943, Kaltenbrunner insisted, for example, on special decrees to permit the property of deported Jews being passed to the state on their death, which put foreign Jews on German-controlled territory on the same legal footing as home Jews, so that those who had foreign passports could be included in the annihilation programme and other similar measures.

When the occupation of Hungary in March 1944 seemed to make it possible to seize Hungarian Jews and deport them to Auschwitz, Kaltenbrunner traveled personally to Budapest to discuss the guidelines for seizing and deporting Jews with the 'Jewish experts' in the new government. That he was not simply acting out of opportunism, but was really convinced that the Jews were Germany's most important opponents, is proved by a statement he made after the war, during his interrogation in the course of the Nuremberg trials, according to which the Jews were not only supposed to be the chief representatives of bolshevik philosophy, but the central pillar of *every* oppositional act; the more so since the Jews were almost the only intellectuals, in exclusive control of all business and 'therefore in general terms the class in society which was sufficiently intellectualised to give the enemy the necessary agent for the implementation of his plans'.[5]

Kaltenbrunner also proceeded against other opponents of National Socialism with the same rigour and ruthlessness. On 5 November 1942, the RSHA had promulgated a decree according to which, with immediate effect, not the justiciary but the police force alone was to deal with crimes committed by Poles and Soviet Russians. The justification for this was that 'alien and racially inferior people' presented a particular danger to the German people.[6] In an ordinance of 30 June 1943, Kaltenbrunner added in an appendix that during the processing of these criminal cases it was to be borne in mind that Poles and Russians simply by the fact of their presence in lands ruled by Germans presented a threat to German 'racial order', for which reason it was 'not so important' to find a suitable punishment for the crimes they had committed as to prevent them from 'further endangering . . . German 'racial order'.[7]

Kaltenbrunner showed little understanding for the German national conservative opponents of the Nazi regime, not only because he thought he knew the type particularly well from his own experience, but also because he criticised them for not having become National Socialists, in spite of their undoubtedly 'racial suitability'. For him, National Socialism was the 'eternal religion' of his own people.[8] For this reason the head of the RSHA, who on other occasions often seemed taciturn, frequently clearly showed his disappointment, which in the case of officers could amount to what was almost pathological hatred, if they, in spite of the oath they had taken to Hitler personally, refused to show loyalty to the Nazi regime, even if only on certain points. He pursued the resistance centred around Canaris to the death, and not just out of duty or professional envy. Kaltenbrunner also followed the announcements relating to the assassination attempt of 20 July 1944 with great interest. He not only used them as a pretext to draw Hitler's attention to the many inadequacies and defects in the Nazi leadership, some of which the SD had been aware of for some time,[9] but also took advantage of the opportunity to warn the 'Führer' persistently about the dangerous attitude of certain 'reactionary' circles, primarily in the officer corps. In one of the relevant reports, dated October 1944, on the supposed politically incorrect attitude of certain 'mere soldiers', the RSHA even went so far as to claim that a certain portion of the officer corps felt itself 'in no way' emotionally bound to the National Socialist Reich and its Führer: the oath of loyalty to Adolf Hitler was regarded no differently from that to Ebert in its day.[10]

His bitterness towards German reactionaries even showed itself before the International Tribunal in Nuremberg. Defended by a Catholic lawyer who felt himself obliged to admit his client's guilt, on one occasion an enraged Kaltenbrunner attacked the defence lawyer for the SS, saying the accused and their 'followers' had tried to 'build a dam against the flood from the east . . . with blood and living bodies'. As the outcome showed, this had not been successful. 'We were still too soft. People like you slipped past us and escaped.'[11] At the end of his life, Kaltenbrunner really seems to have been convinced that he had not acted quickly enough or thoroughly enough in implementing his purge. He drilled into his children that there had been 'so much treachery and shoddiness' that now even 'those who were completely unqualified' felt they could talk of 'degenerate' National Socialism. In reality only a few people had failed and no-one had been there 'to see to them in time'.[12]

It was probably his firm conviction that the 'idea' could not be contradicted by the course of external events which enabled Kaltenbrunner to maintain this attitude until his execution on 16 October 1946. He once remarked to his defence lawyer that he did not take 'words spoken today' terribly seriously. All that mattered for him was to believe in eternity and to express his convictions.[13] He held firm to his principles, as he always had done. Until the very last he professed the view that the political and religious contradictions in Germany could be resolved by National Socialism alone, taking 'race' as its fundamental value. There was no other way of achieving a genuine 'national community'. In his view only National Socialism was capable of reversing the processes of intellectual and social fragmentation and disintegration set in motion by the French Revolution. There was for him no other way of realising the sense of social responsibility and striving for a 'higher community' which would overcome individualism.[14] Typical of Kaltenbrunner's ideological fervor was the wish he derived from these ideas that his own children should only gather those around them who had been taught 'love of others' by National Socialism.[15]

Of course political orthodoxy was not enough to achieve political power. In the bureaucratic confusion of a system which was so finely tuned to the leadership requirements of its dictator, there was certainly no small degree of skill involved in coordinating the implementation of the measures Hitler considered essential with the directing of one's own career. While he was being promoted through the Austrian SS, Kaltenbrunner placed total reliance on his personal loyalty to Himmler. In addition he knew how to interpret the fluctuations in Austrian domestic politics in conformity with the changing interests of his SS superiors 'by being prescient'. Under the influence of the Austrian Nazi State Peasants' Leader, Reinthaller, whom he had got to know well in the Kaiersteinbruch Internment Camp (near Neusiedl am See),[16] Kaltenbrunner recognised relatively early that Dollfuss and Schuschnigg could not be toppled by terror, propaganda or a coup. There seemed to be more prospect of success in the gradual weakening of the machinery of state by means of infiltrating individuals who were 'emphatically national', like Seyss-Inquart. Even before the unsuccessful coup d'état of 25 July 1934, in which Kaltenbrunner did not take part, Reinthaller had used all his influence with the Nazi sympathizers in the 'national' camp to retrieve at least a degree of scope for political activity again for the NSDAP, which had been banned since May 1933, and which had of course, while illegal, persevered in proselytising among its most promising target groups.

It is possible that Kaltenbrunner first got to know Himmler and Heydrich through Reinthaller, by way of Darré. In any case it was through Heydrich that Kaltenbrunner first came into close contact with the 'Carinthians' who took the helm of the Party after the July coup (Rainer, Globocnik, Klausener).[17] As the leader of the SS Regiment 37 (Linz) from 1934, Kaltenbrunner exploited every chance he got, especially in 1936–7, to make himself indispensable to the leading actors. In association with Upper Austrian government offices and under the protection of 'Nationalists' like Seyss-Inquart and Glaise-Horstenau, who were confidants of the Austrian Chancellor, he took care, while rebuilding the Upper Austrian SS, that where possible there was no violence and no deviation from the course of an evolutionary policy of union with Germany. This was in line with Hitler's new Austrian policy, as expressed in the treaty of 11 July 1936 and in the relevant decrees from Himmler. And in some respects it also fitted in with the Schuschnigg regime, which was manifestly only concerned with maintaining a facade of 'law and order'.

Against the resistance of Josef Leopold, the *Gauleiter* of Lower Austria, Kaltenbrunner was at great pains to make Seyss-Inquart fit to appear 'at court' in Berlin (Rainer and Globocnik were also trying to use him as a trojan horse in their dealings with Schuschnigg). When this tactic produced its first successes, in 1937, it was not only the *Reichsführer – SS* who credited Kaltenbrunner with the success. Rainer and Globocnik also acknowledged Kaltenbrunner's services by providing him with more information on internal Party matters and therefore indirectly increased his value to Berlin as an expert on Austria. Kaltenbrunner had many trusted contacts in the Austrian state apparatus and was also constantly kept informed by a small SD formation in Vienna, so that it was not difficult for him to supply Hitler's plenipotentiary for Austrian affairs, the SS General Keppler, 'at least twice a day via Salzburg' with all the latest news.[18]

Because of his firm control of SS Regiment 37 and the strict observance of the treaty of 11 July 1936, Himmler made Kaltenbrunner the leader of the whole Austrian SS in January 1937, while his predecessor, the SS Oberführer Karl Taus, was ordered never to return to Austria. Even in Nuremberg Seyss-Inquart dubbed Kaltenbrunner the 'policeman of 11 July', referring to his role as guarantor of the treaty.[19]

Kaltenbrunner probably owed his later promotion to head of the RSHA, apart from his loyalty to Himmler, whom he revered as more than a father,[20] chiefly to his reputation for being an excellent source of intelligence. Although Heydrich had attempted to a large degree to keep him out of security affairs in Vienna, Kaltenbrunner had always been committed to representing the interests of the SS and the police as opposed to those of the army, Party and state and energetically promoted the cause of the amalgamation of the SS and police in his area, something Himmler had wanted and which did not go unnoticed in Berlin.[21] The question of Heydrich's successor was originally to have been settled in a different way. As late as October 1942, Himmler had suggested sending Kaltenbrunner as Reich Commissar to Belgium and Northern France. One can only surmise why, after much hesitation, Kaltenbrunner was chosen in preference to an in-house candidate. Did Himmler prefer a weaker man because he would have had more to fear from rivals like Streckenbach, Nebe or Müller? Why did he not bring in people with proven experience in the east, like Prützmann or Jeckeln, instead of an alert, diplomatically skilled Austrian, who had spent the entire war in Vienna and therefore had not even acquired any front-line or partisan warfare experience in the Balkans – still the preferred area for Austrian strategies and politicians practising the principle of 'divide et impera'? What role was played in this context by the 'exemplary' conduct of the 'final solution' in Kaltenbrunner's Austria?

The only thing which appears to be certain is that Kaltenbrunner was regarded as an absolutely reliable supporter of Nazi ideology and a particularly loyal follower of Himmler, who was hardly likely to endanger the latter's position. Significantly, Himmler expressly pointed out during Kaltenbrunner's inauguration that he thought that 'a long training period in illegality' was 'always' a 'good school', 'but particularly for a Head of the State Security Office'.[22] So the right-hand man of the *Reichsführer – SS* and Chief of the German Police' ought not to be a dogmatic 'good civil servant', but a flexible, dynamic activist, a pioneer of the Nazi movement, who was not afraid of responsibility, and was sufficiently well trained, where necessary, to 'take the lead' on his own initiative in the spirit of his highest superiors, without being confined by regulations, never resorting to excuses.[23]

As chief of the RSHA, Kaltenbrunner basically only had to continue what others had already started in the field of security and criminal policing. The duties of the SD, which Himmler wanted to be extended, were more controversial. Kaltenbrunner decisively asserted the right of Office VI (SD-Foreign Affairs) to independent reporting in the face of opposition from Ribbentrop's Foreign Office, and with corresponding consequences for Schellenberg's expanding activities abroad. The investigation of 'breakdowns' in the Auslands/Abwehr Office of the OKW under Canaris ended in 1944 with the SD largely taking over the military intelligence service. In Nuremberg Kaltenbrunner's 'sole source of pride' is supposed to have been a remark by Jodl, chief of Staff of the Armed Forces, that Kaltenbrunner did his job better than his predecessor, Canaris, although Canaris had been an admiral and had thirty years' more experience.[24]

Kaltenbrunner had less success in his struggle with the Party Chancellery over the monopoly of intelligence gathering for the Party at home and over control of Party discipline. Of course even Bormann could appreciate the detailed reports on the conspirators of 20 July 1944, but he had made many objections to the relatively forthright series of briefings produced by Office III (SD-Internal Affairs) under Otto Ohlendorf, not just when the SD over and over again, with relish, spread news of corruption scandals and sensational mistakes in leadership made by some megalomaniac prominent member of the Party in the provinces.[25]

Kaltenbrunner defended himself in vain against the expansion in the authority of the *Gauleiter*, who, as Reich Defense Commissars, were, for example, to take over even certain police functions with regard to foreign workers. However the RSHA tried to avoid open controversies with the Party Chancellery, especially since Kaltenbrunner was dependent on Bormann's goodwill if he wanted direct contact with Hitler. Himmler's understandable misgivings about taking severe measures against Canaris provided opportunities for such contact. The *Reichsführer – SS* (Himmler) was not someone who would enjoy approaching Hitler with unpleasant news. But he was all the more ready to bask in the warmth of Hitler's favour when there was any spectacular success to report – something many of his subordinates did not find very fair. A conjuror who profited from the initiatives of his subordinates, who tried to cash in on all the successes and in the case of failures only gave thought to whom he could send out into the wilderness this time as a punishment, must have been a sore trial to the patience of even the most obliging of subordinates. As a practical intriguer, of course, Kaltenbrunner knew ways and means of emancipating oneself from such an uncongenial superior without arousing any suspicion that one was blatantly going behind his back. Why should a man like Kaltenbrunner, as head of the RSHA, deny himself what even his departmental head in Office VI (Schellenberg) took the liberty of doing, namely of sending important intelligence direct to the Führer's headquarters? Since when was it forbidden to nurture contacts in the antechambers of power?

In order to be able to direct reports to Hitler without Himmler's permission, Kaltenbrunner used the support of Walter Hewel, Ribbentrop's contact in the Führer's headquarters, and later of Hermann Fegelein, Himmler's own liaison officer. Naturally Kaltenbrunner was not to be deprived of accompanying his subordinate Skorzeny to make the announcement to Hitler of Mussolini's 'liberation' in September 1943; he even sat down at the table with them while Skorzeny reported on the course of events in full detail in the presence of Mussolini.

However the close cooperation he nurtured with Bormann in the early summer of 1943 was even more significant. Bormann is said to have always arranged matters so that Kaltenbrunner was called directly to Hitler. According to Schellenberg, this went so far that even Himmler himself lived in constant fear, especially after Himmler's 'peace feelers' of 1944–5. It appears, however, that Kaltenbrunner hardly had any secrets from Himmler to justify such fears. In any case, according to Wilhelm Höttl, it was not possible to speak of any dimming in the trust between Himmler and Kaltenbrunner.[26]

From 1944 to 1945, Kaltenbrunner was beyond any doubt among the most powerful men in the Third Reich. He achieved this position of power not only as a consequence of his ideological links to the Führer and the National Socialist philosophy of racial community. His rise was also a consequence of his resoluteness and above all his ability to recognise and realise Hitler's ideological aims and intentions – in spite of all resistance and bureaucratic impediments. In this respect he was the prototype of Hitler's ideal Nazi leader.

NOTES

1. Interview with Dr Werner Kaltenbrunner, Vöcklabruck, dated 25.3.1977; a note from Wilhelm Pöschl to the author dated 24.5.1977; Kaltenbrunner's 'Memoiren', written for his children in July/August 1946, p. 14, 17f., in Kaltenbrunner's papers.
2. Memoiren (see note 1) p. 32.
3. Ibid., p. 38.
4. Kaltenbrunner to Himmler, Feb. 1943 and the reply dated 16.2.1943, RG-242, T-175/22/2527353–56, National Archives (NA), Washington.

5. Interrogation of Kaltenbrunner dated 19.9.1946, in the archive of the *Institut für Zeitgeschichte* (Munich), ZS-673/II.
6. RSHA-express letter dated 5.11.1942, RG-238, L-316, NA.
7. RSHA-circular dated 30.6.1943 in the *Allgemeine Erlass-Sammlung* of the RSHA, part 2 A IIIf., p. 131, Bundesarchiv Koblenz (BA) RD 19/3.
8. Kaltenbrunner's speech on the occasion of his inauguration as chief of the security police and of the SD on 30.1.1943, Kaltenbrunner IRR files, RG-319, XE000440, NA.
9. Kaltenbrunner to Bormann, dated 30.8.1944 and 16.10.1944 in K.H. Peter (ed.), *Spiegelbild einer Verschwörung: die Kaltenbrunner-Berichte an Bormann und Hitler über das Attentat vom 20. Juli 1944* (Stuttgart, 1961) pp. 325, 447f.; for the SD reports see H. Boberach (ed.), *Meldungen aus dem Reich. Die geheimen Lageberichte des Sicherheitsdienstes des SS 1938–1945*, 17 vols (Herrsching, 1984).
10. A secret memo from Kaltenbrunner dated 24.10.1944 with an enclosure titled 'Der unpolitische Offizier – Der "Nur-Soldat"', RG-242, T-175/281/2774921-39, NA.
11. Carl Haensel, *Das Gericht vertagt sich* (Hamburg, 1950) p. 166.
12. Kaltenbrunner, '*Memoiren*', p. 41.
13. Kaltenbrunner to Kauffmann dated 24.6.1946, in Kaltenbrunner's papers.
14. Ibid.
15. *Memoiren*, p. 17.
16. Reinthaller is also said to have introduced Kaltenbrunner to Franz Langoth of the *Grossdeutsche Volkspartei*, the security chief for Upper Austria, Peter Count Revertera, the military historian Glaise-Horstenau and the Viennese lawyer Seyss-Inquart.
17. Kaltenbrunner had probably met Friedrich Rainer while he was studying law at Graz, since they were the same age.
18. Kaltenbrunner to Keppler, dated 3.9.1937, RG-242, T-120/751/344888, NA.
19. IMT, vol. XVI, p. 78.
20. See the speech mentioned above in note 8.
21. See, for example, Himmler's memo to Kaltenbrunner dated 28.1.1941 in Kaltenbrunner's personal file in the Berlin Document Center.
22. Speech by Himmler dated 30.1.1943, RG-319, Kaltenbrunner IRR files, XE0004400, NA.
23. On encouraging SS members to act on their own initiative, see for example, B. Wegner, *Hitlers politische Soldaten: Die Waffen-SS 1939–1945, Studien zu Leitbild, Struktur und Funktion einer Nationalsozialistische Elite* (Paderborn, 1982) and R.B. Birn, *Die Höheren SS- und Polizeiführer* (Dusseldorf, 1986).
24. Kaltenbrunner, '*Memoiren*', p. 41.
25. See Boberach's sources, note 9.
26. Interrogation of Schellenberg on 13.11.1945, RG-242, NG-4728, NA; interviews with Höttl in Bad Aussee on 14/15.4.1977.

BIBLIOGRAPHY

Primary Sources

The Kaltenbrunner Reports on the conspiracy of 20 July 1944 were first edited by K.H. Peter: *Spiegelbild einer Verschwörung* (Stuttgart, 1961). They are now available in a two-volume edition, with a comprehensive documentary appendix by H.-A. Jacobsen. The memoirs of W. Schellenberg are undoubtedly worth reading: *Aufzeichnungen des letzten Geheimdienstchefs unter Hitler*, with a commentary by Gerald Fleming (Munich, 1981), as are those of W. Höttl, the former section chief in the SD (Foreign Affairs) office: *Die geheime Front* (Linz, 1950); *Unternehmen Bernhard* (Wels, 1955). Further references to primary sources can be found in the author's monograph on Kaltenbrunner (see below).

Secondary Literature

There has been some writing on Kaltenbrunner from the point of view of the Nuremberg trials: for example, E. Davidson, *The Trial of the Germans* (New York, 1972). Essays giving psychological profiles are contained in G.M. Gilbert, *Nürnberger Tagebuch* (Frankfurt am Main, 1962); F. Miale/M. Selzer, *The Nuremberg Mind* (New York, 1975). R.W. Houston's work is also worth mentioning: *Ernst Kaltenbrunner. A Study of an Austrian SS and Police Leader*, diss., Rice University, Houston (Texas) 1972. However this study does not give sufficient weight to *völkisch* (populist ethnic) ideology and other links with tradition. For this see the author's work: P. Black, *Ernst Kaltenbrunner. Ideological Soldier of the Third Reich* (Princeton, 1984). For other aspects of the subject see also: G. Cerwinka, 'Ernst Kaltenbrunner und Südtirol', in *Blätter für Heimatkunde* 50/4 (1976) pp. 173–7; R. Luza, *Osterreich und die grossdeutsche Idee in der NS-Zeit* (Vienna, 1977); W. Rosar, *Seyss-Inquart und der Anschluss* (Vienna, 1971); B.F. Pauley, *Hitler and the Forgotten Nazis* (Chapel Hill, 1981); P. Black, 'Ernst Kaltenbrunner and the Final Solution', in R.L. Braham (ed.), *Contemporary Views of the Holocaust* (Boston, 1983).

Note
This chapter is the sole responsibility of the author and should not be regarded as the official view of the United States Department of Justice.

13 Robert Ley: The Brown Collectivist
Ronald Smelser

On 25 October 1945, while he has awaiting trial as one of the major Nazi war criminals, Robert Ley committed suicide in his cell. As a result, he never was brought to trial, the documentation of his behaviour was relegated to the files and the full story of his activities on behalf of Adolf Hitler and the Nazi movement, before and after the seizure of power, did not, until recently, receive adequate scrutiny.

Ley was a prototypical Nazi in one of the most powerful positions in the Third Reich. The social chaos of the immediate post-World War One period, combined with his own psychological traumas to bring Ley early to Hitler and National Socialism. He embraced the movement with a religious fervour; regarded Hitler as the German messiah and remained one of the most fanatical – and successful – agitators as *Gauleiter* of the Rhineland during the late 1920s and early 1930s. His specialty was rabble-rousing and Jew-baiting, something at which he excelled. He was also a Hitler loyalist, something the Führer appreciated highly and rewarded. After the Strasser affair of December, 1932, Hitler replaced the defector with Ley, but did not give him the great power in the party structure which Strasser had enjoyed. Much of Ley's subsequent career during the Third Reich would be devoted to restoring the power of the *Reichsorganisationsleiter* and using it to fulfil his dream of the party as educator and *Betreuer*. His activities in this area took a variety of forms, such as trying to control organisational deployment, in-service training and personnel in the Nazi Party. Some of his successes included organising the elite training schools, the *Ordensburgen*, as well as supervising the annual Nuremberg *Parteitag*. This represented, however, only one of Ley's functions during the Third Reich. Like other Nazi leaders he collected many jurisdictions to augment his growing bureaucratic empire. The most important of these would be the German Labour Front – gigantic bureaucratic edifice encompassing the vast majority of employees and employers, which Ley put in place in May 1933 to replace the smashed trade unions. This Labour Front would become a major power-political contender during the Third Reich, challenging government ministries and industry in its striving to become a kind of Nazi 'superagency' in the socio-economic realm. It would also be the major vehicle designed to keep the workers under control through a combination of carrot and stick. Perhaps most importantly, it would develop within its complex structure the ideas and means by which Ley and

Hitler meant to completely restructure German society according to their vision of a modern, prosperous, racially-pure *Volksgemeinschaft* in which every German might achieve his dream of upward mobility on the backs of subjugated and exploited 'inferior' races.

Robert Ley was born on 15 February 1890 at Niederbreidenbach in the Bergisch Land east of Cologne. The seventh of eleven children, Ley started out his life with some promise, for his parents were solid farm people who had received a generous legacy. His father, however, did not handle money well with the result that he was convicted of committing arson for insurance and briefly imprisoned. This episode, which plunged young Robert and his family into poverty and disgrace was a major life-shaping trauma in the life of the six-year-old. It left him with a vast social insecurity and a vaulting ambition to become 'somebody'. That ambition took the form of pursuing a doctorate in chemistry during the years just before the First World War. By dint of hard work and support from family and teachers Ley had succeeded by 1914 in using the climate of upward mobility during the autumn years of the Kaiserreich to aspire to a degree in food chemistry at the University of Münster. That aspiration was inter-rupted in August 1914 for Ley – and for his generation – by the outbreak of the First World War. Ley joined hundreds of thousands of young Germans in immediately volunteering for service in that conflict. And like all the others soon discovered the horrors of industrial war. For him the war would add another long-term trauma to the one he had experienced as a boy. As a soldier in the artillery, he participated in a number of the battles of attrition on the Western and Eastern fronts, including Verdun and the Somme. In 1917 Ley transferred to the flying corps and that summer went into action as an artillery spotter. On 29 July 1917, Ley was shot down and fell into French captivity. He had been seriously injured in the crash, sustaining a broken leg which required several operations to save, as well as frontal lobe damage to his brain. This latter injury was important for his future for it left him with a pronounced stutter as well as a predilection for alcohol. In January 1920, Ley finally returned home, deeply affected by the stress of combat, injury, imprisonment and repeated surgical invasion.

The Germany to which he returned was also in shock – that of unex-pected defeat and disgrace, of revolution, of political and economic chaos. Ley seemed initially to be able to integrate himself back into civilian life: he completed his degree and secured a well-paying position with Bayer (a branch of the huge IG Farben combine) at Leverkusen. But appearances were deceiving. Ley was unable psychologically to find his way in the kaleidoscopic political and social landscape of Weimar. By 1924, inspired by the story of the Hitler putsch in Munich, Ley gradually disengaged himself from normal bourgeois life and became what he would remain to his dying day – a fanatical National Socialist. For him the movement became a religion, its leader a German messiah. The party gave him valued social and political tasks to perform; the brown shirt provided a sense of community in a chaotic world. The psychologically labile and socially insecure man was drawn to Nazism like iron filings to a magnet. As he himself put it many years later to his psychiatrist at Nuremberg: 'An inner voice drove me forward like hunted game. Though my mind told different-ly and my wife and family repeatedly told me to stop my activities and return to civil and normal life, the voice inside me commanded "you must; you must"'.[1]

Ley soon demonstrated characteristics which propelled him to lead-ership in the Gau Rheinland-South. He was a superb rabble-rouser; one of Hitler's valued *Reichsredner*, he tirelessly agitated for the movement in town and countryside. He was also a fanatic Jew baiter, who did not hesitate to play on popular atavistic fears of Jewish plots and blood libel. Nor did he eschew violence, whether against the Jews, against political opponents or against the officials of the Weimar Republic. Above all he was unshakeably loyal to Hitler, as he demonstrated time and again, whether against the rebellion of Goebbels and the northern Nazis in 1925; against the NSBO agitators in 1929 or, above all, during the Strasser crisis of 1932. Hitler prized Ley's loyalty quite highly and therefore overlooked many of the less salutary aspects of Ley's political life. These were many and included his disastrous press operation, the *Westdeutscher Beobachter*; his chronic financial difficulties; the arbitrariness and highhandedness with which he dealt with members of the party; his verbal public excesses which constantly landed him in court and in jail; and his often scandalous private life, which tended to focus on the over-consumption of alcohol.

Being a successful *Gauleiter* in the Rheinland was no easy job. Much of the area remained under foreign occupation, which tended to put a crimp in Ley's ebullient style. Moreover, the social groups which comprised the Gau tended to be those most resistant to the Nazi message. The northern part had a fairly large working-class population which naturally leaned toward the Socialist and Communist parties, while the small town and rural areas were heavily Catholic and therefore strongly under the influence of the Centre Party. Moreover, the years after Ley joined the party were the brief 'good years' of the Weimar Republic, which witnessed currency reform, a revived prosperity and increased political stability. Under these circumstances Ley had his work cut out for him and he responded ac-cordingly, and in doing so revealed the later Robert Ley, Hitler's powerful paladin during the Third Reich. He was constantly organising and reorga-nising his Gau, as he would the DAF in later years. He was also constantly on the go, making speeches on a daily basis, a custom he would continue during the Third Reich, even though he had a large bureaucratic empire to administer. He gathered around him loyal cronies, men like Claus Selzner, Rudolf Schmeer, Otto Marrenbach, men he would later call upon to occupy leadership positions in the DAF. His concept of what the movement was all about – a tool to reach the masses through propaganda, reeducation and *Betreuung* – would later become the conceptual model for the Labour Front. His proclivity in organising special, entertaining kinds of events would later reappear in the myriad activities of the DAF, while the SA soup kitchens in Bonn and Cologne foreshadowed the lavish social benefits Ley intended to shower on the German worker via the DAF. And his disastrous experience with a Rhenish publishing empire anticipated the gigantomania Ley would later reveal when he had virtually unlimited funds at his disposal. Already the all-encompassing 'brown collectivism' which lay at the heart of Ley's Labour Front empire after 1933 was apparent in a revealing remark to his financial patron, the Prince of Schaumburg-Lippe in 1928: 'Dear Prince, stick with me. I'll make my Rhineland into a social state which the world will scarcely find possible. Through my measures here I'll become so beloved that some day they'll call me the Duke of the Rhineland and everyone will find that completely natural.'[2] There would be, then, an important element of continuity which linked the *Kampfzeit* with the Third Reich.

The coming of the Great Depression and the ensuing paralysis of parliamentary democracy in Germany made Ley's task easier, as more and more desperate, unemployed or economically ruined Germans listened to the radical message of Hitler's agitators. The stunning victory of the Nazis in the September 1930 elections gave renewed impetus to Ley and his activities. His Gau had not performed as well as some others, but the returns both in the northern electoral district (Cologne-Aachen) and the southern (Koblenz-Trier) – which showed the Nazi Party outpolling both Socialist and Communist, although still far behind the Centre – demonstrated the effectiveness of Ley's agitation. But even as the Depression deepened the following year, all Ley's work seemed threatened by a crisis of success: Gregor Strasser, the powerful *Reichsorganisationsleiter* decided to divide Ley's Gau in two, reflecting the two electoral districts which comprised it. The move was a rational one, but the prospect left Ley briefly a threatened and frightened man. His correspondence with Strasser only underscored the importance of his role in the Party to his own psychological and social well-being; to divide the Gau was to 'demote' him, to pull the rug out from under the legitimising activity which had saved him from social uselessness and chaos.

But Ley need not have worried. His master had a place for him. Consequently, in the fall of 1931, as his Gau was transformed into two, Ley was brought to Munich and made first a '*Reichsorganisations-Inspekteur*' and then – in one of Strasser's last reorganisations of the Party in summer 1932 – one of two *Reichsinspekteur* of the Party. In both cases, the scope of Ley's duties was not entirely clear and in the crucial, decisive election year of 1932 he appears, not unlike Stalin during the Bolshevik revolution, as a 'grey blur'. Shorn of his Gau he also lacked an independent power base.

Likely, Hitler used the loyal Ley as his eyes and ears in the Strasser-dominated organisational structure of the NSDAP. If so, the position was important to Ley's subsequent rise. The crucial opportunity came with Strasser's defection in December 1932, just on the eve of Hitler's coming to power. The defection was a devastating blow to Hitler, for it might easily have meant the splitting of the party and an end to the Fuehrer's life's work. Indeed, during the night of 8–9 December, as everything seemed to be unravelling, Hitler contemplated suicide. But buoyed up by his loyalists Goebbels and Ley on the scene, Hitler snapped out of his despair and rescued the situation. In the subsequent election in Schaumburg-Lippe-Oetmold on 15 January 1933, in which Ley was particularly active, the Nazis regained their momentum. After complex behind-the-scenes negotiations, President von Hindenburg named Hitler Chancellor on January 30.

The weeks which ensued were hectic and confusing, punctuated by a series of events which would solidify the Nazis' hold on power, including the Reichstag fire and subsequent emergency decree, the Day at Potsdam and the passing of the Enabling Act, which sounded the final death knell for the Weimar Republic. But one of the most decisive acts in the process which came to be known as *Gleichschaltung* was the smashing of the trade unions on 2 May 1933. The political representation of the German workers had already been eliminated, but the trade unions had remained as the economic arm of labour. It was now that Ley came into his own; for Hitler chose him to preside over the crushing of the unions and to set up whatever Nazi organisation might take their place. This was Ley's big opportunity to build himself an independent power base, one of those castles which would dot the political landscape of the Third Reich. He already had a base of sorts – he had inherited Strasser's title as *Reichsorganisationsleiter* – but very little of the power which Strasser once held. Ley would not abandon this legacy – indeed, tried to expand his powers as time went on against his chief rivals in the party – the Hess-Bormann team. But his real power base, one which, in a sense, would become the tail wagging the dog – was the Labour Front. That Hitler chose Ley for this role was apparent: Ley was completely loyal; had had a profession which would tend to predispose him to favour business over labour; and, so ROL he controlled the organisation best designed to cope with the trade unions and envision a Nazi successor – the NSBO. Although the action against the unions was well-planned, it was, typically for the Third Reich, in a larger sense ad hoc in nature, in that Ley really had no idea initially as to what he would set up in place of organised labour. As he put it: 'I arrived as a bloody layman, and I believe that I myself was most mystified as to why I was entrusted with this task. It was not the case that we had a completed plan which we could haul out and on the basis of this plan build up the Labour Front.'[3]

The ensuing half year after the Labour front had been proclaimed in May was quite confusing. A number of competing concepts vied with one another. The radicals in the NSBO who dreamed of a large umbrella Nazi trade union were strongly represented in the DAF. A number of others saw in the DAF an opportunity to realise the corporativist ideas (*Ständestaat*) that were quite current in Germany. The organisational structure of the early DAF, indeed, reflected these rivalling concepts. Ley himself, initially confused, toyed with a number of these ideas, but, supported by his own loyalists, gradually evolved in his thinking in the direction of a totalitarian mass organisation which both employers and employees would join on an individual basis. By the end of 1933 Ley had mollified his critics in government and business sufficiently to gain their reluctant acceptance of the DAF as the Nazi organisation which would bring together business and labour and end the class struggle which had bedeviled Germany for decades. The Röhm putsch of June 1934 gave Ley the opportunity to purge his organisation of many of the NSBO radicals and to cement his control. In October 1934, Ley wrested from Hitler a decree on which, from that point on, Ley would base his claim to 'totality' for his DAF. Now he could go on to give shape to his ideological dreams.

The DAF empire which emerged after 1933 was partly shaped by Ley's vision of an all-embracing 'superagency' which would educate and 'take care of' (*betreuen*) the Germans; partly by the omnijurisdictional imperialism typical of all such bureaucratic empires in the Third Reich and, in part, by the limitations set by the competitive resistance of economic, state and party rivals.

Ley's vision revealed a combination of idealism and social fear. He really did want to integrate the worker into the nation, to provide opportunities for upward mobility and social reconciliation. Fearing a renewed 'stab-in-the-back' to the regime, he also aimed at creating a totalitarian, conflict-free society which would end the chaos of political pluralism and class antagonism precisely by creating a 'brown collectivism' which would embrace every German from cradle to grave and allow for a completely private existence only in the realm of sleep.

Like a metastacising cancer the DAF continually grew, changed shape and encroached on the jurisdictional turf of government, business and the party. It quickly became a huge bureaucracy with over 44 000 paid functionaries and several hundred thousand part-timers. Many of these men were young careerists who provided much of the dynamic of the organisation. The DAF with its millions of dues-paying members was also bloated with wealth, which enabled it to only to be a powerful party affiliate, but an enormous business conglomerate as well, with holdings in banking, publishing, insurance, construction, automobiles, retailing and leisure travel. With this political, financial and economic base the DAF began to arrogate unto itself the functions of both industry and government – in fact, to become a giant superagency. As such, Ley staked out a number of ideologically and socially independent areas for DAF 'imperialism', including vocational education, housing and settlement, social services and public insurance, and, in a broader sense, sought definitive powers in broad socio-economic areas of jurisdiction such as wage policy and labour conditions.

As threatening to business and government as these activities on the part of Ley were, even more distressing was the fact that the DAF, despite all denials to the contrary, also began more and more to be an advocate in many ways for its labour clientele. It did so in order to legitimise itself in the eyes of workers and to begin the task of integrating them into the Nazi system. Part of this advocacy procedure did result in concrete benefits. For example, the *Schönheit der Arbeit* program did do much to improve the milieu in which workers performed their jobs. The vocational education programme linked up with competition programmes such as the *Reichsber-ufswettkampf* and the *Leistungskampf der deutschen Betriebe* both to im-prove productivity as well as provide opportunities for advancement and upward mobility to individual workers. The DAF also disbursed emerg-ency funds for unemployed, sick and injured workers. Perhaps most im-portant – and most popular – were the Strength Through Joy programmes, which provided unprecedented leisure-time activities to workers, in many cases – as with sea cruises, skiing trips tennis lessons – activities which had hitherto been reserved for the middle and upper classes. Ley, anxious that Germans should not have time to ruminate about the deficiencies of the system, announced: 'We must fashion all free time after work into a gigantic undertaking. It will perhaps be the greatest thing that this revolu-tion produces.'[4] And through it all, the DAF bureaucracy itself, especially at the lower levels and through Ley's notorious 'labour committees', pro-duced a tremendous populist dynamic, as DAF-*Walter* put pressure on businessmen to provide higher wages, longer vacations, better working conditions, longer notice of termination periods and many other benefits for their personnel. No wonder one industry spokesman said that the DAF represented 'the threat of a union of massive force'.[5]

A balanced assessment of Ley's DAF must also, however, point out that these many steps toward labour advocacy really represented the velvet glove which clothed the iron fist. Many other DAF activities in the plants really represented only the sham of labour advocacy as well as a method to practice surveillance and control over the German workers. (We must remember that employers were also DAF members.) These included Ley's ideological factory militia, the *Werkscharen*, as well as the so-called '*Ver-trauensräte*', '*Ehrengerichte*' and '*Rechtsberatungsstellen*'. Nor did Ley neg-lect, as part of the widespread surveillance system, to cultivate his ties with Himmler and the Gestapo.

Ley's myriad activities and vaulting ambition soon conjured up the resistance not only of important party leaders, especially Hess-Bormann, but also business and government. In particular the Ministries of Labour and Economics were objects of Ley's growing encroachment and many battles royal ensued between him and ministers Franz Seldte and Hjalmar Schacht. These struggles, typical of the large-scale turf battles of the Third Reich, were not just personal ones, but of great importance to the subsequent development of German fascism. For Ley's gigantomania really embodied the jurisdictional omnicompetence, the normlessness and the apocalyptic visions of the National Socialist revolution. Implicit in Ley's dreams and schemes was the Nazi vision of the future – a politically driven economic system located between Communism and traditional Capitalism, a new Nazi common law system which would have replaced the traditional juridical system as well as a massive welfare state based on the backs of peoples to be enslaved.

The massive populist thrust of the DAF produced initiatives on so many fronts at once that business and government could scarcely keep track of them. And Ley was the driving force. As he put it:

> There is the Skills Competition, the Performance Competition, the Performance Medals, and so on. . . . Scarcely has one taken place and the new one is already there. Yes, we don't let anyone rest. Where there is life, there must be action, movement, there must be activity. Therefore, the Skills and Performance Competition.[6]

Ley's ambitions and the DAF populist dynamism peaked in 1938 – the last full peacetime year. It was early in this year that Ley produced the drafts of several laws, which, had they been enacted, would have made the DAF by far the most powerful entity in Germany, overshadowing the Nazi party and even the government itself. As Himmler, one opponent, put it, Ley's plans would give the DAF 'the fulness of power which previously state and party have had. . . . The state in the form of its ministries will be downgraded to a handmaiden of the Labour Front, while the party does not even have this helping function.'[7] In the end, only the combined resistance of government ministries, industry and party leaders defeated Ley's exaggerated ambitions.

Ley's grandiose dreams of power were mirrored in his lifestyle as Nazi *Bonze* His driving ambition to be 'somebody' combined with his access to virtually unlimited sums of money to produce a princely style of living. He owned a number of villas throughout Germany, all of them in fashionable neighbourhoods. When he travelled, which was frequently, he had the choice of several expensive cars or a specially refitted railroad car. He dressed expensively, drank the best brandy, smoked choice cigars. Nowhere did his desire to emulate a feudal style of life appear more clearly in his estate near Cologne which he named Rottland. Here he hoped to found a dynasty, to be a representative of the new racial aristocracy, to be 'somebody'. The result was the Third Reich *en miniatur*: a grandiose enterprise marred by corruption, criminality and bad taste.

The war reinvigorated Ley's quasi-religious commitment to National Socialism. Now the great struggle against Jewish-Bolshevism and Jewish-inspired plutocracy could be engaged on a global basis. Ironically, however, the exigencies of war undermined much of what Ley had struggled for during the peacetime years. His grandiose social schemes had to be temporarily shelved; what was needed was commitment and efficiency, not welfare. The grass-roots dynamic of the DAF waned, as its younger functionaries were called en masse to the colours. Labour advocacy gave way to draconian controls as the war made increasing demands on the German industrial plant. The same DAF which once fought for a shorter work week now found itself enforcing 72-hour working weeks. Emphasis on *Betreuung* gave way to efforts to raise productivity. KdF cruise ships now became floating hospitals.

Ley, however, did not forsake his vaulting ambition. His quest for ever more jurisdictions went on unabated. He was even able to win a few victories. Along with a gift of one million RM Hitler gave Ley the important responsibility of formulating the post-war Nazi social agenda for Germany. The resulting *Sozialwerk des deutschen Volkes*, had it ever achieved reality, would have given a post-war DAF and Ley control over extending the Nazi revolution into such crucial areas as social security, national health, housing, vocational education as well as wage and labour policy. Ley would have realised his dream of creating a 'superagency'. Already, early in the war, Ley suceeded in pushing Seldte to the wall in several of these jurisdictions. Hitler also gave Ley specific powers during the war: especially the authority as *Reichswohnungskommissar*, to control housing in Germany. These victories turned out, however, to be pyrric, while Ley's defeats were real. Setting post-war policy depended on victory, and, after Stalingrad that prospect became increasingly bleak. As the demands of the war became more pressing, Ley was ordered to shelve his grandiose social plans for the duration. As for his specific task as Housing Czar, here again Ley suffered defeat. A combination of economic bottlenecks, mounting destruction by bombing and administative ineptness led to his failure to restore any more than a tiny fraction of the housing Germans were losing. Other defeats were more ignominious. The appointment of Fritz Sauckel as Plenipotentiary for Labour Mobilisation in 1942 came as an embarassing blow to the man who had specialised for years in dealing with German workers. And Bormann's success in acting as Hitler's 'gatekeeper' prevented Ley from exploiting Hess' flight to England in May 1941 to successfully reassert his authority as ROL. But all these old struggles became moot as the Allies closed in on Germany in late 1944 and early 1945. Ley, the true believer, never gave up his faith in ultimate victory, and, right up to the end, was concocting schemes to further the Endsieg. These included urging Hitler to use deadly Tabun gas, and to form fanatic fighting units like the 'Adolf Hitler Freikorps' and the 'Werwolf'. But nothing would stave off defeat. Ley, who fled southward in the last days of the war was captured by American troops near Berchtesgaden. He remained an implacable Nazi. His words to his captors were: 'Life doesn't mean a damn thing to me; you can torture me or beat me or impale me, but I will never doubt Hitler's acts.'[8] Incarcerated with other top Nazis, Ley was scheduled to be tried as one of the major war criminals. In the end, though, the destruction of his belief system combined with the spectre of incarceration for criminality, with its concomitant social disgrace – a terrifying re-enactment of his father's fate and the trauma of his childhood – proved too much. Before the Nuremberg trials could begin, Ley committed suicide. He had embodied, more than many other Hitler henchmen, the National Socialist revolution – its apocalyptic quasi-religious spirit, its social idealism, its racist and imperialist core, and its flawed and criminal nature. His dreams showed clearly where it would have gone had Hitler won the war. His restless ambition embodied its dynamism. His venality its corrupt nature. His failures its administrative inadequacy.

NOTES

1. See Douglas Kelley, *Twenty Two Cells at Nuremberg* (New York, Greenberg, 1947), p. 153.
2. Schaumburg-Lippe, Friedrich Christian Prinz zu, *Verdammte Pflicht und Schuldigkeit. Wet und Erlebnis 1914–1933.* (Leoni, Druffel, 1966), p. 170.
3. In a speech given at the Nuremberg Party Day celebration in September 1937. See *Offizieller Bericht über den Verlauf des Reichsparteitages mit sämtlichen Kongreßreden* (Munich, 1938), p. 265.
4. In a speech to NSBO functionaries on 20 November 1933. See Bundesarchiv Koblenz (BAK), NS51/vorl. 256, p. 21.
5. See von der Goltz to Lammers, 26 October 1934 in BAK, R43II/530.
6. Quoted from H.J. Reichhardt, *Ein Beitrag zur Geschichte des nationalsozialistischen Deutschlands und zur Struktur des totalitäteren Herrschaftssystems*, Diss., FU Berlin 1956, S. 149.
7. In a letter to Hess of 17 February 1938 in BAK, R43II. 529, p. 51.
8. *New York Herald Tribune*, 18 May 1945.

BIBLIOGRAPHY

The only full biographical treatment of Robert Ley, one which focuses on his role in the German Labour Front is Ronald Smelser, *Robert Ley. Hitler's Labor Front Leader* (Oxford, Berg Publishers, 1988); important contributions which shed light on Ley as Reichsorganisationsleiter der NSDAP are Dietrich Orlow, *The History of the Nazi Party, 1933–1945* (Pittsburgh, Pittsburgh University Press, 1969); also Peter Diehl-Thiele, *Partei und Staat im Dritten Reich: Untersuchungen zum Verhältmis von NSDAP und allgemeiner inneren Staatsverwaltung* (Munich, Beck, 1971); crucial to understanding social policy during the Third Reich both as analysis and as source are Timothy Mason's *Sozialpolitik im Dritten Reich. Arbeiterklasse und Volksgemeinschaft* 2nd. ed. and *Arbeiterklasse und Volksgemeinschaft. Dokumente und Materialien zur deutschen Arbeiterpolitik 1936–1939* both (Opladen, Westdeutscher Verlag, 1975). For the wartime period very important is Marie Luise Recker, *Nationalsozialistische Sozialpolitik im Zweiten Weltkrieg* (Munich, Oldenbourg, 1985); on the smashing of the trade unions and the emergence of the DAF see Hans-Gerd Schumann, *Nationalsozialismus und Gewerkschaftsbewegung* (Hannover, Frankfurt, Norddeutsche Verlagsanstalt, 1958); also Dieter von Lölhöffel, 'Die Umwandlung der Gewerkschaften in eine nationalsozialistische Zwangsorganisation' in Ingeborg Eisenwein-Rothe (ed.) *Die Wirtschaftsverbände von 1933 bis 1945* (Berlin, Duncker und Humblot, 1965), p. 1–184; old but still very useful is Hans Joachim Reichardt, 'Die deutsche Arbeitsfront. Ein Beitrag zur Geschichte des nationalsozialistischen Deutschlands und zur Struktur des totalitären Herrschaftssystems' unpublished dissertation, FU Berlin, 1956; several important recent studies which illuminate DAF activities are Detlef Peukert and Jürgen Reulecke (eds.), *Die Reihen fast geschlossen. Beiträge zur Geschichte des Alltags unterm Nationalsozialismus* (Wuppertal, Peter Hammer, 1981); Carole Sachse, *et al. Angst, Belohnung, Zucht und Ordnung* (Opladen, Westdeutscher Verlag, 1982).

14 Otto Ohlendorf: Non-conformist, SS Leader and Economic Functionary

Hanno Sowade

Otto Ohlendorf, born as the youngest of the four children of a well-to-do farmer on 4 February 1907 in Hoheneggelsen near Hannover, was interested in politics from his earliest days.[1] His initial inclination, influenced by his father, towards the traditional bourgeois conservative camp (the DNVP), was soon replaced by a more radical orientation. In 1925, while he was still at grammar school, Ohlendorf joined the SA, from where he was transferred to the SS in 1927 (membership number 880). He became a member of the NSDAP with the membership number 6531 (receiving the Party's Golden Badge of Honour). Thereafter he actively dedicated himself to the dissemination of National Socialism. Even while he was still at school, at the Andreanum Grammar School in Hildesheim (1917–28), Ohlendorf helped to build up the local Party organisation in Hoheneggelsen. He abandoned this particular activity when he started to study law and political science at the Universities of Leipzig and Göttingen (1928–31), and initially became involved in the Nazi Student Association and the Party branch in Leipzig. Since he did not find the political activity there satisfactory, he moved to Göttingen after only two semesters. Here, greater political possibilities were open to Ohlendorf. From the summer of 1929 he was given the task of winning the District of Northeim for the Party. Ohlendorf was so successful that the NSDAP was able to win an absolute majority in the election, for the first time at District level, in the Region of Hannover South. Following his qualifying exams in law in the summer of 1931, Ohlendorf received a scholarship, for which the Professor of Economics, Jens Peter Jessen, had put his name forward, to go to Italy for about a year, to the University of Pavia. This stay, which was to enable him to study political science and fascist corporatist institutions, as well as to prepare him for an academic career, left a considerable mark on the future course of Ohlendorf's life. He became a convinced opponent of Italian fascism. His main criticism was directed towards what he saw as the authoritarian, autocratic features of the fascist state institutions, and against corporatism. According to Ohlendorf's ideas, the 'community of the people', as he put it, should be at the centre and take an active part through 'representatives of the people's consciousness'. He rejected the rule of individuals, which he later also regarded as existing in the 'Führer state' of the Third Reich. Ohlendorf took National Socialism's claim to embody a particular philosophy very seriously and developed his own, highly individual philosophy, particularly in the sphere of economics. By so doing he not only came into conflict with the official Party political line on various points, but occasionally even subjected it to quite bold criticism. This willingess to criticise, however, must not be allowed to conceal the fact that Ohlendorf was a convinced National Socialist who gave wholehearted support to fundamental tenets of the Nazi philosophy, like for example its racism.[2]

Alongside his political studies, Ohlendorf had intended to use the stay in Italy as a starting point for his 'lifetime's work', as he put it. By this he obviously meant rapid progress in an academic career at a German university. The scholarship was therefore to form the basis of his doctorate. Ohlendorf was also toying with the idea of a post-doctoral qualification as well. Neither came about. In the summer of 1932 he returned to Germany without having achieved his objects and, initially, proceeded with his lawyer's training. He was saved from this unwanted career by an offer from his tutor, Jessen, who in the autumn of 1933 gave him the opportunity of becoming assistant director of the Institute for International Economics in Kiel. However teacher and pupil soon came in to conflict with the local Party office and the student body. The disagreement became so serious that Jessen was finally forced to leave Kiel in the summer of 1934. Ohlendorf followed him to Berlin at the end of 1934, where he took up the post of departmental head at the Institute for Applied Economics. But in the national capital, too, Jessen and Ohlendorf failed to realise their plans – they wanted to establish a National Socialist University College of Economics. As in Kiel the failure probably had its roots less in practical than in political opposition. Be that as it may, for Ohlendorf the failure meant the final end of his hopes for an academic career.[3]

At this time there was no indication that this moderately talented, but ambitious 'intellectual' would succeed in the Third Reich. His personal ambition might have pointed to success, but his insistence on his own philosophy made it seem less likely. Nonetheless in 1936 Ohlendorf succeeded in taking the step which was to be decisive for his later career: through the intervention of Professor Jessen – and by reactivating his membership of the SS, which he had as good as suspended until then – he joined the SD as director of Department II/23 (Economy). He was fascinated by the aims the SD pursued: the establishment of an intelligence agency, which, in a system of government not accountable to public opinion, was to act as a corrective on the state leadership. As he saw it, this offered a unique opportunity, in close contact with the people, to indicate where the development of Nazi philosophy and the conduct of government had gone wrong, and at the same time to realise his own somewhat convoluted plan to influence the process of development of National Socialist philosophy, for which he believed himself to be particularly pre-destined by his studies of the 'model' of Italian fascism. During the subse-quent period he played an influential part in building up the office for researching public opinion and advanced to be section leader of the entire Central Division. However he only held this office for a short time. He attracted the enmity of Ley and Darré with his 'uncompromisingly critical' reports about the threat posed to the middle classes by the Four Year Plan and his opposition to the National Food Corporation.

For all practical purposes he was 'left out in the cold' in the SD. In order nonetheless to realise his ideas of a Nazi middle class policy, Ohlendorf looked for a job in the economy and applied to be released from his SD duties. Heydrich did not give permission for his request to be granted but did finally agree to reducing his work in the SD to 'honorary duties'. In June 1938 Ohlendorf joined the National Trade Group and created a new platform there for his middle-class oriented economic ideology, which he was again putting forward in latent opposition to the official Party line, to the DAF and to the National Food Corporation. Within a short time he won the admiration of the majority of his colleagues and in November 1939 he was promoted to Chief Secretary of the National Trade Group. Ohlen-dorf probably had the imminent war to thank for the fact that Heydrich recalled him for duties in the SD in June 1939 and remembered his organisational abilities: he conferred substantial tasks in the reorganisation of the higher SS bureaucracy on him, and in September 1939 appointed him Director of Office III (German-settled areas). Thus Ohlendorf was made responsible for all research into public opinion within Germany.

It has to be asked why Heydrich catapulted Ohlendorf of all people, troublesome in many respects, into this position. One reason will in-doubtedly have been the lack of economic experts in the SS. Ohlendorf probably commanded quite a reputation as an expert because of his study of political science and his close contact with the renowned economist Jessen. His 'economic policy', too, which aimed to preserve the middle class, may have recommended him to the National Trade Group. The middle class was ultimately a very important group for the NSDAP. Large sections of the membership and supporters of the Party came from it and during the years of forced rearmament they had had to endure one dis-appointment after another. The lofty promises the regime had made to the middle class when it seized power had all too often been reversed. It was of importance therefore to make sure of the loyalty of a man who had gained great trust among the middle class. In this context it is remarkable that Ohlendorf retained his duties at the National Trade Group and continued to perform both of his other two offices, that in the Supreme National Security Office (RHSA) and that in economic administration.

Ohlendorf will also have recommended himself to a certain extent by his non-conformism; for if the public opinion reports were really to operate as an early warning system – and this was the intention of the security plan of the SS leadership – they had to be handled by a man who dared to articulate disagreeable matters. In this the regime had completely over-reached itself, as was soon to become clear. By the time the difficult initial phase of the war was over, at the very latest, critical voices did not seem at all suited to the mood of victory and soon his superiors focused more on Ohlendorf as a presumptious ideologue than as the economic expert and organiser. In short: Ohlendorf was in trouble again. His relationship with Himmler, especially, became worse and worse. The National Director of the SS (RFSS), who himself had high ideological pretensions, disliked Ohlendorf's 'sense of mission', which he regarded as presumptuous. Personal antipathy will also have played a part. In Himmler's eyes Ohlendorf appeared as the 'insufferable, humourless Prussian', as a 'defeatist' and 'pessimist' and as a consequence of his unwavering ideological stand, as the 'keeper of the Holy Grail of National Socialism'. The disagreements never went so far, however, that Ohlendorf was forced to leave the SS. In due course his career there made steady progress, leading him to the position of SS General and Lieutenant-General of the Police.[4]

In the minds of a wider public, Ohlendorf is known less for his work on security or economic policy than for his involvement in the ideological war against the USSR. From June 1941 until July 1942 he was Leader of Task Force D, in the area of the 11th Army, which, under his command, murdered over 90 000 people. According to his own accounts Ohlendorf resisted this mission, which he traced back to an initiative by Heydrich. The Chief of the Security Office (RHSA) probably intended to force the 'unsoldierly, soft intellectual, who lacked a soldier's hardness and political clarity', into unconditional loyalty to National Socialism by involving him in mass destruction and, under the motto 'we're all in the same boat', to deprive him of the opportunity of opposition as well as making him a docile tool of the RHSA. Possibly the 'other-worldly' theoretician was also to be confronted by 'practice', as cruel as it was dirty. By all appearances Heydrich not only had Himmler's support in this but was also strengthened by the vote of Bormann, the Director of the Party Chancellery, who also disliked Ohlendorf's unorthodox inclination to anthroposophism. Ohlendorf evidently attempted to evade the assignment to Russia on several occasions by pointing out his reserved occupation at the National Trade Group. But it is questionable whether he did this to avoid becoming entangled in the planned mass destruction in Russia, about which he had information through his work in the RHSA. It is possible he was also held back by his concern for the fate of the middle class and his work in the National Trade Group. Nevertheless in the end he was no longer able to avoid the assignment.

Contrary to what might have been supposed from his initial refusal, on his own evidence Ohlendorf endeavoured 'to fulfil all the tasks he was given in Russia . . . honestly, to the best of his ability and with a clear conscience'. For the National Socialist Ohlendorf this meant that he put part of the core of his ideology into practice and tried to destroy life which according to Nazi ideology had no right to existence. He actively strove to deploy his Task Force as 'effectively as possible'. To this end he made efforts, for example, to improve its relationship with the High Command of the 11th Army (AOK 11), which had been bad at the beginning of the campaign, in order to expand his unit's field of action, which was severely restricted by the AOK 11 on the basis of an agreement between the overall Supreme Command of the Army (OKW) and the RFSS, which had been laid down by army officialdom. In addition to Ohlendorf's intervention, the increasing threat from partisans finally made the AOK 11 deploy to the full all the resources at its disposal, and thereby also gave Task Force D more freedom to operate. This step was taken by AOK 11 in the full knowledge of the Task Forces's activities. They had been informed about them from the beginning of the campaign by reports from Ohlendorf and his unit commanders as well as those of their own local commanders. After the initial disputes had been settled, general harmony and cooperation prevailed between Ohlendorf and his outfit and the 11th Army, which had been under the command of Manstein since September 1941. Task Force D's increasing freedom of movement is reflected in a macabre way in the 'Report on Events in the USSR'; that is the collected reports of the Task Forces, which form the basis of our own figures. While about 400 persons were murdered in the first two months, the number doubled for the period from mid-August until mid-September 1941 and reached its high point in the last two weeks of September 1941 with approximately 22 500 victims. In total, from 22 June 1941 until March 1942, Ohlendorf and his men killed around 91 000 Jews, gypsies, communists and members of persecuted groups. Ohlendorf, who by his own account made efforts to minimise the moral burden on his subordinates, did not entertain any doubts about the 'legality' of his activity. He consciously stayed on longer as chief of a task force than any of his colleagues in office who had taken up their duties at the same time as him. In his own words, to begin with, in the summer of 1941, he had been glad no longer to be exposed to the disputes and the inimical surroundings of Berlin. The real reason for his long stay in Russia was that as a convinced National Socialist, he believed in the necessity of the policy of mass extermination. Ohlendorf's racism was 'differentiated' enough to make distinctions which allowed him to recruit units of Crimean Tartars and use them as support troops. But this does not change the fact that Ohlendorf emphatically refused an early recall from Russia, since he was convinced, by his own account, that he could achieve more for National Socialism by his 'activities on population policy' than in office work for the National Trade Group. Moreover according to Ohlendorf, the accomplishment of the 'task' gave him a feeling of being right. He had several opportunities, over the entire duration of his assignment, to return early to Berlin, under 'dishonourable' or 'honourable' circumstances.[5]

He was finally brought back from Russia in the summer of 1942 by the circles which had banished him there a year earlier. To all appearances, Himmler had need of the services of his uncomfortable but tried and tested opinion researcher, Ohlendorf, on account of the smouldering crisis of confidence after the first winter of the war against Russia and after the assassination of Heydrich. The attempt to make him more docile by involving him in mass murder in the USSR had failed. Ohlendorf remained the committed and critical ideologue and his position had been additionally strengthened by having passed the 'test'. His readiness to criticise must not however be seen in the same light as the opposition to Hitler and the NSDAP which increased towards the end of the Third Reich. It was not Ohlendorf's intention to bring down the existing order, but to stabilise the system by pointing out what were in his opinion existing abuses and working against them. Even his old teacher, Professor Jessen, who was a member of the group involved in the assassination attempt on 20 July 1944, was to discover this. Since in Ohlendorf's eyes Jessen might have betrayed National Socialism, he did not use his influence to help him; it is a matter for conjecture whether or not he could have prevented the execution.

The results of the opinion research conducted by the SD Internal Affairs, which Ohlendorf directed until the end of the war, had considerable influence on the leadership of the Third Reich. Concrete measures used to stabilise the system, ranging from the deployment of the Gestapo to Hitler's speeches, can be traced back to SD reports. Nonetheless, without the criteria and orientation of the public opinion research being put into question, the 'Reports from the Reich' increasingly attracted criticism from leading National Socialists. The reason for this is probably that, along with the growing loss of confidence in the face of the threatened defeat, the reports also became more critical and admonitory and this was perceived as defeatism by various people who heard them and who did not know the facts. Since the truth and the exposure of their own mistakes were unacceptable, an attempt was made to keep them from the public. In summer 1943 (after the intervention of Goebbels, who had objected to the manner of the report of his 'Palace of Sport' speech of 18 February 1943) it reached the point where the 'Reports' were replaced by 'SD Reports on Domestic Matters', which were only available to a substantially smaller audience. After further protests in summer 1944 Bormann and Ley prohibited Party and DAF officials from cooperating with the SD. In Ohlendorf's opinion this meant that the duty of the interior intelligence service, to make available reports on the mood of the population at short notice, could no longer be fulfilled. The reports were reduced from the summer of

1944 to reports on single items, with the exception of the reaction to 20 July 1944. Nevertheless the SD-Internal Affairs continued to function until the spring of 1945 and during this time the reporting on, for example, the mood of the workers, reveals the secret fears of the regime as clearly as Office III of the RHSA. Ohlendorf continued to be a convinced believer in the concept of opinion research, and in May 1945 he made an offer to the last functioning government of the Reich to establish a new 'intelligence service on domestic affairs, covering different aspects of life'.[6]

Even after his return from Russia Ohlendorf retained his close links with the economic sphere. In the summer of 1942, Secretary of State Landfried, as the representative of a group within the Ministry of Economics which opposed Speer's economic policy, was already attempting to win Ohlendorf for the Ministry, since he was a proven proponent of policies favourable to the middle class and – as Section Head in the RHSA, a member of the powerful SS. This attempt failed primarily because of Himmler's opposition. He did not want a member of the SS to expound on economic policy in opposition to Speer, thereby allowing any set-backs in the war economy to be put at the door of the SS. One year later, in November 1943, Ohlendorf was allowed to join the Economics Ministry as a Ministerial Director and deputy to the Secretary of State, Dr Hayler, who was newly appointed at the same time. The reason he was now available stemmed from the fact that Himmler, who had taken over the Ministry of the Interior in August 1943, planned to expand his comprehensive plan for state security by attaining potential influence in the Ministry of Economics while at the same time pursuing his ambitions in the realm of internal security. In contrast to the summer of 1942 there were now no obstacles in his way, since after the 'Führer's Decree on the concentration of the war economy' of 2 September 1943, the Ministry of Economics was released from duties relating to the armaments sector of the economy and was responsible for 'fundamental matters of economic policy' and maintaining supplies to the population. There were many indications that Himmler's expectations were primarily supposed to be fulfilled by Dr Hayler, who was among Himmler's personal friends and who had received the post of Secretary of State. Ohlendorf should be regarded more as a 'second string', in view of the personal differences which existed with Himmler, although these were not so great as to prevent his release for duty. However because of Hayler's deteriorating health and weak leadership by the Economics Minister Funk, the restructuring of the Economics Ministry, which began at the end of 1943, was to be basically taken in hand by Ohlendorf. The 'new direction' at the Economics Ministry amounted to the attempt of a group (which aside from Ohlendorf, Himmler, Funk and Hayler, included other leading National Socialists) to find an answer to the crisis of confidence which beset the regime in 1943 after Stalingrad, and which was compounded by the dissent the 'shake-out of personnel' and the closure of non-essential plant had aroused in the middle class. In Ohlendorf's view the prime cause was Speer and the 'un-National-Socialist' armaments policy he was conducting at the time, which was inimical to the middle class.

The aims and duties which were now devolved on the Ministry of Economics consisted on one hand in securing the provision of supplies to the population, undoubtedly important as a means of stabilising the system. Alongside this, however, the Ministry of Economics was to take over the leading role in the conduct of the economy, which meant in concrete terms preserving the possibility of a National Socialist-style economy in the future and developing the basis for the inception of an internal security policy. By his own account Ohlendorf intended to support Speer's economic order during the war – up to a point – since changing it during the fifth year of the war would have led to great set-backs in armament production. At the same time he regarded Speer's ideas as a short-term solution and planned to replace them in the future, that is after the war, by a 'National Socialist economic order'. Until that time the initial phases of this Nazi economic order were to be disseminated by propaganda, for the purpose of stabilising the regime only. The problem for Ohlendorf was that in his view no such Nazi economic order existed, since its theoretical development had been neglected before the seizure of power and this had not been made up for afterwards. In order to correct this Ohlendorf created a kind of 'think tank' to assist him in the Ministry of Economics. In it he gathered colleagues whom he selected on the basis of their achievements, independent of Party membership, and provided them generously with resources.

In spite of his origins on a farm, Ohlendorf's idea of a Nazi economic order was not determined by the agrarian romanticism then widespread, since he regarded industry as necessary for the survival of the Nazi state. He rejected the idea of transferring sovereign state functions to economists, as Speer had done, just as he rejected a planned economy. Ohlendorf saw the basis of the post-war economic structure in private ownership and initiatives by private enterprise. This did not mean a 'free market economy', since the state was to act as a coordinator and purveyor of contracts, without intervening with competition or in the organisational structure of businesses. Towards the end of the war as defeat drew nearer, Ohlendorf came into contact with the post-war planning in industrial circles, since the Ministry of Economics was the agency responsible for internal security measures. In this role he proved himself to be an important mediator and coordinator for the various sections within industry, and in addition was uniquely suited by his office as Chief of the SD-Internal Affairs to give a degree of superficial cover to these illegal actions. For its part, the Ministry of Economics, by virtue of Ohlendorf's commitment, could, for example, share in the results of the work of Ludwig Erhard. In spite of these contacts with the post-war planning of the private sector, in which each side sought to influence the other, and Ohlendorf's intensive efforts to create a Nazi economic system for the future, his work in this area was denied long-lasting success.[7]

On 23 May 1945, Ohlendorf, who had heard of the end of the war while in the service of the last functioning national government, gave himself up as a prisoner to the allies. Within the context of the trial of the SS Task Forces (Case 9), he astonished the court by the open manner in which he gave an account of himself. Even now, Ohlendorf was irremediably convinced of the justice of his philosophy and therefore of his deeds. The court could not fully make up its mind about this 'Dr Jekyll and Mr Hyde' as the chairman of the Military Tribunal called him – the loyally devoted family man, the correct economist and civil servant, who had fought selflessly for the interests of the middle classes, and the mass murderer all in the person of Ohlendorf. According to the relevant guidelines it condemned 'Mr Hyde' to death on 10 April 1948. Otto Ohlendorf was executed on 7 June 1951 in Landsberg/Lech.[8]

NOTES

These references must confine themselves to a few selected facts – some of them are short summaries. Readers are referred to the extensive references in the quoted literature, and especially Herbst (economics) and Krausnick; Wilhelm (Task Force), as well as to the recommended sources as a whole. The overall source for the entire biography is: United States Military Police (USMP) Case 9, Interrogation of Ohlendorf, dated 8.10.1947, University Library Göttingen.

1. For the dates of Ohlendorf's life: Ohlendorf's curriculum vitae dated 26.4.1936, BA NS 20 119–27 B1.106f.; Ohlendorf to Höhn, dated 18.5.1936, ibid., B1.119ff.; affidavit of SS-Brigade Leader Ohlendorf: Personal notes dated 1.4.1947, IfZ NO-2857; draft of a curriculum vitae by Ohlendorf, dated 3.1947, Nachlass Ohlendorf (Na01).
2. Ohlendorf to his brother Heinz, dated 3.7.1932, Na01; numerous other letters to family members in Na01.
3. USMP, Case 9, Dokumentenbuch I der Verteidigung (Dok. Buch I), Dok. 1, 1a, 36, Na01; Ohlendorf to his fiancee K. Wolpers, dated 25.11.1933, Na01. They married on 10.6.1934 and had five children.
4. Dok. Buch I, Dok 2–4, 14–18, 20f., 26.
5. Ohlendorf, letters from Russia Nr. 7, 11, 14, 40, 43, 46 to his wife, Na01; USMP, Case 9, Eidesstattliche Erklärung Dr Braune, Na01; much other material in Na01, for example 'Wie kam es zu meinem Russland-einsatz' (How did I come to be sent to Russia?); 'Der Ablauf meines Einsatzes in Russland' (The course of my deployment in Russia); 'Historische Tatsachen zur Aufstellung, Aufgabe und Tatigkeit der EGr. im Russlandfeldzug' (Historical facts about the setting-up, duties and activities of the Task Forces in the Russian campaign) – all undated (within the time scale of the court case!)
6. Dok. Buch I, Dok. £f., 11, 25; USMP, Case 9, Eidesstattliche Erklärung von Dr Böhmer, Na01; Ohlendorf to Schwerin von Krosigk in May 1945, IfZ MA 660.

7. Ohlendorf to Himmler dated 16.10.1942, IfZ MA 331; marginal note by Himmler dated 21.10.1943, ibid.; Ohlendorf to his wife dated 3.12.1943, Na01; Dok. Buch I, Dok. 1a, 11, 15, 19, 30; Ohlendorf's lecture on 19.4.1944 at the Convention of the Agricultural Councils, Na01; Ohlendorf's lecture to the Chief Advisory Council for Industry, 4.7.1944, ibid.
8. *Das Urteil im Einsatzgruppenprozess*, K. Leszczynski (ed.) p. 145ff.

BIBLIOGRAPHY

Primary Sources

Fall 9. Das Urteil im Einsatzgruppen prozess, gefällt am 10. April 1948 in Nürnberg vom Militärgerichtshof der Vereinigten Staaten von Amerika, edited by K. Leszczynski (Berlin, 1963); F. Kersten, *Totenkopf und Treue. Heinrich Himmler ohne Uniform* (Hamburg, undated) p. 247ff; *Der Prozess gegen die Hauptkriegsverbrecher vor dem Internationalen Militärsgerichtshof Nürnberg, 14.11.1945–1.10.1946*, 42 vols (Nuremberg, 1947ff); Prozessakten Fall IX, University Library, Göttingen; Nachlass Ohlendorf, in the possession of Mrs K. Ohlendorf.

Secondary Literature

There is still no comprehensive scholarly biography of Ohlendorf, but some parts of his life have been covered by studies devoted to broader themes. These can be grouped under the following headings: *SS Activities*: H. Höhne, *Der Orden unter dem Totenkopf. Die Geschichte der SS* (Gütersloh, 1967); *SD Activities*: S. Aronson, *Reinhard Heydrich und die Frühgeschichte von Gestapo und SD* (Stuttgart, 1971); *Meldungen aus dem Reich 1938–1945. Die geheimen Lageberichte des Sicherheitsdienstes der SS*, edited by H. Boberach, 17 vols (Herrsching, 1984); A. Ramme, *Der Sicherheitsdienst der SS. Zu seiner Funktion im faschistischen Machtapparat und im Besatzungsregime des sogennanten Generalgouvernements Polen* (Berlin, 1970); A. Smith, 'Life in Wartime Germany. Colonel Ohlendorf's Opinion Service', in *The Public Opinion Quarterly*, 36 (1972) p. 2ff; *The Task Forces*: H. Krausnick and H.-H. Wilhelm, *Die Truppe des Weltanschauungskrieges. Die Einsatzgruppen der Sicherheitspolizei und des SD 1938–1942* (Stuttgart, 1981); *the Economy*: W.A. Boelke, *Die deutsche Wirtschaft 1930–1945. Interna des Reichswirtschaftsministeriums* (Düsseldorf, 1983); L. Herbst, *Der Totale krieg und die Ordnung der Wirtschaft. Die Kriegswirtschaft im Spannungsfeld von Politik, Ideologie und Propaganda 1939–1945* (Stuttgart, 1982). This work contains the most comprehensive attempt so far at an evaluation of Ohlendorf's life and gives a detailed account of his work in the field of political economy as one of its central themes. This present biography takes up many of the points it makes in the field of economics. *The Trial*: F. Bayle, *Psychologie et Ethique du National-Socialisme* (Paris, 1953) p. 33ff, 462ff; R.M.W. Kempner, *SS im Kreuzverhör* (Munich, 1964).

15 Joachim von Ribbentrop: From Wine Merchant to Foreign Minister
Wolfgang Michalka

The crisis of national identity, brought about not least by two world wars and their devastating consequences, has caused historians to become intensively involved with questions of continuity and/or discontinuity in recent German history. Discussion has centred above all on whether, and to what extent, Hitler's policy, which aimed unambiguously at war, was a more or less direct successor of traditional German foreign policy, so that it is possible to speak of an unbroken line from the Wilhelmine Empire to the Third Reich, or whether National Socialist policy represented a completely new direction, forming a clear break in the pattern of German (foreign) policy.

In confronting this complex of problems, attention inevitably turned to the political and economic elites who were at Hitler's side during the planning and execution of his policy, who attempted to influence and even constrain the 'Führer' in his almost omnipotent role as arbiter and leader.

The following study attempts to describe Joachim von Ribbentrop as a person, his political career, the aims he developed and pursued in foreign policy and finally his role in the decision making process in the Third Reich. He was of course not one of the 'old warriors' of the NSDAP, or one of those personalities who were particularly close to Hitler, like his favourite architect Albert Speer. Nor was he able to achieve the popularity of Hermann Goering or the power of Heinrich Himmler. Instead, Ribbentrop has been regarded until the present day as incompetent and arrogant, moody and unpredictable, entirely Hitler's man and thus completely dependent on him. In short Ribbentrop personifies the cliché of a faceless but malevolent politician.

But precisely because of this negative picture it is all the more astonishing that Ribbentrop himself had such an astonishing career, even if it was of 'almost quixotic incompetence' (Joachim C. Fest), which saw him advance in a few years from being a wine merchant to Hitler's foreign policy adviser and finally to Foreign Minister.

Joachim (von) Ribbentrop was born on 30 April 1893 in Wesel in the Rhineland. His father was a professional soldier who made no secret of his admiration for Bismarck's policies and his own increasing distance from the 'new regime' of Kaiser Wilhelm II and resigned in 1908. Numerous periods abroad – in French Switzerland, Britain and Canada – gave Ribbentrop, who attended school to higher secondary level, a good knowledge of languages and many contacts. When the First World War broke out he was in Canada, where he had various jobs from 1910–14. After an adventurous return to Germany he volunteered for war service with the 12th Torgau Hussars. He fought on the eastern and western fronts, was wounded and decorated with the Iron Cross and finally was sent in 1918 as adjutant to the plenipotentiary of the Prussian War Ministry to Constantinople. After the cessation of hostilities he was assigned to the staff of General von Wrisberg to prepare for the peace conference.

In 1919 Ribbentrop left the army with the rank of Lieutenant Colonel. Bearing in mind the abilities he had as a businessman and his contacts abroad, he joined a Berlin firm which imported cotton, but soon transferred to the spirits trade. One reason for this change was his marriage to Annelies Henkell, the daughter of the famous producer of Sekt, who was well known even in those days. His first – economic – career was taking its course. In a few years he had achieved considerable prosperity, complemented too by social prestige: in exchange for a monthly payment Ribbentrop had himself adopted by a distant aunt in order to give his name the 'von' it still lacked. No wonder that Joseph Goebbels later spitefully said of him, 'he bought his name, married his money and got his public office by a swindle'.[1]

As for most of his contemporaries, for Ribbentrop too the First World War and the defeat of the German Empire in 1918 were the decisive part of his life. He thought the Treaty of Versailles was unjust, did not think much of parliamentary democracy and feared communism. He originally sympathised with the revisionist policies of Gustav Stresemann, but during the course of the Great Depression he moved closer to the NSDAP, which he welcomed as the sole means of salvation from the supposed danger of communism.

He got to know Hitler in the summer of 1932. At the end of 1932 and the beginning of 1933, as a member of the influential Berlin Herrenclub, Ribbentrop played the part of intermediary. On one side were conservative groups around the ex-Chancellor, Franz von Papen, who thought that the crisis management of Papen's successor as Chancellor, General von Schleicher, held out little prospect of success. On the other were National Socialists around Goering, Himmler and Keppler, who were all convinced that only a coalition cabinet 'rallying nationalist forces' made up of National Socialists and conservatives could overcome the political and economic crisis in Germany.

Ribbentrop was not in fact directly rewarded for his offices as an intermediary with an influential political post – he wanted that of Secretary of State in the Foreign Office – but he was soon serving Hitler, who had come to value him as a linguistically gifted, well-travelled man of the world, as a special emissary to France and also especially to Britain. The mutual ground on which Hitler and Ribbentrop met consisted of anti-communism and a desire for the revision of the Treaty of Versailles.

In order to assert himself against the 'old warriors', as a newcomer to the Party, and especially to hold his own against competitors with similar ambitions, who like him were courting Hitler's favour, Ribbentrop, having correctly assessed the leadership struggles in the Führer State, built up his own personal political power base. His so-called 'Ribbentrop Office', which in a short time numbered over 150 members, was an organisation comparable to Rosenberg's bureau, to the foreign affairs organisation and other National Socialist leaders' feudal-style institutions. This meant that the foreign policy of the Third Reich was increasingly characterised by a system of parallel competing institutions and special plenipotentiaries, in which the Foreign Office did have the largest and most effective machinery at its disposal, but little trust among the political leadership. Hitler was entirely of the opinion that the 'company of conspirators' in the Wilhelm-strasse hindered rather than promoted dynamic National Socialist foreign policy, so he assigned important diplomatic tasks to special commissioners – and this in turn further promoted the confusion of authority and the wild proliferation of Party political institutions which were beginning to play a significant role in Hitler's state.

However Ribbentrop did not become known to the public until 1935, when he successfully brought about the Anglo-German Naval Treaty, which the Foreign Office had thought could not be achieved, which made his success extremely welcome to the naval command and to Hitler in particular. From now on he was regarded as a specialist in British affairs – a sphere which was of particular interest to Hitler in view of his foreign policy goals.

In autumn 1936 he was appointed ambassador to London with the task, laid down by Hitler, of delivering an Anglo-German alliance. Although he too was originally convinced that it could be achieved, he was soon forced to recognise the incompatibility of German, that is National Socialist, and British policy and so gradually moved away from the policy towards Britain contained in Hitler's programme and took an anti-British course instead. In numerous reports and discussions the National Socialists' 'England special-ist' tried to explain to his Führer the probability of an Anglo-German conflict which could scarcely be avoided, in order from at least 1937 to make him reorientate his stated policy to Britain. Since London would never be able to accept Germany's disturbing the balance of power in Europe, British politicians would regard the German State as the most dangerous political opponent and so Great Britain would always oppose the German plans for conquest in the East; indeed, Ribbentrop warned, even 'territorial revision involving Czechoslovakia' would mean war. An 'agreement on our terms' was therefore impossible. For this reason it was important for the Reich to prepare in advance for a warlike confrontation with the British Empire and to forge a powerful anti-British system of alliances.[2]

This recommendation suggested exactly how Ribbentrop envisaged foreign policy and what he doggedly tried to persuade Hitler to do: officially they were to continue to court Britain, but at the same time, in complete secrecy and with all urgency, a counteralliance was to be formed, which would be powerful enough either to avoid a future war between National Socialist Germany and the British Empire, which was assumed to be inevitable, or at least to enable the outcome to be in Germany's favour. It was not surprising that he also supported the 'Anti-Comintern Pact' between Germany and Japan, which, especially since Italy had joined in November, was formally anti-communist in its orientation, but de facto anti-British, since according to his understanding of politics all three revisionist powers were hindered in their expansionist plans not primarily by the Soviet Union, but by Britain.

The reports and recommendations of his ambassador in London were not without influence on Hitler, but he still did not by any means believe in the necessity of an anti-British strategy. In his speech on the basis of foreign policy on 5 November 1937, which we know of because of the account given by Colonel Hossbach, the Führer did describe Britain for the first time as a 'hated opponent', and therefore no longer intended to realise his political aims *with* Britain, as he had insisted again and again since the early twenties, but now *without* Britain, although if possible not *against* Britain.

The extent to which Ribbentrop had meanwhile become important for Hitler's policy is demonstrated by the fact that at the beginning of 1938 he replaced the Foreign Minister, Konstantin von Neurath, who had been in office since 1932 but who was no longer prepared to share the responsibility for Hitler's increasingly obvious course towards war as leader of the Foreign Office. Ribbentrop had now achieved the goal he desired.

This new ministerial appointment in February 1938 did not initially result in any spectacular changes in personnel. The new boss chose as his Secretary of State Ernst von Weizsäcker, who as an experienced career diplomat was not just highly thought of in the Foreign Office. Ribbentrop was evidently making an effort to secure the professional competence of the office and to link the Foreign Office more into the foreign policy decision-making process once again. However after a few months more National Socialists were put into key positions. Members of the 'Ribbentrop Office' in particular, which he had kept in existence, moved over to Wilhelmstrasse. Over and above this the influence of the SS in the Foreign Office was increased. It was concentrated on personnel policy, cultural and ethnic policy as well as Jewish policy, especially during the war. Ribbentrop himself had had good relations with Heinrich Himmler since 1932 – he was one of the SS leader's few close friends – and Himmler in return rewarded Ribbentrop's political advancement with correspondingly high rank in the SS.

At the time of the 'union' of Austria with the German state in the spring of 1938, the new Foreign Minister had yet to make an appearance: he was in London, vacating his ambassadorial office. Because of this Hermann Goering was able to seize the initiative and make Hitler adopt a policy of forced annexation. During the Sudeten crisis, however, which followed immediately after this, it was Ribbentrop who was unmistakably one of the 'hawks', advocating an agressive policy in this European conflict. The 'doves' around Goering and the group in the Foreign Office around Weizsäcker were however able to have their way and win Hitler over to the diplomatic solution agreed at Munich.

The antagonism between Britain and Germany, which had become increasingly obvious from at least 1938, made Ribbentrop regard even the Soviet Union, along with Japan and Italy, as an important ally in German plans to become a great world power. At the turn of the year 1938/39, when Warsaw rejected German proposals aimed at resolving the issues of Danzig and the Polish corridor in the interests of National Socialism and to force Poland into the role of a junior partner of the German Reich and when, finally, in March 1939 London and Paris guaranteed the integrity of Poland's borders, National Socialist decision-makers were forced to give greater emphasis in their calculations to the Western powers' opposition to German efforts to become a great power. In this critical situation the proponents of an Eastern option in the Foreign Office and also in economic spheres were given a considerable new impetus, so that Ribbentrop, too, who thought primarily in terms of opportunistic power politics, recognised the Soviet Union as a possible partner for German expansionist policies which would indubitably have to reckon with British opposition, and from now on he conceived of it as a central factor in his policy.

The German-Soviet non-aggression pact, signed on the night of 23/24 August 1939 in Moscow, must surely count as one of the most glittering moments in Ribbentrop's career in foreign policy, for, in the short term at least, he had succeeded in convincing Hitler, who had originally wanted to march with Britain against Russia, that a pragmatic reversal of the fronts was the need of the moment. Ribbentrop regarded the alliance between Berlin and Moscow as the cornerstone of his anti-British plan and the basis of German policies aimed at reviving world power status. He himself compared his policies with Bismarck's: 'In the situation we faced in 1939 the re-adoption of these historical links for reasons of *real politik* was a factor of the first importance in attaining our political security'.[3]

In the same way Ribbentrop was at pains to achieve a 'lasting settlement' with Germany's eastern neighbours. At the end of the Polish campaign he intensified political and economic links. For in the face of the British refusal to recognise Germany's position of hegemony in Europe in the years 1939–1941 and to come to an agreement with Hitler, and with an eye to the threat of America joining the war on the side of Britain, the establishment of a European and Asiatic Four Power Agreement became indispensable for Ribbentrop's anti-British plan. With the help of a power-ful, indeed downright unbeatable continental power block, which was to extend from Gibraltar to Yokohama, Ribbentrop intended to put the traditional sea-power, Great Britain, in its place and lead the German Reich out of its confinement in continental Europe. In his opinion this was the only way that Germany could grow into a world power to match the British Empire and America.

Ribbentrop's foreign policy plans, primarily conceived of in terms of power politics, which clearly harked back to the traditions of Wilhelmine imperialist goals, but were changed to suit the altered political situation after the First World War, so that they were capable of being realised, were in total opposition to Hitler's foreign policy programme, which was determined by racist ideology. The latter's deviation towards this alterna-tive to his original programme was determined solely by events and was short-lived. Hitler held fixedly to his racist ideological policy, the goal being the destruction of the 'Jewish-Bolshevik' Soviet Union, the strategic planning for which occurred at the latest in the summer of 1940, after the defeat of France, and it was to be realised during 1941.

Ribbentrop tried until the end of 1940 to bring Hitler round to his pro-Soviet *real politik*, but in vain. Resignedly he records in his memoirs: 'Even then I had the feeling that I was on my own with my policy towards Russia'.[4]

Although Ribbentrop took his orders solely from Hitler and was com-pletely subordinate to him, he believed after the defeat at Stalingrad in 1943 that Germany would have to seek a separate peace with Russia, an initiative which he pursued until the spring of 1945. His sporadic initiatives for peace, which were certainly undertaken in part to raise his own political profile, can be regarded as vain attempts to end the ideological war by means of calculable *real politik*.

1943 marked the turning point in Ribbentrop's political career. He increasingly lost Hitler's trust and therefore also his political importance. Constantly at pains to remain in the vicinity of the Führer, who was indispensable for his political situation, he devoted himself almost more to increasing rivalry with Goebbels, Rosenberg, Bormann and also with Himmler, whose support he had enjoyed for a long time, than to the affairs of the Foreign Office, which was taking less and less part in the political decision-making process during the war. It should be noted at this point that the Foreign Office was increasingly confronted and pre-occupied with the so-called 'final solution' to the Jewish question. The office responsible for it was the 'Germany Section', created in 1940, the director of which, Martin Luther, took office with the rank of a Secretary of State. He was a member of the 'Ribbentrop Bureau' and initially enjoyed the confidence of his Foreign Minister. The 'Jewish Committee' of this section was respon-sible, among other things, for developing and preparing the ground diplo-matically for, or safeguarding plans for, the deportation and resettlement of German and European Jews which was originally under consideration. The Madagascar Plan, which was drawn up after the victory over France in 1940 but never implemented, according to which European Jews were to be evacuated to this French island and almost put in 'quarantine', should be mentioned in this context. After the attack on the Soviet Union in June 1941, the beginning of the 'ideological war of destruction', deliberations about the deportation of the Jews to the East were put in hand, even at the Wilhelmstrasse office. It comes as no surprise that Luther took part as representative of the Foreign Office at the conference Heydrich called at the Wannsee at the end of February 1942 and learned of the plans to exterminate the Jews. Equally the Foreign Office, and therefore Ribbentrop too, was aware of the murder of the Jews that followed by the Task Forces of the Security Police and the SD.

Within his own Ministry Ribbentrop had long since ceased to be unopposed. Martin Luther, who himself wanted to be Minister, wove a net of intrigue around his superior and those who had originally supported him. However Ribbentrop was able to get rid of this rival in the nick of time – perhaps his last political triumph. He had long since left the arena of political decision-making. Hitler was scarcely accessible to him any more. It was entirely logical that Admiral Dönitz, who was Chancellor for a few days after Hitler's suicide of a Germany which had long since sunk into a coma, did not include Ribbentrop in his cabinet.

He was taken prisoner by British soldiers, prosecuted at Nuremberg as a war criminal and executed on 16 November 1946.

NOTES

1. Quoted from Joachim C. Fest, *Das Gesicht des Dritten Reiches. Profile einer totalitären Herrschaft* (Munich-Zurich, 1986) p. 246.
2. For the broader context see Wolfgang Michalka, *Ribbentrop und die deutsche Weltpolitik 1933–1940. Aussenpolitische Konzeptionen und Entscheidungsprozesse im Dritten Reich* (Munich, 1980) p. 162ff.
3. Joachim von Ribbentrop, *Zwischen London und Moskau* (Leoni am Starnberger See, 1953) p. 184.
4. Ibid., p. 237.

BIBLIOGRAPHY

Primary Sources

In comparison to other leading Nazis, the position with regard to source material relating to Ribbentrop's person and policies is good. The German archives have available a full range of political documents, which make it possible to write a biography firmly based on primary sources. British, French, Italian and American archives – to name but the most important – are accessible to historians. The archives of the Soviet Union are still closed, which is highly regrettable, given the importance of Ribbentrop's policy on Russia.

The edited files of German Foreign Policy (ADAP), series C, D and A present an excellent basis for any study of Ribbentrop. Foreign editions (DBFP, FRUS, DDF etc.) can be consulted to complement the former.

During his time in prison in Nuremberg Ribbentrop wrote memoirs (*Zwischen London und Moskau. Erinnerungen und letze Aufzeichnungen.* From his estate, edited by Annelies von Ribbentrop (Leoni am Starnberger See, 1953)), which in spite of all the criticism which can be levelled at them are of great value as sources.

His wife has published the following annotated collections of source material as an exercise in apologism: *Deutsch-englische Geheimverbindungen. Britische Dokumente der Jahre 1938 und 1939 im Lichte der Kriegsschuldlüge* (Tübingen, 1967); *Verschwörung gegen den Frieden. Studien zur Vorgeschichte des Zweiten Weltkrieges* (Leoni am Starnberger See, 1963); *Die Kriegsschuld des Widerstandes. Aus britischen Geheimdokumenten 1938/39* (Leoni am Starnberger See, 1975).

Secondary Literature

A biography of Ribbentrop which meets all academic requirements is still needed. The brilliantly written biographical sketch by Joachim C. Fest: 'Joachim von Ribbentrop und die Degradierung der Diplomatie', in Fest, *Das Gesicht des Dritten Reiches. Profil einer totalitären Herrschaft* (Munich, 1986), is based solely on secondary material.

In contrast to this Hans-Adolf Jacobsen has described Ribbentrop's origins, his political career and the organisation of his offices on the basis of a broad range of primary sources in *Nationalsozialistische Aussenpolitik 1933–1938* (Frankfurt am Main-Berlin, 1968). Wolfgang Michalka's *Ribbentrop und die deutsche Westpolitik 1933–1940. Aussenpolitische Konzeptionen und Entscheidungsprozesse im Dritten Reich* (Munich, 1980) examines the genesis and quality of Ribbentrop's foreign policy aims on the basis of sources, compares these with Hitler's 'programme' and fits them into the range of political ideas of important decision-makers in the Third Reich.

Important complementary studies are the works of Andreas Hillgruber, *Hitlers Strategie. Politik und Kriegsführung 1940–41* (Frankfurt am Main, 1965) and Klaus Hidebrand, *Vom Reich zum Weltkrieg. Hitler, NSDAP und koloniale Frage* (Munich, 1969) and by the same author, *Deutsche Aussenpolitik 1933–1945. Kalkül oder Dogma?* (Stuttgart, 1971ff) and also Josef Henke, *England in Hitlers politischem Kalkül 1935–1939* (Boppard am Rhine, 1973). These studies are mainly devoted to Ribbentrop's foreign policy goals.

Stimulating analyses of institutions are to be found in: Hans-Jürgen Döscher, *Das Auswärtige Amt im Dritten Reich. Diplomatie im Schatten der 'Endlösung'* (Berlin, 1987) and Peter Longerich, *Propagandisten im Krieg. Die Presseabteilung des Auswärtigem Amtes unter Ribbentrop* (Munich, 1987).

Christopher Browning's study, *The Final Solution and the Foreign Office. A Study of Referat D III of Abteilung Deutschland 1940–43* (New York, London, 1978, gives important insights into Ribbentrop's role in the 'final solution'.

16 Ernst Julius Röhm: Chief of Staff of the SA and Indispensible Outsider
Conan Fischer

At first sight Röhm's personal origins marked him out for conventional success rather than for a career in radical, anti-establishment politics. He was born on 28 November 1887 as the third child and younger son of a well-connected Bavarian senior railway official and, after receiving a grammar school education, fulfilled his boyhood dream of following a military career. A cadet officer in 1906, he attended military academy in 1907 and became an officer in 1908. During the war he served with distinction as a Company commander in the Royal 10th Infantry Regiment and was three times badly wounded, finally at Verdun, before receiving the Iron Cross (First Class) and being transferred as a staff officer to the 12th Bavarian Infantry Regiment. As a man of action he must have regarded this transfer with mixed feelings, but he went about his new, bureaucratic tasks energetically and displayed excellent organisational talent – most notably during the German retreat of September 1918 in Flanders.

This apparently conventional background, however, coexisted uneasily with Röhm's still-latent homosexuality – perhaps the product of an intense attachment to his mother during a childhood blighted by a dominating and austere father for whom, Röhm later claimed, he could find no feelings at all. Finding no emotional satisfaction in a string of affairs with women and eventually despising all women – his mother and sister excepted – and rejecting the civilian society, in which his father had made his career, as venal and corrupt, Röhm found personal and emotional commitment solely within the monarchist Bavarian army. The loss of the war and the collapse of the monarchy came therefore as twin hammer blows for him and out of this personal catastrophe began the overt politicisation of his military and organisational talents.

His role in post-war military affairs left him well-placed to wreak revenge on the hated civilian society which, he believed, had enriched itself during the war and then attained pre-eminence by concluding a dishonourable peace with Germany's enemies. Serving initially as a staff officer in the Freikorps von Epp, Röhm was soon transferred in July 1919 back to the Bavarian 7th Division along with his Freikorps unit. Here he was entrusted with the procurement of substantial weapons stocks and their concealment from the Allies. He assumed a role in military intelligence which provided

173

further connections with the radical Right and, in addition, was a founder member of the clandestine Eiserne Faust (Iron Fist).

This informal association provided a means of liaison between different (para-)military groups and through it Röhm came to meet the army 'V-Mann' (intelligence agent) Adolf Hitler. Suspicious of the lone wolf corporal, Röhm nonetheless believed that his oratorical skills were of use and admitted him to the Eiserne Faust. Shortly after this Hitler joined the fledgling DAP (later NSDAP) and reported his move to Röhm who consequently attended a DAP meeting, was impressed by the manner of its then leader, Drexler, and joined as a passive member. Thus Röhm's personality and background had caused him to gravitate towards that defiance of the Republic epitomised by right-wing radicalism and although he regarded membership of the NSDAP as one commitment among many, Hitler, once leader, was to benefit decisively from his decision. Through the embittered army captain he obtained his first links with Bavarian politicians and with military leaders, some of whom were persuaded by Röhm to join the NSDAP.

During the early 1920s and particularly by 1923 Röhm's importance for the NSDAP became unmistakable. Although the Bavarian government was notoriously ambivalent towards the Republic, it regarded the growth of the right-wing radical leagues on its territory as a decidedly mixed blessing. Recognising that the leagues did not share its arch-conservative values, it wavered between exploiting the common anti-republican bond that united the two and suppressing them, but at such moments the new Nazi leader, Hitler, found he could count on his army friends. A notable example, of which Röhm made much in his memoirs, occured in January 1923 as Hitler planned to include a propagandistically valuable march-past of his paramilitary forces as part of the NSDAP's first congress. The government in Munich resolved to check the rising fortunes of the uncomfortably radical Nazis by banning outdoor parades and thereby humiliating their leader. In the event the government, and not Hitler, was humiliated. Röhm and von Epp lobbied their Divisional commander, von Lossow, to intercede with the government and Röhm even arranged meetings between Hitler and, firstly, von Lossow and, secondly, the authorities. Under this pressure the latter backed down and allowed a triumphal Hitler to take the salute at a march-past of over 5000 paramilitaries as planned.

During the spring and summer Röhm continued to play the role of liaison officer par excellence between the army and the activists, seeing to the equipping and training of the leagues within army barracks and occasionally providing them with arms and ammunition from within the secret hoards he had created. In this he received the backing – sometimes active, sometimes passive – of von Lossow, despite orders to the contrary from Berlin, but the army's support for Hitler was by no means unconditional. Its apparent generousness stemmed from its wish to mobilise paramilitary forces across party lines to serve the interests of Bavarian particularism. This conflicted starkly with Hitler's aim of obtaining military backing for his national revolution which would be accomplished by the NSDAP under his leadership.

These differences between the NSDAP and army left Röhm, as a member of both, in a similarly ambivalent situation. Eventually, as relations between the Reich and Bavaria deteriorated further during September 1923 and both Hitler and the Bavarian conservatives prepared in their own ways for a showdown, Röhm partly resolved his own dilemma by resigning from the army and placing himself at the complete disposal of his paramilitary comrades. Thus was completed the transformation of Röhm from monarchist army officer to paramilitary adventurer. Already involved since 1921 with the SA and for almost a year with organising the Kampfbund, an umbrella organisation embracing the SA, Bund Oberland and the Reichsflagge which sought to achieve the revolutionary overthrow of the state, Röhm openly took command of the Reichsflagge (renamed Reichskriegsflagge) on 9 September. Although these forces claimed loyalty to Hitler and hoped to enable him to repeat Mussolini's exploits north of the Alps, the Nazi leader fell in with this reluctantly. He and the political wing of the National Socialist movement were now overshadowed by their paramilitary allies.

Hitler, who had envisaged the SA on its own as a quasi-terrorist organisation subordinate to the party, instead found himself acting as the gifted propagandist for a broader-based, essentially paramilitary movement. The events of 9 November changed matters decisively, for while Hitler's failed putsch undoubtedly represented a severe short-term setback for Nazism as a whole, it might equally be regarded as the point at which Hitler and his party became the masters of the National Socialist movement and their paramilitary colleagues their servants. Political mass mobilisation under the aegis of the new Policy of Legality replaced the discredited strategy of a military-style assault on the state.

However, while Hitler remained confined in Landsberg fortress Röhm was spared the worst consequences of his own failed strategy; he had displayed his usual competence during the putsch by occupying the War Ministry building and, after five months confinement in Stadelheim prison, was released on 1 April 1924. He became a Reichstag deputy for the NSFB, although by his own admission made little impact, and, more significantly, received permission from Hitler to recreate and command the SA.[1] Because of an official ban on Nazi organisations Röhm established a so-called military sports league, the Frontbann, which represented a compromise between the party army desired by Hitler and a conventional paramilitary league. Despite difficulties with the authorities Röhm built it up to a strength of 30 000,[2] but Hitler's release from Landsberg in January 1925 brought his freedom of action swiftly to an end. He was ordered to dissolve the Frontbann and invited to re-launch the SA which, this time, would be unreservedly under the control of Hitler and the party organisation (PO). Röhm continued to insist on full powers of command over an autonomous league, but Hitler's refusal to countenance this precipitated Röhm's resignation as leader of the Frontbann on 1 May 1925 and his subsequent refusal to re-launch the SA.

Publicly disgraced by his part in the Hitler putsch, estranged from the Nazi movement, and latterly involved in a number of semi-public and controversial homosexual affairs, Röhm withdrew entirely from political life. Not surprisingly he suffered a personal moral crisis living, as he put it, like a sick animal. He failed to establish himself in any civilian career, sought solace in a series of homosexual liaisons and eventually, in 1928, accepted with alacrity an offer from the Bolivian government of a post as military instructor. Receiving the rank of Lieutenant Colonel, the demands of a new lifestyle and exile from the scene of his failures evidently came as a relief to Röhm, but he still hankered after his former love-life and the fellowship of his old comrades.[3]

A crisis within the National Socialist movement provided him with the opportunity to return. Tensions between the SA and PO had persisted in his absence. The SA never abandoned its activist leanings, regarding Nazism's growing political success from 1929 onward as little more than the springboard for its own revolutionary assault on the state, but the PO owed its pre-eminence to the primacy of the Policy of Legality. This basic dispute spawned a series of quarrels over matters such as finance, the delineation of responsibilities and, ultimately, the degree of political power to be enjoyed by the SA within the movement. Matters came to a head in August 1930 when the SA's Chief of Staff, Franz Pfeffer von Salomon, demanded the inclusion of SA members on the NSDAP's electoral list for the forthcoming Reichstag elections, only to be met with a blank refusal from Hitler. He resigned and was replaced provisionally by Otto Wagener, but regional SA leaders regarded the deeper issues as unresolved, all the more so when, in September, Hitler publicly reassured the army that the NSDAP posed no threat to its position in the state. The SA intended to replace the army with a revolutionary people's militia.

In this tense atmosphere Hitler contacted Röhm, inviting him to return to head the increasingly rebellious SA and on 5 January 1931 he became Chief of Staff. Given the obvious political differences between the two men, the move seems at first sight curious and historians have provided varied explanations for Hitler's decision. Certainly the two had always remained personal friends and Hitler was appealing to Röhm to get him out of a tight spot. Röhm conceivably believed that Hitler's problems would enable him to gain concessions for the SA that were unobtainable in 1925. Equally Hitler's move may have testified to his own self-confidence and belief that in the longer term he held the stronger hand. Certainly he retained ultimate control over the SA as its Supreme Commander, whilst Röhm for his part faced an immediate challenge to his authority as Chief of Staff from the existing SA hierarchy. It resented his sudden elevation and resented even more the entourage he brought with him into the SA leadership – men with a reputation for corruptness, debauched perversion, and violent criminality. Furthermore, regional SA leaders, such as the commander of the eastern SA, Walter Stennes, in Berlin, appreciated that these circumstances did leave Röhm particularly dependent on Hitler and, therefore, quite possibly in effect a Trojan horse for the PO and the Policy of Legality within the SA. Stennes rebelled in April 1931, forming an independent SA, but since few rank-and-file stormtroopers followed him Röhm was able to isolate the mutiny and stamp increasingly his authority on the SA, thereby dispelling the doubts expressed by Goebbels, among others, concerning his abilities.

Röhm embarked on a fundamental restructuring of the SA which greatly facilitated its subsequent rapid expansion. It had concentrated from an early stage on recruiting from within the youthful working class and its relative success in this regard became of acute importance during the depression years. Röhm appreciated that young, unemployed workers, as well as white-collar employees and recruits from the impoverished farming population, might have a considerable disruptive impact if they could be organised within the SA to be unleashed against the existing social and political system. In this he was not to be disappointed and, even before the events of early 1933, he earned praise from Goebbels for his personal contribution to the destabilising of Brüning's government in May 1932. Furthermore, Röhm's recruitment policy – willingly endorsed by most other SA leaders – provided the Nazi movement with an organised following from within those circles normally associated with the Communist or the Social Democratic Party. This simultaneously deprived the Left of an element of support while, ironically, providing the National Socialists with an instrument of mass proselytisation and terror which was turned against the Left in particular. Although the SA only enjoyed the support of a minority of the male unemployed before March 1933, it was, in contrast to the KPD (Communist Party), able to organise and exploit its following to great effect.

Even at this stage, however, Röhm's position within the Nazi movement was ambivalent. His homosexual affairs provoked an outraged response from sources as diverse as the Italian fascist government, the Social Democratic press, and elements of the Nazi movement itself who were also concerned by the growing number of senior SA commanders appointed by Röhm from among his ex-Freikorps homosexual acquaintances.[4] With this he seemed at best to have created a potential powder keg. For the moment, these doubts notwithstanding, complaints were brushed aside by Hitler, for Röhm proved an excellent and tenacious SA commander. The latter certainly entertained growing personal misgivings about the prospects for long-term relations with the PO and was uncomfortably aware that the elites of Weimar distinguished between the NSDAP and the SA to the detriment of the latter. He even toyed with the idea of forming an alliance with the disgraced Stennes during 1932 – intriguingly enough to effect the restoration of the Bavarian and Prussian monarchies – but found Stennes unwilling to cooperate. For all this, however, he remained faithful in practise to Hitler and his Policy of Legality and indeed it seems that his personality prevented him from ever branching out on his own. He had always played the role of the loyal lieutenant and during the latter months of 1932 this loyalty was apparent and valuable.

The SA's rank and file had been spurred on during the seemingly endless election campaigns of early and mid 1932 by promises of imminent victory. The failure to win power 'legally' in the July Reichstag election led to mounting frustration and indiscipline within the SA and, during the autumn, to increasing collaboration with the KPD at the grassroots. Röhm was instructed to calm SA excesses; something which he and his senior leaders more or less achieved during the final, difficult months of 1932. The task was unenviable; Röhm himself had lost any personal confidence in the Policy of Legality and his instincts pointed towards the pursuit of a more activist course culminating in a direct assault on the state. Instead, however, he ensured that the SA's activism was harnessed in such a way as largely to contain its impatience, maintain pressure on the NSDAP's enemies and, most vitally, avoid provoking outright state repression. This thankless middle way earned him enemies within the SA, such as the Franconian commander, Stegmann, who eventually mutinied in January 1933, and enemies within Hitler's entourage who resented the SA's ambitions and Röhm's personal lifestyle. At this stage, however, both Hitler and Goebbels stood by Röhm whose value they fully appreciated.

On 30 January 1933 it appeared that Röhm's spadework had paid off and in the immediate aftermath of Hitler's takeover the SA continued to play a pre-eminent role. As the party exercised coercion from above through the organs of government the SA served both as an instrument of overt populist insurrection and of thinly-disguised terror from below, thereby helping the National Socialist regime to by-pass remaining constitutional and legal obstacles to one-party dictatorship. In the run-up to the March Reichstag election the rapidly expanding SA was unleashed upon rival political parties and awkward individuals. In the aftermath of the election the SA, its ranks swollen with new recruits and even deserters from the KPD and its paramilitary wing, the Red Front, vented its wrath on trade union buildings, rival party and church offices and, by staging riots in the non-Nazi south German states, provided the pretext for suspending their constitutions. Equally ominously, the SA's members began to settle personal scores on a grand scale and to indulge in widespread attacks on minority groups, notably Jews.

By late spring the basis of the uneasy alliance between SA and Party, and Röhm and Hitler, was evaporating. Röhm had never concealed his desire to create a people's militia around which the whole of German society would be reshaped – the Second Revolution – while Hitler had, from his days in Landsberg, resolved to collaborate with and exploit existing institutions whenever expedient in order to consolidate his power. And indeed party and SS members were obtaining power and privilege in society as quickly as much of society seemed to come to terms with them, but the proletarian SA found little preferment and its leaders, apart from a few who became local police chiefs, were largely deprived of high office or significant advancement. Certainly control of the armed forces, which they had so long cherished, lay far beyond their reach. Trouble mounted as the SA not only persevered with its campaign of intimidation and lawlessness long after the political benefits of this for Hitler had disappeared, but began to turn against the party itself. At this point, in mid-1933, the question of how far Röhm could adapt to Hitler's programme, or whether he was capable of defying him successfully became all important.

For all his personal bravery and organisational talent, Röhm lacked guile in his political dealings. His hatred of civilian society and ordered bourgeois life remained undiluted in National Socialism's hour of triumph and he observed Hitler's accommodation with elements of civil society and the old army with incomprehension and growing fury. His followers were just as reluctant to break off their widespread petty violence and intimidation which, ominously, began to include strikes in the workplace and attacks on employers and managerial staff. Röhm was unwilling or unable to bring them to order and was just as unwilling to curb his own rhetoric. Frequent speeches aimed at Hitler's conservative allies, including the army, and also at senior Nazi party functionaries were accompanied by private outbursts against Hitler himself about which one of Röhm's subordinates and eventual successor as Chief of Staff, Viktor Lutze, (or so it has hitherto been claimed) kept the Führer informed.[5] Röhm did accept a seat in the Cabinet in December 1933, but this represented an attempt by the party to canalise SA demands through the state bureaucracy rather than a triumph for the Chief of Staff on his own terms.

Even in the spring of 1933 Göring had complained that the SA's ambitions threatened to undermine the new state and by early 1934 he and the Interior Minister, Frick, had lost all patience with the SA. Hitler found himself sandwiched between the PO and conservative groupings in society on the one hand and Röhm and the SA on the other. Ordinary SA members, many of them unemployed, became increasingly impatient with the Third Reich for its failure to provide them with any significant material concessions or reward. Unemployment levels in the SA remained very high long after the national rates had begun to decline markedly. Röhm, meanwhile, showed increasing contempt for his old friend Hitler, and did not baulk from reminding him of his squalid and humble political origins – and by implication of the Führer's debt to him. To make matters worse, Röhm increasingly abused his powers to advance his homosexual preferences and the activities of several other senior SA leaders in this regard became a matter for public concern.[6]

Faced with formidable opposition from the party, the ambitious Himmler and his SS (which was still technically subordinate to the SA), from the armed forces, and with the public heartily sick of the SA's excesses, Röhm could only display embittered defiance towards the Führer whose political friendship he still sought, almost pathetically, to reclaim. Precisely when Hitler decided to curb the SA remains a matter for debate, but by June 1934 a showdown seemed unavoidable. As an experienced military man Röhm must have realised that an effective revolt against the state was beyond the SA's capabilities; at best he might have brought down Hitler and National Socialism along with the SA, but that was never his intention. Indeed, just weeks before Hitler struck against the SA, Röhm sent it on leave.

His enemies, however, had the means and the will to strike at the SA. The army agreed tacitly to stand aside and on 30 June a round-up by the SS of senior SA leaders and some other opponents of the regime was followed by a spate of executions. Hitler sanctioned Röhm's death on 1 July, for his old friend simply knew too much to be allowed into exile or a similar escape. He contemptuously refused a suggestion by his gaolers that he should commit suicide and was subsequently shot down in his prison cell in Munich, deemed a moral and political failure even on Nazism's perverted terms. In gratitude for the purge of their rivals the armed forces delivered up an oath of personal allegiance to Hitler. The bureaucratised terror of Himmler's SS replaced the more spontaneous violence of the SA although the events of June and July 1934 showed that the National Socialist authorities were prepared to operate well outside the bounds of the law – apparently with the approval of the old establishment. Röhm's name disappeared rapidly from standard reference books, the vocabulary and the consciousness of Nazi Germany to the point where historians have only recently come to appreciate the full extent of his malign contribution to the catastrophe of 1933.

NOTES

1. Berlin Document Center. Röhm Papers (BDC). Letter Hitler to Röhm. Munich 1 April 1924.
2. BDC. Correspondence between Röhm and Bavarian Minister of State Stützel. 29 July – 5 September 1924.
3. BDC. Correspondence between Röhm and Heimsoth. 3 December 1928 – 11 August 1929.
4. BDC. Letter from Radowitz to Reichsorganisationsleiter. 30 July 1932. Bundesarchiv (BA) Sammlung Schumacher (Sch)/402. Various letters, autumn 1932. BA, SA Archiv (NS23)/124. OSAF, 18 February 1933. signed Seydel. See also numerous secondary sources.
5. Recent research suggests that Lutze's role in Röhm's downfall may have been exaggerated.
6. BA, NSDAP Hauptarchiv (NS26)/328. Letter Kallenbach to Fiehler. Munich 4 July 1934. BA, Sch/407. Letter Buch to Heines. Munich 16 February 1934.

BIBLIOGRAPHY

Primary Sources

A small collection of Röhm's personal papers and letters are found in the Berlin Document Center. Otherwise one is dependent on material within the extensive collection of SA papers, most notably in the Bundesarchiv, NS23, NS26 and Sammlung Schumacher. Many of Röhm's speeches and other public activities were reported in *Der SA-Mann. Organ der OSAF der NSDAP* (Munich, 1932 to June 1934) available in various archival collections.

Secondary Literature

Biographies
There are very few biographical works on Röhm. His own, detailed, disconcertingly artless autobiography, *Die Geschichte eines Hochverräters* (Munich, 1928) does not cover the later, vital part of his career. This period is included in J. Fest's essay on Röhm and the SA in *The Face of the Third Reich* trans. M. Bullock (London, 1972), but very much as an outline sketch. J. Mabire's *Röhm, l'homme qui inventa Hitler* (Paris, 1983) comprises a very full account of Röhm's life and times, drawing heavily on Röhm's autobiography, but its non-academic, even novel-like style might disconcert readers. Thus there is still a place for a full, academic biography of Röhm's place within the SA and the Nazi movement.

Hitler Putsch 1923/Röhm Putsch 1934
Röhm is given extensive treatment in J. Favez's excellent study, 'Hitler et la Reichswehr en 1923' in *Revue d' Histoire Moderne et Contemporaine* (1970) 22–49. Within the more plentiful coverage of the Röhm putsch one finds frequent reference to him. More recent authors such as C. Bloch, *Die SA und die Krise des NS-Regimes 1934* (Frankfurt-Main, 1970), M. Gallo, *La nuit des longs couteaux; 30 juin 1934* (Paris, 1970) and H. Höhne, *Mordsache Röhm: Hitler's Durchbruch zur*

Alleinherrschaft, 1933–1934 (Reinbek, 1984) investigate inter alia Röhm's role within the context of the political, economic and social background of the purge.

Röhm and the SA

Among general studies of the SA which refer to Röhm: H. Bennecke, *Hitler und die SA* (Munich, 1982) is still useful. More recent works include R. Bessel, *Political Violence and the Rise of Nazism. The Storm Troopers in Eastern Germany 1925–1934* (New Haven, 1984) and C. Fischer, *Stormtroopers. A Social, Economic and Ideological Analysis 1929–35* (London, 1983) in English and P. Longerich, *Die braunen Bataillone. Geschichte der SA* (Munich, 1989) in German.

17 Alfred Rosenberg: National Socialism's 'Chief Ideologue'?

Reinhard Bollmus

Alfred Rosenberg, born on 12 January 1893 in Reval, was regarded as the chief ideologue of the National Socialist movement and the system of rule it represented. At the same time he was never, throughout his whole life, able to exercise the formative and continuing influence on the ideology and policies of the regime which might have been expected from 'the Führer's Commissioner for the supervision of all intellectual and ideological education and training in the NSDAP'. (This was the designation of official duties he had awarded himself on the basis of a commission from Hitler on 24 January 1934.) However the consequences of his activities should not be underestimated. Quite the opposite – the exercise of the function mentioned above alone – and it was only one of several – demonstrated the fateful significance even of an office which was relatively powerless in the Party.

Rosenberg had his roots in the Baltic German bourgeoisie. His ancestors had mainly been craftsmen. His father, the son of a master cobbler from Reval, had achieved the status of director of the Reval branch of a German commercial enterprise; his son Alfred was even able to go to university. All the preconditions for upward social mobility were, therefore, present. Nonetheless the son showed scarcely any of the characteristics of a 'social climber's' mentality; unless it was in the form of his ambition as an ideologue.

Rosenberg's parents died early. An aunt took over the upbringing of Alfred and an older brother (who died in 1928). The younger brother studied architecture and gained his diploma in March 1918 in Moscow, the Riga Technical College having been evacuated there. Shortly after his return to Reval he witnessed the arrival of German troops there. In pursuit of a long-cherished ambition he travelled to Germany on 30 November 1918, after finally having received a permit. In the previous months he had developed a distinct dislike of Bolshevism, which combined with his anti-semitism and a strong aversion to Christianity and churches to form a peculiar ideological mixture. He had become aware of latent anti-semitic attitudes in a student association, the Rubonia Corps, in Riga. However, looking back, in 1935, when one might have expected him to give an exaggerated interpretation, he described his impressions in a lacklustre

manner. As will be shown, his anti-semitic attitudes seem primarily to have
been formed on the basis of his reading of literature on the subject.

Rosenberg did not make any serious attempt to take up his profession.
What he was really looking for was evidently the possibility of being able to
devote himself to the formulation of an all-encompassing ideology. So it
was not by chance that he came across Dietrich Eckart and his anti-semitic
paper *Auf gut deutsch*, and the very first article he published there was an
expression of his ideology: 'The Russian-Jewish Revolution'. In autumn 1919
he got to know Hitler through Eckart; shortly afterwards he joined the
NSDAP. In 1921 he became editor, and in February 1923 managing editor
of the *Völkischer Beobachter*. The following November, after the failure of
the putsch, Hitler, in something of a predicament, made him interim leader
of the Party. In this role he came to grief against more robust opponents
and in mid 1924 he resigned from the *Völkischer Beobachter* too. Nonetheless, from February 1926 his name appeared once more in the list of
editors: Hitler had won him back for tactical reasons. From 1 January 1927
he got a full time deputy. By this time Rosenberg probably only dictated
the general direction of the paper, since now, and more particularly from
April 1933, he was increasingly turning his attention to other spheres of
activity. Nonetheless he still had ultimate responsibility for the *Völkischer
Beobachter*. After a clash with Hitler (probably exaggerated in Goebbels'
account of it) he was demoted from 29 December 1937 to 'publisher'. He
had probably not conformed enough to the Goebbels line.

As far as the period 1920–2, and possibly as far as 1924, is concerned,
however, recent research has provided a basis for the theory that Rosenberg had greater influence on Hitler than had previously been supposed. In
particular, Hitler could have taken his idea about the 'Jewish' character of
Bolshevism, which he spoke of in public for the first time in June 1920,
from the articles which Rosenberg had been publishing since February
1919. Rosenberg's ideas could also have played a part in the transformation of his views on alliances: after 1921 both were of the opinion that
Britain should be fought in alliance with a post-Soviet Russia. But Bolshevism proved to be unexpectedly stable, as was shown for example in 1922
in Rapallo. That demanded an explanation. Rosenberg attempted to give it
in June/July 1922 in his pamphlet 'Plague in Russia', by asserting that there
was a connection between Bolshevism and the Russian character. In the
latter he had detected a 'dormant anarchistic impulse' from its Jewish and
Mongolian inheritance. At the same time he referred to Russia as a
multi-national state and came to perceive Ukrainian separatism as the
means of destroying Bolshevism.[1] From this it may only have been a small
conceptual leap to Hitler's reflections of December 1922, which he still
only gave voice to in confidence, that in future Nazi foreign policy 'there
would be an attempt to reduce Russia to ruins with the help of Britain'. To
this remark was added the comment that 'in Russia there would be enough

land for German settlers and wide scope for German industry.'[2] The new plan for alliances and the demand for 'living space' formed the constant central factor in Hitler's foreign policy planning from 1924 onwards. In 1927 Rosenberg further developed his views on the partition of Russia into independent states in his essay on 'The future course of German foreign policy', and wrote, among other things, of an alliance between Berlin and Kiev. However Hitler completely rejected one central component of Rosenberg's ideology as it was then developing: this was the mysticism with which Rosenberg, in his main work, the *Myth of the Twentieth Century*, attempted to give a religious intensity to a racist interpretation of history. Rosenberg borrowed the historical basis of this from Houston Stewart Chamberlain's *Foundations of the Nineteenth Century*. He had discovered this anti-semitic work as a sixteen-year-old and in retrospect described this youthful experience as follows:

A new world opened up for me: Hellas, Juda and Rome. And to all of it I said yes, yes and yes again. . . . I was in the grip of a fundamental insight into the Jewish problem and it never let me go again. Later political events therefore seemed necessary to me. I did not need to add any subjective experience. And what Chamberlain said about the Germanic world confirmed what I had experienced reading Germanic legends.[3]

So even as an adult Rosenberg still stood steadfastly by the principle that there should be no impirical verification of historical or political theories, as long as the latter agreed with the ideology which had been fixed upon. In his book he proclaimed the overlordship of the 'Nordic' race. It had, he said, created all the substantial cultures of the world, but it was threatened on all sides by the Jewish 'Anti-Race'. 'Juda' had destroyed 'Hellas' and so Rome had emerged. Even today the doctrine of Christianity, imbued with Judaism and orientalism, was still being disseminated from 'Rome'. Its highest virtues of 'compassion' and 'love' undermined the highest Germanic virtue of 'honour'. The 'honour of the German Nation' should take precedence over everything else, he claimed. For it too was an expression of a basic Nordic, Germanic substance and learning, which had been preserved for millenia in a 'mythology of blood', and must now be re-awakened in the twentieth century.[4] Rosenberg saw the formation of a 'German Church', in which, for example, the Nordic legends and fairly tales, to begin with simply related, later conceived of as symbols, should take the place of Old Testament stories of 'pimps and livestock dealers', as the greatest task for this century.[5]

It was set out plainly and simply that what he proposed was an ideology which was anti-Christian as well as utilitarian in the imperialistic political sense. Occasionally this also emerged clearly behind the germanophile mysticism. It was said for example in the *Myth* that in the struggle for 'living space' for the 'future 100 million Germans no allowance could be made for the impotent, worthless and presumptuous Poles, Czechs and so on'. They must be 'driven off to the east, so that the land becomes free to be tilled by the hands of German peasants.'[6]

Although, as can be seen in *Mein Kampf*, Hitler agreed with these demands, from 1929 onwards he expressed his opposition to the *Myth* on several occasions. His concerns were predominantly its pseudo-religious portent. In 1942 Hitler explained in his monologues that like many of the *Gauleiter* he too had 'only read a small part of the book', since in his opinion it was too incomprehensibly written. Even the title was 'off-beam'. For it was impossible to say that one 'intended to compare the mythology of the twentieth century', that is to say, something mystical, with the intellectual ideas of the nineteenth century; instead 'as a National socialist one would have to say that one was comparing the belief and knowledge of the twentieth century with the mythology of the nineteenth century.'[7] This statement also demonstrates a strongly rationalistic component in Hitler's thought. On the other hand in 1943 Rosenberg was once described by Hitler as 'one of the most incisive thinkers on ideological matters'.[8] This remark was made at a time of some excitement; Hitler may have exaggerated somewhat. Nonetheless it demonstrates something important: in spite of the differences of opinion already mentioned, Hitler and Rosenberg were in agreement about the main points of ideology like anti-semitism and the rejection of 'religious faiths' as soon as they came into conflict with 'the feeling of decency and morality of the German race',[9] that is to say did not fit in to national Socialism's claim to be all-embracing.

Rosenberg did not know or did not want to recognise the fact that Hitler rejected his main work and, to a degree, his policies. In any event Hitler usually only addressed himself to Rosenberg indirectly. He avoided naming names in public. Goebbels reports that Rosenberg clapped 'most loudly of all'[10] after Hitler's speech at a Party convention in which the Führer had 'disowned' him. Something similar happened at the 1938 Party Conference. Hitler declared in a speech that racial doctrine did not represent 'a mystical cult, but the care and leadership of a people chosen by their blood'.[11] Rosenberg did not react, but remarked that Hitler had 'ostentatiously . . . shaken him by the hand'[12] for what was admittedly an extremely anti-church address he had given on the same occasion. As an instrument of intellectual, anti-Christian terror he was obviously good enough for the Führer. This use of him as a tool did not by any means only affect the churches but extended to policies for tertiary education and all intellectual activity. On 29 January 1940 Hitler signed the contract for the establishment of the alternative university – the *Hohe Schule* Rosenberg had been planning for a long time. This happened of all times just after a discussion in which Rosenberg and his Führer had exchanged fundamentally differing views on the relationship between scientific knowledge and ideology. Hitler had declared; 'Our ideology must not dictate to the exact sciences but deduce its abstract laws *from* their work'. Rosenberg was surprised but consoled himself: 'The Führer's positivist note was new to me. But since he has a firm faith in providence he *is* at home in *both* worlds'.[13] The wantonness with which they went about revolutionising the entire state education system on the basis of such ill-defined intellectual preconditions had its parallels of course six years earlier when Rosenberg was given an all-encompassing remit to oversee ideology.

Rosenberg did not learn until the Nuremberg Trials in May 1946 that none of the Nazi leaders facing charges there (with the possible exception of Goering who did not face questioning) had more than at best dipped into his *Myth*. Schirach also said, 'the youth leaders had certainly not read the "Myth"'.[14] That is credible, since even Hitler had found the style of Rosenberg's work 'too incomprehensible'.[15] Educated readers were repelled by the abstruse logic in the *Myth*.

At the same time it would be wrong to assume that Rosenberg did not have any effect on ideology. Schirach had proclaimed in 1934 that 'Rosenberg's path is the path of German youth'.[16] By this he meant that young people should leave the Catholic associations – the Protestant one had already been brought into line – and join the Hitler Youth. The comments made at Nuremberg, along with this earlier declaration, show that Rosenberg's name could be used as a watchword in the struggle with the church without people having a detailed understanding of the *Myth*. The frequent use of the name, then, does not allow one to draw any conclusions about the book having been widely read, but on the other hand it does demonstrate the dangers which flowed from Rosenberg's ideology.

However the *Myth* also damaged the regime, since Rosenberg's appointment was perceived by the churches as a declaration of war. In the following period, especially until 1937, there were numerous refutations. They were tolerated by the regime for tactical reasons, as long as the author concerned acknowledged the validity of what was written in the foreword to the *Myth*: that the book contained only 'personal beliefs, not policy details of the political movement to which Rosenberg belonged'. For the Party and the state did not then have to take the criticism of Rosenberg as directed at them. However as a rule they were the real target.

The refutations this procedure legalised have always been the subject of research and recently they have all been thoroughly examined. Their authors all deserve credit for their services in clarifying Rosenberg's ideology. Walther Künneth, for example, author of one of the most widely disseminated ripostes, declared that the concept of 'race', elevated by Rosenberg to the status of ethical yardstick, did not have any 'ethical content' and that in disputed cases it was bound to lead to ethical collapse.[17] Even at that time many readers must have interpreted that as a condemnation of the terror of that era and a warning for the future. Other examples of the refutation of ideological claims were to be found in the Catholic 'Response to the *Myth*'. In this, Rosenberg's historical framework, including the theory that the Etruscans had brought the seeds of the Jewish malady to Italy, were held up to ridicule.

However the refutations also reflected the church's partial failure in confronting the regime: in the case of Künneth in particular, they contained anti-semitic sections. On the Protestant side a national Protestant concept of the constitutional state prevented them from fully recognising the illegal nature of the Hitler state. In 1935 the Protestant pastor Hermann Barth raised the objection that the refutation of Rosenberg's 'mistakes' was spreading the dangerous illusion that the regime was capable of reform. In the latest research this criticism has been emphatically taken up by Harald Iber.

As a politician Rosenberg attempted to put his ideological blueprints into practice, at least in part. He was regarded as a foreign policy expert in the NSDAP, not least on the basis of his 1927 writings mentioned above. After being elected to the Reichstag he represented the Party in the parliamentary foreign policy committee, among other things. After the seizure of power, however, he did not receive the post of Secretary of State in the Foreign Office, but on 1 April 1933 he was commissioned with establishing and directing an NSDAP foreign policy office (APA). The idea of the alliance with Britain against 'Jewish Bolshevism' had been expanded in the *Myth* by the concept of the defence of the white race, hand in hand with the Scandinavian states. The implementation of such ideas foundered on the fact that Rosenberg and most of the experts in the bureau (about sixty in 1939), who had not been educated for service in the foreign office, were unable to come to a precise understanding of the specific interests of other countries. To any informed reader, Rosenberg's foreign policy memoranda were the expression of schematic, ideologically-bound thinking. In practice the office apparently succeeded in providing a few British authorities with information about the 'peaceful' character of the regime, until their rival Ribbentrop put a stop to this in 1935. Apart from Afghanistan, the main campaign ground for this sort of amateur foreign policy was Romania. At the end of November 1937 the anti-semitic politician Octavian Goga, whom the APA had supported for years, was appointed Prime Minister. Rosenberg's triumph was however only short-lived: Goga's lack of success brought about his removal on 10 February 1039 and a coup d'etat by the king.

The APA's activities were fateful for Scandinavia. The 'Nordic Society', which it clandestinely directed held annual, noisy 'Nordic Days' in Lübeck, but in Sweden, for example, it gave the impression that the Reich was pursuing 'secret political and cultural expansionist aims'[18] in the north. Indeed the APA, along with the Navy, was behind the coup carried out by Vidkun Quisling in Oslo on 9 April 1940, the day on which he suggested German occupation should begin. At Rosenberg's suggestion, on 1 February 1942, Hitler appointed Quisling Prime Minister of a government which he however determinedly refused to give any independence, however limited, as for example in the context of a Greater German League. This signified a defeat for Rosenberg, too.

Rosenberg is best known for the part he played as the Party ideologue. The strangely long-winded formulation of his duties quoted at the beginning came about because Hitler did not follow his appointment of 24 January 1934 with any regulations on how his duties were to be carried out. Rosenberg therefore believed he ought to advance his claim to authority in the form of the title he soon assumed. The reasons which led to his appointment are not entirely clear. This is not just because of the inadequate source material which has survived, but is probably also a reflection of the fact that Rosenberg's appointment was as irrational as Nazi ideology itself. Hitler was acting rationally in as far as in appointing Rosenberg he had a functionary who would permanently keep the churches insecure. At least it is possible to assume that this was his motive and the fact that, at the time of the appointment, he was still trying to win the churches over to his regime need not necessarily count against this theory. But it is another testimony to the limits of Hitler's rationality that he appointed as guardian of ideology a man whose chief ideological work he rejected.

The occasion for Rosenberg's appointment was brought about by an internal constellation of interests within the Party: in 1933 the Fighting League for German Culture (KfdK), founded in 1929 and directed by Rosenberg, had succeeded in taking over two organisations for theatre-goers, the *Volksbühne* and the *Bühnenvolksbund*, and making them part of his *Deutsche Bühne* (German Stage). But Goebbels put a ban on its activity. At the end of 1933 Rosenberg saw himself being practically excluded from cultural life, which was dominated by the State Chamber of Culture. Then Robert Ley suddenly appeared, looking for assistance in formulating a syllabus for the training of the NSDAP's body of functionaries, of which he was in charge. He and Rosenberg then formulated the wording of Rosenberg's commission and Hitler signed it without difficulty. The commission also included the supervision of Ley's 'Strength through Joy' group. It is possible that Ley intended to win large numbers of visitors to the 'Strength through Joy' Theatre by this means. In any case in 6 June 1934 he declared himself prepared to subsidise Rosenberg's cultural organisation, at which point it became part of the 'Nazi Cultural Community' (NSKG). However the NSKG and 'Strength through Joy' were competitors. This led to years of violent disputes which ended on 7 June 1937 with

Rosenberg's office losing its most important organisation in the realm of cultural policy to Ley's 'Strength through Joy'.

One of the main reasons for the dispute was that Ley did not allow Rosenberg to play any practical part in training. He stressed until 1945 that 'supervision' meant only the preparation of written material. In spite of intensive negotiations lasting years and countless disputes no solution could be reached. Nonetheless Rosenberg occasionally succeeded in calling conventions of his 'Regional representatives', who were also Ley's 'Regional training directors'. He also frequently spoke at rallies; furthermore the office disseminated extensive publicity. He was one of the publishers of the 'Information on the state of Ideology', an information service opposed to the churches, which was only distributed as far down as the level of District Leader, and on account of the partially confidential information it contained, was a less monotonous read than other 'training' material.

Up to 1940 Rosenberg made four attempts to gain for his office the authority to give directions to the Party and state authorities, and always failed. However at the end of 1940 Hitler signed the commissioning contract for the *Hohe Schule*. Thereafter on 30 May 1940 the National Minister for Education, Rust, gave Rosenberg's office permission to set up so-called branch offices at five universities in the first instance, three of which actually came into being and were staffed by professors who were also employed at the universities. This was a successful breakthrough which would have been bound to have had disastrous consequences. Such consequences had already become evident in the office's activities in the fields of research into pre-history and folklore, where whole academic disciplines and also countless researchers were endangered.

The efficacy which an office possessing little capacity for asserting itself internally within the Party could have, if circumstances permitted, was demonstrated by the 'Task Force of National Director Rosenberg', which exported such quantities of objets d'art, furniture and the contents of libraries from the occupied areas of Europe that up to 17 October 1944, 1 418 000 wagons and 427 000 tons of shipping capacity had been required for the task. Rosenberg was expressly made aware, by the German civil servants responsible for safeguarding works of art, of the fact that his actions were against international law. When, for the first time, in a letter of 1 July 1940, he vigorously dismissed this idea, he stepped over the threshold from ideology to action, from the intellectual crime to one which was committed in fact. In his capacity as State Minister for the Occupied Eastern Territories, to which he was appointed on 17 July 1941, his moral failure was much greater; although he had, as was noted in his Nuremberg death sentence, 'occasionally objected to the outrages and brutality committed by his subordinates', he had permitted the crimes to 'take their course' while he remained 'in office to the end'.[19] On 16 October 1946 Alfred Rosenberg was executed by hanging in Nuremberg.

NOTES

1. A. Rosenberg, *Pest in Russland* (Munich, 1922) p. 38.
2. A. Hitler, *Sämtliche Aufzeichnungen 1900–1924* (Stuttgart, 1980) p. 773.
3. Rosenberg, Wie der Mythus entstand, Manuscript, 1935, BA NS 8/22.
4. Rosenberg, *Mythus*, 4th edition (Munich, 1932) pp. 85, 99–105, 129, 168–170.
5. Ibid., p. 603.
6. Ibid., p. 662 (11.4.1942).
7. H. Picker, *Hitlers Tischgespräche* (Stuttgart, 1963) p. 269.
8. *Hitlers Lagebesprechungen*, edited by H. Heiber (Stuttgart, 1962) p. 258 (8.6.1943).
9. NSDAP Party Programme, 24.
10. *Die Tagebücher von Joseph Goebbels. Sämtliche Fragmente. Teil I*. Edited by E. Fröhlich (Munich, 1987).
11. Quoted from R. Zitelmann, *Hitler. Selbstverständnis eines Revolutionärs* (Stuttgart, 1989) p. 373.
12. Rosenberg, *Tagebuch*, ed. Kempner p. 32 (10.10.1938).
13. Rosenberg, *Tagebuch*, ed. Seraphim, p. 121 (7.2.1940).
14. IMG, vol. 14, p. 494.
15. See note 7.
16. H. Müller, *Katholische Kirche und National-sozialismus* (Munich, 1963) No. 312.
17. Künneth, *Antwort*, p. 57.
18. ADAP, D, Vol. 5, p. 471, note 2 (2.6.1938).
19. IMG, vol. 22, p. 616.

BIBLIOGRAPHY

Primary Sources

Most of the file on Rosenberg are in the Bundesarchiv Koblenz (BA), with a selection of copies in the Institut für Zeitgeschichte, Munich (IfZ); the trial documents are dispersed throughout the Stadtsarchiv, Nuremberg, and some of them have been published in *Der Prozess gegen die Hauptkriegsverbrecher . . .* , 47 vols (Nuremberg, 1947–9), the relevant volume being no. 11, pp. 491–651; *Selbstverteidigung und Verhör Rosenbergs*. Rosenberg's defence is in A. Rosenberg, *Letzte Aufzeichnungen* (Göttingen, 1955) and is put even more strongly in *Grossdeutschland, Traum und Tragödie* by the same author. Rosenberg's *Kritik an Hitlerismus* (Munich, 1970), here edited by the publisher, H. Härtle, a former colleague in the Rosenberg bureau. The following are important – *Das politische Tagebuch Alfred Rosenbergs 1934/35 und 1939/40*, ed. H.-G. Seraphim (Göttingen, 1956 and Munich, 1964) based on microfilm of the manuscript, and R.M. W. Kempner, 'Der Kampf gegen die Kirche. Aus unveröffentlichten Tagebüchern Alfred Rosenbergs' in *Der Monat*, 1 (1948/49) part 10, pp. 28–38 (without any information on the original). Bibliographies of the publications of Rosenberg and his offices can be found in Baumgärtner, Bollmus and to an extent in Iber (see below). His most important works were mentioned in the text. Over and above these his replies to the attacks on the *Myth* deserve mention: *An die Dunkelmänner unserer Zeit* and *Protestantische Rompilger* (Munich 1935 and 1937 respectively).

Secondary Literature

The most important refutations of Rosenberg's *Myth* are a) *Studien zum Mythus des 20 Jahrhunderts* (Cologne, 1934); the important parts are in the 4th and 5th impressions (1935) which also contain a consideration of Rosenberg's *An die Dunkelmänner unserer Zeit* (catholic) and b) W. Künneth, *Antwort auf den Mythus* (Berlin, 1935) (protestant). Numerous other refutations, some parts of which are important, are examined in I. Iber, *Christlicher Glaube oder rassischer Mythus. Die Auseinandersetzung der Bekennenden Kirchen mit Alfred Rosenbergs 'Der Mythus des 20. Jahrhunderts'* (Bern, 1987) and in R. Baumgärtner, *'Weltanschauungskampf im Dritten Reich. Die Auseinandersetzung der Kirchen mit Alfred Rosenberg* (Mainz, 1977). Iber's critique is directed primarily at the refutations, as has been explained above. Baumgärtner accuses the author's book: R. Bollmus, *Das Amt Rosenberg und seine Gegner. Studien zum Machtkampf im nationalsozialistischen Herrschaftssystem* (Stuttgart, 1970) of regarding 'the importance of the ideology as simply being a tool' for Nazi history and Rosenberg, an accusation which is without foundation, since it is based on inaccurate quotations (p. 4 in Bollmus, p. 17, 69) and does not take into account the consequences of the actions of the Rosenberg bureau, something which the author discussed in detail. Baumgärtner largely dispenses with quoting parallel passages in the author's work and does not take issue with them individually. See also R. Bollmus, 'Zum Projekt einer nationalsozialistichen Alternativ-Universität: Alfred Rosenbergs "Hohe Schule"' in M. Heinemann (ed.), *Erziehung und Schulung im Dritten Reich*, Part 2 p. 125–52; by the same author: 'Zwei Volkskunden im Dritten Reich', in H. Gerndt (ed.), *Volkskunde und Nationalsozialismus* (Munich, 1987) p. 49–60.
– Information on Rosenberg's offices's cultural policy, unfortunately largely without references to secondary literature, can be found in the following: Boguslaw Drewniak, *Das Theatre im NS-Staat* (Dusseldorf, 1983), and by the same author *Der deutsche Film 1938–1945* (Dusseldorf, 1987). From the point of view of an East German political scientist: J. Petzold, *Die Demagogie des Hitlerfaschismus* (Frankfurt am Main, 1983) p. 192–216.
– On Rosenberg's Biography and ideology, especially with regard to policies towards the East: R. Cecil, *The Myth of the Master Race: Alfred Rosenberg and Nazi Ideology* (London, 1972) and also F. Nova, *Alfred Rosenberg, Nazi Theorists of the Holocaust* (New York, 1986). Nova's findings, 'that the Nazi holocaust rose inevitably upon its theoretical foundation. And to this Rosenberg contributed substantially . . .' (p. 238) does not appear to agree with the book's subtitle. Both books, although intended for a wide readership, contain useful information on Rosenberg. For thorough information on his foreign policy duties see: H.-A. Jacobsen, *Nationalsozialistische Aussenpolitik 1933–1938* (Frankfurt am Main/Berlin, 1968) p. 45–89, 446–64, 477–94. Essential for an understanding of the Norwegian campaign: H.D. Loock, *Quisling, Rosenberg und Terboven* (Stuttgart, 1970).
– On the Eastern policy: *Das Deutsche Reich und der Zweite Weltkrieg*, vol. 4 (Stuttgart, 1983) especially the contributions by J. Förster, R.-D. Müller and G.R. Ueberschär. Still important are: A. Dallin, *Deutsche Herrschaft in Russland* (Dusseldorf, 1958). On the subject of Rosenberg at Nuremberg: B.F. Smith, *Der Jahrhundertprozess* (Frankfurt am Main, 1977); W. Maser, *Nürnberg: Tribunal der Sieger* (Dusseldorf-Vienna, 1977) (better than its subtitle would lead one to expect). According to O. Bräutigam, *So hat es sich zugetragen* (Wurzburg, no year), the former deputy Nuremberg prosecutor, R.M.W. Kempner, is supposed to have said 'the trial took place at least a year too early. In the meantime we have

found many more documents. Today we would no longer sentence Rosenberg to death' (p. 713f). Kempner wrote an emphatic denial of this to the present author (28.7.1987). This sentence was triumphantly quoted in Härtle, *Rosenberg, Grossdeutschland* . . . (see above), but he omitted Bräutigam's comment: 'but I believe he did deserve to die'. Kempner wrote on this matter to the present author (28.7.1987): 'It was more my intention to express the fact that later material was found against Rosenberg which fully justified the death sentence.' See also R.M.W. Kempner, *SS im Kreuzverhör*, new, revised edition (Nördlingen, 1987) p. 116, 224–28, 271f.

18 Fritz Sauckel: Plenipotentiary for the Mobilisation of Labour
Peter W. Becker

It was problems in the German labour market which brought Fritz Sauckel, then *Gauleiter* of Thuringia, to the controls of the German war economy, brought him ignominy, and ultimately his death at the end of a rope in Nuremberg.

Ernst Friedrich Christoph Sauckel was born on 27 October 1894 in Hassfurt (Lower Franconia), the only son of postal official Friedrich Sauckel. His parents brought him up in the spirit of the Christian faith and to love his Fatherland. His mother was a seamstress; the extra income she brought in enabled her son to go on to high school. When she had to give up work because of a serious heart complaint, Fritz left school at the age of fifteen. Following his inclination for seafaring, he became a cabin boy and sailor on Norwegian and Swedish sailing ships and came to know all the oceans and continents At the outbreak of World War One he found himself on a German sailing ship bound for Australia, which was sunk by a French warship. Sauckel spent the next five years as a prisoner of war.

In November 1919, he returned to Germany. He decided to become an engineer and financed his studies by working as a lathe operative in a ball-bearing factory in Schweinfurt. In 1923, he married and in the course of a happy marriage he fathered ten children, two of whom were killed in the war.

During his life at sea he had not been interested in politics, but this had changed while he was a prisoner of war. In 1923, he attended an NSDAP meeting and it was here that he heard Hitler speaking for the first time. In his speech Hitler demanded that the contradictions between workers and the bourgeoisie should be eliminated in a 'national community' which stood over and above the classes. Only if one succeeded in overcoming the division of the German people into a multiplicity of parties and philosophies could the burning issues confronting Germany be dealt with. This idea made a deep impression on Sauckel and he joined the NSDAP.

As one of Hitler's faithful followers, he also remained loyal to him during the time when the Party was banned after the Hitler Putsch. He tirelessly won over new adherents to National Socialist philosophy, and in 1927 Hitler rewarded him for his zeal with the job of *Gauleiter* of Thuringia. His predecessor in this job was Arthur Dinter, a religious

194

sectarian, who regarded a Christian religious revival as the necessary prerequisite for national rebirth. Hitler, on the other hand, was of the opinion that the Party should keep itself out of religious controversies. Dinter, who was not prepared to follow Hitler's line on this issue, was dismissed as *Gauleiter* of Thuringia on 30 September 1927 – 'because of overwork', as they put it – and a year later he was expelled from the Party. Sauckel, who thought on far more pragmatic lines than Dinter and, moreover, had distinguished himself as regional administrator, seemed to Hitler to be a fitting successor. In 1929, he was elected to the Thuringian Parliament and after the elections in June 1932, in which the NSDAP won 26 of the 60 seats, he acted as Minister President of Thuringia and Minister of the Interior. After the states were integrated and coordinated within the Reich, he became governor and a member of the Reichstag. At the beginning of the war he became one of the Commissioners for the Defence of the State. In spite of all this he remained a simple man of the people.

In fact he would rather have served the Fatherland in the armed forces, and when Hitler turned down his requests for this he hid himself as a stowaway on a U-boat, in order to demonstrate his willingness to fight to his children and friends. Dönitz felt obliged to recall the U-boat. The possibility of serving his Führer in soldierly fashion arose at the beginning of 1942, shortly after Hitler had nominated Albert Speer as successor to Fritz Todt in all his duties. On 21 March 1942, Hitler appointed Sauckel Plenipotentiary for the Mobilisation of Labour, a position which, according to Speer, was beyond him both ethically and intellectually. While it had been possible in the so-called Blitzkrieg period of the war for Germany to mobilise sufficient numbers of soldiers as well as workers for the armaments industry, the situation changed drastically with the Russian campaign, and more and more rigorous measures were called for.

Between May 1939 and May 1942, 9.7 million men had been mobilised and had theoretically left behind the same number of vacant jobs. In fact, however, there were only 7.5 million unfilled jobs: the difference is explained by the mobilisation of foreign workers and prisoners of war (the Geneva Convention permits states at war to put captured soldiers to work at jobs which do not directly benefit the war effort). Foreign workers were originally enlisted as volunteers in Poland, Holland, Belgium, France, Luxembourg, Norway, Denmark and Russia, but as early as January 1940 Hermann Goering ordered Governor-General Hans Frank to recruit a million Polish workers, if necessary by force. In August 1942, Frank announced that up to that time it had not been possible for him to find more than 800 000 workers. In the western occupied territories by the end of 1941 around 300 000 people had responded to the inducements of the German recruiters; after this compulsory measures were introduced here too.

However, right from the outset, there was a difference between workers from the east and those from the west. This was the consequence, firstly, of the fact that the western countries had a greater pool of skilled workers, as well as highly developed industry, which Speer intended to harness for the German economy. Secondly, the National Socialists regarded the inhabitants of the western and northern European countries as racially related, while they arrogantly looked down on the Slavs in the east as 'subhumans'. This racist motive, as well as Hitler's fear that all Russians were disciplined and convinced communists, intent on undermining the German will to fight, held the German leadership back from deploying as workers the 3.5 million soldiers taken prisoner during the first four months of the Russian campaign. In February 1942, only 1.1 million of them were still alive; the others had starved to death in German prison camps. Hitler did not exploit the labour potential of the Russian prisoners of war until November 1941, and then with great reservations; but even by February 1942 only about 400 000 of them were working in Germany.

The same sort of ideological blinkers prevented Hitler from deploying German women in the armaments industry. He was of the opinion that the church, the kitchen and motherhood provided the proper contexts for women's tasks and was reluctant to widen their range of functions in the face of looming defeats. Goering supported him in this view, making him uneasy with accounts of the decline in sexual morality in World War One, and these were fears which Sauckel, too, shared. On the other hand, he was ignoring the reality of the approximately 15 million women who were in employment, a figure which barely changed throughout the war. Six million of them worked in the countryside and were therefore involved in an activity which was ideologically acceptable to Hitler, since it involved the land. Over and above this, however, nine million women worked in other areas, from which one can only conclude that pragmatic considerations weighed more heavily than ideological reservations. Before the war the national Ministry of Employment had worked out plans to deploy 5.5 million unemployed German women in the war economy and to move a further two million women from civilian into war-related employment. Ultimately the possibility of the extensive deployment of foreign workers released Hitler from having to come to terms realistically with the issue of women in the labour force. While the numbers of working women in Britain and America doubled during the war, the German leadership depended on forced foreign labour.

The recruitment of the necessary foreign workforce became Sauckel's duty. He had been singled out for this not because he had any special abilities (later, in Nuremberg, he thought it to his credit that he had never read a book), but because he was a *Gauleiter*. The *Gauleiter*, who were also Commissioneers for the Defence of the Reich, had made life difficult for the armaments ministers, Todt and Speer. The conscription of millions of German men for military service, the closure of factories not essential to the war effort, the conversion of other facilities from civilian to military production, as well the conscription of millions and the relocation of hundreds of thousands caused problems which were not solely economic, creating work for the *Gauleiter* in particular. They felt themselves responsible for the social and political concerns of the residents of their region, were unwilling to allow themselves to be told what to do without protest by the national authorities, and thwarted measures which were in the interests of the warring nation. Only one of *them*, it was thought, could overcome such resistance. Speer would have liked to see his friend, Karl Hanke, the *Gauleiter* of Lower Silesia, take on this role, but Bormann was afraid of power becoming concentrated in Speer's hands and suggested Sauckel instead. Hitler's decree of 21 March 1942 made Sauckel directly responsible to him and made him responsible for the mobilisation of the entire labour force, including foreigners and prisoners of war.

The growing losses on the eastern front, increasing conscription and the heightened demands on the war economy constantly forced Speer to turn to Sauckel with steadily increasing demands for more workers. Sauckel did his best to fulfil Speer's requirements. Earlier, he had received backing from Hitler for his task: approached about the legality of the planned compulsory recruitment, Hitler declared to Sauckel that he had no need to comply with the Geneva or Hague Conventions. In the west the army's decrees or agreements entered into with the French government would prevail, while in the east the surrender of Poland, it was said, had deprived it of all rights. Since Russia had not signed the Geneva Convention in any case, Germany was not bound to observe it there either. Sauckel acted accordingly. In his 'Report on the Mobilisation of the Labour Force in 1942' he pointed proudly to the fact that in the first two so-called 'Sauckel Initiatives' he had brought 2.7 million people into the Reich.

As events reached a critical stage in Stalingrad and North Africa, and also with the conscription of German men this involved, it became evident that the numbers of foreign workers were no longer sufficient. It became necessary to fall back on the German workforce to a much greater degree. And so, in January 1943, the 'Führer's Decree for the comprehensive Deployment of Men and Women for the Task of Defending the Reich' was proclaimed. Now all men between the ages of 16 and 65 and women between the ages of 17 and 50 who had not yet registered with the employment offices were to be mobilised. The result was inadequate. During the first six months, Sauckel announced that 1 332 000 people had been mobilised, 1 235 000 of these being women. However only 688 000 of them were in full-time employment. On the other hand, at the end of 1943, Sauckel announced that in the third 'Sauckel Initiative' he had recruited 1.4 million foreigners.

At the beginning of 1944, a conference which had been called by Hitler came to the conclusion that during that year the German economy would require a further four million workers. Sauckel believed he could mobilise half a million in Germany itself, but doubted whether he would succeed in finding the missing 3.5 million abroad. The outcome proved him right. During the first six months he recruited 1 482 000 people, of whom 96 600 were prisoners of war, 537 400 were foreigners and 848 000 were Germans, mainly women and young people. During the second six months of 1944 he added a further 449 000 foreigners.

When the retreat from the east began, the area from which Sauckel could win recruits became steadily smaller, until there were practically no more Russians available to him. However he believed he could recruit more workers from western countries to replace them, and, after the defection of Germany's Italian ally, from German-occupied Italy too. He only had a limited degree of success in this, however, mainly because Speer had in the meantime established so-called restricted enterprises in these countries, which worked for him alone and were not accessible to Sauckel.

Nonetheless Sauckel managed to bring approximately 5.3 million foreign workers to Germany during the three years he was active. The largest western contingents came from the Netherlands, Belgium and, particularly, France. However the great bulk of the foreign workers came from Poland and Russia. At the end of 1944, at the height of the mobilisation of the workforce, 20 per cent of all workers in Germany were foreigners. It is important not to underestimate these figures. Up to 1940, four million men had been conscripted into the armed services and the civilian workforce had been reduced to 36 million. A further seven million German men were called up between May 1942 and September 1944, but nonetheless, thanks to the foreigners, the size of the civilian workforce remained constant at 36 million.

Just as important as the quantity was the quality of the workers. An examination of the aptitude of 12 000 workers in a steel factory gave the following ranking among men: first the French then Russians, Germans, Poles, Yugoslavs, Dutch, Norwegians and Italians. In the case of the women the Russians came in first place, followed by the Poles, Germans, French and Yugoslavs. In the spring of 1944, the National Chamber of Commerce made available a study of the productivity of foreign workers. Measured by a German standard of 100 per cent, female workers from the east scored 90 to 100 per cent, trained Czechs scored 80 to 95 per cent, men from the east 60 to 80 per cent, Italians 70 per cent and workers from the Netherlands, Denmark and the Balkans 50 to 70 per cent. All in all, the contribution of the foreign workers to productivity was astonishing; there is no doubt that it was the decisive contribution to the German war economy during the last years of the war.

However recruitment was anything but voluntary. Sauckel himself admitted that, of the five million foreign workers, at most 200 000 had come to Germany of their own free will. It was forced deportation and the treatment of foreign workers in Germany which landed Sauckel in the dock in Nuremberg after the war.

Sauckel had no reservations about going about his duty with tireless energy and ruthless brutality. He had promised Hitler in 1942 that he would execute his task with fanatical conviction and he kept this promise until the end. In the beginning he had no difficulty in fulfilling his quotas: until mid-1942 the number of voluntary registrations was more than sufficient. The first trains filled with laughing Ukrainians arrived in German stations decked with flowers. After this, however, it was necessary to hunt down people in order to produce the required millions. Raids were conducted at night, in railway stations and in the streets and public places, even during religious services. Men, women and children were herded together like cattle, brutally and in humiliating fashion. Villages were surrounded, the inhabitants loaded into goods wagons and transported to Germany. In occupied Russia in 1943, an order went out that all people between the ages of 14 and 65 were required to register. Additional regulations made it possible to deport them more easily to Germany, but did not make the deportation any more humane.

Word had naturally got round about how bad the treatment of forced labour in Germany was. However, wherever there was the slightest resistance, it was broken with the use of extreme force; on one occasion 45 Ukrainians were shot, among them 18 children, ranging in age from 3 to 15. And that was by no means the only time that German forces acted so barbarously. The calls to the target age groups to report for transportation to Germany were always linked to threats. If those concerned refused, then members of their family lost their ration cards or were taken to prisons, punishment camps or even concentration camps. The execution of Sauckel's initiatives was the responsibility of the army, the SS and the SD. Criticism of Sauckel's methods was voiced increasingly loudly, particularly by the army. With some justice, he was held responsible for the steady growth in the number of partisans: instead of allowing themselves to be freighted off to forced labour in the Reich, the Russians preferred to join the partisans in the forests.

However no easy fate awaited those who were rounded up and transported to Germany. The first difficulty was in accommodating the foreign workers, as they were called. The main responsibility for this lay with the firms who employed them; the German Labour Front had the task of supervising the building and maintenance of the lodgings. All over Germany barracks grew up in the vicinity of workplaces. In 1944, there were 22 000 of these camps, 16 400 of them in the countryside. Until the first Sauckel Initiative, conditions in them were relatively good, but the sudden influx of several million Russians changed the situation considerably. For all practical purposes the workers were treated like prisoners; they were not allowed to leave the camps without permission and were surrounded by guards. The camps were overcrowded and facilities for hygiene inadequate.

The provisioning could at best be described as unsatisfactory. Initially the Russians and Poles received less to eat because it was thought that, as 'sub-humans', they could be treated in this way. After Sauckel was put in charge of the mobilisation of the workforce the workers were better provided for, but the differences between workers from the west and from the east and the German workforce remained: the workers from the west received less to eat than the German workers and those from the east received only about half of the Germans' rations. The workers normally only had one hot meal a day. The German authorities found themselves in a particular dilemma with regard to provisions: on the one hand, they wanted to give the foreign workers as little to eat as possible; on the other hand, it was plain to them that they could only get the maximum out of the workers if they provided them with a reasonable amount of food, the more so since the workers from the east were often undernourished when they arrived in Germany.

The workers were similarly disadvantaged in the matter of payment. Although the workers from eastern Europe nominally earned as much as the workers from western Europe, their wages were subject to special levies, the result of which was that only 7 to 22 per cent of their wages was left for them. Apart from this, the eastern workers in particular were subjected to merciless discipline in their workplaces. They were often beaten and handed over straight away to the police or even the SS for even minor crimes. If they attempted to escape they could even be publicly executed.

Sauckel knew that slaves who were undernourished, ill, obstinate, despairing and full of hatred never work as well as those employed under normal circumstances. From the beginning, therefore, he gave orders to the agencies carrying out his policies that during recruitment they should give truthful information about wages, accommodation and food. Over and above this he demanded that the foreign workers be well treated and housed. He was partly motivated by humanitarian considerations, partly by purely pragmatic ones. He also tried a few times to improve the appalling conditions by his own intervention, but these efforts did not last for long. Sauckel was fully informed about the deficient living conditions of the foreign workers but, leaving aside sporadic attempts to alleviate them, he preferred to do nothing. It was certainly not his intention that his compulsory conscription should result indirectly in the death of thousands and the suffering of millions, but these considerations paled before the necessity of producing millions of new workers. Germany's victory was more important than behaving justly. Over and above this, as far as he was concerned foreign workers were only second-class people.

On these grounds, he was found guilty in Nuremberg of having committed war crimes and crimes against humanity. He was unanimously condemned to death and executed. In certain respects the verdict was questionable. In the final analysis it was Speer who spurred Sauckel on to more and more conscription campaigns, and it was Funk's Ministry of Economics which was directly responsible for the treatment of the foreign workers. Accordingly both Speer and Funk should also have received the death sentence; however Funk was only sentenced to life imprisonment and Speer only to 20 years. The considerations the individual judges took into account in coming to their judgments are unknown, but it is certain that Sauckel was no more and no less guilty than the other two.

BIBLIOGRAPHY

Primary Sources

The main sources for Sauckel's role in the mobilisation of labour are the transcripts of the proceedings of the International Tribunal in Nuremberg and the related collections of documents. The documents are held in the *Bundesarchiv* Koblenz and in the *Institut für Zeitgeschichte*. Further insights into Sauckel's activities are to be found in the files of the Armaments and Economics Ministries, the archives of the Four Year Plan and those of the Ministry of Employment, all of which are held in the *Bundesarchiv* Koblenz. Speer's 'Memoires' are an interesting primary source, but can only be used with due reservations.

Secondary Literature

The best accounts based on archival research are: A.S. Milward, *Die deutsche Kriegswirtschaft 1939–1945* (Stuttgart, 1966) and G. Janssen, *Das Ministerium Speer. Deutschlands Rüstung im Zweiten Weltkrieg* (Berlin, 1968). Both works concern themselves with the German war economy, and pay particular attention to the question of the mobilisation of labour. On the question of the 'foreign workers' see also: E.L. Homze, *Foreign Labor in Nazi Germany* (Princeton, 1967); H. Pfahlmann, *Fremdarbeiter und Kriegsgefangene in der deutschen Kriegswirtschaft 1939–1945* (Darmstadt, 1968); U. Herbert, *Fremdarbeiter. Politik und Praxis des 'Ausländer-Einsatzes' in der Kriegswirtschaft des Dritten Reiches* (Berlin–Bonn, 1985). Books which are concerned with the Nuremberg trials and devote chapters to Sauckel include: E. Davidson, *The Trial of the Germans* (New York, 1966); B.F. Smith, *Reaching Judgment at Nuremberg* (New York, 1977); G. Wysocki, *Zwangsarbeit im Stahlkonzern. Salzgitter und die Reichswerke 'Hermann Goering' 1937–1945* (Braunschweig, 1982); R.E. Conot, *Justice at Nuremberg* (New York, 1983). See also the following articles: D. Eichholtz, 'Die Vorgeschichte des "Generalbevollmächtigten für den Arbeitseinsatz"', in *Jb. Gesch.* 9 (1973) pp. 339–83; J.L. Wallach, 'Probleme der Zwangsarbeit in der deutschen Kriegswirtschaft', in *Jb. Inst. Dtsch. Gesch.* 6 (1977) pp. 477–512; D. Petzina, 'Die Mobilisierung deutscher Arbeitskräfte vor und während des Zweiten Weltkrieges', in *VfZ* 18 (1979) pp. 443–55.

19 Baldur von Schirach: Student Leader, Hitler Youth Leader, *Gauleiter* in Vienna

Michael Wortmann

Baldur von Schirach was born on 9 May 1907 in Berlin, the youngest of four children. However it was his childhood years in Weimar which formed his character. His father Carl took over the directorship of the Grand Duke's Court Theatre there the following summer. Up until then Carl Baily Norris von Schirach had served in the Royal Prussian Hussar Guards Regiment. He left with the rank of captain. Schirach the elder's decision to go into the theatre did not come out of the blue. He had long felt attracted to art, literature and music. From time to time he had taken leave of absence from military service in order to take lessons with the famous stage director Martersteig. Schirach's skills as a director were 'highly commended'. Within the musical sphere he was regarded as 'extremely talented'.[1] The change from being an officer to a theatre manager was not exceptional in the Wilhelmine period. The officer as artist, the artist as officer: Schirach always claimed that 'as director he was a cavalier, not a comedian', thereby contributing his share to the intellectual sterility of the era.[2]

Baldur von Schirach's mother was an American. Emma Middleton Lynah Tillou had married Carl in 1896 in Philadelphia. The Schirach family had close ties with America. Carl's father had spent several years in the United States, fought for the North in the Civil War and married the daughter of a locomotive manufacturer. Emma, too, came from this family.[3] Several anecdotes are told of her which give the impression of a self-confident, wilful woman. The fact that throughout her life she spoke only broken German contributed considerably to making Baldur an outsider from his childhood onwards. By his own account at the age of six he still could not speak 'a single word of German'.[4]

The Schirachs established themselves in Weimar in imposing style. The director's salary alone of course was scarcely adequate for the way of life which went with the job. However Carl and Emma had sufficient private means to enable them to enjoy the life style of the grand bourgeoisie. Schirach's bourgeois origins are documented in family history. The upper class 'von' had been awarded by Maria Theresa to a learned ancestor,

Gottlob Benedikt. He had written a biography of her father, Charles VI.

In cultural terms, Weimar at the beginning of the century was still just a shadow of its former self and the classical literary period of Goethe and Schiller had atrophied into rigid monuments. It was dominated now by literary reactionaries, led by Adolf Bartels, who had come to the seat of the Court in 1895. Bartels and his confederates preached the ideal of 'home-grown art', symbolically expressing the intellectual isolation and rigidity of Weimar. They blocked modern literary trends. The Bartels group was characterised above all, however, by an extreme anti-semitism. Hans Severus Ziegler, Bartels' pupil and secretary, later to be deputy *Gauleiter* in Thuringia, became the young Schirach's first National Socialist mentor. Baldur von Schirach singled out his time in the Wald Institute at Bad Berka as the formative phase of his schooling.[5] This country boarding school was run according to the rules of the educational reformist Hermann Lietz, who wanted to replace schools based on 'instruction' with schools which emphasised 'character building'. Lietz taught that the development of the body and the character must rank equally alongside the mediation of knowledge. Lietz too was anti-semitic.

The defeat in the First World War resulted in drastic and painful changes for the family. Carl von Schirach was dismissed. In October 1919 Baldur's brother Karl shot himself. In his farewell letter he gave 'Germany's misfortune' as the reason for his decision.[6] The actual reason, however, was his own misfortune, the career as an officer denied to him by the Treaty of Versailles. Without a doubt this double catastrophe for his family was one of the decisive formative experiences in Schirach's life, with far-reaching consequences for the development of his personality. He had been made receptive to the National Socialist doctrine of salvation.

However Schirach did not become a National Socialist at any specific time. Within the *völkisch* (populist ethnic), anti-semitic atmosphere he lived in and took for granted, his perceptions of the enemy were simply radicalised under the influence of these personal and political upheavals, and his hopes for deliverance intensified into fanaticism. At the age of seventeen Schirach developed an intensive interest in anti-semitic literature. He read Chamberlain, Bartels and Ford. In July 1925 Hitler's *Mein Kampf* appeared. Schirach devoured the book straightaway at one sitting. For him it was like 'a bible, which we learned by heart, in order to have an answer to the questions of doubters and critics cleverer than us'.[7]

Hitler, who was still banned from public speaking in Bavaria, made repeated visits to Weimar in the spring and summer of this year to make public appearances. In Thuringia the *Völkische* had a considerable pool of people at their disposal. At national and state elections they gained around ten per cent of the votes. Schirach was present at Hitler's first public meetings. He was a member of the *Knappenschaft*, a *völkisch* youth defence league led by Ziegler, which provided the security services for the meeting. Schirach and his family soon came into closer contact with the leader of the NSDAP through Ziegler. Baldur admired Hitler and soon became his unconditionally devoted follower. Countless poems in praise of him which begin to appear from then on, bear testimony to this. Schirach's relentless production of poetry, which was superior to the outpourings of other *völkisch* versifiers, laid the early foundation of his reputation as the movement's bard and in the early years in particular it furthered his National Socialist career.

Baldur von Schirach joined the NSDAP on 29 August 1925. His membership number was 17 251.[8] In the years that followed Weimar remained an important stronghold for the National Socialists. In 1926 the NSDAP held its Party Conference there. On that occasion, at Ziegler's suggestion, the youth organisation was given the name 'Hitler Youth'. The name was descriptive, and at the same time an indication of the extreme personality cult of the Weimar National Socialists, even in the early days. The socially revolutionary views which dominated wide sections of the Party at that time were alien to them. Schirach followed decisively in this tradition.[9]

After finishing his Higher School Leaving Exam, on Hitler's suggestion he went to study in Munich. He attended lectures and seminars in German Literature, English, art history, psychology and Egyptology, without however gaining any final qualifications. The straitened financial circumstances of the majority of his fellow students were alien to him. Schirach socialised in the upper-middle-class salons, which by that time had long since opened their doors to Hitler, and tried, at first in vain, to find a foothold among the Party leader's closest following.

Soon he came across the National Socialist German Students' League. The basic tenets of National Socialist ideology, anti-semitism and anti-Marxism determined the policies of this organisation too. But over and above this it was dominated by strong social revolutionary traits. Soon Schirach became leader of the Munich University group. In summer 1928 he took over the leadership of the entire Nazi German Students' League. The social revolutionary tendencies were supressed and the League opened up to the corporations which then dominated student life. At this time, when the NSDAP could still only claim to be a splinter party, the Students' League launched upon a series of electoral successes at the universities, which led to the National Socialists dominating the German student body in the summer of 1931. This also gave Schirach an official mandate for his battle against the Republic. This victorious campaign strengthened his position in the Party and assured him of Hitler's backing. Repeated attempts to remove Schirach from power were therefore condemned to failure.

Even at that time Schirach was looking around for new duties to increase his power. He cast an eye on the Hitler Youth. Under the leadership of Kurt Gruber it was being built up only slowly. It hardly gained any recruits from among middle class youth. In the schools and colleges the National Socialist League of School Pupils, founded in 1929, was becoming established under the leadership of Adrian von Renteln. In the university towns he worked closely together with the Students' League. Gruber's position was worsening visibly. Finally he was dismissed. On 3 October 1931 Hitler appointed Schirach National Youth Leader of the NSDAP, but transferred direct responsibility for the Hitler Youth to Renteln. However in June of the following year Schirach succeeded in having Renteln removed from power and forcing his resignation. Schirach himself took over the Hitler Youth and made the School Pupils' League an integral part of it.

His efforts were now concentrated on building up the Hitler Youth as quickly as possible. At that time it was one youth organisation among many, and by no means the biggest among the numerous assortment of groups, leagues and associations. Only a strong position would give him a chance of taking over the leadership of the entire youth movement after the expected seizure of power. The so-called State Youth Day in Potsdam in October, in which 70 000 young people took part, was a demonstration of his claim.

However after 3 January 1933 Hitler was initially dependent on his Conservative coalition partners. So Schirach had to be patient in his battle against the other youth organisations and confine himself to propaganda and tactical moves, like taking over the state committee for German Youth Associations. The plan considered in the spring of creating a Ministry for Youth and the merging of countless groups within the 'Greater German League' considerably weakened Schirach's position. Things only changed when Hitler appointed him as 'Youth Leader of the German State' on 17 June 1933. Now Schirach vigorously asserted his claim to power wherever possible. The 'Greater German League', with 70 000 young members, was scrapped. An agreement between Schirach and Reich Bishop Müller on the organisation of Protestant Youth brought 700 000 young people into the Hitler Youth in December 1933. The membership total was further increased by deals, coercion and new members joining voluntarily to stand at 1.9 million boys and 1.26 million girls by September 1935.[10]

However there were limits on Schirach's expansionist plans. For example, Hitler's Concordat with the Vatican prevented him from getting the Catholic youth organisations within his grasp. The development of the organisation did not keep pace with the rapid increase in membership. Leaders, premises and money were all in short supply. At that time the Hitler Youth would not have been capable of dealing with the compulsory membership of all young people. In this early phase of the dictatorship Schirach repeatedly underlined the socialist mission of his organisation, the claim to be 'Adolf Hitler's Revolutionary Youth Movement'.[11] But this meant nothing other than that he intended to encompass and lead all young people.

He stayed at a careful distance from the SA, although he was an SA General and for a while before the seizure of power was immediately subordinate to Röhm. He survived the assassination of the leadership of the SA on 30 June 1934 unscathed. Schirach's position had been further strengthened at that time, but was based entirely on Hitler's goodwill. Since he had married Henriette Hoffmann in March 1932, the daughter of Hitler's close friend and personal photographer, Heinrich Hoffmann, he belonged at last to the inner circle around the Party leader. Among the leader's followers, however, he continued to be controversial.

Schirach was consistent in his pursuit of his political and pedagogical strategy. He proclaimed it endlessly in his two slogans: young people must be led by young people and have their own state. Schirach could point to Hitler himself as the originator of this strategy.[12] It represented an attempt to create, as it were, an autonomous copy of the Nazi state within the Hitler Youth: a 'Liliput' in the Third Reich, answerable to Hitler alone. This meant in part warding off or canalising the influence of the Party and the state, while at the same time usurping greater and greater areas of education. Cooperation with the Party, army, SS, SA, ministries and other organisations was regulated by contracts, which were always designed to guarantee the sovereignty of the Hitler Youth. Cooperation with any one organisation immediately brought the other competitors into the fray, since they feared losing influence and new recruits. The alternating attempts of the army and the SA, and later the SS, too, to take in hand the pre-military training of the Hitler Youth and Schirach's efforts to extricate himself are all impressive testimony to this.[13]

After the seizure of power, Schirach was responsible first to the Minister of the Interior, Frick, and then to the Education Minister, Rust. His efforts to establish the Hitler Youth as the third factor in upbringing, alongside the parental home and school were reflected from summer 1934 in the so-called State Day of Youth. Saturday was to belong to the Hitler Youth alone. However this arrangement proved to be unsuitable becasue of organisational difficulties and was abolished after the promulgation of the law regulating the Hitler Youth. With this law of 1 December 1936 Hitler made the National Youth Directorate a senior office of state and Schirach Secretary of State. Schirach was now directly responsible to Hitler. The Hitler Youth was reorganised as an independent educational power. However he did not achieve his aim of establishing the National Youth Directorate as a shadow ministry within the educational sector – led by 80 civil servants, a leadership corps paid by the state and with a state budget. The Hitler Youth did not become the State Youth, but remained a branch of the Party. Hitler only allowed the National Youth Directorate a few civil service posts. Financial jurisdiction remained with the Party Treasurer, Schwarz.[14] Compulsory membership was not enshrined in law until March 1939. Nonetheless the law represented a success for Schirach. He had now obtained a platform for the most ambitious phase of his career: he intended to bring school education, too, under his control. In January 1937 he, and the National Organiser, Robert Ley, announced a programme for the establishment of 'Adolf Hitler Schools'. In these, selected Hitler Youths were to be educated to Higher School Leaving Certificate standard and the principle of self-government implemented. Rust was beside himself about this competition. The strain which already existed in their relationship escalated into open conflict. Hitler considered replacing Rust with Schirach, but then left everything as it was.

Schirach continued his show-down with the schools, demanding 'unity of education', the unspoken meaning of which was: under his direction. However the only result of all his efforts was that the gulf between the National Youth Directorate on the one hand, and the Education Ministry and the National Socialist Teachers' League on the other, became deeper and deeper. Even Rosenberg became involved in the conflict. He was already in dispute with Schirach. They had differences on ideological matters, in their evaluation of the philosophers Klages and Kant. Rosenberg accused the National Youth Directorate of attempting to form 'as it were an intellectual party alongside the Party'. Now the Party ideologue publicly took the teachers under his protection, in the face of the attacks from the Hitler Youth. Schirach did not give in. Finally Rosenberg temporarily even subjected Schirach's journalistic mouthpiece 'Wille und Macht' to his censorship.[15]

Schirach's pedagogical policy was very inadequate. In the final analysis, behind the jumble of phrases his plans related to the few fixed points of Lietz's teachings. However he did want more than simply to fulfil Hitler's much quoted adage, by which the Hitler Youth were to be 'as swift as greyhounds, as hard as Krupp steel and as tough as leather'. Schirach also claimed for himself the 'intellectual and moral education of youth'. This reflected his intention of encompassing 'all spheres of life' for young Germans.[16] At the same time, alongside sporting and pre-military training, cultural work gained in significance in the years before the war. Schirach took a comparatively independent line in cultural policy, with which he intended at the same time to underpin his claims to leadership in the sphere of National Socialist education.

However control of education in the Third Reich was only a staging post for him. Instead Schirach wanted to 'seek out that German person who is capable of leading the world power called Germany'.[17] On 20 April 1939 he declared to his deputies:

> The German people is called on to rule the world. Of course we will heed this call. . . . If we dispute the British nation's claim to leadership, then we don't need people who have the outlook of moles, but people who have trained themselves to conceive of great territories. . . . Within this territory we have millions of Czechs. We will yet have millions of other peoples.[18]

However the outbreak of war put a temporary end to Schirach's ambitions. While all eyes were on Poland, he attempted, in a surprise move, to secure for himself sole control of the education system. Goering, who was conducting government business, appeared to greet his intentions approvingly. But when Hitler learned of his plans he stopped Schirach just before he achieved his goal. Most of the Hitler Youth leaders had at that time entered military service. Control of Youth was increasingly slipping out of his grasp. The number of illegal youth groups increased by leaps and bounds. Increasingly, criminal tendencies came to the fore. During this phase, supervision of the Hitler Youth passed in practice to the Party. The 'failure of the leadership of the Hitler Youth' was blamed on Schirach.[19] When exactly Hitler made the decision to dismiss Schirach can no longer be determined today. However the decision was final by the beginning of April 1940 at the latest. By this time Schirach had already entered active service in the army. After participating in the French campaign, on 10 August he took up his new post as *Gauleiter* and Reich Plenipotentiary in Vienna. At the same time he was appointed 'Commissioner for the Inspection of the entire Hitler Youth'. However his influence on youth training was severely limited.

At this time there was a sense of dissatisfaction among wide sections of the Viennese population. The initial euphoria after the annexation into the Reich had evaporated. Living conditions had become worse since then. The pivotal positions in the Party, administration and economy had been filled with German functionaries from the Reich. There was a general feeling in many places that they had been downgraded into a Prussian provincial town. Schirach's task was to divert the Viennese from their social problems by developing a glittering cultural life, and to blind them to the fact that their city had indeed become politically insignificant. Over and above this Hitler delegated him with the task of deporting the 60 000 Jews remaining in Vienna.

At first Schirach was successful in his efforts to fulfil these tasks. Vienna soon seemed to outshine even Berlin in cultural terms. In the process Schirach continued to pursue policies which were avant-garde even by National Socialist standards. Goebbels, who was responsible for cultural policy and at the same time *Gauleiter* of the capital of the Reich, observed Schirach's work with the greatest attentiveness and gradually became more and more critical. However his first attempt to undermine Schirach's cultural supremacy in Vienna, in June 1941, missed its mark.[20] By that time 10 000 Jews had already been sent to Poland in the first wave of deportations, after Governor-General Frank had objected in vain to Schirach's demand that he must 'relieve him' of the Jews.[21] Although Schirach knew by May 1942 at the latest, that Jews were being murdered in the gas chambers, even after this he still publicly celebrated their deportation as his 'active contribution to European culture'.[22]

Even from Vienna Schirach made attempts to strengthen his influence on the education system. In September 1940 Hitler had charged him with the evacuation to the countryside of children from cities at risk from bombing. Initially the evacuation was to apply only to children of school age from Berlin and Hamburg who lived in suburbs and parts of the cities which did not have sufficient air-raid shelters. Schirach gave responsibility for teaching in the camps exclusively to the National Socialist League of Teachers. The project soon became more and more extensive. In April 1942 there were already 850 000 boys and girls in the evacuation camps.[23] In them it was possible to some extent for Schirach to implement his 'unity of education' ideas. His attempt in March 1942 to have Hitler entrust him with the conduct of the mobilisation of young people and by this means to achieve pre-eminence in the field of education was unsuccessful.[24]

At this time, in spite of the increasingly violent attacks from Goebbels, Schirach still enjoyed his Führer's patronage. However Hitler was becoming more and more dissatisfied with Schirach's cultural policy. Even the establishment of a 'European Youth Association', to which he had invited delegates from fascist youth organisations of thirteen countries to Vienna in September, was almost unanimously rejected in the capital of the Reich. Schirach was increasingly pessimistic in his assessment of the prospects of winning the war. Therefore he declared in front of his subordinates that Germany should not exercise 'power through force', but should instead aim to act as the 'premier security power' within the context of 'voluntary cooperation between nations.'[25] By this time the defeat at Stalingrad was already taking place. He fell into disfavour in summer 1943 because of misgivings about his cultural policy, complaints that he had not been energetic enough in putting Vienna on the necessary footing for total war, and an attempt he made at least once, although in vain, to inform Hitler of his ideas on alternative foreign policy and policy for the occupied territories.[26] Schirach remained at his post, but from now on he no longer played any political role. When the Russians were outside Vienna in April 1945 Schirach stood down and disappeared but later gave himself up to the Americans. At Nuremberg he was sentenced to twenty years imprisonment for 'crimes against humanity'. He completed his sentence on 1 October 1966. Schirach died on 8 August 1974 in Kröv on the Moselle.

NOTES

1. Leonhard Schrickel *Geschichte des Weimarer Theatres von seinen Anfängen bis heute* (Weimar, 1928) pp. 256 and 251.
2. Carl von Schirach to the editor Christ, 5.6.1943, Archive of the Hesse State Theatre, Wiesbaden, Carl von Schirach's personal file.

3. For the family history see Max von Schirach, *Geschichte der Familie von Schirach* (Berlin, 1939).
4. Schirach in conversation with Jochen von Lang. Transcript in the Institut für Zeitgeschichte, Munich, vol. I, p. 12.
5. Ibid., p. 20, vol. II, p. 47.
6. Schirach, *Ich glaubte an Hitler* (Hamburg, 1967) p. 15.
7. Baldur von Schirach, *Die Hitler-Jugend. Idee und Gestalt* (Berlin, 1934) p. 17.
8. Berlin Document Center, file on Baldur von Schirach. According to this Schirach did not, as is frequently claimed, join the Party on his eighteenth birthday.
9. See Konrad Studentowski, *Wie die Hitler-Jugend ihren Namen erhielt. Weihnachtsgruss an die Thüringer Hitlerjugend-Führer im Felde* (Weimar, 1941). According to other information in Nazi literature, the naming of the Hitler Youth can be traced back to Julius Streicher, who was then conducting a meeting about 'matters concerning schooling and the organisation of youth'. He evidently put Ziegler's suggestion to a vote.
10. These figures were given during a conference of Hitler Youth financial managers in the context of the Nuremberg Party Conference on 12.9.1935 (BA/NS26/395). The officially announced figures for the end of 1935 are as follows: 3 943 303 boys and girls from a total population of 8 172 000 young people within the German Reich.
11. Radio speech, 1.1.1934, Allgemeines Verwaltungsarchiv, Vienna (AVW)/Reichsstatthalterei/Ordn. 1394.
12. Adolf Hitler, *Mein Kampf*, 743rd–747th edition (Munich, 1942) p. 461 and p. 317f.
13. See the Bundesarchiv-Militärarchiv Freiburg (BA-MA)/RH37/1351/1379 and the Bundesarchiv Koblenz (BA)/R43II/520b/522b/526 and NS/336, Institut für Zeitgeschichte Munich (IfZ)/MA325.
14. See the letter of Graf Schwerin von Krosigk, 6.5.1936, Politisches Archiv des Auswärtiges Amtes Bonn/Inland I Partei/Reichsjugendführer, Plan für den Aufbau der Reichsjugend, BA/R43 II/525, Bericht über die Geldverwalterta-gung der Hitlerjugend, 12.9.1935, BA/NS26/395, Vermerk zur Hitlerjugend, 25.2.1937, BA/R43II/525.
15. Compare the references in BA/NS8/212.
16. Speech to the press, 5.4.1939, AVW/Reichsstatthalterei/Ordn. 1396.
17. Speech to the departmental directors of physical education, 21.4.1939, AVW/Reichsstatthalterei/Ordn. 1398.
18. Speech at the opening of the Academy for Youth Leaders to its first students, 20.4.1939, ibid.
19. Friedrichs, in front of the deputy *Gauleiter*, 5.3.1940, IfZ/91/3.
20. Schirach to Lammers, 25.6.1941, AVW/Reichsstatthalterei/Org. 569/208 II.
21. Note by Bormann, 2.10.1940, quoted from IMT, vol. XXXIX, p. 435.
22. Speech on the occasion of the establishment of the EJV, 14.9.1942, AVW/Reichsstatthalterei/Ordn. 1406.
23. Landverschickung schulpflichtiger Jugendlicher, no date (September 1940), AVW/Reichsstatthalterei/Presse/unsigned, speech to the participants in an officers' training course, 22.4.1942, AVW/Reichsstatthalterei/Ordn. 1406.
24. Printed in IMT, vol. XXXIII, p. 558f. Schirach was evidently reacting in this to the appointment, which was announced shortly before, of the Thuringian *Gauleiter* Sauckel to the post of 'General Plenipotentiary for employment'.
25. Speech to a regional leaders' conference in Braunschweig, 13.1.1942, AVW/Reichsstatthalterei/Ordn. 1406.

26. Compare Nicolaus von Below, *Als Hitlers Adjutant 1937–1945* (Mainz, 1980) p. 340.

BIBLIOGRAPHY

Primary Sources

An impression of Schirach's output of lyric poetry is given in a book published in Munich in 1929: B.v. Schirach, *Die Feier der neuen Front*. Schirach's book, *Die Hitler-Jugend. Idee und Gestalt* (Berlin 1934) was described by his press agent, Günther Kaufmann, in 1941 as being entirely 'outdated in all sections'. Schirach himself was not interested in a new edition, because 'various fundamental questions concerning education will have to be thoroughly looked into after the end of the war'. A collection of the speeches of the Hitler Youth Leader appeared in 1938 in Munich: B.v. Schirach, *Revolution der Erziehung. Reden aus den Jahren des Aufbaus*. This collection was intended to provide the written programme for the Hitler Youth, which up till then had been lacking.

Schirach's memoirs can only be used with considerable reservations: B.v Schirach, *Ich glaubte an Hitler* (Documented by J.v. Lang) (Hamburg, 1967). The book is based on conversations Schirach had with Jochen von Lang after his release from prison. The transcripts of the tapes are in the Institut für Zeitgeschichte, Munich. Schirach attempts to take refuge in the role of an innocent young man, seduced by Hitler, who only learned of the crimes of National Socialism when it was too late.

Secondary Literature

There are two comprehensive biographies of Schirach: M. Wortmann, *Baldur von Schirach. Hitlers Jugendführer* (Cologne, 1982); J.v. Lang, *Der Hitler-Junge. Baldur von Schirach: Der Mann der Deutschlands Jugend erzog* (with the collaboration of Claus Sybill) (Hamburg, 1988). Wortmann shows in his study that Schirach consistently followed a political and educational policy which had as its aim the unrestricted control of education in the Nazi state and the formation of a new leadership elite. Lang's biography is based on the 'oral history' method. Lang had already collaborated on Schirach's memoirs. However the results of recent research are also taken into consideration. Unfortunately Lang does not give any detailed source references. A sketch of the Nazi Youth Leader which contains many salient points can also be found in J.C. Fest, *Das Gesicht des Dritten Reiches. Profile einer totalitären Herrschaft* (Munich, 1963) p. 300–18. However large parts of this contribution no longer reflect the latest findings of research, and Fest also underestimates Schirach's desire for power. There is as yet no satisfactory history of the Hitler Youth. The best study to date is: A. Klönne, *Jugend im Dritten Reich. Die Hitler-Jugend und ihre Gegner* (Dusseldorf/Cologne, 1982).

20 Albert Speer: Cultural and Economic Management
Jost Dülffer

No other leading personality of the Nazi era has expressed himself as explicitly and critically about these years as Albert Speer has done. Because of this none of the actors of the time has had such an impact on the interpretation of the Nazi system as a whole as he has. This does not make it easy for a historian to give a picture which is independent of these distorting factors.

Albert Speer was born on 19 March 1905 in Mannheim. He grew up there, and from 1918 in Heidelberg, in an upper middle class milieu imbued with liberal values. His father was a respected architect in the area. It seemed reasonable for his son to chose the same subject. Albert studied in Karlsruhe, Munich and, from 1925, in Berlin, where he was a student of Heinrich Tessenow at the Technical University. Tessenow was neither a modernist nor a traditionalist in his field and aimed for a policy of self-determination, closeness to nature, simplicity and a vernacular style, but also a renunciation of mere rationality. Speer was immediately enthusiastic about his teacher, writing in 1925, 'To look at he is just as unimaginative and sober as I am, but nonetheless his buildings have a sense of profound experience.'[1] This personal affinity probably also explains why Speer became Tessenow's assistant in 1928. This also gave a material basis for his marriage to a childhood sweetheart, which produced six children. A circle of friends of the same age formed around Tessenow and these later became Speer's close colleagues, but the National Socialist students also gathered around him and soon became dominant as they had done elsewhere. In this milieu, open to radical change and new experience, which provided a sharp contrast to the sufferings of the Great Depression, Speer found his way into the NSDAP. His later description of the effect of one of Hitler's public speeches bears all the marks of a personal conversion: 'He had taken hold of me, before I realised'.[2]

Speer's admission to the Nazi Party in January 1931 was not just a formality; he attempted immediately, both in Berlin and Mannheim, to make himself useful to this cause which he had recognised as good, primarily in the National Socialist Drivers' Corps. He was also interested in the SS, but did not become a member. Since he was financially secure, because of his parents' property, Speer became an independent architect in 1932 and received his first commissions through Nazi contacts. The young architect's uncertain prospects improved considerably with the National

Socialists' seizure of power. The Berlin *Gauleiter*, Joseph Goebbels, had his new propaganda ministry, a Schinkel building, converted and furnished. Speer, an industrious worker, achieved this in three months. At the same time he was commissioned to set the scene for the Berlin Proclamation of 1 May 1933, and a little later for the Party convention in Nuremberg. For this purpose Speer used over-sized swastika flags which could be lit up at night. From this he developed the idea of projecting a 'cathedral of light' by using many spotlights directed upwards. This created a pseudo-sacral element within the aesthetic concept of National Socialism which remained a constant part of the ritual thereafter. He had created a gigantic and exhilarating framework, impressive for the media world of its day, which made the individual appear small but at the same time part of a collective national greatness.

Hitler noticed Speer and had him supervise the conversion of the Reich Chancellery which had been planned by Paul Troost. In this way he entered into the most decisive association of his life. It was probably the young man's vigour which Hitler liked; but Speer himself proved to be so impressed by his personal proximity to the Führer that other perceptions of the centre of power and the exercise of power paled by comparison. The architect soon belonged to the Führer's artistic entourage, took part in Hitler's bohemian life style, travelled with him and moved to be close to Hitler's alpine home on the Obersalzberg. Hitler, for his part, as a self-taught architect, made use of Speer's expertise. If Hitler had had a friend, it would have been Speer, was how Speer later interpreted the points of contact between the two personally reserved men, which also contained elements of homosexuality. This also points to the most important criterion for Speer's varying positions of power until 1945: the Führer's goodwill or lack of it, which formed the basis for departmental power within the Nazi hierarchy and for competition between National Socialist rivals. The arrangement was reminiscent of courtly ritual, but on the whole this 'court' had petty-bourgeois characteristics. Furthermore, the ability to enforce obedience to one's own decrees also played a part, as did personal assertiveness, ambition, intrigue and the cold-blooded exploitation of opportunities in competition with others in positions of power; the vehicles for this were legal regulations, decrees and authorisations, best of all from Hitler himself. They were formulated specially for a given sector, but were at the same time vague as to the delineation of authority and were scent marks which were placed at the individual boundaries of those in positions of power.

At the beginning of 1934, after Troost's death, access to the Chancellor meant he had the opportunity to advise him on his hobby, a hobby, however, which related in the closest possible way to the dictator's overall political aims. Hitler wanted to anticipate German greatness, indeed its position as a premier world power, in a corresponding monumental design for buildings and whole cities, like Berlin and Munich. His ideas for town planning were determined by his intention of demonstrating that the German nation did not 'represent some sort of second-class power, but is the equal of every other people in the world, even America'.[3] For Hitler, buildings were a source of pride for all peoples in the history of the world. The architect experimented with this concept and then suggested the idea of building in natural stone, so that even thousands of years later there would still be imposing ruins remaining of this German Reich which they were to build anew. 'The Führer is building as head of state . . . . His great buildings, which are today beginning to rise in many places, are intended as *one* expression of the character of the movement for millenia to come, and so are a part of the movement itself,' Speer wrote in 1936 in a book of photos which was distributed in hundreds of thousands.[4]

First of all, however, he had to impress Hitler with monumental designs which the latter found to his liking and which reproduced the forms of classical antiquity, to make plans for individual builings and develop parade routes for city centres. In Nuremberg Speer extended the National Party Convention ground. Hitler had been negotiating with Berlin's National Socialist administration since 1933 about a monumental transformation of the city and he was looking for a man suited to the task. In 1935 he was still sceptical about whether Speer would do. He in the meantime had been commissioned with building projects by other Nazi leaders and was producing various buildings as examples of his work, of which the foremost was the German Pavilion for the Paris World Exhibition in 1937. Furthermore he undertook the office of 'Beauty of Labour' in the German Labour Front (DAF) in 1937 and established himself in the NSDAP on Rudolf Hess's staff as the Commissioner for Buildings.

On 30 January 1937, the fourth anniversary of the seizure of power, Speer became General Building Inspector for the National Capital (GBI). With global authority for all the necessary measures which fell within this remit, authority he himself established in accordance with Hitler's wishes, Speer set himself to the task of establishing an axis of parade streets and boulevards in the centre of the capital, at the central point of which was to be built a mighty triumphal arch, and at its nothern end a monumental Great Hall for 180 000 people. The remaining overall plan for the transformation of the capital into the world imperial capital, Germania, which was to be completed by 1950, fared badly by comparison. Alongside the design work for the larger buildings which were to be situated on the axes, there began a ruthless programme of evicting tenants and tearing down established streets. Later the seizure of the appartments of Jewish citizens was also part of this process. They had to vacate their appartments initially to make way for those affected by the demolition work, then for those decorated in the war and finally for victims of the bombing. What happened to them was beyond doubt. Energetic negotiations with other authorities underline the fact that the Führer's dynamic architect was endeavouring to fulfil the expectations made of him. This became even more obvious during the rebuilding of the Reich Chancellery, which was completed within a year at the beginning of 1939, more quickly than normal planning procedures and the careful handling of money and materials should actually have allowed. This seemed to be an expression of genuinely National Socialist get-up-and-go and secured his superhuman reputation. Speer's position became so strong that in the middle of 1940 he brought about the dismissal of Berlin's mayor, who had demanded rights of consultation: 'The unique nature of my task demands the clear pre-eminence of the one post necessary for the overall concept. That means me.'[5]

In addition to this Speer made efforts to coordinate building plans in the rest of the Reich too. Hitler had commissioned other architects elsewhere – for example Hermann Giesler; for their part party leaders attempted to gain building permits within the context of a law promulgated in 1937. In February 1941 the talk was of twenty-three regional capitals and four other towns, and building projects in the National Socialist style were scheduled to be undertaken in forty-one towns. On 18 October 1940 Speer did in fact gain authority for the overall coordination of these plans, but when he tried to become 'Commissioner for Town Planning' as a whole, he had overreached himself. After intrigues against him he threw in the towel and declared on 20 January 1941 that in future he intended to concentrate on his real life's work, the buildings in Berlin and Nuremberg, and gave up the Party buildings. Speer saw himself being cast back on the source of his power, on Hitler. There is something to be said for the theory that the latter wished to retain alternatives to his chief architect, so that all strands of building work had first of all to pass in front of him.

If before Speer had repeatedly rejected requests from other offices for the provision of all monies required, and especially for natural stone and building materials, as not being in line with the Führer's wishes, in 1940 he fought his way to the position of being able to assert the precedence of what was practicable over all other requests.

On this basis five Führer cities' – Berlin, Munich, Hamburg, Nuremberg and Linz on the Danube – were given overall precedence, and the – defunct – general plenary powers for city planning were to be used to achieve this. This endeavour may have appeared to Hitler as the first stage of bureaucratic torpor. Of course in the meantime Speer had built up an apparatus, even including a fleet of trucks, which were to be used to transport suitable natural stone from all over Europe for the planned major buildings. It was the enormous requirement of raw material which brought Speer closest to the terror inherent in the system. Concentration camps were newly established or expanded at the demand of the General Inspector. In close cooperation with the SS economic concern 'German Earth and Stone Works', brickworks were built from Oranienburg to

Neuengamme, stone quarries worked from Natzweiler to Flossenbürg. As late as March 1945, Speer's deputies were calculating costs with the SS for a new works in Oranienburg. They were fully aware that the work was done as forced labour by detainees in concentration camps, and in the same way the GBI gratefully accepted the offer of the SS to put detainees at their disposal to exploit deposits of Norwegian stone should the need arise. This was more than 'technical immorality' (J. Fest), clinging to a grand task which was primarily artistic, and not caring about or not noticing the crimes which surrounded it. Speer, the capable organiser, was central to the expansion of the system of concentration camps.

The war, which was intended to win, by military means, the German greatness which Speer was building in stone, did not initially drastically interrupt his activities, for in the summer of 1940, after the victory over France and then again after the first battles against the Soviet Union in summer 1941, the hope was that the war would soon be over. Hitler urged the architects to keep working. Trondheim in Norway was added to the list in 1941 – planned as a future naval base and a city of several hundreds of thousands of people. However a proportion of the workers were withdrawn from Speer's building sites to be put in to armaments production and assigned as a unit to the factories concerned, and then in 1941 sent as Speer's Building Staff to rebuild railways and roads in the Ukraine. In so doing the GBI had taken over activities which were normally the duty of the Todt Organisation (OT).

When Fritz Todt died on 8 February 1942 in a plane crash, Hitler at once appointed Speer as his successor in all offices. This was undoubtedly a central turning point in Speer's career. Along with Road Building and Fortification, Speer's chief task was to take over the Ministry for Armaments and Munitions. Further duties were added, like that of General Inspector for Water and Power, and General Inspector of German Roads. At the same time Speer became chief of the Todt Organisation. It was an empire with responsibilities which extended right across Europe and 70 000 public sector employees had been earmarked to work in it. Speer was no expert in the specialist problems it dealt with, but he was in possession of Hitler's trust and had considerable organisational talent. He promised to fulfill the duties conferred on him, by-passing the establishment elites and bureaucracies – and that included the military. Some principles should be stressed. Speer knew how to delegate: the OT for example de facto continued to be directed by Franz Xaver Dorsch. But since the Minister did not bother with the details, and even brought the 'experts' along to discussions with Hitler, they were, because of their relative independence and access to the centre of power, gradually able to undermine the Minister's role. The more duties Speer had, the more he lost an overall view of them. It was possible to build up power bases against him via access to Hitler, the legitimising basis of authority and the signatory of Führer's Decrees, who stubbornly pursued his favourite ideas, even in the field of armaments, and distributed his favour according to the extent to which they were implemented. From 1942 Hitler's relations with Speer were no longer predominantly based on art and friendship, but on matter-of-factness and impartiality. Hardly anything is more characteristic of the dynamic aggressive style of the thirty-six-year-old Minister than his declaration, shortly after he took office, that 'a deputy, not over forty years old, must be appointed for every executive over the age of forty-five'.[6]

Speer subsequently made much of the fact that the number of colleagues directly responsible to him remained comparatively small. They consisted predominantly of architects, municipal officials and entrepreneurs. Below his ministry Speer built up a system of which his predecessor had already developed the central features: the 'self administration of industry' or, in Marxist terminology: a new level of state monopoly. Committees were formed with responsibility for some military goods – as Todt had already done for weapons, munitions and heavy armour – under the honorary control of an industrialist. They were responsible for the armaments deliveries requested by individual customers (mostly the military); between these 'rings' were formed for the relevant sections of industry, and these in turn set up main and branch committees or 'rings'. So self-administration only meant that industry was responsible for production and it did not plan for a specific market. What was to be produced was decided by others. Nevertheless industrialists took up more prominent state functions than in World War One. Chairmen were usually directors of industry, representatives of the big firms, and with the express support of the minister they pushed through a dynamic rationalisation of the German economy. Small and medium-sized concerns were specifically sought out and shut down, using a decree obtained by Speer on 28 June 1943, among other methods. This trend towards big business and rationalisation of production was the consequence of an intended change in armaments policy which only happened to coincide with what Speer had been entrusted with doing. If the war had until then been designed in economic terms for campaigns which imposed only slight material deprivation on the German population and mobilised far fewer resources than the First World War, the bogging down of the German advance on Moscow at the end of 1941 symbolically signalled that a longer and more total war would have to be waged; the alternative of peace did not exist for Hitler. What Goebbels tried to bring about by propaganda, Speer did for armaments.

1. His first aim was to expand his spheres of competence. In April 1942 he received from 'central planning' (of the Four Year Plan) the responsibility for the provision and administration of raw materials; one month later the Defence Economy and Armaments Division of the Army Supreme Command was put under his control and completely abolished the following

year. In July 1943 Speer and the Commander-in-Chief of the Navy, Karl Dönitz, agreed the former would now take over naval armaments; on 1 August 1944 Speer took over the Air Force armaments, by making General Erhard Milch, who had hitherto been responsible for it, his deputy. In this way Speer also brought about the rationalisation of military output down to fewer types of a given arms product, at least in as far as Hitler did not intervene with his own ideas. The results were considerable. The index of armaments production (1942=100) reached its highest point during the war (226) in June 1944, the index for armour got as high as 462; the index began to decline after June 1944, while production by subcontractors reached its highest point slightly earlier. Over and above this Speer took over responsibility for civilian output from the Economics Ministry. This was announced by a decree from Hitler on 2 September 1943, aimed at 'the concentration of the war economy' and at the same time it transformed Speer's Ministry into a 'Ministry for Armaments and War Production'. As a result the 'Super Minister' now held the chairmanship of an inter-ministerial committee. Powers to manage the armaments industry in the parts of Europe under German rule were added, powers which on the whole were easier to implement in France, Belgium and the Netherlands, and in the Protectorate of Bohemia and Moravia than in the east. Finally from 1943 he gained increasing influence on the remaining German foreign economic policy.

Speer became the second most powerful man in the regime, and this because Hitler let him have his way. The young man began to think he was probably the one whom the 'Führer' would name as his successor, in a Nazi regime of course.

2. However the extent of Speer's power already contained the seeds of its destruction, that is the construction of opposing power blocks. On 1 March 1942 Speer skilfully took up a formal position subordinate to Hermann Goering as 'Commissioner for Armaments in the Four Year Plan' and was able in this way to bring about a bearable relationship with the former second man in the regime, although it was repeatedly upset by petty jealousies. Speer could only occasionally evade the triumvirate which regulated personal access to Hitler – Wilhelm Keitel, Hans-Heinrich Lammers and Martin Bormann – and he failed in particular to neutralise Bormann. The Armaments Minister was aware that for the moment he was in agreement with Goebbels in the endeavour to run the Reich more efficiently and achieve total mobilisation, and was even willing to be put on public show by him. Nonetheless personal enmity outweighed this. Speer's relationship with Heinrich Himmler was originally characterised by effective cooperation. Speer could depend on the SS leader when he threatened insufficiently cooperative colleagues or competitors with the concentration camp. He fully understood the significance of the system of forced labour,

which contributed to the efficiency of his activities, when he demanded armaments workers from Auschwitz, for example, or had concentration camp workers work on the building of underground factories in the Harz mountains. Later he stepped back from this position. The few improvements, for example in hygiene, which Speer implemented for the concentration camps, were solely for the purpose of increasing productivity. What the Armaments Minister only dimly grasped was that Himmler was proceeding to build up production bases and positions of power which did not come under Speer's control, precisely in the sphere of the armaments economy, through the Economics Ministry.

The final authority for the mobilisation of the population into employment was held by Fritz Sauckel, the Thuringian *Gauleiter*. With him, too, Speer originally worked well, as long as he came up with the necessary workers for the armaments industry. But Speer occasionally arranged things directly with Hitler, as with the transportation of 200 000 Russian miners into the Reich. It was not the system of forced labour, as such, which led to disputes with Sauckel, but its lack of efficiency vis-à-vis the requirements of the defence industry. Speer came more and more to favour production in the parts of Europe controlled by Germany, especially in France, while Sauckel continued to support forced deportation into the Reich. Plans for Europe in the case of permanent German rule after the war, too, were developed in Speer's ministry. Finally, the fact that Speer was increasingly getting into difficulties with the *Gauleiter* (who were also the Commissioners for the Defence of the Reich) was added as a source of conflict.

Speer became ill in the course of this permanent struggle for power, in January 1944, because he was exhausted/overworked; but his illness had a psychosomatic background. During his convalescence, which lasted several months, aspects of his power base in the Reich were lost to him and even within his department colleagues were able to make themselves permanently independent.

3. Speer's success in armaments is all the more astonishing if one considers that with the retreat of German troops before the victorious Allies, access to raw material and workers they had previously exploited was lost, the willingness to cooperate disappeared and, most importantly, bombing raids destroyed or damaged German towns and utilities important for the armaments industry. Armaments planning now gave rise to an increasing number of special committees and commissioners, who, although they were given precedence over earlier priorities, were only able to plug gaps. The first of these was the 'Fighter Staff' for the production of fighter aircraft, set up on 1 March 1944, which became a miniature ministry in its own right and slipped from Speer's control under the leadership of Saur, on the authority of SS leader Kammler. Speer was at first officially involved in the

making of 'wonder weapons', rockets, and other missiles, but gradually had to give up his role to the SS. It was, for example, necessary to have a special commission for the maintenance of synthetic oil production in summer 1944; in autumn 1944 a Ruhr commission was set up to alleviate the worst of the bomb damage in that area. Industrialists filled the most important positions in it, up to the point of intervening in municipal administration. 'The armaments industry, which had been unified within my ministry from the spring of 1944, began to disintegrate again in the late autumn.'[7]

Speer personified to a very high degree the endeavour to bring technical efficiency into the armaments industry, and its inhumanity as well. Some of his disputes with other potentates can be traced back to this. Speer wanted to involve women in greater numbers in the total war and was frustrated by Hitler's ideological reservations. From a very early stage, Speer had trouble with a form of 'regional particularism',[8] which he attacked, and which seemed incompatible with the principles of 'the unity of the Reich'. *Gauleiter* (of whom Sauckel was one) were opposed to the total mobilisation he aimed for, partly out of consideration for the population, but probably also because of anti-capitalist resentment about Speer's clientele from large-scale industry. It made no difference, if Speer, for his part, complained to the *Gauleiter* as he did for example in his speech in Posen on 6 October 1943, that some industrialists did not want to conduct the war on such an all-embracing footing as he did. When, after he assassination attempt of 20 July 1944, Goebbels and Hitler concentrated more powers in their own hands, that too was a consequence of Speer's demands. Shortly before – at the high point of war production – he had demanded 'that now even the last reserves should be mobilised' and that 'in Germany all measures which are appropriate for increasing German armament, should be taken with all vigour'.[9]

Speer described himself as a bad speaker, but he learned how to overcome this handicap within the Party and in public. He described himself as shy, but he seemed to be arrogant; 'He is cold right through to his heart. All that counts for him is the cause. He will extract everything from us right down to the last drop', was the opinion of one close colleague (Schieber) even as Speer took office.[10] He conducted the numerous meetings in a cavalier manner. Another colleague (Kehrl) noted; 'His wealth of ideas, his dynamic activism, the impatient pressure for speed, his ability to throw customary practice into question and to find unconventional solutions for apparently insoluble problems were the source of his success'. 'I was infected and intoxicated by the exercise of power, pure and simple, organising people, making decisions on important matters, having billions at my disposal,' was how Speer later analysed his 'intoxification with leadership'.[11] In retrospect, Speer claims he had given the war up for lost by 1942/43. His attempts to achieve the greatest degree of material and psychological mobilisation, however, can be traced as far on as January 1945. There is evidence of public pronouncements on endurance, which were probably required of a man in his position in the Nazi movement, right up almost to the end. However because of the war situation and his own reduced power base, thoughts were taking shape in Speer's head during the course of 1944 about the time after the war, now no longer regarded as the epoch after the final victory. As early as 11 October 1943 Speer had had himself entrusted with the rebuilding of the bomb-damaged cities. In this way the architectural team of the Thirties, the core of which remained, could plan for the period after the war. The pre-war idea of cities planned for traffic, but now without monumental buildings, became their guiding strategy, as Speer had wished. In contrast to the pre-war era, he now made a stand for the preservation of historic buildings. As the allied troops moved increasingly closer to Germany, Speer employed himself not in completely destroying industrial sites which were about to fall into the hands of the enemy, but in making them temporarily unusable, paralysing them. This policy, which was still pursued under the pretext that those areas would soon be regained by military action, became, in two long memoranda dating from March 1945, decisively opposed to Hitler's 'burnt earth' policy.

Although in the preceeding months he had barely taken any notice of his duties, and on his travels had only been punctual at the point of departure, he now declared that the war would be lost in four to eight weeks. 'We ourselves have no right, at this stage in the war, to undertake destruction which might affect the lives of the people [. . .]. It is our duty to leave all possibilities open to the people, which might secure their revival in the distant future'.[12] This outspoken, and even then daring stand, had no personal consequences for Speer, who began to prepare for a future without National Socialism.

Adventurous plans to flee to Greenland were weighed up and rejected; for in May 1945 in the 'Dönitz government' Speer undertook the duties of Minister for Economics and Production. He used this activity, fictitious in most respects, mainly to build up good contacts with the Americans, who were trying him, by means of providing them with experts in armaments matters. As an apolitical expert, he probably expected to play an authoritative role in a new German government. Therefore the blow was all the greater when, after his imprisonment and the subsequent hearings, charges were brought against him in the trials of the major war criminals at Nuremberg, and when he was finally sentenced to twenty years imprisonment, which he served, for his involvement in the system of forced labour. Speer differed from most of the accused at Nuremberg in that he did not only (like Goering) admit his responsibility, but also his *guilt*. He understood this in a very limited way in the general sense of being a senior member of the government who took no notice of the crimes of the system outside of his own sphere of work. It was at this time that he developed an image of himself as a man who was essentially only ambitious in an artistic sense, and then of the technician who had acted in an immoral way precisely because of his limited insight. Although this self-analysis of a senior Nazi potentate was rare, it must be emphasised that he was more actively involved in the shaping of the system of terror and mass destruction than he admitted to himself. In prison, and from his release on 1 October 1966 until his death on 1 September 1981, Speer reflected on and published works on his activities. His pride in his unprecedented architectural achievement and his success in the armaments economy remained.

Speer was a National Socialist, even though he was not a Party organisation man, or even if he did have disputes with *Gauleiter* or Martin Bormann. Speer boasted in his last memo to Hitler that, 'without my work the war would perhaps have been lost in 1942/43'.[13] In this he may well have been right. Speer was not personally bound to an ideology of conquest based on racial theory, but he was more than an apolitical technocrat. His rise to power came because of his personal faith in Hitler, which was unique because of the artistic component in it. In his role as an architect Speer actively promoted the expansion of the concentration camp system, the erosion of traditional government. As manager of the armaments industry he was one of the most important figures in the implementation of the total war, with all its consequences for the German state and Europe as a whole. And at the same time he was always aware of the significance of his own actions for National Socialist rule and the inhuman system it espoused, even if he only thought about it later, and then partially distanced himself from it.

NOTES

1. Speer, Memoirs, p. 37.
2. Ibid., p. 34.
3. Dülffer/Thies/Henke, *Hitlers Städte*, p. 297 (a remark made by Hitler on 10.2.1939).
4. Adolf Hitler. *Bilder aus dem Leben des Führers*. Cigaretten-Bilderdienst (Altona-Bahrenfeld, 1936) p. 72.
5. Speer to Lippert, 1.6.1940, Bundesarchiv R 120/3984.
6. Speer, Memoirs, p. 225.
7. Ibid., p. 420.
8. Bleyer, *Staat und Monopole*, p. 123.
9. *Deutschland im Zweiten Weltkrieg*, vol. 5, p. 360 – memorandum dated 12.7.1944.
10. Kehrl, *Krisenmanager*, p. 344, the following quotation from p. 330.

11. Speer, *Memoirs*, p. 353.
12. *Internationaler Militärgerichthof*, vol. XLI, Document on Speer 23, p. 421, 425.
13. Ibid., Speer to Hitler 19.3.1945, document on Speer 24, p. 426.

BIBLIOGRAPHY

Primary Sources

Speer's own works begin with his memoirs, which are themselves based on source studies: *Erinnerungen* (Berlin, 1969). They are continued in his diaries, which one suspects have been heavily edited: *Spandauer Tagebücher* (Frankfurt am Main, 1975), an extensive interview in *Technik und Macht*, edited by A. Reif (Esslingen, 1979), and end with a work written entirely from a historical perspective: *Der Sklavenstaat. Meine Auseinandersetzung mit der SS* (Stüttgart, 1981). In addition Speer published his artistic work in a magnificent volume with an introduction by historians: *Architektur. Arbeiten 1933–1942* (Berlin, 1978).

Important sources for evaluating Speer's life are contained in: W.A. Boelcke (ed.), *Deutschlands Rüstung im Zweiten Weltkrieg. Hitlers Konferenzen mit Albert Speer 1942–1945* (Frankfurt am Main, 1969); J. Dülffer/J. Thies/J. Henke, *Hitlers Städte. Baupolitik im Dritten Reich. Eine Dokumentation* (Cologne-Vienna, 1978).

Secondary Literature

So far the only attempt at a critical biography of Speer based on a careful examination of Speer's own writing is by M. Schmidt: *Albert Speer. Das Ende eines Mythos. Speers wahre Rolle im Dritten Reich* (Bern-Munich, 1982). The sketch on Speer in: J.C. Fest, *Das Gesicht des Dritten Reiches* (Munich, 1963) pp. 271–85 should also be mentioned here, as well as the two more recent contributions on the same theme: A.C. Mierzejewski, 'When did Albert Speer give up?', *The Historical Journal*, 31 (1988) pp. 391–7; J.J. White Morris, *Albert Speer: The Hitler Years. Views of a Reich Minister*, dissertation, Ball State University, 1987.

On the subject of Speer as an architect see: J. Petsch, *Baukunst und Stadtplanung im Dritten Reich. Herleitung/Bestandsaufnahme/Entwicklung/Nachfolge* (Munich-Vienna, 1976); W. Durth, *Deutsche Architekten. Biographische Verflechtungen 1900–1970* (Braunschweig-Wiesbaden, 1986); W. Durth/N. Gutschow, *Träume in Trümmern*, 2 vols (Braunschweig-Wiesbaden, 1988); J. Dülffer, 'NS-Herrschaftssystem und Stadtgestaltung: Das Gesetz zur Neugestaltung deutscher Städte vom 4. Oktober 1937', *German Studies Review*, 12 (1989) pp. 69–89. On the subject of the war economy or Speer as Armaments Minister, the following works should be consulted: D. Eichholtz, *Geschichte der deutschen Kriegswirtschaft 1939–1945*, Vol. II: 1914–43 (Berlin (East), 1985); W. Schumann (director of the authors' collective), *Deutschland im Zweiten Weltkrieg*, vols 3–6 (Berlin (East) and Cologne, 1983–5); G. Janssen, *Das Ministerium Speer. Deutschlands Rüstung im Krieg* (Frankfurt am Main, Berlin, 1968); E.R. Zilbert, *Albert Speer and the Ministry of Arms* (London, 1981); L. Herbst *Der Totale Krieg und die Ordnung der Wirtschaft. Die Kriegswirtschaft im Spannungsfeld von Politik, Ideologie und Propaganda 1939–1945* (Stuttgart, 1982).

21 Gregor Strasser: Nazi Party Organiser or Weimar Politician?

Udo Kissenkoetter

Gregor Strasser came from a farming family in the Chiemgau. He was born on 31.5.1892 in Geisenfeld near Plattenhofen on the Inn. His father, Peter Strasser, served as counsel in the courts in Windsheim and Deggendorf. He loved discussing history, political economy and politics in private with his three sons at the end of the Wilhelmine era, and so, for example, they all read Maximilian Harden's *Die Zukunft* (The Future) together. Strasser the father also published polemical political tracts himself. When the First World War broke out, Gregor joined up as a volunteer in the 1st Bavarian Light infantry Regiment and was demobilised at the end of the war with the rank of First Lieutenant. This was the decisive formative event in his life, as it was for a whole generation. From the experience of life in the trenches, where all social distinctions seemed to have been abolished, there developed the idea of 'German Socialism'. The 'miracle of August 1914' and the 'organic' national community, as experienced by a whole generation as they fought through a total war side by side, made a deep impression on him:

> It was a profound experience for me when, during patriotic instruction in the field, one of my gunners asked me: 'What does it mean, this Fatherland? It is surely the land which belongs to my father and one day will belong to me, which gives me the chance to work and feeds me; in the same way I have been defending this patch of land for three years. But neither my father nor I has ever had even a patch of land, and all our desire to work has never yet protected us from going for weeks and months without bread and from existing our whole lives through in a constant state of worry, about whether we will still have a job tomorrow'

From this Strasser draws the following conclusions:

> It is deceiving oneself to believe that a nation of sixty million people in the rational Twentieth Century can be induced to make the endless sacrifices a national war of liberation requires simply out of exalted feelings of honour, love of the Fatherland and national pride, if the nation does not become a unified tolerant whole, with equality of opportunity and reward.

He wanted to draw all of society, but especially the workers, into an organic national community, structured along corporative lines. In the 'German working people's social struggle' he saw 'the German nation's struggle for freedom'.[1] These ideas, which derived as much from the social-revolutionary ideas of his parental home as from the 'miracle of August 1914' accompanied Strasser throughout his political career. As a member of the *Freicorps* Epp, he took part in the founding of a 'National Association of German Soldiers' and in Landshut, where he set himself up as a pharmacist in 1920, he built up the 'Lower Bavarian Storm Batallion'. This brought him into contact with the patron of all the patriotic defence leagues, General von Ludendorff, and also with the early Munich NSDAP under Hitler. On 11.3.1923 he was appointed leader of the 'Lower Bavarian Storm Troops'[2] (SA). He took part in the demonstration by National Paramilitary Leagues in Munich on 1.5.1923 with the largest SA formation from outside the area. On 9 November 1923, he was the only leader to arrive punctually in Munich with his Storm Troops. He accomplished his task, which was to occupy the strategically important Wittelsbach Bridge, and returned in good order to Landshut with his unit, where, without trying to escape, he allowed himself to be arrested at home. After the Nazi leaders had been put in jail and the NSDAP had been banned, Strasser's greatest hour arrived.

On 6.4.1924 he was elected to the Bavarian Parliament from the list of the *völkisch* (ethnic populist) faction. In a triumvirate with Ludendorff and von Graefe he founded the National Socialist Freedom Party in Weimar at the conference which unified their movement, and entered the Reichstag after the elections of 7.12.1924. While Hitler was in prison he had become one of the most important *völkisch* leaders in the country. As a member of the Reichstag, and as one of the leaders of the *völkisch* camp, he began to collect experience and knowledge in both organisational matters and parliamentary work at a national level. Having been released from prison, Hitler received permission to re-establish the NSDAP on 4.1.1925, and this took place at a meeting in the Munich Bürgerbräukeller on 27.2.1925. Strasser was not present at this inaugural meeting. He was holding an event of his own in Straubing at the same time. A few days earlier, on 21/22 in Hamm/Westphalia Strasser had chaired a conference of leaders of National Socialist groups from North and West Germany. Here, five days before the actual founding of the party, he was able to show them a power of attorney signed by Hitler, and appointed 'suitable' local leaders as the *Gauleiter* of a party which did not yet exist. With a slight exaggeration it is possible to say that the NSDAP was founded twice: once on 27.2.1925 – the official legal founding within the context of the old Munich-Bavaria organisation, from those remaining who had stayed loyal to Hitler, and for the second time at national level in a conversation between Hitler and Strasser, probably on 17.2., which led to the conference at Hamm.

Here, in the organisation at national level, was to be his sphere of activity for the next few years. For him, questions of ideology and propaganda, on the one hand, and organisational work on the other, were simply two sides of the same coin. His manifest ability to attract able colleagues stood him in good stead here. Throughout his political life he was accompanied by an increasing number of able and obviously devoted colleagues and friends, some of whom left the Party with him after his downfall, or remained friends or in contact with him, or his family after his murder. It was typical of him too, that in his search for colleagues, those of like mind and discussion partners, he did not by any means stop at the boundaries of the NSDAP. In principle, everyone who was willing to help in the nationalist reconstruction or create equality within the terms of a national German socialism were possible partners for him. Strasser's organisational work, and the development of his policy statements which ran parallel with it, can be divided into three phases. During the initial phase of building up the Party, which was basically his duty outside Bavaria, Strasser at first had no official legitimisation apart from Hitler's power of attorney. With the support of a few active young National Socialists, who wanted the Headquarters of their Region in Elberfeld to become the 'Mecca of German Socialism', and who included Karl Kaufmann, Joseph Goebbels, Franz Pfeffer von Salomon, Viktor Lutze, he founded the Study Group of the North West German Regions of the NSDAP. At the same time he attempted to establish a quality, mass circulation newspaper and he tried to win over Oswald Spengler for this purpose. On 2.6.1925, he wrote to him: 'One way I see of achieving this is by publishing a political and academic newspaper, like the socialist monthlies . . . which clarifies and explains problems of National Socialist foreign, domestic and economic policy independent of any official influences'. In the same exchange of letters he also pointed out the fundamental differences between the NSDAP and other völkisch groupings:

The *völkisch* movement, including its so-called political statement of intent (represented in organisational terms by the *Völkisch* Freedom Party) and National Socialism's political and economic aspirations to power! (For better or for worse, and unfortunately rather more the latter, this is represented by the National Socialist [German] Workers' Party). If in the first case what we are discussing is a movement fed by a thousand sources of dissatisfaction, which considers the primitive solution of anti-semitism to be adequate, and is satisfied by a nationalism which is usually as loud as it is honest, and driven by an understandable reaction to war and revolution, then the second is nothing other than the conscious desire to bring about a true revolution to make up for the results of one which failed because of the cowardice and inability of its leaders and because of the doctrinal limitations of Marxist theory![3]

There was much enthusiastic discussion in the Study Group North West (AG) about a new Party manifesto and efforts to formulate it as a means of bringing about this German revolution. This draft manifesto, which propagated the model of a corporatist state, and which foresaw controls on, and common ownership in the economy, industry and agriculture, was rejected at the Bamberg Conference of 14.2.1926. To this extent the North West AG had failed to become a policy-making circle within the NSDAP. However in Strasser's view the AG also, over and above this, had the duty to be a pressure group within the Party and it was by no means unsuccessful in this role. On 16.9.1926 Strasser took over as Director of National Propaganda in Munich, replacing Hermann Esser, precisely the man whom the AG had targetted in most of their attacks when they referred to the 'stinking rotten state of affairs in Munich'.

For Strasser, propaganda meant covering the greatest possible area of the country with speakers, propaganda materials and demonstrations by the Party. In the Party, which was still short of members, and most of all, money, this meant that the few existing available speakers had to be engaged in tours which were well prepared with regard both to dates and themes. This was exactly what had already been formulated in paragraph two of the statutes of the AG: 'The greatest possible degree of uniformity of the attached Regions in organisation, propaganda, the creation of uniform propaganda tools, exchange of speakers . . . where necessary the exchange of ideas on political and organisational matters.'[4] Strasser had taken his Regional business manager, Himmler, with him into the director's office for national propaganda. In accordance with Strasser's ideas, Himmler acted by and large independently in the thematic and geographical organisation and timing of propaganda. This did not change when Strasser gave up the directorship of National Propaganda at the end of 1927 and Hitler himself finally took over the running of propaganda, or when Joseph Goebbels was entrusted with the control of propaganda on 27.4.1930. Goebbels and his collaborators did not take over until after the Reichstag elections of 14.9.1930, although at the same time the National Propaganda Directorate was hived off under Fritz Reinhardt, who was responsible for the training of speakers and continuing to supply them with materials for speeches. In January 1928 Strasser took control of National Organisation. At the elections of 20.5.1928, which turned out unfavourably for the whole of the right, the NSDAP alone received almost exactly as many votes as it had had in December 1924, when the trend was favourable to the *völkisch* parties, in a coalition with Ludendorff and von Graefe. Although at that time only four National Socialists had entered the Reichstag, now it was twelve. This result was judged a great success, not only by Gregor Strasser, but also by Hitler and Goebbels. However the organisational structure was still in the form dictated by circumstances as they were at the time of the Party's founding. Strasser, who was attempting to introduce uniformity, had to overcome two hurdles. First of all, internal financial problems had to be cleared up. The national leadership financed itself fundamentally from the huge Bavarian Region, since dues from other Regions were paid only irregularly. Secondly, the personal resistance of Hitler, who regarded Bavaria as his home power base, had to be overcome. Strasser succeeded in achieving both at the leaders' meeting of 31.8. to 2.9.1928. In the new Party guidelines it was determined in point four that 'the local branches are to be concentrated in Regions in such a way that those branches within the area of a national parliamentary constituency form a Region of the NSDAP which bears the name of the constituency'. Accordingly on 1.10.1928 five Regions were set up within Bavaria and had *Gauleiter* appointed. On 1.3.1929 Strasser himself gave up the post of *Gauleiter* in Lower Bavaria and on 1.11.1929 Greater Munich became the last area to be transformed into a Region. The Otto Strasser crisis caused an upset for Gregor Strasser. It reached its climax on 4.7.1930 when the press of the Kampf Verlag announced: 'The socialists are leaving the Party'. However the significance of this event for Gregor Strasser has clearly been overestimated. For one thing many articles in the Kampf-Verlag Press attributed to Gregor Strasser were in fact written by Otto, and for another Strasser had withdrawn from the affairs of the Kampf Verlag by 1928 at the latest. Now he quickly took up a critical position to this secession and in this way by and large prevented it from having a greater effect within the Party.

Soon this crisis too, was overshadowed by other events. Subjected to the full impact of the Great Depression, the parliamentary elections of 14.9.1930 turned into a debacle for the Weimar parties. If the NSDAP up to now had ultimately only been a sectarian party with twelve members, now, with 107 members of parliament, it was the second strongest grouping in the Reichstag. It had, so to speak, arrived at the outer gates of power. Strasser was prepared for such a situation. A decision had been taken, at the special conference for organisational matters in 1929, that:

> at the suggestion of the National Organiser, Strasser, an Organisation Department II will be set up under the direction of Party Comrade Colonel (retd) Hierl, with the purpose of collating, studying and clarifying all matters concerning the development of the movement and the National Socialist concept of the state.[5]

Hierl, whom Strasser had known for a long time from the Tannenberg League, was standing in for him in this capacity, in the construction and expansion of his power base in the Party. While Strasser himself retained control of the immediate Party organisation in Organisation Department I, Hierl's Department II had two important tasks from his point of view.

Firstly, important matters relating to the domestic and economic policies of the future government were to be developed here. Here, for example, were to be found departments for justice, social policy, international economics, the creation of employment, trade and industry and economic theory. Secondly, however, Strasser was creating here a think tank which would be able to pursue further his policy ideas and aims. At the same time these 'specialists' gave him the possibility of making contact with groupings outside the NSDAP, without him having to appear in person. This happened to a particularly great degree with the creation of an economic and job creation programme in 1931 and 1932.

In summer 1932, as a final step in the construction of the Party administration, came the implementation of a clear vertical steering and command structure.[6] The most important visible evidence of this Party reform, during which Organisation Department II was re-absorbed, was the emergence of national State inspections. The chief, Strasser, and his two national inspectors, Schulz and Ley, had under their control Senior Division III with, among other things, education and the national press office, IV economy, V agriculture, VI NSBO (National Socialist Factory Cell Organisation), VII civil servants, VIII women, IX care of war victims. The state inspectors were subordinate to National Inspector I, Schulz, for North Germany and II, Ley, for the South. They had great power over the roughly three to five Regions under their control, in respect of personnel as well. It was compulsory for all Party organisations, and for *Gauleiter*, too, to follow 'official channels', set up in parallel with this new administrative structure, in cases of complaints, requests or suggestions. By means of a decree aimed at controlling Nazi fractions,[7] it was established that fractions were to be controlled uniformly from the centre. 'All petitions to elected bodies, from local council to Reichstag, are to be presented to me (Gregor Strasser) *before* they are submitted.' However he did not stop at passive control, but had parliamentary petitions formulated in advance in the specialist department of his administrative headquarters (ROL), which he then made binding on the various Nazi fractions. He delegated specialists from the ROL to support Nazi parliamentarians in promoting these petitions. 'I forbid all offices and Party members . . . from dealing with publications about job creation or its financing . . . in local newspapers . . . independently.'[8] He also intervened increasingly in Nazi propaganda:

> The preparatory work required by the ROL's head departments for propagandistic use will be carried out within the ROL. Individual consultants who are members of the ROL may not make any preparatory drafts available to the National Propaganda Directorate without having obtained the approval of the National Head of Administration or his deputy through official channels.[9]

In addition Strasser now possessed a kind of house press again – he was the publisher of the weekly and monthly papers of the corresponding chief departments of the ROL: 'National Socialist State Post', 'Nazi Women's Watch', 'Care of German War Victims' and 'Working People'. The last named in particular, the organ of the NSBO, became increasingly important, since this organisation was growing quickly and he was increasingly becoming the idol of its members. For many he became a point of reference, since it was possible to become a member of this mass organisation without even belonging to the NSDAP, so that a direct means of relating to Hitler was lacking for many. From this power base Strasser presented his 'Economic Immediate Programme' (*Wirtschaftliche Sofortprogramm*) of the NSDAP to the public and made it binding on the Party. First of all he introduced it in his speeches in the Reichstag on 10.5.1932 and then it was published as a series of points to serve as material for speakers in the campaign for the elections to the Reichstag on 31.7.1932. Strasser attacked the existing economic order, against which 'the great anti-capitalist longing . . . which is spreading through our people' was directed and 'which has today already encompassed 95 per cent of our people'. 'This was,' he claimed, 'the protest of a people against a corrupt economy, and the people demands of the state that it should stop thinking in terms of export statistics and National Bank interest discounts and should be in the position once more to produce an honest livelihood for an honest day's work'. Since workers and tools and the need for goods, too, all existed, these factors had to be slotted together. He saw this as a cumulative process: 'I am utterly convinced that it is only a question of starting up the motor. Work produces work.' He suggested that the following tasks were in the interest of the state as a whole: 1) agricultural work; 2) private house building; 3) road building, the construction of dams and drainage canals, the expansion of the economy in the field of energy, the renovation of apartments.

The most important point was naturally the financing of this programme. For this he recommended the following model: since all the measures were wage intensive, approximately thirty per cent of the costs could be financed from the unemployment benefit which would no longer be taken up, and a further five per cent from the increased flow of unemployment insurance contributions. A further fifteen per cent was to be financed from additional tax income. Twenty per cent was to be paid by the beneficiaries of these measures, for example those who received their own home, or the farmers whose lands were improved. The remaining thirty per cent should be paid by 'productive credit creation'. Strasser explained this in the following terms: the expansion of credit occurs on the basis of credit advanced to the Reich by the National Bank and those banks subject to state control. The expansion of credit occurs by way of a state-run bookkeeping exercise, and as such is to be included within the bounds of state finance and in the newly-created financial and credit system of the future. Exchange of goods and state credit would become the basis of currency in circulation.[10] The origins of these ideas for a National Socialist economic policy which Strasser put forward and which later also became the basis of early National Socialist government policy-making, in the form of the so-called Reinhardt Plan, cannot be examined any more closely here. None-the-less the circles in which these plans were discussed, interesting in themselves, reflect, in the wide range of the figures involved in them, Strasser's view of the possibility of a political seizure of power. The 'Study Society for Systems of Finance and Credit' founded by the industrialist Dräger and finance specialist Dalberg became the platform for the economic reformers, whose thinking took its impetus from both the economic and financial doctrines of Silvio Gesells and perceptions of the development of the German State economy during the First World War. Trades unionists, like Woytinski and Tarnow, who later presented the WTB plan in association with Baade, met here, and bourgeois industrialists and politicians alongside Dräger and Dalberg like Grotkopp, Gräwell, Professor Wagemann, Friedländer-Prechtl, and also National Socialists, predominantly from Strasser's political economy department, like Fritz Reinhardt, Werner Daitz, Hermann Tholens, Arthur R. Hermann, Walther Funk and Cordemann. In summer 1932 it became possible to recognise the political constellation on which, six months later, Schleicher attempted to base his government. Strasser himself had reached the zenith of his power in the NSDAP in the summer and autumn of 1932. Dominating the entire party apparatus as a quasi 'general secretary', he himself regarded this power as a form of division of labour with Hitler. While he was the man for practical political work, Hitler embodied the idea of the National Socialist movement. Therefore he probably did not seriously consider breaking with Hitler at any time, for he realised that by so doing he would also destroy his own base. Over and above this he was also sure right to the end that in the final analysis he had the greatest influence on the Führer against his opponents in the Party.

At the same time as his power in the NSDAP was developing, Strasser had also grown beyond the Party. He had become a Weimar politician. For many in Germany, from bourgeois conservative politicians to various union representatives, he was considered well-suited for government, indeed for many he had become a possible integrating figure, who pointed to a third way of saving Germany from the emergency of 1932. From the time of the Presidential Elections in spring 1932 at the latest, Strasser himself had come to perceive that the NSDAP by itself could not achieve power by legal means. If plans for coups d'état were disregarded, there remained outside parliament only the possibility of a minority cabinet dependent on the 'auctoritas' of the President. But as Strasser saw it, this made for dependence on the goodwill of the President and his camarilla. After the NSDAP's great electoral successes of 31.7., Hitler tried to follow this path, carried along by the enthusiasm of his followers, when he demanded the office of Chancellor for himself from Hindenburg on 31.8. However the President refused and – so it seemed – finally. There remained therefore only Strasser's route to power, and that was to enter into coalitions in order to achieve a parliamentary majority. And for this purpose the NSDAP's prospects at that time – the strongest fraction in the Reichstag with 230 members – were excellent. In the short term this could only mean entering a coalition with the Centre Party and making the job creation programme put forward by Strasser the basis of government policy. But for the long term he had visions of a 'front of working people'. He believed he saw Germany's future in a corporatve model and regarded the various trade union organisations as its central core. By agreement with the 'potestas' of the army they would take over the administration of the state and by so doing make Germany independent of the swings and roundabouts of a parliamentary democracy. He probably also saw the possibility that one day the NSDAP alone might be able to dominate a state based on this model. Until such a time he was willing if necessary to 'throw himself into the breach' if Hitler himself, perhaps as Vice Chancellor, was unwilling to enter such a cabinet.

When, after parliament was dissolved again, the NSDAP remained the strongest fraction in the elections of 6.11.1932, but suffered serious losses, the situation as Strasser saw it became increasingly urgent. Once again he attempted to implement a 'Labour Front' as a practical solution to Germany's continuing crisis, on one hand by bringing immense influence to bear on Hitler, and on the other by negotiating with the powerful man in the army, General von Schleicher. The *'Tatkreis'* and above all Zehrer and Elbrechter, played a part behind the screens in this. However it must be emphasised that these ideas, and the attempts to translate them into fact, were never directed against Hitler, or even without Hitler knowing of them. He did not want to split the Party – for the Party administration was ultimately his life's work – nor did he want to separate himself from Hitler, to whom he was attached by a remarkable personal devotion. Instead he wanted to convince him of the way he had recognised as the correct one. And it was precisely in this that he failed. Instead of coming to Berlin on 30.11. to arrange the final details of a Schleicher government with Strasser and Schleicher, Hitler went to the hustings in Thuringia. It was here that Strasser suffered his decisive defeat within the inmost circle of the NSDAP leadership. Hitler did not want to go down Strasser's road. Deeply resigned, he gave up all his posts on 8.12 and went to the Tyrol on holiday. Returning hesitantly once more to the political stage in the middle of January, his only significance and last chance would probably have been in being the rallying point for his supporters in the event of parliament being dissolved again. But since there were no new elections, Hitler took power in his own way on 30.1.33 and as Strasser stayed clear of any further involvement in politics, the grievances within the Party soon dissipated. On 30.6.1934, Strasser was murdered by the Gestapo on the basis that he still represented a possible threat to Hitler.

NOTES

1. Gregor Strasser, *Freiheit und Brot* (Berlin, no date).
2. VB, 22 March 1923.
3. Letter from Strasser to Spengler dated 2.6.25 and 8.7.25 in, Oswald Spengler, *Briefe 1913–36* (Munich, 1963) p. 291f. and p. 397f.
4. BA, NS 1–340–319.
5. VB, 12.9.29.
6. VB, 9./10.6.1932, negotiations about deputies within the National Organisation Departments dated 18.7.32 BA/ns22/348.
7. Decree dated 9 June 1932, VB 15.6.32.
8. Circular to the Nazi press 21.11.32, BA, NS22/356.
9. Letter of the National Organiser dated 5.12.32 to the Senior Departments I–IV in the ROL, BA/NS/348.
10. Speech in the Berlin Palace of Sport dated 20.10.1932.

BIBLIOGRAPHY

Primary Sources

Important documents relating to Gregor Strasser's activities are to be found in the Bundesarchiv Koblenz, the Institut für Zeitgeschichte and the Berlin Document Center. Reference should also be made to the numerous publications which appeared at the end of the twenties and the beginning of the thirties. For the early period, approximately the period before 1930, however, it is important to bear in mind the danger of confusing the activities of Gregor Strasser, on the one hand, and the circle round Otto Strasser on the other, something which is not always taken into account in the literature. In 1932 the *Eher-Verlag* published a collection of speeches and essays by Gregor Strasser from the period 1924 until 1932: Gregor Strasser, *Kampf um Deutschland*. This collection also contains the important 'Arbeit und Brot' (Work and Bread) speech of 10 May 1932. The 'Economic Immediate Programme' (*Wirtschaftliche Sofortprogramm*) of the NSDAP was distributed throughout the entire Party organisation in the form of 'outline material for public speakers' and can therefore be found in many archives relating to this period.

As far as the publications which appeared during the Nazi era are concerned, it is important to be aware of the fact that references to Gregor Strasser were often subsequently erased and sources falsified, if the disgraced former National Organiser was mentioned in them.

Secondary Literature

The study by the present author, U. Kissenkoetter, *Gregor Strasser und die NSDAP* (Stuttgart, 1978) concentrates basically on the period 1930–2. Its most important theme is Strasser's activities as National Organiser and his links to parties, associations and individuals in the Weimar Republic. Over and above this it investigates the origins of the NSDAP's 'Economic Immediate Programme'. The study by P.D. Stachura, *Gregor Strasser and the Rise of Nazism* (London, 1983) is based on a wide range of sources. Nonetheless the author underestimates the basis of Gregor Strasser's power around 1932. Stachura's interpretation of the context of Strasser's policies is rather unconvincing, especially the questionable thesis that the NSDAP regarded the results of the Reichstag elections of 20.5.1928 as a defeat and as a reaction to this underwent a swing to the right. The two following dissertations should also be looked at in a critical light: J. Murdock, *Gregor Strasser and the Organisation of the Nazi Party, 1925–32*, Stanford University 1966, and U. Wörzt, *Programmatic und Führerprinzip. Das Problem des Strasser-Kreises in der NSDAP* (Erlangen-Nuremberg, 1966). Murdock's dissertation rests on an extremely narrow base of sources, and mainly uses secondary literature. Strasser's significance for the NSDAP is insufficiently developed. Wörtz is mainly concerned with matters of ideology. In the process he inaccurately lumps Gregor Strasser together with his brother Otto and the other members of the 'Elberfeld circle' and the 'Kampf-Verlag'.

22 Otto Strasser: Nationalist Socialism versus National Socialism
Patrick Moreau

The history of the National Socialist left wing in the years 1925 to 1938 is primarily that of its leading figure, Otto Strasser. Strasser, who was born into the family of a civil servant in Bavaria, a conventionally Christian family with socialist and nationalist leanings, volunteered for military service in 1914. His military exploits brought him countless honours and a commission as an officer.

After the war, with no clear sense of direction, he joined the *Freicorps* Epp, along with his brother Gregor, and took part in the liquidation of the 'Red Army' in Bavaria. While Gregor Strasser began his nationalistic agitation in June 1919, and met Adolf Hitler for the first time as a result, his brother made his way to Berlin, joined the SPD there and began to study economics. The following year he founded the 'Academic War Veterans Association of the SPD' and had himself elected to the students' parliament. In addition to this he wrote as a freelance journalist for *Vorwärts* and led three Red Hundreds in their resistance to the Kapp Putsch. In April 1920, Strasser broke with the SPD, accusing it of having betrayed the workers in the Ruhr uprising; in fact they had been left in the lurch by the Social Democratic government under pressure from the *Freikorps*, led by Watter. Returning to Bavaria, Otto Strasser, too, met Hitler for the first time, but the relationship between the two men was stamped from the beginning by antipathy and Otto refused to join the emerging National Socialist movement. Somewhat later he got to know one of the leaders of the Russian Revolution, Grigori Zinoviev, at an Independent Social Democratic (USPD) meeting in Halle, and he seems to have convinced Strasser of the importance of the Bolshevik revolution as such, of its role as a model for Germany's future course of development and of the necessity of Russian-German rapprochement.

At the end of 1920 Strasser was under the influence of a variety of approaches to politics: revolutionary socialism, nationalism, Christianity, moderate anti-semitism and finally, an as much romantically as ideologically motivated pro-Soviet position are some of the facets he later attempted to integrate into the philosophical stock of ideas in his political writings.

Between 1920 and 1925 Strasser took a doctorate in economics and became an executive in an industrial concern. In his free time he intensified his knowledge of politics both by his contacts within the circles of conservative and National Socialist youth and particularly by his critical reading of the works of Oswald Spengler and Moeller van den Bruck. He still resolutely refused to join any organisation, however it was structured.

In the meantime, Gregor Strasser, for his part, had left Bavaria in order to put himself at the disposal of the German Nationalist Freedom Party (DNFP) in north Germany as organiser and Propaganda Chief for the elections in May and December 1924. Since the gradual restabilisation of economic life threatened considerably to reduce the chances of a National Socialist protest movement in the longer term, it was now becoming even more urgent that its various currents should converge. With Hitler, now released from prison, at its head, the newly founded NSDAP had a born leader, but nonetheless the transformation of the National Socialist movement from a putschist grouping into a mass party was to throw up serious problems with regard to policies.

On the basis of his activities as leader of the election campaigns of 1924, Gregor Strasser was well aware of the difficulties there would be in developing a predominantly racist and National Socialist movement, given North Germany's particular economic and social structures. A numerically strong industrial proletariat solidly organised by the SPD and KPD did not produce a very favourable milieu for the expansion of National Socialism. The Party's Twenty-Five Point 1920 manifesto was quite obviously unsuited either to conquering the middle classes or winning over the working class. Gregor, whose strengths lay more in the area of strategy, rather than ideology, therefore asked his brother for help in working out a Nazi ideology, which was to be reworked and renewed in order to suit it to the altered political and economic situation. This was a task which Otto Strasser, who had in the meantime been convinced of the theories of Moeller van den Bruck, undertook with enthusiasm. The two brothers shared out their work according to their talents: Otto became the 'North German ideologue' and wrote articles for his brother which he published under his name. In his role as an 'eminence grise' Otto Strasser forgot to take the trouble to gain an official post in the Party for himself, with the result that his role in laying its foundations was largely unrecognised and his influence limited to the North German leadership cadres.

In September 1925 Gregor organised a Party conference in Hagen, Westphalia, the goal of which was to define and agree on a common policy, independent of Munich, for the whole of the North German NSDAP, suited to the economic and social preconditions for regional propaganda there. The founding of the Study Group North and North West of the NSDAP, led by the Strasser brothers, Karl Kaufmann, Viktor Lutze (later Chief of Staff of the SA) and Joseph Goebbels, was to proclaim and establish in writing this 'Right to our own Way'.

In 1926 the left-wing functionaries introduced a programme they had been working on since October 1925, which gave the Study Group's policies a more precise orientation in economic, domestic and foreign affairs. This formed the basis of the doctrine which was retained in its essentials until the leftist wing of the NSDAP was wiped out in 1934, and it was to undergo extensive further development in the ideologies of the groups led by Otto Strasser from 1930–8. The left wing of National Socialism agreed to a large extent with the Party's Twenty-Five Point Plan and laid particular emphasis on nationalisation and putting curbs on private ownership. But over and above this it demanded the creation of a Soviet-German alliance for a national war of liberation against the western imperialist powers.

Hitler, who was convinced of the necessity of purging the Party of these 'Bolsheviks', as they were called, tried from 1926–30 to weaken the Nazi left and drive a wedge between the Strasser brothers, without however risking the breakaway of the North German Party organisation. He struck his first successful blow at the end of 1926, with Joseph Goebbel's unconditional change of sides. Hitler's declaration that the Party's Twenty-Five Point Plan was unalterable and could neither be modified nor expanded through the inclusion of new theories meant for Strasser that he could be marked out as a renegade in the Party if he continued to elaborate his ideology.

In spite of this, for tactical reasons Hitler offered Gregor the post of Propaganda Chief and in January 1928 that of National Chief of Party Organisation. He accepted the offer in the (vain) hope of being able to convince Hitler of his socialist ideas.

That meant there were only Otto Strasser and a handful of functionaries left to defend the socialist programme in the Region of Berlin, the leader of which, Goebbels, had received orders to increase the propagation of socialist theories, in order to take the wind out of the sails of anti-Hitler tendencies. As a parallel move, all high ranking left-wing cadres, like the *Gauleiter* of Silesia, Rosikat, Pomerania, Vahlen and Saxony – von Mücke – were expelled from the NSDAP and replaced by leaders loyal to the Party line.

The Great Depression, which began in 1929, finally put an end to the equilibrium between the various National Socialist tendencies. Within the changed social and economic context, Hitler defined the strategic axes for his Party's policies: respect for institutional legality and the principle of elections, restrictions on anti-capitalist agitation, an opening towards conservatism and the Catholic Church and an increase in anti-marxist and anti-semitic propaganda.

In the face of this strategic plan and the NSDAP's closer relations with the German National People's Party, there remained for Strasser in his writing only the steadfast repetition of the criticism that Hitler was betraying socialism in favour of reaction. The 'founding of a Third Reich' he proclaimed, was only possible by means of a national revolution, side by side with the Marxists, whom the National Socialists had meanwhile persuaded of the futility of class warfare and proletarian internationalism.

A power struggle between Otto Strasser and Goebbels was then to lead to a final breach between Strasser and his followers and the NSDAP. When Strasser succeeded in March 1930 in transforming his *National Socialist*, which had previously been published weekly by the Berlin Kampf Verlag, into a daily paper, Goebbels feared for his influence in the Region and demanded several times that Hitler should put Strasser in his place and force him to give up the Kampf Verlag. Although Hitler subsequently decided to have two conversations with Strasser in May, in which the inevitability of the breach between them became apparent, Hitler succeeded in delaying it for tactical reasons until the state elections in Saxony. Not until the fourth of July 1930 was it finally announced 'the socialists are leaving the NSDAP', and the 'Battle Group of Revolutionary National Socialists' (KGRNS) was called into being. In spite of an appeal by Gregor Strasser, who reminded the NSDAP members of their oath of loyalty to their leader, the KGRNS developed substantially faster than the Munich headquarters had expected. The rise of the KGRNS can be divided into two periods: in the first, during the months of July and August, the framework of the KGRNS leadership structure was created from the influx of people who had left the NSDAP, while the second period, from August to December 1930, is characterised by the consolidation and strengthening of its basis, although it was limited by the 'national bolshevist' crisis in September/October 1930.

The KGRNS, under the leadership of Otto Strasser, Herbert Blank and Bruno Ernst Buchrucker, the former leader of the Black Army, registered 5000 members for the first time in December 1930, among whom were the *Gauleiter* of Brandenburg and Danzig, Emil Holz and Bruno Fricke, cadres from the Hitler youth and the SA, as well as numerous NSDAP local branch leaders from Thuringia, Saxony, Brandenburg, Schleswig Holstein and the Ruhr. At the end of May 1931, after a phase of administrative consolidation, the KGRNS turned again to seeking new members, with the result that it finally numbered 6000 members in ninety local branches. For them the weekly *Die Deutsche Revolution* was published in an edition of 10 000 copies and also a theoretical monthly entitled *Nationalsozialistische Briefe*.

However tensions soon emerged within the KGRNS: a national bolshevist left wing demanded radical socialisation and the establishment of a planned economy. The supporters of this approach criticised the economic ideas of the KGRNS leadership as being 'reformist'. In spite of these internal conflicts, however, Strasser's group was able to record further successes in April 1931 during the revolt of the Berlin SA.

At the time of the Stennes Putsch the KGRNS was able to count on allies who would spread revolutionary ideas outside the confines of its own organisation into the senior ranks of the SA, where it stirred up disatisfaction still further. Apart from this, the Strasser group was cooperating at this time with the 10 000 member strong para-military *Wehrwolf* League and the Hamkens wing of the *Landvolkbewegung*, which had 2000–3000 members in Schleswig Holstein and Saxony. From 1931 onwards there was widespread unrest and loud protests in the SA about the Party's legality policy. When at last no wages were paid in the months of March and April, Stennes, the leader of the North German SA, set himself at the head of an uprising which was joined by most of his general staff and about 10 000 members of the SA, thus threatening a breach with the NSDAP. However the intervention of Hitler and Goebbels and immediate financial measures quickly took the wind out of the revolt's sails. In the end only about 1000 active SA members decided to break away.

In May 1931 Ehrhardt, well known from the *Freikorps* in the Twenties, initiated the merging of the Stennes group and the KGRNS into the 'German Nationalist and Socialist Fighting Association' (NSKD). However Ehrhardt was a government agent. This explains why resources accrued secretly to the NSKD from state sources. Ehrhardt aimed to gather all active paramilitary groups which opposed Hitler around the NSKD and its allies.

However July 1931, when the NSKD increased its public demonstration of power, manifestly put an end to the revolutionary national socialist dynamic. By this time the ideological bases of revolutionary national socialist thought had reached their final form and the coalition of the Stennes wing of the SA, the *Wehrwolf*, the remains of Ehrhardt's brigade and a few peasants' groups had developed into a force which stood unambiguously apart from the NSDAP.

On the basis of this alliance, however, there was a series of feuds and personal rivalries: Stennes was fundamentally an activist, Strasser a socialist intellectual and Ehrhardt was a government agent. The opposing nature of their aims made lasting cooperation within the NSKD leadership impossible. The break-up of the NSKD was therefore preprogrammed into it, and each of the separate tendencies in it had to re-establish its own tactical autonomy.

When the failure of the NSKD, caused by the opposing characters and interests of its protagonists, became obvious, the Strasser group plunged once more into a 'national bolshevik' crisis, whose consequences were clearly greater than those of 1930. Since its founding the KGRNS had had to accept a series of splits or the loss of former NSDAP members who afterwards joined the KPD. With this trend, which continued to a greater or lesser extent until the KPD was banned in 1933, the KGRNS had involuntarily taken over the role of a sort of staging post between Hitler's National Socialism and communism.

The reason for this 'national bolshevik' crisis probably lay in the weakness of the ideology, which could not hold its own in the intellectual battle with Marxism; but it was unmistakably also the result of the inability of the Strasser group to assert itself against the power of the NSDAP and the SA. Neither the elitist theories of the 'Officers and NCOs of the German Revolution' of 1930, nor the alliance with Stennes, nor the *Schwarze Front* in 1931/33 made Strasser's supporters capable of resistance or even of reacting to the blows of Hitlerite terrorism. The climate of uncertainty increased with every raid by the SA on the meetings of the Revolutionary National Socialists or against individual members, and drove the local branches of the KGRNS into the protective arms of the communists at precisely the same time as the leadership was forced to intensify its criticism of communism in order to secure its capacity for ideological survival. Thanks to its influence and its nationalistic propaganda, the KPD soon appeared to be the only political force which could materially and intellectually defy Hitlerite terrorism.

The KGRNS, which after the break-up of the NSKD had lost both the activists around Stennes as well as its entire left wing, did not seem likely to survive much longer in autumn 1931. Therefore Otto Strasser decided to establish the *Schwarze Front* (Black Front), which consisted of an informal alliance of the *Wehrwolf*, several local branches of the Oberland League and remnants of the Hamkens Movement.

At the periphery of this alliance, *Die Tat*, a newspaper edited by Ferdinand Fried gave it an intellectual point of reference. It threw its weight behind the establishing of a front line against Hitler, which was to extend from the Revolutionary National Socialists by way of trades unionists like Leipart and figures like Kurt von Schleicher, into the Christian conservative camp. In May 1932, the KGRNS, which had already dwindled by the end of 1931 to a hard core of 800 active members and about 1500 supporters, was sleep-walking into a serious crisis, forcing it to fall back on dogmatic positions, which it continued to defend by a permanent appeal to irrational *völkisch* (populist ethnic) feelings and by a belief in the cyclical course of history, in which they placed all their hope. At that time the KGRNS could only be regarded as a sect around Strasser.

The internal crisis in the NSDAP in autumn 1932 and Gregor Strasser's resignation at the beginning of December resulted in a wave of resignations from the Party, which also contributed to the revival of the anaemic KGRNS. Up to the end of 1932 it won 4000 new supporters for the fight against Hitler, but still could not prevent his unstoppable rise to the Chancellorship. This triumph of Hitler's legality tactic even won applause from Otto Strasser, who, blinded by his belief in his destiny, could only see in it the first, reformist phase of the inevitable national socialist revolution which he intended one day to bring about.

After Strasser's troops had been decimated in the first months of 'integration and standardisation' by police raids and arrests, he conducted a resistance struggle on two fronts, at home and abroad, in the years between 1934 and 1938, from Austria until 1934 and afterwards until 1938 from Czechoslovakia. Thanks to the support of conservative circles around Edgar Jung, Strasser was able to maintain illegal groups in a state of readiness in Germany until 1935/36 and continue agitation against the regime with their help. The effectiveness of the repression, however, caused his influence to disappear almost completely from 1936/37 and a little later it drove him right across Europe and as far as America, as he fled the Gestapo.

What was ideology which drove Strasser on, and how different are his theories from Hitler's philosophy? Strasser was a believer in the life cycle. He saw every society as being tied into such a life cycle of birth, development and death. Since there was no place in his philosophy for a heroic meaning to life, as Nietzsche formulated it, for Strasser the individual had to find his social and ethical fulfilment in sacrifice for the community. The motif of readiness for sacrifice is therefore omnipresent in Strasser's writings and is used to justify both the First World War and the inevitable losses in a future conflict which would be necessary to liberate Germany from the chains of the Treaty of Versailles.

Strasser's point of departure was the existence of regular biological cycles, for individuals as well as for social systems, in the course of history. The present time was still a waiting time, but an 'Us' revolution would certainly come, marking the final point of a swing of the historical pendulum which every one hundred and fifty years led western civilisation first in the direction of individualism and then back in the direction of collectivism.

In contrast to Ernst Jünger of Moeller van den Bruck, however, Strasser devoted little attention to the political present, since for him it was only a transitional phase within the context of the cyclical development of history. This 'logic of destiny' led him completely to lose sight of the industrial society of his day – with the exception of the contemporary agricultural crisis. He contented himself with diagnosing the bankruptcy of society and evaluated the failure of the Weimar Republic and the Great Depression as manifestations of a predetermined degeneration. On the basis of the unavoidable return of social values, the future for him belonged to the Revolutionary National Socialists and 'leader figures' – like Cromwell, Lenin and Strasser – were to hasten the inevitable course of history.

Strasser, like Jünger, dreamed of a new type of 'worker', who was however to be explicitly peasant-like in nature, be it the peasant-worker, the peasant-intellectual or the peasant-soldier, – facets of a social revolution brought about by the destruction of industrial society and compulsory re-education of citizens towards regenerative work in the countryside.

In his theoretical works, Strasser's ideology comes over as extreme agrarian conservatism. His goal is the abolition of heavy industry and its breaking down into small decentralised structures which would bring peasant workers together in units within the framework of village communities. Consumption was confined to the near autarchic satisfaction of the primary necessities of life, by which means a clear reduction in industrial production would be achieved in the medium term. Capitalism, already weakened by a process of employees taking a share in capital assets and decision making processes, which Strasser foresaw, was in this way to be abolished step by step. Great landed estates were to be divided up into several smaller feudal holdings, and banks were to disappear gradually in favour of international barter.

It should be pointed out here that the significance of Strasser's 'socialism' has often been undervalued. Of course Strasser's 'socialism' differed markedly from the Marxist concept of socialism. However, putting his ideas into practice would have led to just as radical a transformation of the existing social order as had been brought about by the Bolshevik October Revolution.

In his own view Strasser was following a third way between liberalism and Marxism – the two classic hate figures of the National Socialist revolution. At the same time he regarded a tactical alliance with the KPD and the partially semantic adoption of many of its theories as tolerable, indeed even necessary for the speedier development of a desire for revolution in the working class. Strasser's judgement of the NSDAP, too, bore the strong imprint of his cyclical view of history. In the NSDAP, as Strasser saw it, were gathered in a mass party those Germans who had become aware of the imminent change in the times, or felt it coming intuitively. This coming together took place as yet under the auspices of a programme defined by liberalism, but its nationalistic, league-oriented and *völkisch* aspects were bound to produce a new public spirit. Hitler, who beat the drum of the German revolution, was for him only a Kerensky, who would have played out his role in fomenting and intensifying a collective rejection of the existing regime at the watershed of the revolution and with the re-entry into the conservative cycle.

The 'School of Officers and NCOs of the German Revolution', the KGRNS and their allies in the *Schwarze Front* were to gather up from the ranks of the mass parties all the leaders who had grasped the logic of the historical cycles and were intellectually prepared, not necessarily to *bring about* the revolution (which was in any case unavoidable), but to lead on the masses after the downfall of Weimar.

Strasser therefore found himself in a dilemma. With Jünger or Goebbels he would have recognised the usefulness of propaganda as a means of mobilising the masses, and Hitler's unique gift of acting as a political catalyst. However, crippled by his sterile political theories, he could only wait for the end of what he regarded as the necessarily short dynamics of the predetermined upheaval. This explains his impotence in the years after 1933, when Hitler was able to an increasing degree to personify a far-reaching consensus and the social and economic stability desired by the German people.

Among the most modern aspects of Strasser's ideology is indisputably still his vision of nationalism as a factor for undermining the imperialism of the western powers. The weakening of Germany's opponents, like France and Britain, was based, in his view, not only on supporting all the national liberation movements in the colonies but also on the break up of pseudo 'national states' like France. Strasser was probably the first to emphasise consistently the importance of the independence movements of an ethnic linguistic type, like those of the Bretons, Flemings, Welsh and Scots – ideas which were to be taken on ten years later by the General Staff of the SS, too. So for left wing National Socialists, nationalism is a tool for the reorganisation of Europe on an ethnic and linguistic basis and a political model for all peoples on the earth. Within the movement, nationalism was the point of reference for all political activity for Strasser's supporters, but in contrast to Hitler's ideas it was not based on racism.

Strasser does emphasise the importance of the natural inclination to endogamy and the rejection of all foreign cultural influence (be it on the German national character or on any other) and for this reason he too wanted to reduce the political and cultural influence of the Jews, but he never considered systematic persecution of the Jews, far less a 'final solution'.

The anti-modern character of many of the traits of Strasser's ideology is as clear as the contrast with Hitler's philosophy and goals. Hitler was too clearly aware that the industrial transformation of Germany in the nineteenth century could not be reversed for Strasser's agrarian extremism to be attractive to him. He saw himself as the authoritarian leader of an industrial society, on which he wanted to force certain strategic options; Strasser on the other hand felt called on to bring about a fundamental transformation of the social, economic and political system and underestimated not least its stability and capacity for resistance. And this explains why Hitler's realism ultimately triumphed over Strasser's idealism.

BIBLIOGRAPHY

Primary Sources

Of all of the Strasser movement's newspapers and journals, we should first of all mention *Die Deutsche Revolution* (Jan. 1931 to Aug. 1931), which was the most important organ of the KGRNS. The two daily papers of the National Socialist left wing, *Die Faust* (1929–30) and *Der Nationale Sozialist* (1929 to Dec. 1930), document the conflicts between the varying ideas of the two Strasser brothers and the official line of the NSDAP. *Die Schwarze Front* (Sep. 1931 to Feb. 1933), the organ of the organisation of the same name, contains important information about co-operation with groups like the *Wehrwolf* and the 'Peasants' Movement'. Insights into the ideological development of the Strasser group are best found in the *Nationalsozialistiche Briefe* (1929–31), the theoretical organ of the National Socialist left and the KGRNS.

The most important publications in book form from the ranks of the Strasser movement are: H. Blank, *Weichensteller Mensch* (Leipzig, 1932). This book give a good insight into the theory of history which ultimately led the 'revolutionary national socialists' into a serious misjudgement of the Hitler phenomenon. Complementary to this work is: R. Schapke, *Die schwarze Front* (Leipzig, 1932). The most important of Otto Strasser's own works is the book *Aufbau des deutschen Sozialismus* (Leipzig, 1932). Here Strasser developes the economic and social ideas of the *Schwarze Front*. Both the radicalism of his concept of revolution and the distinctions between this and the bolshevik model of revolution are evident here. On the breach between Strasser and Hitler see Strasser's own account: *Ministersessel oder Revolution* (Berlin, 1930). Strasser's great ignorance of Marxism, the language of which he nonetheless adopted, is documented in his publication: *Mit oder gegen Marx zur deutschen Nation* (Leipzig, 1932).

Secondary Literature

Fundamental to an understanding of Strasser are the studies by R. Kühnl and the author's dissertation: R. Kühnl, *Die nationalsozialistische Linke 1925–1930* (Meisenheim am Glan, 1966); P. Moreau, *La Communauté de Combat National Socialiste Révolutionnaire en Allemagne, Tchéchoslovaquie et Autriche 1930/1938*, 2 vols (Paris, 1978) (the edited German version appeared under the title: *Nationalsozialismus von links – Die 'Kampfgemeinschaft Revolutionärer Nationalsozialisten' und die 'Schwarze Front' Otto Strassers 1930–1935* (Stuttgart, 1985)). Kühnl's analysis gives exact and detailed information on the 'Strasser wing', even if one may not wish to accept the author's marxist approach to the material. The French edition of the present author's work deals very fully with Strasser's ideology and also gives information on the Strasser group's resistance in Austria and Czechoslovakia. These sections are not reproduced in the German version, but are about to be published in a German translation. An excellent description of the 'national bolshevist' tendency is given in the study by L. Dupeux, which also deals with the KGRNS: *'Nationalbolschewismus' in Deutschland 1919–1933. Kommunistische Strategie und konservative Dynamik* (Munich, 1985). However one major shortcoming in this work is its underestimation of the seriousness of the socialist claims and the light in which many 'national bolshevists' saw themselves.

23 Fritz Todt: From Motorway Builder to Minister of State

Franz W. Seidler

ENGINEER AND POLITICIAN

Fritz Todt was a successful civil engineer in the firm of Sager and Woerner in Munich, when Hitler sent for him in Berlin in 1933. He specialised in tar and asphalt roads. A Swabian, born in Pforzheim in 1891, he had completed his education at the Technical University in Karlsruhe, and afterwards served throughout the First World War, finally as an air force officer. For a while he was impressed by Friedrich Naumann's vision of a European economic community under German leadership, but as early as 1920 he was drawn under Adolf Hitler's spell. He was engrossed by 'how much the people actually love this leader and how devoted they are to him, and look to him full of hope and trust.'[1] Todt did not come into Hitler's circle from a royalist or imperialist, reactionary standpoint, but because of his social and national inclinations. Put another way, he came to the NSDAP from the left and not from the right. At that time many technologists were choosing to join the Party. At the end of 1922, Todt and his wife submitted application forms to the Party and were admitted in January 1923. Todt immediately founded a local branch of the NSDAP at Eitting near Erding, where he was at that time supervising the construction of a power station on the Isar.[2]

After the NSDAP was banned because of the failed November coup attempt, Todt's political zeal went into abeyance. He remained a member of the Party, but in the second half of the twenties he devoted himself exclusively to his career and his family. In 1931 he even disregarded the rallying call made on the occasion of the establishment of the 'Fighting League of German Architects and Engineers' (KDAI). Todt did not become active in party politics until the winter of 1931/32. He joined the SA Reserve Regiment R16 and took part in the customary propaganda marches. During the Presidential elections in March 1932 he became an active proselytiser within middle class circles for the candidate Adolf Hitler. Within the KDAI he took over leadership of the engineers' section. He worked as consultant and assessor for the NSDAP's 'Office for Economic Technology and Creation of Employment', which was run by Gottfried Feder. In this capacity he vehemently opposed the demonisation of the

245

machine as the main cause of unemployment in Germany. In the building trade, at least, he considered the slogan 'Down with Machines: Create Work for the Unemployed' to be a pernicious demand. He clarified his thoughts on the abolition of unemployment in December 1932 in a report for the leadership of the NSDAP: 'Roadbuilding and Administration'. He expounded the view that roadbuilding was a part of the 'overall task of rebuilding the Reich' and that the communications network must be expanded. He estimated the costs at five billion Reich Marks, if 600 000 workers were employed. Technical responsibility for road-building in Germany should be given over to a higher national office empowered to impose guidelines on the states – not an administrative body in the traditional sense but an office made up of specialists with a real leader at its head.[3]

ORGANISATION OF TECHNOLOGY

When Todt delivered the 'Brown Report' he already held the Party office of 'Personal commissioner to the Führer's deputy for all matters of Technology and their Administration'. In this capacity he came into competition with Gottfried Feder, who as leader of the KDAI was ruthlessly bringing into line all technical and scientific organisations. Todt was against abolishing existing specialist professional associations. He aimed to preserve their specialist abilities 'but to realign them with National Socialism'. In August 1934 at Todt's suggestion, Hess founded the 'National Socialist League of German Technology' (NSBDT) as an umbrella organisation for the many varied forms of technical associations. Therefore of the eighty-four specialist associations in the Weimar Republic, sixty survived until the end of the Third Reich. The most powerful was the 'Association of German Engineers' (VDI) and Todt himself became chairman of it in 1938.[4] Todt exercised decisive influence on the development of technology and the orientation of technologists and engineers in the Third Reich through his nexus of roles and responsibilities. As director of the 'Head Office for Technology' in the Brown House he had to be involved in all regulations and decrees concerning technical matters. As the national chief of the NSBDT he was responsible for the furtherance of technical and scientific projects and the training and orientation of its members 'in the interests of applying German technology according to the demands of people and state.'[5] As Director of the 'Office for Technical Sciences' in the German Labour Front (DAF), he gained an overall picture of technical innovation and secured the right to be consulted on the care of technicians by the DAF. Todt drew the final line under the reorganisation of technology in the German Reich in April 1937 with his mass meeting at the Berlin Palace of Sport. In front of more than 10 000 engineers he argued that the committed co-operation of technical specialists was indispensable for the rise of the Third Reich. However, in spite of this appeal, the degree of organisation within the NSBDT remained relatively slight. In autumn 1937, with the total number of engineers standing at 220 000, it only had 81 000 members.[6] From March 1936 the Plassenburg near Kulmbach was made available to Todt for the purpose of specialist political training. Here, the political implications of their profession were to be made clear to technicians and natural scientists. Todt demanded of them that they should not just think as experts, but also in political terms. In his speeches he emphasised again and again the importance of technology for Germany's destiny. Striking sentences and apt turns of phrase from Todt's speeches were collected in the so-called 'Plassenburg speeches' and kept in readiness for future publication.[7]

According to Todt's ideas, Plassenburg was to become an academy of engineering in Germany, the stronghold of the National Socialist concept of technology. In it 'the achievements and cultural significance of technological endeavour at the time of Adolf Hitler were to be brought before the German people in a worthy setting'.[8] The museum building, on a 90 000 square metre site between Corneliusstrasse and Zweibrückenstrasse was to be planned in such a way that it was the expression 'of a higher cultural understanding of technology'.[9]

ROADS

The 'Decree for the Establishment of a National Motorway Enterprise' of 27.6.1933 commissioned the German Railways to set up a subsidiary called 'National Motorways' for the purpose of establishing an efficient network of transport routes under the control of the Reich. Hitler appointed Fritz Todt as Inspector General of this enterprise in July 1933. Todt was enthusiastic:

> The contract to build a network of interconnecting motorways offers challenges which the master builders of many centuries have longed for in vain. The task of constructing a network to a unified plan and, moreover, to the shortest timescale, of building roads many hundreds of kilometres long all in the same style, and of imbuing the overall character of the roads with grace, toughness and singleness of purpose is one which is bound to give rise to enthusiasm among those entrusted with it.[10]

Todt set to work with unprecedented energy. By the middle of 1934 he had set up fifteen building directorates, which were to take care of all the matters which arose from the implementation of building work. The 'Society for the Preliminary Work on National Motorways Inc' (known as

Gezuvor) was commissioned to plan the routes. It had developed out of the 'Association for the Preliminary Work on the Trunk Route Hansa Towns–Frankfurt–Basel' (*Hafraba*). Work began on the Frankfurt–Darmstadt–Heidelberg stretch on 23.9.1933. In 1936, 125 000 workers were employed on motorway building sites. 120 000 worked in quarries, or for suppliers and subsidiary companies, an unknown number in the extensive road-building equipment industry.[11] By the beginning of the war more than 3065 kilometres of motorway were ready and 1689 under construction.

It was Todt's ambition to make the motorways not only technically perfect but also artistically pleasing. They were to blend into nature and be suited to the form of the landscape. The new roads were not intended in the first instance to convey travellers as quickly as possible from one place to the other, but to show them the beauties of Germany. All the building directorates were allocated landscape architects as advisers. These took care of the alignment of the curves, the correct management of topsoil, the restoration of the edges of forests which had been torn up and suitable planting for preventing sun dazzle. They were not only to preserve the countryside but to enhance its effect through road-building:

> The road itself should be beautiful in the same way as the countryside which surrounds it. Embankments and cuttings are to merge into the land by means of soft curves. Drainage ditches are to be avoided where possible. Only native varieties are to be used for planting, that is, plants which grow and flourish by themselves without human intervention. . . . Care should be taken with the line and construction of the roads so that the landscape is seen to advantage and the sequence of landscapes is harmonic and rhythmic.[12]

Hitler was enthusiastic about Todt's work. While inspecting the Dresden-Chemnitz-Meerane stretch of motorway in June 1937 he enthused – 'These roads will never disappear. There is something grand and wonderful in living at such a time and being able to take part in work such as this!'[13] Hitler did not have military or mobilisation routes in mind. In the thirties a visit to the motorways was part of the tourist agenda of many foreign visitors to Germany and was a part of the agenda of all congresses.

Hundreds of journalists and correspondents were stunned and enthusiastic. Abroad they represented Todt's masterpiece as symbolic of the rise of the new Reich. In National Socialist propaganda the roads were called the 'Führer's Roads'. Todt did nothing to damage the legend that Hitler had already sketched out transport routes suitable for cars in the 'Era of Struggle'.[14] Hitler and Todt were in agreement: the Reich's motorways were not economic products but national artistic monuments. They should not just be judged by fiscal criteria. All the great cultural monuments of past centuries had broken the budget of their builders, the churches of the Middle Ages as much as the buildings of classical antiquity. 'But the German people, indeed all of humanity, would be the poorer today without these immortal works of art'.[15]

THE BUILDING OF THE WEST WALL (THE ŚIEGFRIED LINE)

The 'Czechoslovak crisis' of May 1938 made Hitler speed up the building of a fortified belt on the western border as a defence against Czechoslovakia's ally, France. Since the fortification pioneers did not think they were capable of building bunkers in the numbers required by the Führer in the prescribed four months, Hitler transferred the commission to implement the project to the Inspector General for German Roads. He was to contrive the chain of fortifications according to the military and tactical plans of the Pioneer Staff, employing the Motorway Directorates in such a way that 5000 concrete structures were complete by 1.10.38. Todt directed the twenty-two senior building executive committees which were commissioned to undertake the construction work from the Central Office for Western Fortifications in the Hotel Kaiserhof in Wiesbaden. Along with the Pioneers and the National Labour Service, about 1000 firms with their depots and staff worked under his overall direction on the West Wall. At the end of the day there were 430 000 building workers employed on it. Their working day could be as long as thirteen hours.

Hitler's commission to Todt to build the West Wall was seen by the military as an unprecedented assault on their authority. Hitler took every opportunity to make it clear to the army generals that Todt was to take the credit for the West Wall. 'If I had given this task to the army alone, the West Wall would still not have been ready in ten years'.[16] Todt played his part in the West Wall propaganda in agreement with the general objectives. He interpreted the Wall as a measure 'to re-establish the might of the Reich'. He regarded the edifice as a 'chess move by our Führer, by which he has compelled our opponents to declare unambiguously whether they want to live in peace with Germany or whether they no longer want this peace!'[17] Hitler appeared twice at building sites in Todt's company. In an order of the day of 20.5.1939 he expressed his satisfaction. 'An inspection of the West Wall has convinced me of its impregnability. The German people joins me in thanking all those who by their unstinting efforts have in the shortest of time built the basis of Germany's security in concrete and steel.'[18] With the West Wall Todt proved that he was able to fulfil commands which would be regarded as impossible by the standards of normal technical expertise. After this Hitler's trust in Todt was as great as for few others within National Socialist leadership circles.

WORK ON THE FOUR YEAR PLAN

Since the building of the West Wall had had a considerable deleterious effect on the construction sector of the Third Reich's economy – shortages of raw materials, labour shortages, rising wages, price increases, fierce competition – Hermann Goering, in his capacity as Commissioner for the Four Year Plan, decided on 9.12.1938 to appoint Todt as Plenipotentiary for the Regulation of the Construction Sector (GB). Todt was to restore order to the construction sector, 'under a unified leadership' and to throttle the volume of building work back to a normal level. The GB's most important measures for stopping the boom in the construction sector, which had already reached a level of 11.5 billion Reich Marks in 1938, entailed an increase in the use of machines, while restricting the range of makes, the fixing of quotas for raw materials and the direction of labour. In the list of priorities which Todt made for the building sector, fortifications, docks, locks and harbours for the defence of the Reich were pre-eminent. In second place was building of production facilities important for the armaments industry. The building of dwellings took last place. The slogan of the building industry in 1939 was 'increased production with simultaneous savings in raw materials.' Todt flooded entrepreneurs, engineers and workmen with appeals to their national conscience. 'Now there must be a quite different type of education. Concepts like enthusiasm, enjoying one's work, comradeliness within companies must be required to a far greater extent than before'.[19]

Todt prohibited three shift working at building sites because of the increased danger of accidents, but other than this he considered every way of increasing production: moves to rationalisation, the management of building materials, transfers of building workers, mothballing of building sites, the punishment of builders who broke regulations, suspension of lists of priorities. In spite of this Todt was only partially successful. The civil service, the army and the NSDAP tried again and again to escape his restrictions. Nonetheless the Commissioner for the Four Year Plan, Hermann Goering, was impressed by what had been achieved. On 23.2.1940 he ordered Todt to take on technical and economic problems outside the building industry. In his new office as Inspector General for Special Tasks in the Four Year Plan, it was his duty to examine all the measures of the Four Year Plan with a view to their being successfully implemented in the economy. To this end he was able to make use in the first instance of the offices of the Head Office for Technology, that is of the Party apparatus. From this time onward technical engineering arguments came to the fore in the planning of economic enterprises. In all companies the machinery depots were inspected to see if they were being used to capacity. Time and motion specialists supervised the pursuit of national working methods within factories. Instead of putting up costly new buildings, firms had to make do with huts. Even armaments factories were shut down if they met no urgent requirements.[20]

THE TODT ORGANISATION

The name Todt Organisation (OT) was used by Hitler for the first time at the National Party Convention at Nuremberg in 1938, when he was informing the public about the building work on the West Wall. But it he meant the 430 000 men who were building fortifications in the West of the Reich under Todt's direction. During the Polish campaign from September 1939, and to an even greater extent during the French campaign from May 1940, the squads of building workers who had until then worked on the motorways or the West Wall were brought into the occupied territories to support the army engineers and pioneers. One of their particular tasks was the reinstatement of roads behind the front. Wherever they were deployed their company links were maintained. The contractor, workforce and machinery stayed together. Transport and mobility were guaranteed by the OT. The men were now called 'front line workers'. At the beginning of the Russian campaign Todt placed 20 000 men in units of 2000 each, with the necessary fleet of transport, at the disposal of the army. In the winter of 1941/42 the organisation grew to a strength of 800 000 men, including foreign workers. After the collapse of the rail transport system because of winter temperatures the OT ensured that the front line was re-supplied and the wounded removed by road. Alongside maintaining the road transport system, in Russia, as in all occupied territories, it took over the exploitation of sources of raw materials, the reinstatement of factories and the transportation of strategic products back to the Reich. At the same time it was commissioned in France with the constructing of bunkers for the Navy's U-Boats and with the fortification of the Channel coastline. Up to 800 000 tons of concrete were used up in one month there. The total number of workers deployed by the OT's Western Action Force rose to 264 000 men.

ARMAMENTS

The appointment of a 'National Minister for Weapons and Munitions' on 7.3.1940 fulfilled one of Hitler's long-cherished desires. He had wanted to centralise the production of munitions as early as 1939 on the basis of his perceptions of the First World War. The supreme commanders of each of the armed forces had torpedoed this plan. When the armaments industry complained more and more openly about the ponderous and pedantic methods of the weapons offices, the Führer took up the idea once more.

He chose neither an officer nor an armaments expert, but Fritz Todt.

The latter took up the post without enthusiasm, because he had no technical qualifications in this sphere. In industrial circles, however, the new minister met with a very favourable response, because it was expected that he would promote the development of entrepreneurial initiatives. Todt did. First of all he reduced the demands of the armed forces to correspond with what was possible for industry. In order to increase production he ordered that companies which produced similar weapons, munitions and tools should be merged into production communities or work groups. For each broader area of production, for example weapons or tanks, the relevant contractors formed committees as autonomous, responsible bodies for the industry. These co-ordinated production by securing supplies of raw materials, workers and machinery. Todt's task was limited to executing the planning of Hitler's political changes, of course, and to giving the committees realistic planning targets after discussion with the Armed Forces High Command and the Army High Command. If the armaments industry did not achieve the expected degree of efficiency during Todt's time, this was caused by countless changes of direction which resulted from the changing priorities set by Hitler according to the military requirements of the moment. Besides this there was an increasing lack of trained workers in the factories because of the growing volume of conscription into the army. The only help Todt could offer was to deploy huge numbers of prisoners of war and civilian workers from the occupied territories. For the summer of 1942 he promised the armaments industry 800 000 foreigners.

ENERGY SUPPLIES

Todt's appointment as Inspector General for Water and Energy on 29.7.1941 represented a decision by the Führer against the ministries which had hitherto dealt with these matters. In his new capacity Todt was to centralise the Water and Energy industries in the Reich, open up new sources of energy and draw upon the occupied territories as a source of supply for the German armaments industry. His appointment as Inspector General for Water and Energy fulfilled one of Todt's most heartfelt wishes. He believed that in this office he would be able to apply his technical building experience in the same way as he had done for road building since 1933. He regarded hydraulic engineering, too, that is to say exploitation of the power of water, as a cultural task. No more buildings for the water and energy industries were to be constructed without first having regard to biological, geographical and anthropological consequences.[21]

However Todt's short period in office was not sufficient to reform the energy industry. The shortage of coal and gas in the Reich increased month by month. The Army High Command did intend, at Todt's insistence, to exempt coal miners from conscription. Todt planned to build new hydro electric power stations, he did attempt to equalise supplies between the various consumer areas in the Reich by setting up a grid system, he did fall back on the energy reserves of the occupied territories, but he could not prevent the threat of an energy crisis.

THE END

Only a few men in the leadership of the Third Reich understood Germany's economic inadequacies as well as Todt did. By the time the USA entered the war, in December 1941 at the very latest, he was forced to admit to himself that the Allied armaments potential was so great that Germany could not win the war, no matter how the campaign against the USSR ended. To these insights were added in the winter of 1941/42 depressing human experiences, for example when Todt learned of the wretched fate of Russian prisoners of war in the Soviet Union's icy deserts, and when he registered the collapse of the German transport system with his own eyes. All the evidence points to the likelihood that Todt spoke alone with Hitler before the end of 1941 about the hopeless situation of the German Reich. The latter remained deaf to all arguments.[22] Even the increasingly obvious inferiority of German weapons, particularly the tanks, to Russian armaments, did not open his eyes. He ordered modifications in design and improvements in materials, although the one was impossible in the short term and the other was hopeless in view of the increasing shortage of raw materials.[23]

On the afternoon of 7.2.1942 Todt was with Hitler for the last time at the Wolfschanze. He expected the conversation to provide him with, among other things, the Führer's reaction to a report he had presented to him containing a comparison of German industrial capabilities with those of the Allies. What happened during the six hours that Hitler and Todt were alone together remains unclear, because there are no minuted statements about it in existence. It seems at times to have been a noisy discussion. After a short night, which Todt spent in the guest bunker at the Führer's headquarters, he intended the following morning to fly to his family in Munich. Shortly after take-off the plane, a Heinkel III, crashed. Hitler gave the address at the state funeral in Berlin. After a detailed appreciation of Todt's achievements for the National Socialist movement and the Third Reich, he concluded with the words: 'In this man I have lost one of my most loyal colleagues and friends. I see his death as a contribution by the National Socialist movement to our people's war of liberation.'[24] Since no announcement was circulated about the cause of the accident, there were soon rumours that Todt had been the victim of an assassination.

Some spoke of it as the planned work of enemy secret services, others of sabotage by army officers, who wanted to stop Todt breaking in to military concerns, and finally a third group believed that Hitler himself had had a hand in it, to sweep the defeatist Todt out of the way. Yet others suspected that Bormann, remembering the flight of Hitler's deputy, Hess, to Britain, feared that Todt would take off for Sweden and for this reason had had an explosive charge built into Todt's aircraft.[25] However, as the experts at the office for Air Safety and Equipment in the National Air Transport Ministry established, Todt's crash was caused by a technical fault. It left open simply whether the cause of the accident lay in the icing up of the wings or in oversteering the aircraft.[26]

NOTES

1. Facsimile of a letter by Todt in *Deutsche Technik*, March 1942, p. 14.
2. See Berlin Document Center, NSDAP-Akte Todt.
3. Todt's memo '*Strassenbau und Strassenverwaltung*' dated December 1932, Brauner Bericht, Bundesarchiv RW65I/1a.
4. See *Völkischer Beobachter* dated 31.5.1938.
5. See *Rundschau Deutscher Technik* 14/1939.
6. See *Deutsche Technik*, October 1937, p. 470.
7. See Bundesarchiv NS14/78 and NS28/1188.
8. See *Mitteilungen aus dem Haus der Deutschen Technik*, ed. by Haus der Deutschen Technik e.V. Munich, supplement to the journal *Deutsche Technik* October 1938, p. 495ff.
9. *Leistung und Schönheit der Technik im Dritten Reich*, series 1, pictorial supplement to the journal *Deutsche Technik*, January 1939, p. 2.
10. Quoted according to Eduard Schönleben, *Fritz Todt. Der Mensch. Der Ingenieur. Der Nationalsozialist* (Oldenburg, 1943) p. 56.
11. Fritz Todt, '*Der Strassenbau im nationalsozialistischen Staat*' in *Grundlagen, Aufbau und Wirtschaftsordnung des nationalsozialistischen Staates*, ed. by Hans H. Lammers und Hans Pfunder, vol. 3: *Die Wirtschaftsordnung des nationalsozialistischen Staates* (Berlin, 1937) p. 3.
12. Fritz Todt, as above, p. 26.
13. *Die Strasse*, second July edition 1937, p. 6.
14. See Heribert Menzel, '*Das Erlebnis der Reichsautobahn*' in, *Die Strasse*, 23–24/1941, p. 372.
15. Lecture by Todt at Plassenburg on 7.10.1938; see *Deutsche Wasserwirtschaft* 1938, p. 397.
16. *Heeresadjutant bei Hitler 1938–1943. Aufzeichnungen des Major Engel*, ed. by Hildegard von Kotze (Stuttgart, 1974) p. 27.
17. See *Die Strasse*, January edition, 1940, p. 28.
18. Bundesarchiv NS16/1190.
19. Rundschau Deutscher Technik 24/1939.
20. See Deutsche Technik, March 1940, p. 99.
21. See Fritz Todt, '*Schönheit der Technik*' in *Kunst im Dritten Reich* 1/1938, p. 14; see minutes of the meeting of 9.11.1941, Bundesarchiv R4/4, sheet 302f.

22. See statements made to the author by Xaver Dorsch and Heinrich Classen.
23. See the proceedings of the leaders' meeting of 29.11.1941, Bundesarchiv/ militärarchiv RW19/822.
24. See *Der Frontarbeiter* dated 14.2.1942, p. 3; *Die Strasse*, February edition 1942, p. 26; *Deutsche Technik*, June 1942.
25. See the Akten des Spruchkammerverfahrens Todt, Amtgericht Munich.
26. See a condensed version in Franz W. Seidler, *Fritz Todt* (Berlin, 1988) (Ullstein-Taschenbuch 33095, p. 365ff.)

BIBLIOGRAPHY

Primary Sources

Fragments of written sources material on Todt's life can be found in nearly all the German archives, but mainly in the Bavarian Hauptstadtsarchiv, the Institut für Zeitgeschichte and the archive of the Deutches Museum, Munich. The vast majority of the files did not survive the war. A substantial proportion of them were destroyed by fire during the bombing of Berlin. Another part of them, especially files on the West Wall and the Atlantic Wall, was apparently entrusted by Speer in January 1944 to Todt's widow for safe-keeping. Colleagues of Bormann and Speer were supposed to go over the material with her 'with a view to seeing which of the files were the late Dr Todt's personal property and could be handed over without further ado to his widow and which were to be regarded as official files'. Mrs Todt, who died in January 1986, in her one hundred and third year, claimed to have seen nothing of this. A third parcel of files, 'especially those which had to do with the personal influence of Dr Todt on the design of buildings and the transformation of the road system' were taken to Schloss Steinach near Straubing on Speer's instructions. This building had been bought by the building directorate in Munich as a rest house on the planned Regensburg-Passau motorway. The director of the then building directorate in Munich, President Hafen, was given the task of keeping safe 'the most important files, those which would one day be essential for Todt's biography or for editing his letters'. Mrs Speer was informed of this in a letter from Speer dated 15.9.1944. Shortly before the end of the war Schloss Steinach was bombed by the Allies and burned to the ground. The files which were being kept there were lost.

Of Todt's writings only one long essay is worthy of mention: '*Der Strassenbau im nationalsozialistischen Staat*' in volume three of the publication *Grundlagen, Aufbau und Wirtschaftsordnung des nationalsozialistischen Staates*, which was published by Hans H. Lammers and Hans Pfundner in 1937 in Berlin. Salient quotations from his speeches at Plassenburg were collected and today they are kept in the Bundesarchiv NS 26/1188. Many details on the person of Todt can be gleaned from the files and evidence from the tribunal proceedings against Todt's widow during the years 1946–50.

Secondary Literature

The biography of Todt by the present author which appeared in 1987 was published as a paperback in a revised version in 1988. Franz W. Seidler, *Fritz Todt. Baumeis-*

ter des Dritten Reiches (Munich, 1986; by the same author, *Fritz Todt* (Ullstein Taschenbuch 33095). In the second edition in particular it is made clear that Todt was not the victim of an assassination, but of a navigational error by his pilot. Todt scarcely plays any part in the literature on the Third Reich. Not even the literature on architecture, road-building, engineering, armaments, job creation or the building of fortifications gives more than references to the minister. Among these are: D. Eichholtz, *Geschichte der deutschen Kriegswirtschaft 1939–1945*, vol. 1 (1939–41) and vol. 2 (1941–3) (East Berlin, 1984/85); G. Hortleder, *Das Gesellschaftsbild des Ingenieurs. Zum politischen Verhalten der technischen Intelligenz in Deutschland* (Frankfurt am Main, 1974); K.-H. Ludwig, *Technik und Ingenieure im Dritten Reich* (Dusseldorf, 1974); A.S. Milward, *Die deutsche Kriegswirtschaft 1939–1945* (Stuttgart, 1966); W.F. Renn, *Hitler's West Wall. Strategy in Concrete and Steel 1938–1945*, dissertation, Florida State University 1970. Even the author's essay on *Die Organisation Todt. Bauen für Staat und Wehrmacht 1938–1945* (Cologne, 1987), had to put the main emphasis on Todt's successor, Albert Speer, since it was only under the leadership of the latter that this organisation gained a 'European dimension'.

Index

DATE DUE

GAYLORD   #3523PI   Printed in USA